CONFLICT AND TENSION IN TRIBAL SOCIETY

About the Author

DR. SURENDRA PRASAD SINHA currently is Professor Behavioural Sciences-cum-Joint Director in Bihar Institute of Rural Development, an apex State institution of training and research located at Ranchi. Born in 1933, Dr. Sinha was educated at Patna University, Patna, and took his D.Litt. from Ranchi University. He taught in Patna University and was a Visiting Professor at Centre of Advance Studies, Anthropology Department, Ranchi. He served for three decades in Bihar Tribal Welfare Research Institute, Ranchi, where he published his work on "Life & Times of Birsa Bhagwan", "Problem of Land Alienation", "Santal Hool" Papers relating to Santal Insurrection", "Peasant Movement in Chota Nagpur" and "Munda Land System", "Tribal Gujarat: Some Impression", etc. He has a number of research papers and reports on tribes and their movements to his credit. He has edited volumes on "Impact of Industrialisation", "Tribals and Forest", "Administering the Prehistorics", "Educating the Preliterates". He is editing the Journal of Bihar Institute of Rural Development (*Vihangam*) and the Journal of Bihar Tribal Welfare Research Institute.

CONFLICT AND TENSION IN TRIBAL SOCIETY

S. P. SINHA

CONCEPT PUBLISHING COMPANY, NEW DELHI 110059

ISBN 81-7022-493-4

First Published 1993

Published and Printed by
Ashok Kumar Mittal
Concept Publishing Company
A/15-16, Commercial Block, Mohan Garden
NEW DELHI 110059 (India)

Lasertypeset by
Printing Express
H-13, Bali Nagar
NEW DELHI 110015

PREFACE

THE CONFLICT and Tension in Tribal Society is primarily an elementary source book for those who are interested in knowing the details of tribals in ferment in mid-India and can be used as basic material on this branch of knowledge. Its purpose is to give well rounded view of Social History as a discipline as well as providing necessary ground-work for further study in the field of Social Anthropology and Sociology concerning various movements gripping the tribal society in mid-India.

This book is an edited version of "Conflict and Tension in Tribal Society in Chota Nagpur and Santal Parganas (1858 to 1990) — A Case in Social Perspective" which was originally submitted for the award of D.Litt. Degree of Ranchi University — which the author was awarded in 1978. The author was awarded financial assistance of Rs. 5,000 by the Indian Council of Social Science Research, New Delhi.

This book has its origin in the experience of the author in researching in the aspects of freedom movement studies in which he was involved from 1953 to 1956 as research worker. The author's teaching in history in Patna University and later on taking up paid research work in Bihar Tribal Welfare Research Institute gave him an opportunity to write about Birsa Bhagwan at the behest of the late Sri M.S.M. Ayanger, Governor of Bihar in 1962. The Government of Bihar published his work as *Life and Times of Birsa Bhagwan* in 1964. Since then author remained actively engaged in collecting materials in National Archive, New Delhi, State Archive at Calcutta and Patna, National Library at Calcutta and various record rooms at District and Commissionary levels in Bihar. The author tried to piece together all the relevant materials to integrate them into a whole using the Postanian methodology, the historical method in social science, i.e., taking microcosmic view of the microscopic problem of historical research. The struggle of the tribal communities, such as Santals, Korwas, Gonds, Khonds, Mundas, Ho, etc., against the injustices is a microscopic account of what may be seen as microscosm, a great world represented in small one. Looking at these little histories in Redfielddian sense is a historiography of their accomplishment, their development, it would call for a look at history as a whole. This may be a happy addition to the field of Social History and Social Anthropology.

Faculty of Behavioural Sciences
Bihar Institute of Rural Development
Ranchi

S.P. SINHA

ACKNOWLEDGEMENTS

THE AUTHOR takes this opportunity to express his thankfulness and gratitude to Member-Secretary, Indian Council of Social Science, New Delhi, for making a grant-in-aid of Rs. 5,000 available for this project and to the late Dr. L.P. Vidyarthi, University Professor of Anthropology, Ranchi University, for ungruding help in formulating the Project and arriving at crucial conclusions. The author is also thankful to his mentor the late Dr. K.K. Datta, Ex-Vice-Chancellor of Patna University and his teachers Dr. R.S. Sharma, University Professor of History, Delhi University, Dr. Bimla Prasad, Dr. Sachchidanand and Dr. Yogendra Mishra, in the then Department of History, Patna University for their valuable contribution in shaping the abiding interest in him for "little history" of this region of Chota Nagpur and Santal Parganas. Dr. P.N. Ojha, University Professor of History, Ranchi University has been this author's great support in sustaining this effort. The author is grateful to the late Sri Nihar Ranjan Ray, Dr. B.D. Sharma, Dr. Bhupendra Singh, Dr. Sachchidanand, Dr. S.C. Dube, Dr. B.B. Mishra, Dr. Surjit Sinha, Dr. K.S. Singh, Sri P.S. Krishnan, Sri Ranjit Gupta, Dr. P.K. Bhowmick, Dr. L.K. Mahapatra, Dr. B.K. Roy Burman, Dr. D.P. Sinha, Dr. B.K. Sinha, Dr. Rath, etc., for their help in theoretical formulation of the Project. The author's esteemed colleagues, the late Mrs. R.O. Dhan, Director of the Bihar Tribal Welfare Research Institute and the late Sri T.R. Sharma, Assistant Director of the same Institute, the late Sri B.N. Jha, Sh. Balbir Datta, Dr. Amar Kumar Singh, Vice-Chancellor Ranchi University, Sri C.S. Prasad deserve his gratitude for their comments and constructive criticism. The author is also very thankful to the late Sri Kartik Oraon, M.P., Sri N.E. Horo, M.L.A., the late Sri S.K. Bage, M.L.A., Sri Bhaiya Ram Munda, Ex M.P., the late Sri Narayanji, Secretary, Adimjati Seva Mandal, Ranchi, Dr. S.M. Pathak, Dr. A.B. Saran, Dr. Dilwar Hans, Dr. Ram Dayal Munda, Dr. A.K. Sinha, etc., for their help in so many ways in collection of materials for the work.

Director-General of the National Archive of India, New Delhi, Directors of West Bengal Secret Record Room, Calcutta and the State Central Record Room, Patna, and the Librarian, The National Library, Calcutta, have been very considerate to this author for providing all facilities in their organisation and the Secretary to the Government of Bihar in the Welfare Department, Patna, for permitting him to take up the Project in his individual capacity. Sri S. Prabhakaran, Sri S. Patankar, Sri M.C. Subarno, Sri C.K. Basu, Sri A.R. Bandopadhya, Sri K.B. Saxena, Sri G.R. Patwardhan and Sri Chintu Nayak helped the author with their constructive advise to the author. Author's thanks are due to Sarvashri Ranchor Prasad, Sri Kamla Prasad, B.L. Das. S.V. Saran who have been great inspiration to him.

The author is extremely thankful to Dr. John MacDoughall, Lowell University, Lowell Massachusetts and Dr. Machael York, School of African and Indian Studies, London University, for their ready help not only in procuring materials for this work but also providing many insights into the problems of this work. Dr. Savitri Sinha, Dr. Saileshwar Prasad and Sri Sisir Kumar helped this author which is gratefully acknowledged.

The author is thankful to large number of informants who ungrudgingly co-operated with him in getting the information. Lastly, M/s Concept Publishing Company is to be gratefully acknowledged for publishing this book.

S. P. SINHA

CONTENTS

Part IV
Conflict and Tension in Gujarat Mahal (Tributary States)

Part V
Resolution of Conflict, Analysis and Conclusion

LIST OF TABLES

LIST OF MAPS AND FIGURES

GLOSSARY

Abkari farmer — Collector of excise duty.

Abwabs — Miscellaneous dues.

Ading — Sacred taberancle.

Batta — Discount in general sense but specially an allowance for the exchange of *sicca* (currency of local rulers) rupees into East India Company.

Baraik — A jagir awarded by the Raja of Chota Nagpur. See also *Bhaiyas, Jamadar, Ohdar, Pandeyas.*

Banias — Community of traders, money-lenders.

Beth begari — Compulsory labour without payment which was renderable by the raiyots to their landlords for the cultivation of their *majhihas* lands and as personal service.

Bhatta — A charge to meet the expenses of the landlord and his servant, wherever they visited a village to collect rent etc.

Bhandari dhan — Contribution of *dhan* made by the raiyots for the support of the village *bhandari* or landlord's local agent in former time but later on it was turned into an impost.

Bhaiyas — A jagir awarded by the Raja of Chota Nagpur. See also *Baraik, Jamadar, Ohdar, Pandeyas.*

Bhuinhar — Original settlers of the village; pioneer; a local variant of the word Khuntkatti.

Bhuinhari Survey — A survey ordered in 1858 to prepare a register of all *Bhuinhari* lands.

Bhutkheta — Land held by Pahan for the performance of certain sacrifices made to appease malign effects and devil's forces. See also *Pahnai.*

Chanda — Subscription.

Chattisa — A type of tenancy consisting of lowland *(don)* with a quantity of upland (*tanr*) thrown in, called *lagan* or complementary *tanr.*

Chuars — A Bengali opprobrium for the Bhumijs and the tribals of the Manbhum and Tamar areas who rose against the British Government and the non-tribal Zamindars and money-lenders during the closing years of eighteenth century.

Dali Katari — Land held by Pahan for certain specified sacrifice.

Daroga — Police officer.

Dhangars — Young boys engaged in the Munda household for cultivation works, a Kurukh word signifying a "youth".

Dharti Aba — Father of the Earth, a name by which Birsa Bhagwan was hailed by his people.

Diku — Landlord, of late taken as persons of non-tribal origin.

Ghatwal — A new tenancy introduced by the British Government to guard the various *ghats* in Chota Nagpur and Santal Parganas.

Har — A type of begari for ploughing the landlord's land.

Jamadar — A jagir granted by the Raja of Chota Nagpur. See also *Baraik, Bhaiyas, Ohdar, Pandeyas.*

Karai-dhan — Same as *Bhandari dhan.*

Khorposdar — Dependent of the Raja of Chota Nagpur who used to get jagir for their maintenance.

Khuntkattihatu — Village of the original settlers of the area.

Khuttkattidars — Offsprings of the original clearers of the forest and settlers in Chota Nagpur.

Killi — Exogamous unit of tribe.

Mangan — A type of demand by the Zamindars on the *raiyots.*

Majhias — Privileged land of the landlords.

Mauki — Head of the group of Munda villages.

Mati — The ghost finder.

Misni — A type of *beth begar* taken by the Zamindars from the *raiyots* for thrashing grain.

Morabandhi — A type of *beth begar* taken by the Zamindars from the *raiyots* for storing the grain.

Namak dhan — Paddy taken by the Zamindars in lieu of salt.

Nawakhani or *Sarai Chaul* — A kind of levy of rice taken from the *raiyots* on an auspicious day, when the winter rice had been harvested.

Neg — Means *dasturi*, customary payment which was made on certain occasions such as marriage etc.

Orga dhan — A kind of levy of rice taken from the *raiyots* for the support of the village official who guarded the jungles.

Ohdar — A jagir awarded by the Raja of Chota Nagpur. See also *Baraik, Bhaiyas, Jamadar, Pandeyas.*

Padris — Christian Missionaries.

Panbhara — Land held by Pahan's assistant for carrying water and cooking during sacrificial ceremonies.

Pandeyas — A jagir bestowed by the Raja of Chota Nagpur. See also *Baraik, Bhaiyas, Jamadar, Ohdar.*

Panriai — A kind of levy paid by the *raiyots* towards the tax which the Jagirdars had to pay for Maharaja's Panre, record-keeper.

Pagri — Turban.

Pahan — Eccelesiastical head of a Munda village.

Pahnai — Those land held by Pahan for the performance of cetain specified sacrifices. See Also *Bhutkheta.*

Panchayat — Tribunal of the village.

Parha — A cluster of ten to twelve Munda Villages.

Pracharak — Preacher of religion.

Rajhas — Land of the Jagirdar or Raja or "the Raja's Share" in Munda village.

Rakumat — The rent of an ordinary *raiyot* tenancy was found to consist of cash payments and customary paraedial condition, locally known as *rakumat* and *begari.*

Rashid Likhai — A charge on the *raiyots* for getting rent receipt.

Sanyase — Hindu saint.

Sing Bonga — Supreme God of the Munda Pantheon.

Topped Buru — Where guns were fired in queling the agitators on Dumbari hill in Khunti Subdivision.

Thikadars — A jagirdar used to allot some villages to the *Thikadar* (contractor) for collection of dues.

Tanr — Highland.

Thana Kharcha — Charge for the upkeep of the Police levied on the *raiyots* by the Zamindars.

PART I

Theoretical and Historical Aspects of Conflict and Tension in Tribal Bihar

1

RESEARCHES IN TRIBAL HERITAGE OF INDIA

THE PERSISTENCE of conflict and tension among the tribes of Bihar is not an isolated phenomenon. The tribes in different parts of the world have reacted to their indifferent situations in their own characteristic manners which have caught the attention of social scientists from time to time. But seldom has any systematic treatment of the great theme of the 'archaic phase' of the history of social movements ever been done. The objective of this study is to examine the situation of Bihar tribes after the great upheaval of 1857. It was the time when the tribals of Bihar became greatly attuned to the extension and intensification of European administration and their region underwent a common political authority. The initiation of developmental work on various plantations, mines and railways, which also happened to start about this time, brought together members of previously widely scattered tribes. The development of trade, transport and other media of communication increased. This time also saw the mission converts brought into communion groups which were formerly discreet and often divided by cultural and political differences. The study of these factors in small compass with a view to understand their riddles in tribal society of Bihar will not only be a fruitful exercise in interdisciplinary approach to the problem in time perspective, but it will also be rewarding to an inquisitive mind engaged in studying the course of integration of the tribal society with the wider Indian community.

It is surprising that the concepts of tension and conflict which are of central importance for an understanding of major areas of social relations have been almost wholly neglected. Coser explained the reasons of this neglect by American sociologists[1] over the past fifty years. Ghurye[2] also recorded the same phenomenon and quoted large number of titles in course of his survey, but in Indian context hardly any study can be said to have been made in the background of tribal situation. However, some attempts to focus attention on the gravity of group tensions and their consequences were made by the Indian as well as non-Indian writers after Indian Independence.

The study of conflict reminds one of the class wars and the class struggles. Marx and Engels very forcefully placed the agrarian questions and prepared some sort of creed for class struggle. Taking a diametrically opposite position, Pitrim Sorokin[3] identified the concept of conflict taking shape out of cultural change. Indian sociologists such as Surjit Sinha, Stephen Fuchs, Roy Burman, Vidyarthi, Oran, Sachchidanand, Bhowmic, Jha, Sinha, Singh and many others have endeavoured to unravel the riddle of tension among the tribes specially in Bihar. In his Presidential Address to the Anthropology Section of 49th Indian Science Congress held in 1959, Surjit Sinha repudiated, Oppenheimer's typical 'Conquest Theory' which held that invasion of peasants by hordes of herdsmen is an essential historic prerequisite to the formation of a State. In this hypothesis, Sinha cited a number of examples, how the tribes of Central India such as Bhumij of Manbhum district (major part since transferred to West Bengal from Bihar), Munda of Chota Nagpur and the Gond of Bastar among whom there is no tradition or record of large scale invasion of the agriculturists tribal territory by aggressive nomads. Sinha has carried out very important and meaningful researches in his subsequent studies.[4] Stephen Fuchs[5] published his valuable work *Rebellious Prophets : A Study of Messianic Movements in Indian Religions* in 1965.

A seminar on tribal situation in India was convened in 1969 at the Indian Institute of Advanced Study, Simla in which apart from this author scholars such as Surjit Sinha, L.P. Vidyarthi, Jyoti Sen, Phillips Ekka, L.K. Mahapatra, B.K. Roy Burman, K.S. Mathur, S.L. Doshi, Alamchiba Ao, G. Chattopadhyay, D.P. Sinha, N.K. Bose, Sachidananda, Martin Oran, D.N. Dhir, M.N. Srinivas, I.S. Negi, Nitya Nand Das, S. Bhattacharya, L.M. Shrikant, Sirsalkar, O.K. Moorthy, D.R. Pratap, T.N. Pandit, and so on, contributed papers on the tribal situation in North-east India, Nagaland, Bihar, Orissa, Central India, Western and Eastern Deccan Tribes, Maharashtra, South India, Andhra Pradesh, Andaman and Nicobar Islands, etc., respectively. The proceeding of the Seminar was edited by Dr. K.S. Singh in 1972.[6]

Coming to the specific subject of tribal movements, it is B. K. Roy Burman who made a very useful survey of 'National Movement among the Tribes' in 1971 in which he tried to bring out some conceptual framework of those movements.[7] In the same year, he wrote

'Modernisation among the Tribal Population, Particularly of the Borders of India'. In 1972 he contributed his valuable paper on 'Social Process in the Hills of North-east India : An Ecological perspective' in the National Seminar on Social Change. His has been the important contribution in this branch of study which ranges from his thesis in 1960 on 'Dynamics of persistence and change of a small community, the Totos'. In 1968 he wrote on 'Some dimensions of Transformation of Tribal Society in India'. P. C. Joshi prepared a mimeographed report in 1972 on 'A Survey of Research on Land Reforms in India' under the auspices of Indian Council of Social Science Research. It gives an idea of the land problems in India. As early as 1958, F. T. Januzzi submitted a thesis to the University of London on the agrarian problems in Bihar. Divakar Jha prepared an Evaluation of Land Reforms in Bihar, in 1965. Bansidhar Singh submitted his thesis on 'Land Reforms in Bihar' to Bihar University. V. P. Singh submitted his thesis on 'Some Economic Aspects of Tenancy with special reference to Bihar' to the Delhi School of Economics in 1967. Gyan Chand wrote as early as July 1946, in the *Journal of Agricultural Economics* on 'Land System in Bihar'. S. R. Bose wrote in August 1954 on 'Land Distribution in Bihar'; Satish Kumar Bose wrote on 'Land Reforms Legislation in Bihar and its implications' in 1962; Indradeep Sinha contributed 'Struggle for Agrarian Reforms in Bihar' and 'Land Liberation Movement in Bihar' in *Mainstream* in 1968 and 1970 respectively; R. N. Sinha published his 'Bihar Tenancy 1783-1833' in 1963; R. O. Dham wrote 'These are my tribesmen : The Oraon' in 1967 in which she examined various historical forces at work in forging a new tribal identity in Chota Nagpur context; in 1972 Eastern Zone Seminar on Land Reform was held in A. N. Sinha Institute of Social Change, Patna under the auspices of the National Institute of Administration, Mussoorie.

But no specific reference to Chota Nagpur region was made in all these studies. P. C. Bose was the earliest writer to write on 'the rural life of Chota Nagpur' in the *Indian Journal of Economics*, 1918-19. S. P. Sinha[8] wrote on 'The Problem of Land Alienation in and around Ranchi District' in 1965 and discussed the Chota Nagpur agrarian problems in the last century in his book on '*Life and Times of Birsa Bhagwan*' published in 1964. This was followed by K. S. Singh[9] history of Birsa movement in 1966. Kol Insurrection and Bhumij Revolt by J. C. Jha, which were published in 1964 and 1967 respectively.

Apart from these secondary sources and others, certain printed archival materials such as Indian Finance Commission Reports of 1880-81, 1898, and 1901, extracts from papers connected with the Bengal Rent Bill, various reports on condition of the lower classes in India in 1881-91, confidential reports on condition of the agricultural population in India, papers relating to Bengal Administration (1905-1912), Commission on Agriculture in India (1920), Royal Commission on Labour in India (1931), Government of India Resolution on Land Revenue System and memorials to Secretary of State for India (1902) and other such Government reports give a very comprehensive and competent picture of the time though not dealing on the tribal problems since that alone was never the terms of reference for these various commissions and committees. Of the printed materials special mention may be made here of a bunch of documents printed by the Government of Bengal in 1890 for restricted use under the title *Papers Relating to Chota Nagpur Agrarian Disputes*, Vol. I and II (1890). These papers deal with the causes of disputes between tenants and landlords with descriptions of land system prevalent in different parts of tribal districts, tenancies of paraedial conditions, working of Chota Nagpur Tenure Act, (Act II of 1869) and effects of Bhuinhari Survey, agitations and disputes between converts and their churches etc. These are in the form of long letters with enclosures containing long reports, memoranda, government resolutions up to 1890. These are veritable mines of information on dependable materials. Various land tenure reports were prepared by very able civilians of the times and were forwarded in original by the Commissioner of Chota Nagpur to the Government of Bengal in 1875.[10] In them we find a wonderful marshalling of facts relating to land tenure prevalent in the respective area and are anchorsheet of our knowledge about the material condition of Plateau. E.T. Dalton's *Descriptive Ethnology of Bengal*, Calcutta (1872), H. Risley's *Tribes and Castes in India* give information regarding tribes of this area. Apart from these documents available only in the State Archives, our knowledge can well be supplemented by Survey and Settlement Reports by Forbes, Bridges, Saunders, Reid, Taylor, Tucky, Shifton, and others of different districts of Chota Nagpur Division and Santal Parganas. Of course, gazetteers and their revised editions of different districts place before us a resume of what should one know about the district in a nut-shell.

Besides these valuable materials, we have certain recent

publications by the State Central Record Room, Patna, under whose auspices old records have been serialised and compiled. Mention may be made here of (i) Selection from the Judicial Records of the Bhagalpur District Office (1772-1805), Patna (1968), (ii) Selections from Unpublished Correspondence of the Judge-Magistrate and the Judge of Patna, 1790-1857, Patna (1954) and (iii) Unrest against the British Rule in Bihar 1831-1859, Patna (1957). Many more volumes are about to be published which will throw ample light on the matters of such research projects. Special Officer, Revision of Gazetteer, Patna, published "1857 in Bihar", Patna (1959) and Selection from Old Singhbum Records, Patna. Dr. Jagdish Narain Sarkar published a paper 'Palamau Jagirdars' in the *Journal of Bihar Research Society*, Dr. K.K. Dutta compiled the *History of the Freedom Movement in Bihar* in three volumes published from Patna in 1958. R.R. Diwakar's compilation[11] *Bihar Through the Ages* published in 1958 is another worthwhile publication. These materials are very important from the point of view of our study. Beals dealt with conflict resolution in South Indian village and F. G. Bailey studied Orissan village and expounded his tribe, caste and nation theory. Martin Oran took interest in Santals and political question of Chota Nagpur in the context of urbanisation and industrialisation in 1965. P. Ganguly devoted his studies on Separatism as a factor in Indian polity and took Adivasi Mahasabha as a case study. A. F. C. Wallace, the father of concept revitalisation movement was followed by Edward Jay[12] who used situation in Chota Nagpur-Santal Parganas for formulating his theoretical framework.

Ethnographers such as S.C. Roy, D.N. Majumdar, L.P. Vidyarthi, K.K. Leuva and others have done yeoman service in bringing forth the tribals from the dark nitches of oblivion. S. C. Roy had been a pioneer in making use of historical materials in understanding the riddles of tribal life and his monograph on *Munda and their Country*[13] published in 1912 still stands out as a unique monument of his diligence and scholarship. Some studies have also been made on tribal rebellion. Prominent among these are: K.K. Dutta's *Santal Rebellion of 1855* (Calcutta, 1940), S.P. Sinha's *Life and Times of Birsa Bhagwan* (Patna, 1964), K.S. Singh's *Dust Storm and the Hanging Mist* (Calcutta, 1966), J.C. Jha's *The Kol Insurrection of 1832* (Calcutta, 1966) and *Bhumij Rebellion of 1833* (Delhi, 1968), Muchi Roy Tiru's *Birsa Bhagwan* (Ranchi, 1948), and P.G. Purti's *Shaheed Birsa Munda* (1955), S.P. Sinha's *Birsa Bhagwan aur Unka Kal* (Patna, 1988) in Hindi, and S.P. Sinha's *Santal Hul* (1990). But they could never give an all-comprehensive picture of the situation and they selected one stormy petrel or other for eulogisation.

Among the works of European missionaries, John Hoffmann's *Encyclopaedia Mundarika* stands out very prominently for its richness and scholarship. It is an on-going work and its thirteen volumes were published between 1930-50 and future volumes are in preparation. It mirrors the social life of the Munda people and depicts the social and political problems of the Mundas and other people in a most scholarly way. Hoffmann represents the extreme school of tribal extension due to the modern contact. He has very ably discussed Khutkatti system and its breakdown, emigration, Birsa, village and many topics depicting tenurial situation in tribal society of Munda community. No writer on Chota Nagpur, whether he is a historian, a sociologist, ethnographer or a social anthropologist can afford to miss these volumes. Similarly other missionaries like Lusty, Nortrott, Bodding, Skrefsrud, Campbell, threw ample light on the problem of their own time in their own way but they wanted to justify their own proselytising activities. Newspaper clippings preserved in private collections and the National Library, Calcutta, are very interesting indeed and they can be looked into with profit.[14] *Gharbandhu*, an organ of G.E.L. Church dealt with the problem of conflict between landlords and the tribal tenants on the one hand and on the other it exhorted the tribals to join G.E.L. Church to fight the 'alien landlords'.

Government of India from time to time appointed Parliamentary Committees to look into the tribal situation and then to suggest remedies to solve their problem. In 1958, a Study Team on Social Welfare and Welfare of Backward Classes was formed under the Chairmanship of Mrs. Renuka Ray who submitted the report in 1959. Similarly, a Scheduled Areas and Scheduled Tribes Commission under U. N. Dhebar went into the problems of the tribes in India in 1960 and submitted its report in 1961. Earlier Simon Commission Report (1928) and Backward Classes Commission under Kaka Kalelkar in 1956 and Commission on Multipurpose Tribal Blocks under Verrier Elvin were commissioned to look into the problem. Their reports are indeed valuable materials on the applied side for the study. The Backward Classes Commission for Bihar under Mongeri Lal has submitted its report which was published in 1976. S.C. Dube[15] edited *Tribal Heritage of India* in 1977 which contained valuable research papers on Tribal self-image and identity. The proceeding of the ASI Seminar on the Tribal movements in India held in 1976 was published in 1982 in

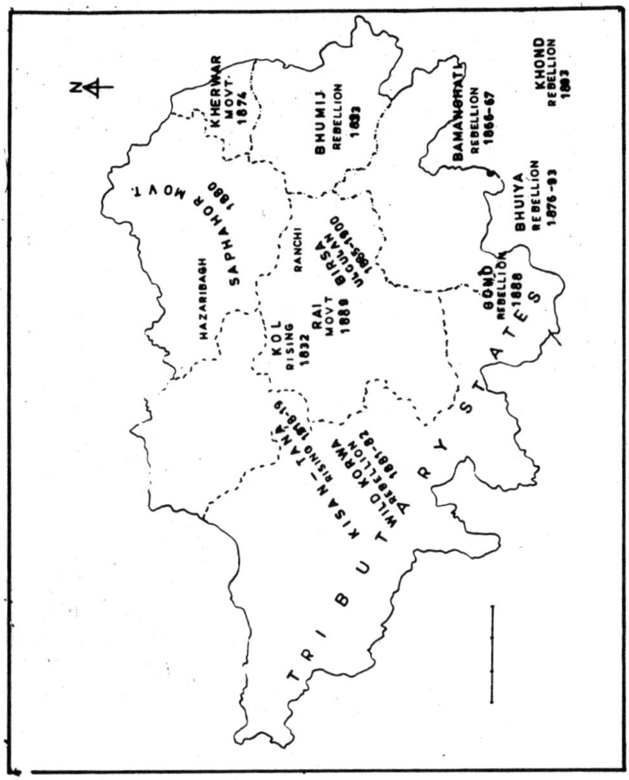

FIG. 1.1: Rebellion Map of Chota Nagpur and Tributary Mahal

two volumes. In 1985 shortened version of John Macdougall Ph.D. thesis written in 1974 was published as *Land and Religion.* A.K. Singh (Ed.) *Social Change in 1989* had number of papers on Jharkhand. S.P. Sinha (Ed.) *Tribal Leadership in Bihar* gives in 1990 the genesis and development of tribal leadership and other papers.

Thus we have seen that for a study like this and also with a time perspective right from 1858 to the present time, one has to piece together all relevant materials from all possible disciplines to integrate them into a whole. We have to make the best use of the published and unpublished archival materials, we have to seek help from background materials published by indigenous and foreign scholars. We have to look to ethnographers, social anthropologists, sociologists and social psychologists for various interpretation of the phenomenon of conflict and tension in tribal society of Bihar. Thus in this way the originality of this work is thought to be maintained since no exclusive work on this problem has ever been made. In the references cited above, one has to search out some allusion to this problem in the heap of materials scattered here and there.

Theoretical Framework

In this study, we shall have to take this into account that the rebellions after the ascendence of the British Crown on Imperial India were certainly typologically different from what we found those during the days of East India Company administration. While the early British penetration in the area met with violent retaliation and fighting in Tamar Insurrection (1795-1800), Chero Rising (1802), Kol Rising (1832), Bhumij Revolt (1833) and Santal Hul (1855), the rebellions during the period of Crown's early administration were that of a movement of a "prayer, protest and petition" (Santal Discontent of 1860 and 1871; movement of Bhagirath, Dubia Gossain, Sardar Movement of Munda and Oraon etc.). If there were some violence in Birsa Rebellion, it was negligible in comparison with Santal Hul, Kol Rising and other such risings of Company's days.

Roy Burman has suggested four types of unrest typologically:

1. Revolt against Territorial Encroachment.
2. Revolt against Loss of Resources leading in to Agrarian Revolt.
3. Revolt against Extension.
4. Ideology-oriented Revolt.

The first three types of the tribal revolts occurred in Bihar, but it is very difficult to accommodate the fourth since when tribals are impelled by ideology to rise they themselves no longer remain tribal. Ideological acceptance is definitely a very advanced situation which could not be expected from pre-literate groups of Chota Nagpur and Santal Parganas. Therefore, we can say that the tribal rebellions in Bihar were the outcome of the agrarian causes due to loss of their land by territorial encroachment by the new settlers who were termed as 'Diku'. Sometimes, it is more than agrarian as in the Kol Rising. In all rebellions, agitations and movements, agrarian question reigned supreme while other factors of revitalisation were among the subsidiary causes. Sinha and Mahapatra have tried out models which would be good for their use in understanding the present day tribal solidarity movements, but historical facts point out the existence of unsatisfactory agrarian situation which invariably goaded one group of tribes or the other to rise throughout the nineteenth century in Bihar. These rebellions were not against the violent intrusion of a different people, but it is a clash of a culture in peaceful meeting of two different cultures. Such clashes could be found among the traders peddling the petty trades, business men settling in interiors with their wares, introduction of *zamindari* system of land settlement and revenue, missionary activities, enhancement of rent, ejectment, under-weighing, over-weighing etc. These were the peaceful process of exploitation to which the tribals sometime violently reacted. They reacted because they had the tradition of leading an isolated life, living in a 'commune system' and well developed indigenous social system. Therefore, in all the eventful main clashes such as Paharia Rebellion, Kol Rising, Santal Hul, Birsa Rising, we find the economic and social degradation mostly resented by the tribals. Their leaders retaliated to see that encroachment is put to an end, forced *begari* is not taken and *rakumat* are not paid, injustice is not meted out to them in courts and their land is not further alienated. That much is their ideology, that much is their philosophy of rebellion. The salient features of tribal rebellions in Bihar are the following :

1. Early British penetration was reacted violently by every tribal groups in Bihar in their own way as it entailed loss of liberty. Even if they were suppressed and given an administration they intermittently resented the slightest fault in the working of that machinery which sought to provide protection to them. Therefore, whole nineteenth century in Bihar is a saga of furtherence of

British administration as well as wresting of various concessions and safeguards that go to make up the personality of a tribal Bihar, alienated, withdrawn and somewhat hostile against the people with whom they had the tradition of living more or less peacefully for centuries. Government administrative machinery, land laws, western education and western Christian missionaries, etc., acted as catalytic agents.

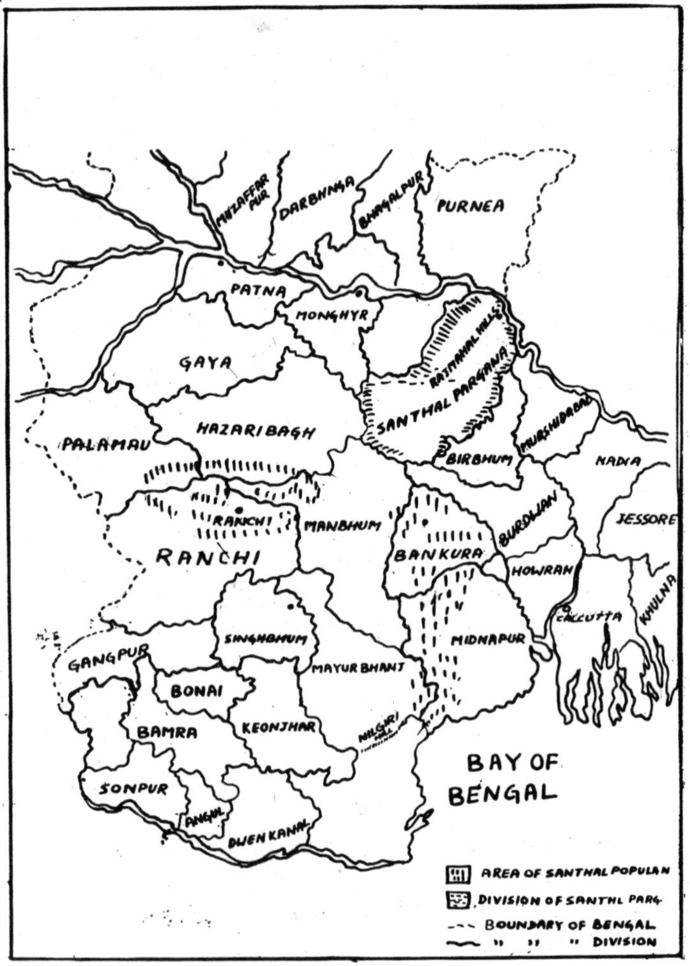

IMPERIAL GAZETTIOR OF INDIA VOL XXVI OXFORD 1709

FIG. 1.2: Map of Bihar, Orissa and Bengal

2. The aftermath of the extension of Permanent Settlement was not followed by preparation of Records of Rights which the settlement envisaged and, therefore, the whole nineteenth century tribal Bihar is beset with the agrarian clashes between the two groups, the tribals *raiyots* and the group composed of landlords, money-lenders, big cultivators, missionaries and local petty administrators.
3. On the level of leadership, the traditional leaders like Manki, *Munda, Parganait* supplied the initial lead to any movement which remained confined in their own realm, but region of influence, if sought to be extended, required the help of other modes of communication which may not be invariably confined to indigenous traditional leadership.
4. If the minor tribes like Korwa, Gond, Bhuinya, Khond preferred to rebel, these are apt to be local affairs, an isolated event in a particular area marked by the geographical feature of inaccessibility from the seat of administration.

Universe of Study

The universe of study is the tribals of Chota Nagpur-Santal Parganas in the State of Bihar and that of Gajarat Mahals of Orissa and tributary States in the then Central Provinces. Taken together they have been categorised into two broad groups major and minor tribes in the following manner:

Major Ttibes

Santal

1. Santal Discontent, 1861	Santal Parganas
2. Bhagirath's Kherwar Movement, 1870	Santal Parganas
3. Dubia Gossain's Kherwar Movement, 1872	Santal Parganas and Hazaribagh
4. Sapha Hor Movement, 1872-1990	Hazaribagh, Giridih and Santal Parganas
5. Jharkhand Movement, 1912-1990	Chota Nagpur Division and Santal Parganas
6. Shibu Soren Sarkar, 1971-78	Giridih, Hazaribagh, Dhanbad and Giridih

Munda

1. Rai Movement, 1884-87	Ranchi
2. Sardari Larai, 1869-1895	Ranchi
3. Birsa Rebellion, 1895-1900	Ranchi, Singhbhum
4. Jharkhand Movement, 1912-1990	Chota Nagpur Division and Santal Parganas Division

Oraon

1. Tana Bhagat Movement, 1914-1990	Lohardagga, Gumla, Ranchi and Palamau
2. Jharkhand Movement, 1912-1990	Ranchi, Lohardagga and Gumla

Minor Tribes

Kisan

1. Kisan Rebellion, 1919	Palamau, Ranchi, Sirguja

Korwa

1. Wild Korwa Rebellion, 1881-82	Sirguja (M.P.), Palamau

Khond

1. Khond Rebellion	Khondmal (Orissa)

Bhuiyan

1. Bhuiyan Rebellion of Keonjhar, 1867-93	Keonjhar
2. Bamanghati Movement, 1866-67	Mayurbhanj, Bamanghati

This is based on the attempted or the fight against the British Government by the tribals themselves and whatever materials available in archives have been categorised in the above manner.

Unit of Observation and Sample Size

Tribes are the unit of observation. Taking the census figures of 1961, we find that 72.24 per cent of the tribal population have been included in the sample frame (Table 1.1).

TABLE 1.1: Population of Major/Minor Belligerent Tribes

Tribes	1961	1971	1981
Major Tribes			
1. Munda	628,931	723,166	845,887
2. Santal	1,541,345	1,801,304	2,060,730
3. Oraon	735,025	876,218	1,054066
4. Ho	454,746	505,172	536,523
Minor Tribes			
1. Kisan	12,011	16,903	23,420
2. Korwa	21,162	18,717	21,940
3. Khond	814	596	1,264 (Bihar Figure)
4. Bhuiyan	118,636	— (No enumeration as S.T. in Bihar)	—
5. Gond	33,521	48,869	96,574

Note: (Bhuiyan were in the table of aboriginal or tribal people before they were descheduled in Bihar in 1956. Figures of Tributary Mahals not available).

The shortfall of about 27.76 per cent is due to the fact that the tribes falling within it did not have the records of fighting in any rebellion.

NOTES

1. Lewis A. Coser, *Toward A Sociology of Social Conflict*. Columbia (1954) and *The Functions of Social Conflict*. Glencoe, (1954), pp. 16-31.
2. G. S. Ghurye, *Social Tension in India*. Bombay (1968).
3. P. Sorokin, *Social and Cultural Dynamics*. London (1957).
4. Surjit Sinha, "Bhumij Khatriya Social Movement in South Manbhum", *Bulletin Department of Anthropology*, Indian Museum, Calcutta, Vol 8, No. 2 (1959). Surjit Sinha etc., "The Concept of Diku among the Tribes of Chota Nagpur", *Man in India*, Vol. 49 (1969), pp. 121-138.
5. Stephen Fuchs, *Rebellious Prophets: A Study of Messianic Movements in Indian Religions*. Bombay (1965).
6. K. S. Singh, ed., *Tribal Situation in India*, Simla, Indian Institute of Advanced Study, (1972).

7. B. K. Roy Burman, "National Movement among the Tribes" *Secular Democracy Annual Number*, 1971.
8. S. P. Sinha, *Life and Times of Birsa Bhagwan*, Patna, Government of Bihar (1964) and *Problem of Land Alienation in and around Ranchi City 1955-1965*. Patna, Government of Bihar (1968).
9. K. S. Singh, *Dust Storm and Hanging Mist*. Calcutta, Firma KLM (1966).
10. Letter dated 8th April 1875 from G. K. Webster, Manager of Chota Nagpur Estate to the Deputy Commissioner of Lohardaga.
11. R. R. Diwakar, ed., *Bihar Through the Ages*. New Delhi, Orient Longman (1958).
12. Edward Jay, "Leadership and External Relations in Tribal Community of Middle India" in *Leadership in India*. Bombay, Asia (1967).
13. S. C. Roy, *Munda and Their Country*. Calcutta (1912).
14. S. P. Sinha, "Calcutta Press Reaction on Birsa Rising", *Calcutta Review*. (1959).
15. S. C. Dube, ed., *Tribal Heritage of India*, Vol 1. Delhi, Vikas (1977).

2

ADMINISTRATIVE RIGMAROLE AS A SOURCE OF CONFLICT

ADMINISTRATION IS one of the factors which could be responsible for conflicting situations in the tribal areas of Bihar because the pattern of technological progress of advanced civilisations, when foisted on a relatively primitive people, sometimes created havoc. But at the same time this factor of conflict serving as the kingpin in the process of social change makes an interesting study because the older technology is so thoroughly fused with the prevailing culture that the newly introduced technology threatens, in part or in whole, the cultural life itself.[1] The introduction of an alien culture through the media of administrative machinery, industrial products, laws and regulations and missionaries, etc., leads to cultural clash, conflict of opposing value systems, creeds and ways of life. It introduces alien values, different standards, different goals.[2] A cultural clash becomes inevitable. The threat to the very existence of indigeneous mode becomes more apparent and pronounced. This phenomenon is very common and frequent in pre-literate and unsophisticated tribal societies.

The situation in Chota Nagpur and Santal Parganas, the heartland of different tribes of Bihar during the initial years of British advent, was such that it created ripples of great tension in the area because the tribes constituting the masses of the area reacted sharply to the innovations in the administrative pattern. Rebellion against the rule and defiance of the authority became the order of the times. The history of this region is dotted with one rebellion or the other because the aborginals resorted instinctively to prayer and battle-axe, both symbolising the sense of dissatisfaction among the tribals.

In an atmosphere where despotism was justified on higher plain as a moral principle and the cry for any sort of representative and responsible government was very feeble, the mode of political operation adopted by the hapless tribal masses was necessarily that of battle-axe for the first instance. But, subsequently, some educated people in the community preferred the course of 'petition and appeals' for reform in administration and also for the removal of the grievances of the people. It was their genuine belief that the defects of the governments and the consequent hardships of the people like *zamindari*, oppression and allied pin-pricks would be remedied if the attention of the higher authorities both in India and England was drawn to these. In this study, a detailed narrative account of all such commotions is given. But it will not be out of place here to look into the bulk of records in archives which gives bewildering situation for the British administrators first to initiate the laudable measures and then be wiser after it had created ferment. It will be profitable if we make some references to events in Santal Parganas and Chota Nagpur as case study for which the responsibility squarely lay at the doors of British administration.

Administrative History of the Santal Parganas

The British rule was very firmly established in Birbhum District as early as 1786 and this district lay adjacent to the Santal Parganas. The invocation of the law of Permanent Settlement in 1793 helped in increased output of agricultural commodities which had gone down due to recurring famines and predatory habits of the Paharias of Rajmahal Hills. The Santals were hired to clear the jungles and also to secure the countryside against the onslaught of ferocious wild animals. The reclaimed areas were freed from the ambit of taxation. This gave fillip to land-reclamation activity and permitted the landlords to demand a comparatively lesser rent from their Santal tenants. Buchanan, who visited present Bhagalpur and Santal Parganas in 1810-11 reported that:[3]

> Whenever the land has been brought into full cultivation, and the customary rent is demanded, they (the Santals) retire to the wastes belonging to some other Zamindars (rent-collector landlord). A whole village always moves at once, and their headman (*Manjhi*) makes a bargain with the new landlords for the whole, agreeing to pay a certain sum for as a much land as they can cultivate. At first they pay a trifle, but this is gradually increased until the full sum become due. If any attempt is made to take more from any individual the whole run off. The *Manjhi* levies tax assessment on the individuals, according to the stock which each possesses.

MacPherson's Settlement Report on Santal Parganas District in 1907 stated that the first wave of migration occurred during the period 1790-1800 and the Santals presumably settled in the present Jamtara and Deoghar Subdivision. The Santal settlers entered here from about 1810 onwards. They were pushed further north, because Buchanan found 500 Santal families in Dumka Subdivision in 1810. In 1818, Southerland found them in Godda Subdivision and that part of Dumka Subdivision which lies within the Damin-i-koh area. In 1827, Ward encountered Santals in Northern Godda because the Santals wanted to escape from the disturbances in Singhbhum district.[4]

Besides the Santals, we should know something about the Paharias who are the dwellers of north-central part of Santal Parganas in Rajmahal Hills. The Paharias, the scions of the Dravidian people, are the indigenous inhabitants of these hills and had the tradition of plundering the Hindus in the plains for centuries. Paharia raids became very common affair and affected the cultivation very adversely. The raids became intensified particularly when the plains were depopulated by the Great Famine of 1770. The famine did not affect the Paharias so much as the people in the plains because the Paharias could also live on forest products for considerable time.

The British administration could not have allowed this region of strategic importance to remain like a paradise of plunderers, since the main trade route between Calcutta and northern India passed along the narrow plain between the Ganges and the Rajmahal Hills. So the Paharias had to be contained. Between 1770-1784, the British developed a system under the collectorship of Cleveland (popularly known as *Chilmili Sahib* among the tribes) whereby the Paharias were exempted from the payment of land revenue; but in return were responsible for restraining their people from raiding the plains.[5] The Cleveland system was applied to Rajmahal Hills and also to the fiscal division of Belpatta to the south-west of the Ambar Hills and Sultanabad Parganas of the east. In 1826-32, this area was marked by a line of pillars and named the Damin-i-koh as 'skirts of the Hills'. The Paharias were given certain internal autonomy of following their own way of life and hill rangers were raised from among them. The British encouraged to settle agriculture among the Paharias and non-Paharias were not allowed to settle in the Damin-i-koh area.

But from 1820 particularly the Santals began to settle in the Southern Damin-i-koh which created necessarily a great tension among the Paharias and the Santals. Carstairs, who was a Deputy

Commissioner in the Santal Parganas for 13 long years, has beautifully depicted this situation in his novel *Harma's Village*. Perhaps the Santals were allowed to settle in Damin to clear the forests in the valleys and to start rice cultivation. But they were not exempted like the Paharias from paying revenue to the government. Damin-i-koh was considered the Government State and the rent payable to the Government was fixed at a low level. The Santals were themselves given some sort of autonomy to run their own life and their traditional leaders like *Parganait, Parmanik* and *Subas* were held responsible for collection of land revenue. The rent was about one-quarter of a rupee per acre or less than half the rate in Ranchi District. This policy was vigorously enforced by Pontet, a non-commissioned British officer, who was the Superintendent of the Damin-i-koh. He also tried to encourage cash crops such as potatoes but without any success. But he could not legally prevent Dikus (non-tribals and money-lenders) from lending money to the Santals or doing business with them, because the Santals got their money either for paying rent or for personal purposes like wedding from the Dikus. It appears that the economy already was or had become monetised to some extent. The small traders could make good profits by buying rice or oilseeds from Santals and selling them in plains and this profitability invoked the process of land alienation. Money-lenders trapped Santals into debts and used to get their property attached. They even kept false accounts and used false measures and weights. The rate of interest charged was sometimes to the extent of five hundred per cent[6] per annum and many Santals ran deep into debt so much so that they became bonded labours for life which was made hereditary.

Not only the petty traders and money-lenders but the local *Zamindars*, *Khetwaris*, *Bhuiyans*, *Ghatwalls* and others vied with each other in exploiting the Santals by enhancing their rent and taking different types of extractions. O'Malley says that the rivalry between the traditional landlords and unscruplous adventurers from outside sought to give the Santals outside the Damin some protection against the latter even though the aliens even ousted the old landlords. But no such protection was given to them against Dikus in Damin-i-koh. It is not clear whether the Santals were better off inside or outside the Damin. O'Malley thought that they were better off outside; but according to Bidwell,[7] it was the other way round. The Santals kept flooding into the Damin-i-koh during the forties and fifties of nineteenth century despite the increased exploitation by the Dikus.

Bidwell reported that the government rental income in this area had increased from Rs. 6,682 in 1837-38 to Rs. 28,033 in 1854-55. In 1838, there were about 3,000 Santals in Damin whereas in 1851, this number had risen to an estimate 83,265 Santals and over 33,780 Paharias. According to 1881 Census the Santal population went up to 3,26,613 out of the total population of 12,14,680.[8] The Santals moved into the plains of Bengal from the districts of Birbhum, Bankura and Singhbhum but in 1855 they were yet to leave the Damin.[9]

Although the Santals did not attempt to grow commercial crops like indigo and other things yet from 1854 when construction started on the railwayline from Calcutta to Patna, they turned out in large numbers for employment on this project. The demand for Santal labour increased dramatically because they were very popular with their employers for their truthfulness and their hard work. To quote Hunter:[10]

> The contractors sent their recruitors to every fair, and in a few months the Santals who had taken service came back with their girdles full of coin, and their women covered with silver jewellery, "just like Hindus" as their astonished clans-people remarked. Every man, woman and child could get work and boys of ten earned higher wages on the line than men had earned in the village. It was then that the distinction between slave (i.e. bonded servants) and the free man began to make itself felt. The entire free population who had not land of their own went forth with their women and children, their bows and arrows in their hands, and the national drum tatooing in front, to work for a few months on the railway, and then to return and buy land and give feasts to their clansmen. The slaves, who were compelled to remain working for their masters at home, contrasted their own lot with that of the prosperous adventurers. Running away became common, and the Hindu masters had recourse, in self-defence, to a much stricter and more vigilant system than they had ever before practised.

The cash brought from employer in the railways created all the more greater stir in the Santal's life because that gave an opportunity for comparison between the life of bonded man of petty traders, *mahajans* and *zamindars,* left on starvation level, and the life of a free wage-earner in railway construction, full of future prospects, full of joy and mirth and ornaments for their wives. This increased Santal solidarity without creating real class divisions between the bonded and the free men.

The Pontet had no legal power over the police or the courts in so far as the dealings with the Santals were concerned because they were initially within the jurisdiction of the Commissioner of Bhagalpur and consequently under the Magistrates and Collectors of the Districts of Bhagalpur, Birpur and Murshidabad. The nearest courts were held at the towns of Deoghar and Suiri which were at a distance of forty and twenty miles respectively from the Damin-i-koh. The headquarters of Bhagalpur District were thirty miles from the Damin and the areas were predominantly non-tribal. A handful of officials, however sincere their intention might be, could hardly maintain close contact with the tribals. Not surprisingly, exploiters such as *Naib Sazawals*, *Amalas*, *Mukhtiars*, *Darogas*, *Berkandazes*, etc. levied illegal taxes, acted as money-lenders' agents, and manipulated British court system to their own and the money-lenders' advantages.[11] Pontet was immensely popular with the Santals who affectionately called him *Palteen*. But his ability to help the Santals was limited. Besides this, he himself never exercised his powers to eject the *mahajans* from Damin because he knew that he had to gain some cooperation from the Dikus since his orders had to be carried out by the Diku officials, and that was why he was lenient to them. The Santals harboured hatred towards the Dikus because the Santals were allotted some territory by the British on the understanding that they would be able to live their traditional forms of life without any external interference. The personal guaranteer of this right was Pontet and in Santal eyes he was to give them direct access to the distant British authority whom they called *Kupinee.* Therefore, Pontet was never held responsible by the Santal villagers for the injustice wrought by the subordinates of the British authority. Secondly, the Santals being recent settlers had to define themselves in relation to the existing inhabitants of the area. The Paharias and Santals had an egalitarian form of social structure but; since their economy was different, they had little cause for either cooperation or conflict. But with regard to the semi-Hinduised tribals living in Santal Parganas, the issue of identity was quite acute. The *Bhuiyans* and other such castes aspired to go higher in the ladder of Hindu caste hierarchy, but such people were frequently poor and were themselves engaged in struggle against the Dikus. Thirdly, the work on railway construction no doubt brought home to many Santals the misery of being a bonded labour and in contrast the great economic opportunities open to those who could find better employment elsewhere. The existing new economic opportunities opened up by work on railway may well have turned many Santals to think of rebellion. In 1854, several petitions against the oppression of *mahajans* were addressed to Pontet and some *mahajans* were robbed by some Santals and some Santals were punished for this by the local police. The Santals began to gather for revenge from Birbhum, Hazaribagh, Ranchi and Bankura districts under the leadership of four brothers Siddhu, Kanu, Chand and Bhairab of Bhognadihi. They called a mass meeting on 30th June, 1855 which attracted about 10,000 people. It was here that the idea of setting up of a Santal Raj was mooted.

After encounter with Diku Police, the group of about 20,000 Santals roamed about killing, looting and destroying. The authorities wavered between leniency and severity in their methods of dealing with the rebellion. The coordination between civil and military authorities was poor until 1856 when ultimately martial law was clamped. In the next four months, the remaining resistance was stamped out in a systematic but ruthless and barbaric manner and an account suggests that tens of thousands of people were killed in the uprising.[12] The main target of rebels were money-lenders and local police and court officials. The British officers were spared unless found involved actively. Bidwell and others reported that the fighting was the most fierce at Damin-i-koh among the newer Santal settlers. This was sought to reflect the fact that the Santals had greater expectation of Damin-i-koh being protected by the Government. This rebellion of the Santals popularly known as *Santal Hul* further brought the Santals together by strengthening in them the sense of solidarity, born initially in their employment in railway construction. The Santals in Damin-i-koh succeeded in securing a kind of homeland for themselves as assured by the Government. The Hul, unlike the Kol rebellion had to its credit some revitalising and millennial attributes. It was in the face of stark poverty and humiliation that the Santals came to imbibe a sense of territoriality which saved them from losing their identity.

The north-east portion of Santalia near Rajmahal known as Damin-i-koh had no *zamindar* because it was a government settled State. The remaining Santal districts were permanently settled with *zamindars*, and the difficulty arose there. The Lieutenant Governor had told the officers that he saw nothing in Act VIII of 1859 or Act X of 1859 or in any other statutes which could render it really necessary that they should permit oppression of the Santals, if they exercised properly the powers which they possessed, but the fact was that administration of law had been tinctured by the views prevailing in Bengal.[13] The late Commissioner Mr. Money, though an excellent officer, took, as his letter showed, a strong view of the rights of the *zamindars* and was said to have ruled some questions which arose in that sense. The *zamindars* of the Santal country were people who in some sort held a wild uncultivated and inaccessible country on *Ghatwalis*, and similar tenures, paying very little revenue, but being found to protect the plain country against the hill robbers. "Now things are changed, they did not protect us but we protect them and they take advantage of that protection to exact the utmost rights of absolute proprietors from the little civilised but very industrious Santal people who have by their own labour reclaimed the wastes. These people exercised the sacred right of rebellion, and for a time government introduced an exception regime in consequence." Somehow or the other, most of the estates were taken under the government management in the Court of Wards. Sir George Yule[14] had a strong belief in the energy and enterprise of the European character and he gave farms of some estates to European gentlemen, a system which may have answered well as long as they were under the control of his absolute and active rule. But those farms have since been renewed under totally different conditions under the reign of law or what is supposed to be law, and the farmers have pushed their claims as far as they can for the sake of profit. "One of them has been unfortunate in his affairs, and is absentee, standing," the Lieutenant-Governor believed "much in need of the income he derives from his holding in the Santal Parganas, which are notoriously mismanaged". "The other is a prosperous manager but is stated to have left the management of the Santal estate to a brother, who seems to be driving the people to rebellion. The *Zamindars* who have resumed the management of their own estates are quick to copy European energy, so far as concern enhancing rents and increasing the income, though the copy no other European virtue."

As a matter of fact, the Santals and other inhabitants too of the Santal districts always have since insurrection been accustomed to look upon the Lieutenant Governor of Bengal as their last resort when dissatisfied in a way the *raiyots* of the other districts never had done until they began to throw the Indigo Yoke in Krishnaghur and elsewhere. The Lieutenant Governor of Bengal, Mr. Halliday,[15] had several interviews with the bodies of Santals, soon after the insurrection and he talked freely to them. The Santals addressed direct petitions to him. Therefore, the character of the administration in Santal Parganas on the eve of Sepoy Mutiny in 1857 was something like that of an administration deeply alienating the tribals to look to Lieutenant Governor for succourage.[16] The Government of Bengal discussed the steps taken by the Santals to right themselves as not 'illegal, violent and improper', but it was a matter of great surprise and regret to them that the Santals did not make their appeal to the Deputy Commissioner or to the Commissioner. The Lieutenant Governor suspected the existence of a weak point in the existing administration of the Santal Parganas. Such weak points lurked in the administration exactly there where it was hoped that this administration was specially strong, viz., the mutual relation of the people and the public offices, the freedom of intercourse between them, the intimate knowledge by the officers of the feelings of the people and the confidence of the people in the protection of the authorities. For this, the administration administered annoyance to the local officers many a time.

Similarly the administration of justice in Santal country in those days was far from satisfactory because the Santals were greatly oppressed by the money-lenders and most of the cases instituted by them ended in the prosecution of the Santals through crafty means followed in the courts set up by the administration. Carstairs in his novel *Harma's Village* draws a characteristic picture of British helplessness in administering justice to the tribals. Hunter, the District Magistrate of Birbhum with headquarters at Suri, wrote a book *The Old Missionaries* in 1896 and this work contains a few allusions to the British justice among the Santals.[17] The Santals were awarded rigorous imprisonment and the older people among them even died in their first year of confinement. The prisoners worked happily growing vegetable for the whole station as well as the jail because they thought that they had to serve the Queen Empress for the period of their sentence and then go back to their village with honour. Trafalgar Douglas a missionary, brought round the Lieutenant Governor to reconsider the cases of some of the Santals who were undergoing imprisonment.

More precisely the administration of justice in general and among the Santals in particular was such that one can find the real anomaly by which the Santals suffered. Arthur Ayliffe,[18] the Magistrate of Birbhum who was credited to have suppressed the Santal Risings of 1856, set his face against the series of Code promulgated by the Calcutta Secretariat for legal symmetry and worked with fervour in one of his protests against applying a uniform procedure to races in widely different stages of human society. He was alleged to have gone beyond the decorous limits of official remonstrance. This outspoken Commissioner was demoted to the Judgeship of the District of Birbhum. In those days District Judgeship was held in small esteem. The District Judges were usually elderly gentlemen who had not been able to make their mark in administration. To this rule there were indeed brilliant exceptions. But, generally speaking, the abler men regarded the district judgeship as an unavoidable halt in their promotion from the magistracy of a district to commissionery of a division; or as locus penitential for a Commissioner who had differences with the Government or had made a mistake. Aylliffe set himself to discharge the duties of his office strictly and consciously. The subordinates native Magistrates could not bring to bear such diligence in their judicial work because they were usually men of the dignified old type and their unaquaintance with English made it difficult for them to master the new penal and procedure codes. Their judgments were now consistently reversed on an appeal to the Judge owing to flaws in the proceedings, and, thereby, the notorious offenders got off. Already the difficulties of the Magistrate and Executive responsible for keeping down the crimes in the districts were increased by the circumstances that the Bengal Police had also been reorganised by law on entirely fresh basis. The system was full of novelties both for the officers and men and they found their efforts checkmated by technicalities which they imperfectly understood. A sense of discouragement seized the whole executive cadre of the District. This trend greatly alienated the tribals and created frustration and tension among them because they were not getting justice properly.

The experience of nearly fifty years brought home the lesson that the Regulation system was unsuitable in Santal Parganas and thereby Act XXXVII of 1855 was passed. The district was exempted from the operation of general regulations and acts as well as any laws passed subsequently in which the district was not specially mentioned, except in regard to civil suits above Rs. 1,000 in value, the collection of revenue in permanently settled estates, the sale of lands for arrears of revenue, etc. The exempted tract was placed under the Commissioner of Bhagalpur Division assisted by a Deputy Commissioner and a number of Assistant and Extra Assistant Commissioners. In 1856, a few simple rules for civil and criminal administration were laid down for the guidance of these officers and thus for some years the Santal Parganas were administered on a strict non-Regulation System which summarily meant :

(i) no advocates, no pleaders or *mukhtiars*, and no middlemen between Government officers and the people were permitted;
(ii) the contact with the people was direct;
(iii) there was no regular police; and
(iv) the spirit of the laws not in force was regarded, but no technical forms were allowed.

Thus this system was introduced to suit the occasion created by the Santal Hul, and it worked so well under Deputy Commissioner Ashley Eden, and Commissioner George Yule that the Santals remained generally unruffled during the Sepoy Mutiny. Eden drew up police rules and subsequently these came to be known as Yule's Rules.

When the memory of the Santal rebellion grew fainter, the Government grew complacent and changed its policy. The *zamindars*, especially the European *zamindars* like C. H. Barnes and others, started taking steps to enhance the rent, a natural source of irritation to the tribal tenants. In 1861 an excitement among the Santals was caused by Barnes' action and official apathy. The rules in regard to the administration of criminal justice remained in operation till 1862, when the Penal Code was introduced; and although the Code of Criminal Procedures was not formally extended to the district, its officers were directed to act in accordance with its spirit. In 1863 a question arose whether the Stamp Law could not be enforced in the Santal Parganas, and the then Lieutenant Governor, Cecil Beadon,[19] expressed his opinion that the Santal Parganas should also, as soon as practicable, be administered on the system in force in the rest of Bengal. These instructions and views were followed for some years, with the result that the Santal Parganas drifted more or less under the ordinary law and procedure of regulation districts. The Rent Law, the Civil Procedure Code, the Stamp Act and other Acts were considered to be in force, and the Deputy Commissioner was practically transformed into a judge with headquarters at Bhagalpur.

This change had a seismographic effect. The dissatisfaction caused by this change of system culminated in the disturbance of 1871. An enquiry was held, which showed that the Santals had real and substantial grievances, and the Government came to the conclusion that the indiscriminate extension of some of the acts of the legislature to the Santal Parganas had worked much mischief, and that the district still required a simpler form of administration than the rest of Bengal. Lieutenant Governor George Campbell accordingly recommended that the Santal Parganas should be exempted from the operation of the laws applicable generally to Bengal and suggested that the best mode of effecting this object was to bring it within the scope of Act 33 Vic Cap 3 of March 1870, which enabled local Governments to make regulations "for the peace and good government of territories" to which the Act might be applied by the Secretary of State. This measure followed by a suitable regulation, would, it was believed, place the action of the Government on a legal basis, which would be wholly unassailable and which would best enable the Government to apply from time to time the exact remedies for evils which had been or might be shown to exist, without violently or unnecessarily; disturbing the law or general administration of the district.[20]

Having received the approval of the Secretary of State on this measure, the Government of India issued a notification announcing the extension of the provisions of section 1 of Act 33 Vic. Cap. 3 to the Santal Parganas. The Government of Bengal then submitted, and the Government of India sanctioned, a regulation for the peace and good Government of the Santal Parganas, which passed into law as Regulation III of 1872. This Regulation gave the Lieutenant Governor full powers to appoint officers to make a settlement of landed rights, to restore dispossessed *manjhis* and others, to settle rent and to record the customs and usages of the people. It also introduced a usury law limiting the accumulation of interest on debts. It also specified the matters that were left to the discretion of Government to be introduced or withdrawn as might be found desirable from time to time. The Lieutenant Governor further took away from the Deputy Commissioner his powers as Sessions Judge and assigned them to the Sessions Court of Birbhum and Bhagalpur. At the same time he brought within the Santal Parganas the administration of civil justice, which for suits of over Rs. 1,000 in value had hitherto been exercised by the Civil Courts of the two districts. He further removed the Deputy Commissioner from Bhagalpur and posted him at Dumka, in the heart of his district, in order that he might be able to control its affairs adequately.[21] Brownwood was made settlement officer who defined and recorded the rights and duties of landlords and tenants and where necessary fixing fair rents between 1873 to 1879. One of the results of this settlement was to preserve the Santal village community system, under which the village community, as a whole, held the village lands and had collective ownership over the village waste.[22] These settlement operation created excitement which coupled with revivalistic Kherwar movement under Bhagirath Manjhi and Gyan Parganait posed a problem for the administration. Campbell's ideas were to be translated. Probably there could not be other officer so well adapted for this than Deputy Commissioner John Boxwell (1873-79). It is said about him,

> "Not only did he thoroughly grasp and appreciate them, but he brought to them fulfilment of both qualities and attainments of a high order. To the people he was a veritable *avtar* and he set himself to study and master the Santal tongue."[23]

This exercise of trial and error of measures led the authorities to devise new ways. It was subsequently found necessary to define more clearly the status of the Courts, and this was effected by the enactment of Regulation V of 1893. In regard to criminal jurisdiction, that Regulation constituted the Santal Parganas Session Division, the Court of the Deputy Commissioner, the Court of Sessions of the Division and appointed the Deputy Commissioner as the Judge of the Court of Sessions. The High Court at Calcutta was to confine itself to matters relating to jurisdiction in regard to European British subjects, to all cases in which sentence of death had been passed, and to all appeals.

In 1899 a regulation amending Regulation V of 1893, was brought into force. The new regulation converted the Court of the Sessions Judge of Birbhum into the Court of Sessions for the Santal Parganas Sessions Division and the Sessions Judge of Birbhum into the Judge of the Court of Sessions. The powers of a Sessions Judge exercised by the Deputy Commissioner were withdrawn. It further provided that the High Court at Calcutta, in addition to its jurisdiction under the Regulation of 1893, should exercise appellate and revisional jurisdiction in respect of all Sessions cases tried by the Judge of Birbhum; that the Deputy Commissioner should have appellate jurisdiction over the subordinate courts of the district, and that the Commissioner should have appellate jurisdiction over the Deputy Commissioner and revisional jurisdiction over all the courts of the district. By Regulation IV of 1912 and by notification No. 11-A of 1st April, 1912, issued in pursuance of that Regulation, the Court of Sessions and the Sessions Judge of Bhagalpur were declared to be

Court of Sessions and the Sessions Judge for Santal Pargana Division, the Session Court sitting within the district. The Regulation V of 1893 was further amended by Regulation IV of 1933, which empowered the local government to appoint any officer as a subordinate judge and to empower any Magistrate with powers under Section 30 of the Criminal Procedure Code. It further provided (i) that when in any case of a Magistrate specially empowered under Section 30, passed any sentence of imprisonment for a term exceeding four years or any sentence of transportation, the appeal of all or any of the accused convicted at such trial should go to the Commissioner, and (ii) that the Deputy Commissioner might direct that any appeal by any persons convicted or sentenced under Section 349 by any Magistrate other than the Deputy Commissioner of any class of such appeals should be heard by any first class Magistrate subordinate to him and empowered by the local government to hear such appeals.[24]

It is needless to recount the names of various Deputy Commissioners who worked uncessantly with untiring zeal in safeguarding the tribal sentiments and interests. But nonetheless the Indian counterparts of these British bureaucrats could not reach the standard of governance causing cracks and fissures in governmental machinery and this process became more conspicuous after the independence. The umbrella of protection and paternalism slowly started giving way to impersonal general type of administration in usual course creating a lot of stir, anguish and hardship to the *raiyots* in general and tribals in particular. However, the Santal and Paharia systems continued with little modification. In 1949, the Santal Parganas Tenancy (Supplementary Provisions) Act was passed incorporating earlier regulations passed to suit the exigencies of time. In 1969, the Bihar Scheduled Area Regulation was passed to restore the alienated tribal land to the non-tribals. But all these legislative measures did not considered as show the penchant of seriousness of British officers when protection of the tribal *raiyots* was an onerous task by every official under the supervision of Commissioner, who mostly acted as a saviour and a Great Patriarch for these tribals. The tribes, now mostly harassed by an army of developmental staff and other enterlopers, wistfully look back to the British days of Carstairs, Oldham, Boxwell etc. The steel frame of administrative machinery of Santal-Paharia system exists but it is souless being without a patriarch, the Santal Courts are still there but the judge is not there in the real sense of the term to dispense ready and speedy justice to the tribals.

The real merits of these courts with their simple procedure was that it gave definite advantages to the poorer classes of litigants. Their worth is based on the principle that the poor classes of people in the area should be tried in the simplest, the cheapest and the most expeditious manner as far as possible by direct dealing between the parties and the court. The Santal Parganas being a poor district deserves a speedy justice. Cheap and speedy justice is more important to the people than technical perfection, because simple procedure of the courts means less harassment, delay and expenses to the parties, and in these courts the rich have not the advantages over the poor that they have in regular courts.

On 4th April, 1965, the Bihar State Law Commission visited Dumka, the headquarters of Santal Parganas and heard the views of the members of local bar and others. Accidentally no tribal leader of repute came to place his point before the Commission. Even Deputy Commissioner also somehow or other acquiesced in the strong views of closing the Santal courts; but later on when the Commissioner, Bhagalpur pulled up the Deputy Commissioner he changed his mind. The matter is still to be finally decided by the Law Commission and the State Government.

From time to time such situations have arisen. In 1937 a Committee[25] under G. R. E. Russell was appointed to enquire into the system of administration of Santal Parganas and to suggest such changes and improvement in it as will best conduce to the well-being of the inhabitant. Bihar Legislative Assembly passed a resolution on 2nd September, 1937 in which the question of continuance of the Santal Courts was raked up. The Committee visited Santal Parganas from 29th January to 8th February 1938. The general criticism made on the Santal Civil Courts was (i) that the Officers lacked that training in civil law which did not enable them to decide cases correctly, (ii) that their decisions are often arbitrary and summarised and (iii) that the Santal Civil Rules under which they work are deceptive and inadequate. These led to injustice and the government has often been urged, therefore, to abolish these courts and place all civil courts under the rule of the High Court and the Civil Procedure Code. The legal profession was particularly opposed to that system and all the Bar Associations of the District have suggested its abolition. The Russell Committee though agreed that injustice has occurred and may recur owing to the ignorance of officers or the adoption of the summary methods, but very strongly believed that "regular courts also are not immune from the infliction of injustice" and therefore, the Committee opined that "the good features of the Santal Civil Courts are as valuable to the great mass of poor litigants that they should not be abandoned". But the Committee suggested many points of improvement which have been incorporated in this system.

The present day opposition of the Santal Courts stems from innate apathy towards the system being nursed by the lawyers from one generation to another. It also emanates from the desire of aggrandisement of judiciary over the executive and therefore, the worst battle between the executive and the judiciary is being fought here. Time alone will tell as to who will emerge victorious, but for us it is the question of the survival of the tribals of the district who could remain secured only when their system is allowed to function. The Constitution of India has made specific provisions for the tribal welfare through its Fifth Schedule and many sections in the Fundamental Rights and Directive Principles. Therefore, the continuance of the system governing tribals is not at variance with the programmes of social justice, equity and welfare as envisaged in the Constitution of India. In 1982 Santal Parganas was declared as Division and put under a Commissioner and the old district was parcelled into four divisions, viz. Dumka, Gadda, Sahebganj and Deoghar. Except in its Scheduled area portion (Dumka, Sahebganj and parts of Gadda) the Non-Regulation spirit is being eroded.

Administrative History of Chota Nagpur

Having seen historically the situation in Santal Parganas, a similar review of the situation in Chota Nagpur may be taken up to see how frequent administrative changes and decisions were responsible for the creation of conflict situations. This can be traced fruitfully if we study the story of early British contact in this Division and evolution of the administrative edifice.

The first initial impact by the British was made by Captain Jacob Camac in 1771 when he intervened in Palamau on behalf of Patna Council. Warren Hastings transferred Palamau (with Ramgarh and Chota Nagpur) from the charge of Patna Council to that of Presidency and entrusted both revenue collection and the administration of justice of the *zamindars*. In 1781, the Civil and Criminal Courts were opened at Chatra. Fluctuating and inefficient pattern of British administration contributed over many years to the mismanagement of the estate. The

Cornwallis system was applied to Chota Nagpur with little questioning of its suitability. However, Cornwallis was a Whig and was opposed to the concentration of executive and judicial powers in the hands of a district officer. As a matter of fact the Permanent Settlement of Bengal in 1793 was a frank attempt[26] to apply the English Whig philosophy of Government "having as its central belief that political power is essentially corrupting and inevitably abused; that power to be exercised with safety must be reduced to minimum, and kept divided and counter-balanced". However isolated attempts were made by some British officers to exempt this area from the general application of the regulations. Opposing the extension of the Permanent Settlement into this area, Mathew Leslie on 20th June, 1789 expressed an apprehension that "extending these Regulations to this district will be attended with very bad consequences",[27] and Sir John Shore, concurred with this view.[28] So this resolution dated 18th September, 1789 of the Bengal Government which confirmed the Decennial Settlement in Bihar precisely mentioned "that the Regulations do not extend to this district (Chota Nagpur) but that the Settlement be continued on the present footing and be extended to a period of 10 years".

Hunter, the Judge-Magistrate of Ramgarh corroborated Shore's anxiety about innovations and he wrote to the Board of Revenue testifying to the "simplicity of the character of and ignorance of the generality of the people". Therefore, on his motion in 1794 a modification of section II of Regulation VI was introduced to suit the need of the people of Ramgarh District. In 1800, regulation X similarly modified the rule of inheritance to suit the special needs of the chiefs of the area. Half-hearted governmental measures could not save the indigent tribals from being exploited by hordes of 'outsiders' which ultimately led to the Great Kol Rising in 1832.

When military operations ended in Jungle Mahal, as the area was known in the then official records, it was found necessary first to reorganise the administration of the tribal areas. The mood and thinking of the Home authorities ran counter to the spirit of the Cornwallis Code and seemed to be the expression of the general approbation of the Munro system of district administration.[29] What was needed most was the imagination and sympathy of a Brooke or a Brown or a Cleveland. The newspaper correspondent of the ***Bengal Harkaru*** dated 14th April, 1832 rightly remarked "to send a **Cleveland** to the Coles and you will have no occasion to augment **the Ramghar** Battalion". W. Dent and T. Wilkinson, in their capacity of Joint

Commissioners, submitted a note to the Bengal Government incorporating many benevolent recommendations for a new police and judicial system which could expect to bring justice to every man's door, embodying thus Bentham's idea of "a summary non-technical method in which the suitor would orally state his plea and personally confront the defendants".[30] This presupposed a concentration of undivided power in the hands of an European officer in-charge of Chota Nagpur endowed with high special powers. Here was the genesis of the Non-Regulation system which was to be applied to the South-West Frontier Agency, and of the special position of the Political Agent who was, with his assistants, to administer it.[31]

In these suggestions of the Joint Commissioners, more specially of Dent, one can see the application of some of the ideas of Munro, Elphinstone, Metcalfe and even Bentham to solve the problems of the tribal areas. The Collector would have none of the Cornwallis' division of judiciary from executive. He would have no one glued to his chair in court or office. The man who collected the revenue was also responsible for law and order. In a nutshell he was a policeman, magistrate and a judge. Metcalfe deplored "the continued separation of the office of Judge, Magistrate and Collector and believed that the best form of government in the interest of the people was that which was most simple and most free from artificial institutions. He devised the pattern of field administration which was military in form, personal in orientation. Munro, Elphinstone and Metcalfe were the three principal representatives of what may be called the patriarchal, unitary system of administration.[32] They stood for the following ideal:

> To the ryot, government must be represented simply; not by a multiplicity of officers and a multiplicity of written forms, but by a single officer, who had powers to enquire, to judge and to punish, without the delay and intricacies of the western legal process. This officer was not to be a distant and awful figure, presiding in his *cutchery* like a deity in his temple, but a familiar lord, visiting and speaking with them of their quarrels and their crops, and looked up to as *ma-bap,* father and mother. In practical terms, this meant a union of powers, at least at the district level.[33]

The weaknesses of the Bengal system was further exposed in view of the emergence of new ideas, viz., liberalism, utilitarianism, and humanism which called for "a new view of the functions of

Government. The combination of magisterial and revenue functions in the person of the Collector would be most desirable because it was in consonance with the contemporary philosophy of liberalism which advocated functionalism on the one hand and centralism on the other".[34]

Dent might have been influenced by these ideas and might have belonged to anti-Cornwallis school but his and Wilkinson's thinking were more due to the direct experience they had in running administration in tribal areas, Wilkinson had served at Nagpur for more than a decade and directly dwelt on his experiences as well as on the ideas propounded by Munro and Elphinstone. But his model was W. Blunt[35] who had considerable experience of tribal administration and had been famous for his framing of rules relating to the administration of civil justice in Arracan in 1828. As a matter of fact such ideas were also likely at that time to be well received by those in power in India, for under the Lord Bentick were ranged such men as Charles Metcalfe, the Vice President of the Council, W. Blunt, the third member of the Council, and James Thomason, the Deputy Secretary of the Judicial Department. Of them Blunt played a key role in pushing up the views of the Joint Commissioners for he was out and out paternalist who attacked Permanent Settlement vigorously.

On 22nd December, 1833, the Government announced that "whereas considerations connected with the present state of certain tracts of country now included in the district of Ramgarh, Jungle Mehals and Midnapore, the nature of disturbance which presently prevailed in various parts of those districts and the character of the inhabitants, have rendered it expedient to separate these tracts" and proceeded to pass a Regulation for "abolishing the courts of *Dewany Adawlat* of *Zillah* Ramgarh Jungle, Mehals and Midnapore".[36] The tracts included in the new charge were in the Ramgarh District, Chota Nagpur, Palamau, Kharakdiha, Ramgarh, Kunda, in the Jungle Mahals all the Mahals except Seainpahari, Shergarh and Bishunpur, in Midnapore, Dhalbhum. The new jurisdiction was placed under an officer known as Agent to the Governor-General who would administer justice and superintend the police and revenue services under the rules to be framed for the area which was later known as Wilkinson's Rules. Those parts of Regulation III of 1793 and Regulation XVIII of 1805 and all other Regulations which had hitherto been applied to the area were rescinded.

It deserves to be particularly noted that no civilian officer was preferred for this area. The criterion seems to have been efficiency as a military officer in suppressing the unrest as well as the then prevailing notion that military officers were suited the best for administration and pacification of such turbulent areas. This attitude came in such a bold relief that the provinces in which military officers were employed were known as Non-Regulation while civilians were exclusively employed in the Regulation provinces.[37] Thus by the middle of December 1833 under Captain Wilkinson a paternalistic non-regulation system of administration for this underdeveloped area, at the apex of which he would stand with very considerable powers, was set up. The swing of pendulum away from the complex machinery and regulations of Cornwallis was thus complete.[38]

By Act XX of 1854 the name of South-West Frontier Agency was replaced by Chota Nagpur on the reports of Ricketts and was placed under the administration of the Lieutenant Governor of Bengal as a Non-Regulation province. The Governor-General's Agent was turned into Commissioner and Principal Assistant Agent into Principal Assistant Commissioner and other senior or junior Assistant Agents were designated as senior or Junior Assistant Commissioner. The British Government had subjugated the *Hos* of Singhbhum and brought them under direct rule recognising their *Manki-Munda* system of administration. But the extension of Act XXXVII of 1855 to this part of the country was opposed.

On the examination of the early history of Kolhan, it was found that in 1837, 23 Kol pirs or parganas belonging to the three chieftains of Porahat, Seraikella and Khoraswan were detached from their states and with four others taken from Mayurbhunj in Orissa were, for the first time, brought under the direct control of the British Government under the name Kolhan. Regulation XIII of 1833 had then already been passed and it seemed very likely that the Kolhan was added to the Regulation Agency by an order of the Governor-General- in-Council issued under Section 7 of that Regulation, though no trace of such an order can be found, for after the date of its having been brought under the control of the British government it continued to be administered both as regards criminal and civil matters in the same way as the rest of the division, under the rules framed by Captain Wilkinson, the Agent to the Governor General-in-Council and duly approved by the Governor General-in-Council under Section V of the Regulation.

The rules framed for the administration of criminal justice were, however, superseded by the Code of Criminal procedure which was extended to the entire province of Chota Nagpur by the Government Order No. 3167 A, dated 26th December, 1861 and as Kolhan was held to be an integral position of the province of Chota Nagpur, the appellate Criminal Procedure jurisdiction over the Kolhan was transferred from the Commissioner to the Judicial Commissioner of Chota Nagpur. Subsequently, the Penal Code and the Code of Criminal Procedure were again formally extended to the Kolhan by notification No. 1384 dated 21st October, 1881 so that in criminal matters both the Judicial Commissioner and the High Court legally exercised control over the Kolhan. The same thing cannot, however, be said of civil matters as neither the Civil Courts Act nor the Civil Procedure Code were ever extended to the Kolhan. It, therefore, follows that the rules framed by Captain Wilkinson in 1833 for the administration of Civil justice in Chota Nagpur, which were duly approved by the Government and as such had the force of law, were then operative in Kolhan. Thus neither the High Court nor the Judicial Commissioner could interfere in civil matters connected with Kolhan so long as these rules were not superseded by the formal extension of the Civil Court's Act and the Code of Civil Procedures to it. Therefore Forbes, the Commissioner of Chota Nagpur in 1897, advised the Deputy Commissioner of Singhbum to follow the rules framed by Captain Wilkinson.[39] He was positive that neither the High Court nor the Judicial Commissioner had any jurisdiction there because Wilkinson's Rules were simple and adapted to the requirements of a primitive people like the Hos of the Kolhan.

The Commissioner advised the Deputy Commissioner to make judicious use of his authority in matters of allowing pleaders or *vakeels* so that they are of material assistance to the tribals rather than otherwise. The following are his observations regarding the extension of Act XXXVII of 1855 which are also noteworthy:

> In the Kolhan already, a large number of enactments have been formally extended under the notifications of the 21st October, 1881 and so far their extension has not resulted in any administrative inconvenience. The Criminal Procedure and the Penal Codes have been in force in it for more than the past 32 years and the High Court and Judicial Commissioner have been exercising appellate criminal control and jurisdiction over it during all this period without creating any administrative difficulty. The extension of Act XXXVII of 1855 the Kolhan would place the criminal administration of the tracts entirely under a special officer

> (presumably the Deputy Commissioner) working under the appellate control of another special officer (Commissioner) instead of as at present under the District Officer acting under the appellate control of the Judicial Commissioner and the High Court. Such a measure would in my opinion be a retrograde one. While as regards civil matters the gain from the extension of the Act would practically amount to nothing, for the Deputy Commissioner as Special Officer would continue to decide civil suits, as he is now doing, under the rules of Captain Wilkinson and the Commissioner will hear the appeals from his decisions as he is now doing under the rules. If the Act be formally extended to the Kolhan the Special Officer or Officers appointed under clause of Section II of it, will, in the administration of both civil and criminal justice, under the Section III be guided by the spirit and principle of the civil and criminal laws administered in the rest of Bengal so that in the criminal matters instead of Penal and Criminal Procedure Codes themselves their spirit and principle will have to be followed which in civil matters instead of the rules framed by Captain Wilkinson the spirit and the principle of the Code of Civil Procedure will have to be followed. I do not see what advantage would be derived from this.[40]

Apart from this, a post of Kolhan Superintendent was created in 1874 for looking after the interests of *Adivasis* and he was made the principal revenue officer of this area. He had been running the affairs in Kolhan successfully and administering the civil justice there. His relationship with *Manki-Munda* was such that he was all in all for them. He implemented various schemes, settled government waste lands and was, in short, the sole custodian of the tribals in the area, even arbitrating in domestic and private matters such as the family disputes or even the quarrels between husbands and wives. He also discharged the functions of a *Munsiff* in Kolhan, tried civil suits up to the value of Rs. 3,000. He had an elaborate staff and his task was accomplished by permanent hierarchy of time-honoured agencies such as *Mankis* and *Mundas*. *Manki-Munda* looked after the police organisation in Porahat and Kolhan. *Manki* had powers of Sub-Inspector of Police, *Munda* as Assistant Sub-Inspector and *Dakua* as police constable. This worked well till 1950 when the system was relaxed and police work of Kolhan was taken over by the police department by establishing Police stations of Jhinkpani, Manjhari,

Majhgaon and Noamundi.

In matters of judicial administration *Manki-Munda* served the processes. Civil cases were referred to arbitration of the *Mankis* and their unanimous award for the decree was final and not questioned in any court. When the decision was divided, the decision by Deputy Commissioner became final. Of course, the appeals lay with the Commissioner of Chota Nagpur Division and the Board of Revenue. The Miscellaneous cases were also referred to the *Mankis* for investigation and reports or for adjudication. The *Manki* and *Munda* arbitrated the family disputes, partition of lands and properties, and quarrels in a Village Panchayat and decided the claims etc.

But the post-Independence period has now again started witnessing the conflicting views on introduction of general laws and regulations. People have started questioning the utility of the plethora of Rules created by the military officers about a century ago. But efficacy of the paternalistic non-regulation system bequeathed by a Brook, a Brown, a Cleveland, a Munro, an Elphinstone, an Outram, a Wilkinson, a Dixan, an Evans or a MacPherson still holds good because the tribals in Kolhan as in the other areas require the leadership, sympathy and goodwill of such officers as are still enshrined in their hearts.

What a heartless attack could be made on the time-honoured system can be well imagined if we follow the proceedings of an application under Articles 226 and 227 of the Constitution of India made by Jotindra Nath Roy in Patna High Court.[41] Roy was evicted from the premises of A. C. C. Ltd., Jikpani on the orders of Kolhan Superintendent in his capacity of *Munsiff* in Kolhan area. Against this order Roy obtained a writ in the nature of *certiorari* on the grounds that the Kolhan Superintendent was never invested with any power by any notification or under any law to try the suit in question under Wilkinson's Rules. The learned judges found that no express words are to be found in Wilkinson's Rules indicating that Kolhan Superintendent or any other officer appointed as such can try a suit in Kolhan area. Several adjournments were allowed to the State Government and ultimately Roy won the case because the inherent lack of jurisdiction was proved by his counsel in the absence of positive pleadings from the State in this regard. The result was that the whole basis of Wilkinson's Rules and Kolhan system were jeopardised. Kolhan courts suspended their activities and ultimately the State Government had to pass a Revalidating Act in 1976. The Manki-Munda Sangh, Singhbhum[42] memorialised to the State

Government for steps to restore the functioning of the Kolhan Superintendent and thereby Kolhan system. But it said that the lawyers as a class have started clamouring for the abolition of the Kolhan system because they felt that conditions in Kolhan and Kolhan courts obtaining now, are absolutely different from what they were in 1833.[43] There were pressures from other quarters also.

The Kolhan Enquiry Committee appointed by the State Government in 1948 under M. M. Philip, Commissioner of Chota Nagpur Division held that the Wilkinson's Rules were out of date, but still they did not recommend the adoption of the Civil Procedure Code straightway. Instead they recommended the adoption of Santal Civil Rules. In 1956 L. Dayal, the Deputy Commissioner, Singhbhum was of the opinion that only a portion of the Wilkinson's Rules were out of date so far as the non-existence of *Sadar Dewany Adawlat* or the Governor General-in-Council were concerned, "but the essence of Wilkinson's rule still holds good".[44] He argued "The essence of the rule is that civil justice is administered". Over and above, he said that "by now Kolhan system is a social organisation of the Hos community and it will immediately touch off an agitation amongst the Hos if this system is to be changed". The third argument that the Deputy Commissioner placed was that "the Hos have a community way of living and the system of arbitration or speedy decision by the Kolhan Superintendent seems to be working well". He also recommended that the "lawyers should not be allowed to appear as a matter of right".[45]

In his other letter the Deputy Commissioner, Singhbhum advocated for the continuance of the system and in case any change was envisaged it should be done by proper legislation. His solution was only a gradual change over because *Manki-Munda* was an established institution in the society and any decision to replace it must radiate serious repercussions. He was sure that the whole idea of this system was to prevent the Hos from being exploited by intermediaries either in bureaucracy or in judiciary, and also by outsiders and *non-Adivasis*.

But a decade later in 1956-57, the sympathetic attitude shown by the Deputy Commissioner gave way to innate apathy and negligence inherent in bureaucracy in a disorganised parliamentary set up. The result was that the weapon of litigation was used to defeat the time-honoured tribal institutions. Working of different plans and the Acts in the area slackened the integrating bonds and the litigation referred to above took away altogether the seriousness of the Kolhan system of administration. The result is that Kolhan is restless.

Integrative forces are giving place to separatist tendencies. Parochial slogans are getting popular and "hate Diku campaign" is on its zenith. It is in the weakening of the Kolhan tribal system that we can search the explanation for the presence of large number of Naxalites or extremists in the jungles of Singhbhum where they have the audacity to wage gun battles against the government. The shots of gun battle in Ruam jungle was still reverberating, but distant Patna hardly hears. The anti-State acts being committed in Singhbhum by those who follow the politics of extremism could have been easily apprehended and stopped with the force of *Manki-Munda* system. But the question is could they try it?

People complain that *Manki-Munda* system is based upon the principle of inheritance and as such is against the democratic goals. But perhaps they do not like to remember that rights and privileges of a *Manki-Munda* emanate from *Hakuknamas* signed by the Deputy Commissioner, Singhbhum. The selection of a *Manki* or a *Munda* is based upon the principle which is half way between inheritance and election. Tyrants are to be removed by the Deputy Commissioner. Therefore, the trouble is not with the system. The system is not rapacious. But those who run the system forget their rights and duties and treat them in most *ad hoc* manner without the spirit of an officer of a Non-Regulation Area. Kolhan is a scheduled area also. But very few remember this fact, simply for the want of will. Dr. S.P. Sinha prepared a Report on Wilkinson Rule in Kolhan in 1978. The matter was examined by an Expert Committee headed by Member Board of Revenue, Patna and the report on updating of Wilkinson's Rules are under the consideration of State Government since 1984, which was submitted by that Committee then.

But now when Bihar Panchayat Raj Act, initiated a scheme of Community Development under the slogan of "service through guidance and assistance and inspiration of self-help" and the areas were demarcated for the location of funds and personnel, we find that indigenous system came into sharp clash with the new system. Each area contained a block of some 50,000 acres of cultivated land embraced about 100 villages. By 1955, the Community Scheme went into full swing. New blocks were created at the rate of 10 to 12 at a time and the officers were given full powers under the Community Development Department of the State Government. The District Development Office was set at district headquarters and Block Development offices were set up in the block. The blocks tended to be smaller than a circle. Where a circle is divided into two blocks, then only one of the Block Development Officers was also the Circle Officer. Under him there were Agricultural Supervisor, Cooperative Officer, *Gram Sevaks* and others. A viable link between these officers and the villagers was the village level worker whose job was to keep liaison between the village and the block. Armed with the *Karamchari's* records and the advice of the experts, his function was to supervise the realisation of the development schemes in the villages and to gauge all the modifications that were necessary in respect of particular needs. He was also the incharge of supervising all contracts for schemes done by the villagers and to communicate their desires and requests to the block offices. It would appear that village level worker was a crucial link in the allocation values. He is torn between political involvement and responsibility towards the village panchayat and the administrative responsibility towards the Block Development Officer. This viable link often tends to be a weak one. However, it is a common experience that Panchayat Raj has changed the basis of local leadership pattern. Hundreds of blocks were selected for greater allocations especially of those predominantly tribal. Tribal Development Blocks were created but now in the recent circular in December 1975, they have brought uniformity in the block administration. But, nonetheless, the idea of community acting as a self-governing body either through *Manki-Munda* or Pargana system are now given lip sympathy and the highly respected *Manki* and others of the old system were paled into oblivion. The two systems, the block system representing the State Government's allocative activity, and the *Manki-Munda* system representing the residual political organisations are now organisationally separated. Both the systems have suffered at the expense of each other and have created a great ferment and tensional situation.

NOTES

1. Maciver and Page, *Society* (Macmillan), p. 577.
2. *Ibid.*, p. 579.
3. F. H. Buchanan, *An Account of Bhagalpur District in 1810-11* (Patna : Bihar Research Society, 1939), pp. 264-65.
4. W. W. Hunter, *Annals of Rural Bengal* (London, 1868), pp. 424-25.
5. W. W. Hunter, *A Statistical Account of Bengal*, Vol XIV, Bhagalpur and Santal Parganas (London, 1877), pp. 307-08.
6. Anonymous, *Calcutta Review*, 1856.
7. Letter No. 827 A dated 10th December 1858 from A. C. Bidwell, Special Commissioner for the Suppression of Santal Insurrection to the Secretary,

Government of Bengal.
8. *Census of India*, 1881, Vol. VIII, pp. 728-29.
9. K. K. Datta, *The Santal Insurrection* (Calcutta 1940), p. 2. See also Michael Yorke, Tribal Density among the Santal, 1770-1885 (Unpublished Thesis, London) & Dr. S.P. Sinha, *Santal Hul of 1855*, Ranchi, (1990), Dr. S.P. Sinha (Ed.) Paper relating to Santal *Hul*, Ranchi, (1990).
10. W. W. Hunter, *Annals of Rural Bengal*, p. 235.
11. A. C. Bidwell, *op. cit.*
12. F. H. Buchanan, *Journal Kept During a Survey of District of Bhagalpur, 1810-11*, ed. C. E. A. W. Oldham (Patna, 1930), pp. 22, 45, 64, 132-33.
13. L. S. S. O'Malley, *Santal Parganas District Gazetteer* (Calcutta, 1910).
14. *Ibid.*
15. C. E. Buckland, *Bengal under the Lieutenant Governors* (Calcutta, 1901), pp. 1-64
16. Letter No. 337 dated 20th June, 1861 from J. D. Gordan, Junior Secretary, Government of Bengal to the Officiating Commissioner, Santal Parganas.
17. W. W. Hunter, *The Old Missionaries* (Oxford, 1896).
18. *Ibid.*, p. 67.
19. C. E. Buckland, pp. 272-397.
20. L. S. S. O'Malley, *District Gazetteers of Santal Parganas* (Patna, 1938), p. 328.
21. *Ibid*, pp. 328-29.
22. L. S. S. O'Malley, *Santal Parganas District Gazetteer* (Calcutta, 1910), pp. 58.
23. W. B. Oldham, *Laws of the Santal Parganas*. (Patna, 1889). Introduction.
24. *Ibid.*, p. 33.
25. *Santal Parganas Enquiry Committee Report* 1938. (Chairman : G. R. E. Russell).
26. Eric Stokes, *The English Utilitarians and India* (Oxford, 1959), p. 4.
27. Note dated 12th April 1832 from J. Thomason. para XIV.
28. Firminger's Fifth Report. Vol. II, p. 498.
29. Hardwar Rai, "Politico-Administration Bases of Indian Field Administration: The Pattern of the District Officer System under the British" *Indian Journal of Public Administration,* XVI, p. 474.
30. Stokes, p. 71.
31. J. C. Jha, *The Bhumij Revolt* (Delhi, 1967), pp. 158-59.
32. Hardwar Rai, *op. cit.*
33. Stokes, p. 20.
34. B. B. Misra, *The Central Administration of the East India Company* (Manchester, 1959), p. 289.
35. Letter dated 16th June, 1828 from W. Blunt, Special Commissioner for Arracans to H. Shakespear, Acting Chief Secretary to the Government of Bengal.
36. Regulation XIII dated 2nd December 1833 para I. Judicial General Progress p. 99.
37. L. S. S. O'Malley, *The Indian Civil Service* (London, 1965), p. 53.
38. Jha, p. 170.
39. Letter dated 15th September 1897 from A. Forbes, Commissioner of Chota Nagpur to the Deputy Commissioner, Singhbhum.
40. *Ibid.*
41. Patna High Court. Miscellaneous Judicial Case no. 548 of 1962.
42. Memorial dated 12th October 1964 of Manki-Munda Sangh, Singhbhum to the Bihar State Government.
43. Resolution dated 22nd May, 1957 of Chalisbasa Bar Association.
44. Letter dated 17th October 1956 from L. Dayal, Deputy Commissioner, Singhbhum to Commissioner Chota Nagpur Division.
45. *Ibid.*

3

THE LAND TENURIAL SYSTEM AS A SOURCE OF CONFLICT

LAWS IN general and land laws in particular are concrete factors of social change. It is needless to dilate in detail as to how legislation can bring about social transformation, more so, in tribal areas of Chota Nagpur and Santal Parganas. Some of the laws had temporary pacificatory effect, but they always tended to create some new tension symbolising some new aspiration which ultimately paved the way for further amendments in the legislation concerned and, thereby, the cycle of legislation and tension went together simultaneously. This chapter surveys the historical development of different concepts of land and land tenure in this part of India and the present day tenurial tensions have only survived from the distant past.

India has been a country of villages with peculiar oriental features of Indian social organisation. In pre-British rural India, we come across self-sufficient cultivators using plots of land in the village on a hereditory basis with village community system, the most dominant form of socio-economic organisation in India. Under village community system characterised by self-sufficient and autonomous village unit, land was held communally by the entire village so that each household lived on subsistence production on the land allotted to it under usufructuary rights. Such was the state of affairs in Indian society from about the fourth and fifth centuries A.D.

Agriculture was the main occupation of the villages, but each of them had usually its own compliment of weavers, potters, carpenters, oil-pressers and goldsmiths. Thus forming a self-sufficient economic unit was nothing less than village republic with *Grameyaka* or *Gramadhyaksha* presiding over *Gramsabha*. The organisation which made for the continuity of life and tradition, held society together and carried it safe through the storms and turmoils of political revolution was the autonomous self-sufficient village.[1]

"Old communes" like self-governing villages existed in Tribal areas of Bihar according to Rakhal Das Halder[2] who wrote about it in 1872. He found Chota Nagpur dotted with village republics with strong sense of community feeling, community ownership of land and great cohesive purposefulness in the village agencies. Virtually land was then, only for possessive use by the rural households for subsistence production, and, in a broad sense at least, the self-sufficient and autonomous village communities were based on "possession in common of the land".[3]

The decentralised strength of the village community system, although new forces, had begun to emerge in society from about the fifteenth century.[4] In order to break through this institution, they could not completely do away with it even by the middle of the eighteenth century. The village community thus gave a special imprint to Indian feudalism whereby the self-governing, self-sufficient, self-possessing type of cultivator represented the characteristic form of production-relation prevalent in the agrarian economy of those days. Within the sphere of a subsistence economy and joint possession of land by the entire village community there was very little scope for the development of the landholder-cum-share cropper and supervisory farmer-cum-agricultural labourer relationships.

Some British scholars asserted that "proprietorship of lands" existed before the introduction of the Permanent Settlement in 1793, but even if there were some, their presence was insignificant and Fifth Report categorically stated that previously *zamindars* were essentially "accountable managers and collectors, and not lords and proprietors of the land"[5] and that "the sale of land by auction, or in any other way, for realising arrears of land revenue, appears to have been unusual, if not unknown in all parts of India, before its introduction by the British Government into Company's dominions".[6] If Baden-Powell is to be believed the Moghul revenue system is the direct cause of the growth of the *zamindar* landlord of Bengal, but he agreed with Ghulam Hassan, the celebrated author of *Sayyarul Mut Akhirin* that the Emperor is proprietor of the revenue, he is not proprietor of the soil.[7]

It is true that Turko-Afghan and the Moghul Emperors created noble fief-holders out of their associates and settled territories on them but these fief-holders, notorious for their intrigues in the power politics and their conspiracies in the overthrow of one monarch or the other, did not have a direct control within the villages and of the peasant since *altamgha* was rather an assignment of the revenue of cultivated land and grants under *suyur-ghal* were assignment of revenue only.[8]

This could not and did not affect the continuance of the subsistence economy in the rural areas governed by the village community system and these feature in Indian history did not fundamentally affect the usufructuary right of the village community to its land and that of the individual possession of cultivable plots by the villagers. Shelvankar[9] has rightly assessed that Indian feudalism was fiscal and military in character but it was not manorial. Mishra further elucidates this point when he says:

> "But their *(Zamindars)* seigniorial rights arose from their tax farming and the military and fiscal fiefs of a bureaucratic state rather than from any legal recognition of the same in respect of village lands."[10]

It was in this state of affairs that the East India Company obtained the Dewani of Bengal, Bihar and Orissa in 1765 and after a series of experiments made in the administration of revenue Cornwallis gave statutory recognition to them as proprietors and permanently settled the lands with them in 1793, of course, on imperialistic consideration because he wanted to win the attachment of a powerful group to the government. According to Mishra the question of the rights of *Zamindars*, or of the grounds upon which those rights were founded did not seriously engage his attention. In fact with the introduction of the Permanent Zamindari Settlement of land in 1793 the landlords were created and the concept of private property in land was fully established. Consequently, the village community system was lost for ever.[11] The basis was thus laid for the new innovation like sale of land by auction or in other way for realising arrears of land revenue.[12]

Furthermore, with the disintegration of rural industries as a part of the concerned plan to reduce India into a supplier of raw materials only to the British industrialists and a consumer of British manufacturers, the pressure on agriculture went on increasing[13] and thus resulted in further impoverishment of the rural population. Incessant demands of landlords led the peasant to borrow from the money-lenders and frequently lost their land-holdings being unable to repay the ever increasing amount of debts and usurious interests. Loss of land, the primary means of production in agrarian economy naturally precluded the possibility to the rural people to remain as self-possessing, self-working and self-sufficient peasants and thereby whetted them for tensional situation. Thus the agrarian crisis was due to the colonial system imposed on the country and the role of the parasitic land-owning class as an appendage to that system, whereby their profit-making motive could find ample satisfaction while preserving the 'peasant' cultivation without any capital outlay in order to improve the state of the productive forces.

The land tenurial system in Santal Parganas and Chota Nagpur are of peculiar interest because the two represent one of the centres in which can be traced pretty clearly one of the earliest methods of land-holding in relation to the State. Baden-Powell opined, just as Oudh and Rajputana and to some extent Orissa, give us the best information regarding the Rajput or Aryan organisation which has profoundly affected the constitution of village communities, so Chutiya Nagpore is a centre which enables us to reconstruct the organisation of Kols and Dravidians, the latter being great colonisers and conquerors, like the Rajputs, and this organisation is probably identical with what once existed in Gondwana (now the Central Provinces of India) as well as in Southern India.[14] With the grant of Dewany in the year 1765, Chota Nagpur or Junglemahals being the part of Subah of Bihar, passed to the British, but it was not till 1772 that Captain Camac made the presence of British felt on the soil of Chota Nagpur. Although Thomas Rumbold, Collector of Bihar Revenues pleaded many times with the authorities of Fort William[15] for permission to subjugate Palamau Fort and Ramghur Fort for many tactical reasons but all in vain. Gopal Rai was reinstated on the *Gaddi* of Palamau Raj with Camac's help and in return the *Raja* acknowledged himself as the vassal of the British, paid a *Nazarana*, received *Khillat* and promised to pay annual tribute of three thousand rupees, and undertook to assist the Company against the Marhattas.

Raja Ramgarh used to pay an annual tribute of Rs.27,000 to the British Government also as *Malguzar* of Raja of Chota Nagpur. But Captain Camac recommended a direct deal with Chota Nagpur Raja due to political consideration and Patna Provincial Council made a settlement for three years at Rs.12,000 per annum (Rs.6,000 as *Nazarana* and another Rs.6,000 as rent). This was raised to Rs.14,000 at the Decennial Settlement, and later on to Rs.15,041. The internal administration of his dominion was left entirely in the hands of the Maharaja, who thus because a tributory chief. But Raja always remained in arrears.[16]

Ramgarh Hill Tract

In 1780 a new district under the name of 'Ramgarh Hill Tract' was established with its headquarters alternately at Sherghatti and Chatra with Chapman combining Judge-Magistrate-Collector of Revenue. The new district comprised of the present districts of Hazaribagh, Palamau and parts of present districts of Gaya, Manbhum and Monghyr, while Chota Nagpur proper under its own tributary chief owed a vague allegiance to the East India Company and formed but a nominal part of this huge district. Grant[17] the then Chief *Sheristedar* in 1781, describing the dominions of the Rajah of Chota Nagpur as "an elevated region which forms part of Subah Behar, containing nearly 18,000 square miles, though proportionately (to Behar and Tirhut) of very inconsiderable value. The highland district, including the modern sub-divisions of Palamau, Ramghur and Chutia Nagpur, bounded on the west by the Subah of Allahabad, on the south Orissa, and on the east Bengal, hath since the age of Ptolemy been geographically termed the Three Bellads and Cantons, in Arabic".

In the beginning, the Bengal Regulations were enforced in this unwieldy district, without any consideration for the widely different conditions of these parts from that of Bengal. Appeals from the decisions of the District Officers who was Judge-Magistrate-Collector lay direct to the Governor General. Permanent Settlement was promulgated in this area in 1793, by one stroke of pen without little questioning of its suitability. However, isolated attempts were made by the some British officers to exempt this area from the general application of the regulations. Earlier Mathew Leslie on 20th June, 1789 opposing the extensions of proposal of the Permanent Settlement into this area, expressed an apprehension that :

> extending these regulations into this district will be attended with very bad consequently to which Sir John Shore showed great concern. Therefore, the Resolution of the Bengal Government on 18th September, 1789, which confirmed the Decennial settlement in Bihar precisely mentioned that the Regulations do not extend to this district (Chota Nagpur) but that the settlement be continued on the present footing and be extended to a period of 10 years.

In the year 1800, this area was included under the Collector of Behar. The Collector in his letter of 22nd July, 1800 to the Board of

Revenue, found 20 grounds for exempting Chota Nagpur from the operations of the ordinary Regulations, and proposed for the realisation of excise tax there and the issuing of licences. Stamp papers were introduced in that year into Chota Nagpur. Evidently, these along with the system of collection of revenue through Suzawals created unrest among the tribals. Tamar rebelled intermittently.

According to the Regulation XX of 1793 and Regulation XVIII of 1805, Raja of Chota Nagpur was ordered in 1809 to keep up police stations in his dominions and appoint *Thanedars* and *Chowkidars*. The police arrangements took effect from 4th June, 1809 Raja paid the police, but the Magistrate of Ramgarh controlled them. From now on the feudal authority of the Nagpur Chief began to disappear. The civil and criminal processes, which had been, hitherto, ineffective, began to be enforced. The Raja was unwilling and he withheld the payment for police arrangements in arrears. In 1812 there were six *thanas*, one each at Maharajganj, Jhikochutti, Borwai, Tamar, Barkagarh and Tori. In 1819, a woman who was supposed to have practised magical arts upon the lives of the Raja's son and daughters was murdered with four others. The Magistrate received no assistance in the detection of the criminals, who could not be traced. As a consequence he recommended that the Raja should be deprived of his control over the police and that a superintendent should be appointed on behalf of the government. The proposal was sanctioned. But this led to the aggravation of discontent which led to the Rising of Mundas and Uraons in the year 1811. The result was that by 1817 this tract was brought under the direct administration of the East India Company as part of the Ramgarh District by depriving the Raja of Chota Nagpur his status as a tributary chief. The presence of a horde of outsiders, traders and adventurers who got *theka* or temporary lēase added fuel to the fire (Appendix I). Therefore, it was no wonder that in the year 1820, the ferment of unrest, seething so long all over the country, again burst out in open revolt under two Mundas Rugdeo or Roadan and Konta. It took Major Roughsedge several months to quell the insurrection with great severity and restore tranquillity.[18]

Great Kol Rising of 1832

When the horrors of the insurrection of 1820 were still green in the memory another outbreak vastly more formidable in its magnitude, convulsed the entire length and breadth of the country like bursting of a fire that had long been smouldering. This is known as the Great Kol Rising of 1832. The rising was against the incessant increased demands and atrocious behaviour of the *Thekedars* and their aids. The quelling of this insurrection ushered in a new epoch in the administration of the country . The ordinary Regulations that had hitherto been in force in the district were withdrawn and replaced by a new Regulation XIII of 1833 to be operative in the parts of the country known as Chota Nagpur proper, as well as Palamau, Kurrukhdeha, Ramgarh and Korunda which were separated from the old district of Ramgarh, and these together with the *Jungle Mahals* (the present district of Purulia, Dhanbad and the Manbhum) sub-divisions and the dependent Tributary Mahals, were formed into a "Non-Regulation Province" and was called the South-Western Frontier Agency. Captain Wilkinson was appointed as an Agent to the Governor General for the Agency on consolidated salary of Rs. 36,000 and Lieutenant R. Ousley and Dr. Davidson as his Principal and Junior Assistant respectively on Rs. 1,000 a month. He was to exercise the same power and authority for the time being as were vested in a Commissioner of Revenue and Circuit and a Civil and Sessions Judge. *Sadar Dewani Adalat* and *Nizamat Adalat* and Sadar Board of Revenue and Board of Customs, Salt and Opium were not to interfere normally in the affairs of the Agency, and their powers of control would be ordinarily exercised by the Agent or any of his assistants.

Thus by the middle of December 1833, all preliminary consultations had been completed and Captain Wilkinson had emerged as the sole official head of the new administration. He was to set up a paternalist non-regulation system of administration for this undeveloped area, at the apex of which he would stand with very considerable powers. The swing of the pendulum away from the complex machinery and regulations of the Cornwallis system was complete. Wilkinson laid down his rules which are still known as Wilkinson's Rules. One can perceive the influence of Munro school in them. The salient features[19] of the new system were once again the creation of a hierarchy of authority with powers and responsibilities clearly defined at each level, and the Agent at the apex of pyramid, and the creation of elaborate safeguards against the abuse of authority. It was decided that no transfer of land on account of claims for rent, etc. would be legal unless previously authorised by the Agent or Assistant, by a certificate upon the back of the bond. In subsequent years, Wilkinson and his Assistant made the protection of tribal interests even more complete by using powers to interfere whenever the estate of an hereditary proprietor was "so deeply involved as to render such interposition desirable". Thus the Agent could adjust accounts and regulate interest charges, to release mortgage property where necessary, and to sequester an estate for the payment of debts. To quote Jha,

> If *Rajas* and *Jagirdars* were saved by Wilkinson and Davidson from the clutches of the money-lenders, the *Mankis* and *Ghatwals*, the junior members of the chiefly families, and the minor *Zamindars* were saved from oppression by their *rajas*. The result was 20 years of peaceful development in the Agency.[20]

Earlier in 1849 W. Settonkar, Under Secretary to the Government of Bengal wrote to the Secretary, Sadar Board of Revenue "The Control hitherto exercised by government over the Agent, in his revenue management of these four districts has not been very plain or systematic, and the Deputy Governor anticipates much benefit from the change of system now determined upon".[21]

Chota Nagpur: A Non-Regulation Area

Consequent upon Ricketts report, a further change in administration was introduced by Act XX of 1854 under which the Agency was abolished and Chota Nagpur passed under the Lieutenant Governorship of Bengal as a non-Regulation Province and the country was to be administered by a division of Bengal under a Commissioner. The main contention of Ricketts was :

> but it cannot be concealed that it must be a hopeless contest between a middle man of any degree and a *Zamindar* incharge of the police. However carefully his rights may have been ascertained and recorded, if the *Zamindar Darogah* is resolved he shall go, he must go, his ruin may be affected in a hundred ways, and if he resist, will be effected, though the officer incharge of the District be his friend.

Thus rapacity of "outsiders" continued and there was need of Code of Law in force prescribing a procedure for the disposal of revenue suits or for the realisation of revenue in intricate cases like that of Tekait

Pekhram Singh of Gadi Gawen in Pargana Khurreckdeah in Zilla Hazaribagh.

Lal Lokenath Sahi's Survey

But the establishment of Commissionership was not the final answer to the ills from which the Chota Nagpur *raiyots* suffered. Rather, the embers of discontent continued in the different aspects of the social and economic life of Chota Nagpur. Through the exertions of missionaries a new class of converted *raiyots* with great vigour and enterprise had attracted the wrath of the *zamindars* and their aids. How Christian preaching contributed to the creation of tension and conflict in the Chota Nagpur is itself a subject-matter of an independent chapter in this study? But this much can be said that the missionaries were successful in getting the government order passed. It is because of the missionaries that special tenures of the tribals like Bhuinharis were ordered to be registered. The authorities were actuated by this proposal that the only effectual mode of preventing a repetition of such affrays and riots which had rocked the Parganas of Sonepur and Bassia in the year 1858, would be to remedy the grievances that had been the cause of them. Accordingly, under Government orders dated the 15th April, 1858, Lal Lokenath Sahi, a local *zamindar* and a Sub-Assistant Commissioner was deputed to prepare a register of all Bhuinhari lands. Lal began his operations in August 1860, and continued till his death on 13th August, 1862 during which period he could complete the register of 429 out of 572 villages, leaving remaining 143 villages incomplete. He was able to complete his work for Lodhma, Khukra, Udaipur, Sonepur, Doesa, Korambe and Basia Parganas.

British Land Policy

While the local administrators and the European Missionaries advocated pro-*raiyots* policy, the land policy at higher level became the part of the imperial policy designed to develop agriculture produce to feed the British industry and in many ways supported the interest of superior *zamindars*. In a dispatch of the 31st December 1859, the Secretary of State for India stressed this object and advised the Government of India to consider favourably the several applications of persons. "Who, either on behalf of themselves or on Companies, proposed to establish or were desirous of obtaining grants of unoccupied land for the purpose of carrying on the cultivation of cotton and other exportable products for the supply to manufacturers in this country."[22]

In drawing up the Rules the Council was guided by the desire to promote the attainment in India, "a complete ownership and soil free of all demand by the State on account of land revenue so far as this may be done without injury to the interest of the State and without detriment to the rights of the third party".

In short "the political aspect of the British Land Policy was aimed at in creation of a landed middle class in India, who from motive of all self-interest might support British in the development of country material resources".[23]

The grant of waste land in perpetuity, redeemable at the discretion of grantee was, therefore, not confined to European Settlers. The redemption of land revenue signified absolute right in property redeemed. Lord Stanley was aware of the fact that this obviously clashed with the trends of the past 50 years of the Company's rule which had in effect reduced the power of big land holders by recognising the rights of the middle class landed gentry including also a body of joint proprietors and resident peasants, many of whom belonged to upper castes and possessed public spirit and enterprises. But since the system of periodical settlement of land revenue led to increase the demand from time to time Lord Stanley considered it responsible for breeding poverty. He believed that if the public demand were to be limited and *zamindars* allowed to retain the land tax on the basis of existing rates of assessment this might encourage the accumulation of agricultural capital. His successor Sir Charles Wood, in his Revenue Dispatch of the 9th July 1862, confirmed that :

> the security, and, it may almost be said the absolute creation of property in the soil which will flow in limitation in perpetuity of the demands of the State with owners of land, cannot fail to stimulate or confirm their sentiments of attachment and loyalty to the Government by whom so great a boon has been considered, upon whose existence its permanency will depends.[24]

But the Crown could not undo the work of the Company. Sir Charles Wood desired the growth of the landed middle class but without dispossessing the peasant proprietors and occupants. Mishra rightly observes that the post-mutiny concept of middle class was thus richer in its major economy content and broader in social basis.[25] Wood's declared policy was based on the fact of success of the British Rule in keeping up the contentment of agricultural classes who constituted the great bulk of the population. Wood argued if they are prosperous and "any casual outbreak on the part of the other classes or bodies of men less likely to become and element of danger and the military force and its consequent expenses may be regulated accordingly". Sir John Lawrence also stressed on the contentment of the agriculturists on whom the security of British Rule to a large extent depended. "If they are prosperous the military forces may be small and not otherwise." Thus the interests of the superior class of *zamindar* was uppermost in the minds of the new policy-makers because the proposed perpetual settlement was to benefit that class most. But the benefits that might arise from the limitation of the public demand were to be extended to other agricultural classes also under the proper regulations. The new land policy confirmed the integral part of the policy of *laissez faire*. Its object was to create by conferring free property rights, a composite landed middle class which might participate in the development of the imperialist economy and form a contented and stable social element to support the British Rule in India.[26] But could this materialise? The subsequent events showed that it fell through on financial grounds and ultimately the abnormal necessity of the Government required the agriculturists to bear the burden. "Thus the proposal for Permanent Settlement was killed before being put into effect."[27]

The re-opening of the question of Permanent Settlement affected the peasantry in Bihar more seriously than elsewhere.[28] Though it made no progress beyond the stage of correspondence and exchange of views, it lent support and added strength to the claims of the *zamindars* in a province where, in the absence of education among the lower orders of society, they could indulge in the rapacity without fear of punishment or public opinion. It was agreed that Chota Nagpur required special deal and special attention for the regulation of land and land tenure. Close at the heels of 1857 uprising, the Bengal Tenancy Act of 1859 was passed which was the first serious attempt to protect the interests of *raiyots* by granting occupancy rights and limiting the enhancement of this rent. It was found that it could not be made applicable to Chota Nagpur unless certain modifications suiting the special position of the area were made. Commissioner E. T. Dalton in consultation with the Assistants Incharge of the districts of

Lohardaga, Manbhum and Hazaribagh, informed the Board of Revenue the desirability of modifications to suit the local situation. He explained "that law of protection from sale of all kinds of immovable property as administered in Hazaribagh and Manbhum districts was of the regulation provinces, but due to some peculiar circumstances the cultivators in the Lohardaga district were exempted from distraint and no sale. *Ameens* had, therefore, been appointed in this district". He was, therefore, of the opinion that until the rights of cultivators of the soil in the Lohardaga district were in a better way than what they were, he did not consider it to be expedient to confer the power to distraint on the different clauses specified in Section XVII. But it might be held out as some endducement to landlords to give their ownership and the distraint clauses would be extended to them when it was found that it had generally been done.[29]

Past experience had taught that the local conditions always required some special law regarding land. Dalton, therefore, reported :

> I consider, however, that officer-in-charge of districts should not be content to allow the Act to make its own way. If so, it would first be known to those who least require its protective clauses, who will derive from it themselves all the advantage they can, but to their utmost to keep in the background the benefits intended for the cultivating classes.[30]

The Commissioner hoped that "the protective clauses will, when fully understood, be considered as a great boon by cultivating classes in this division prevented under our rule from resenting infringement of their rights in the manner that was not frequently resorted to when they had only their land-lords to contend against, and debarred by excessive ignorance from seeking such redress as our courts could have afforded. Many have of late years silently submitted to burden which should never have been imposed on them.

Dalton, therefore, suggested that following reservations should be made in application of the Act to Chota Nagpur:

I. That it has been deemed proper for good and sufficient reasons to continue the restriction on the sale of landed property observed in the above districts, it is declared that no sale shall take place under the provisions of Sections CV, CVIII, CIX, and CX without the sanction of the Commissioner of the province had and obtained thereto.

II. That as it has hitherto been considered expedient to exempt cultivators of land in the district of Lohardaga from distraint otherwise by the order of Court, the provisions of sections CXIII to CXLV inclusive shall not at present be enforced in that district.

III. That the appeals under which section CLX of the Act, are allowed to the Zilla Judge, shall lie to the Deputy Commissioner of the Province. (This is necessary, as the district officer is *ex-officio* Zilla Judge as well as Collector, and these appeals from his decision as Collector cannot lie to himself as Judge).

IV. That as all officers in this province, having powers as Deputy Collectors, have also police powers, the restrictions contained in section CLXIV in regard to this class of officers shall not be observed.[31]

Webster, ex-manager of Chota Nagpur Raj and well acquainted with the land system and problem of this part of the country also expressed similar opinion. He observed,

> The rise in the value of produce can of course, be applied to enhance the rents, but in a district like Lohardaga, part of which has scarcely yet emerged from barbarism, legal proof of price many years ago is very hard to obtain.[32]

He concluded:

> . . . the prohibition on enhancement, where the productive power of the land has been increased at the labour and expense of raiyot, is not suited to a district in which cultivation is constantly being extended. Various customs prevail in different parts of the district with reference to the rate of rent ultimately payable by the improving ryot. In some cases he holds three years free, three years at half rents, but this latter rule has come to force since Act X was passed. The three years and six years rule fair in most cases in which no special agreement has been made, but each case should stand on its own merits, and no hard and fast rule can apply.[33]

It was thus decided:

> with such relations existing between landlord and tenant as those

described in Webster's note, the ground of enhancement of rent prescribed under Section XVII of the Act X appears altogether inapplicable to the three districts of Lohardaga, Hazaribagh and Singhbhum, in which much of the same characteristics, in regard to tenancy and relation between landlord and tenants seem to obtain. The Member-in-charge expressed himself, in a separate letter, averse to any change in the principle which then governed the enhancement of rent in Bengal, where relations between the two classes were on a more complicated and settled basis. But in the districts above-named where a far more simple and primitive state of things existed, the Member-in-charge would advocate the adoption of a principle and prospect based on the suggestions contained in the ninth paragraph of the note. As those districts assimilate themselves to the more advanced and intricate condition prevailing in Bengal, the law, of course, will need to be modified to keep pace with that alteration.[34]

As expected the *zamindars* as a class presented a stiff opposition to the Bill which caused a serious controversy and Legislative Assembly became sharply divided. Maharaja of Darbhanga, Pyare Mohan Mukherjee, V. N. Mandalik and Amir Ali advocated the causes of *zamindars* while the Lieutenant-Governor of Bengal and other official members such as Bayley, Reynolds, Hunter and Gibbon pleaded for tenants. Through the intercession of the Viceroy the Council made, a number of concessions which watered down the effect of the original bill in favour of the *zamindar*. Mishra rightly says that even in its diluted form, the bill, which resulted in the Bengal Tenancy Act of 1885, became the first effective landmark in the history of Tenancy Legislation in the Bengal. It repaired the defect in the law governing occupancy rights by providing that a *raiyot* who had been in a possession of any land for 12 years either himself or through inheritance, would become a settled *raiyot* of the village with occupancy rights in the land he already possessed and would immediately acquire those rights in any new land which he took into cultivation. It also provided for the introduction of Survey and Settlement Operation as the only means to form what Sir Ashley called the trustworthy record of rights.[35]

Another important question arose during this period regarding the estates of *Ghatwals*. The Chota Nagpur having great mineral potentialities attracted the cupidity of English miners as well as the administrators. C.G.D. Betts went into the question of *Ghatwali* tenants. Considering legal aspects of the rights of the owners of the land containing rich minerals, C. Beadon, Secretary to the Government of India wrote to W. Grey, Secretary to Government of Bengal that Government had no claims to the minerals.[36] Therefore, the rights of *zamindars, elakadar* in such minerals were recognised in the year 1862. The necessity to amend the Rent Law Act X of 1859 was felt by the Bengal Government and consequently in the year 1859, Act II was passed by the Council which concerned the sale of land on arrears of Revenue. It was not made applicable to certain parts of Chota Nagpur i.e. in the districts of Hazaribagh, Lohardaga and Manbhum Parganas and Kolhan in the district of Singhbhum.[37]

In the year 1860, the problem of reviving the quit rent or tribute of *Tributary Mahals* was felt because Commissioner Dalton was of the opinion that rents in such Tributary Mahals were of nominal nature and would yield a large sum. On 2nd July, 1860 he wrote to the Secretary of the Government of Bengal,

> I have shown that most of Tributary Mahals in Chota Nagpur were temporarily settled and in regard to them the properties are, under the Bill, to be held liable to the tax, the estimate of profits at one-third of the *Jumma*, Government demand would be very favourable.[38]

Dalton had no objection regarding districts which were to be assessed under Act XXXII of 1860, but he was very particular about the Tributary Mahal. The Government of Bengal was not in favour of enhancing the rent or imposing an extra tax presumably because it had tasted the terrible uprising during 1857-59. W.S. Seton-Kar, Secretary to Government of India wrote,

> Although the chiefs and people were subject to little interference but sometimes they were required, to refer all heinous cases to the Commissioner. It meant, practically it depended upon the will of the British Government. But for the tribute, no tax was ever imposed by the British Government on the Mahals, although the chiefs were at liberty to arrange their own taxation.[39]

In 1862, Act VIII of 1862 was passed by the Bengal Council to improve the system of *Zamindar Darogas* in the province of Bengal and it was enforced wholly in the districts of Hazaribagh, Lohardaga, Manbhum and Singhbhum. Another important Act to amend the law for alienation of such under-tenures which were transferable by sale title deeds for the recovery of arrears and rent (due in respect thereof) in accordance with the established practice of the region, was enacted by the British Council and received the assent of the Lieutenant Governor on 10th May, 1865 and of the Governor General on 27th May, 1865. All the sections of this Act were applicable only to the districts of Hazaribagh, Lohardaga, Manbhum and Parganas Dalbhum of Singhbhum.[40]

In 1868, a trouble between landlord and *Adivasi* Christians of Chota Nagpur began on gigantic scale. Finding the position difficult, the Legislature had to intervene in order to define and record these incidence by passing Chutianagpur Tenure Act (Act II of 1869) on 26th July, 1869. The passing of this Act was the most important milestone in the history of land revenue administration of Chota Nagpur. This Act was enforced only in the entire district of Lohardaga. It received kudos at the hands of Rev. H. Onasch[41] and others, when A. W. B. Power, Deputy Commissioner, Lohardaga wrote to the Commissioner of Chota Nagpur, on 18th June, 1880, "In the prolonged struggle, which took place before Act II of Bengal Council of 1869 was passed, the Kols had but two fitful gleams of success once after their rebellion of 1833, the other after the Mutiny of 1857. The warning afforded by such dangerous lessons was not disregarded and the result was what may well be called a noble effort to administer impartial justice and put an end to the burning question."[42] Colonel E. T. Dalton, Commissioner of Chota Nagpur held "it was bill to restore peace and make amends for past shortcomings, and it was deemed to make litigation under it costly to either side".[43]

Now the Special Commissioners were required to prepare the accurate registers of land which they might ascertain to belong to *Bhuinhari* and *Majhias* respectively, all the conditions to be fulfilled and rents and services to be rendered in respect of several lands of those classes which they might ascertain to be held subject to any condition rent or services, and of the rights and privileges to be enjoyed in respect of any such land.[44] They were also empowered to restore possession to the persons or their heirs wrongfully dispossessed of any land under Bhuinhar or Majhias tenures, within 20 years prior to the passing of the Act and to cause the names of the persons; thus, any possession to be entered in the register as occupant of the said land as the case might be.[45] Besides this, many more sections of the Act dealt with different aspects of the tenancy question.

The operations under the Act commenced on 1st April, 1869 and were concluded on 31st March, 1880. Babu Rakhal Das Haldar was appointed a Special Commissioner under this Act and he started his proceedings in Lodhma where Lal Lokenath Sahi had also conducted survey two decades ago. It was perceived that immediate effect of Chota Nagpur Land Tenure Act was that it gave impetus to false litigation. Therefore, the Act was misunderstood by the people and they started gathering at the courts of the Special Commissioner to put forward their real and unreal claims by trying to get registration. This traditional outbreak of the aboriginals of Chota Nagpur was all the more blurred by the confusion of the Government Official at Lodhma in a position to make and unmake the ownership of *Bhuinhari* land real and unreal. Therefore, apart from people of Lodhma, people of Sonepur, Basia, Doisa and Khukhura encamped near the Special Commissioners' camp in hundreds. They held Council and sent their emissaries in all directions. It was really a difficult situation which has been graphically described :

> None can only justly blame persons determined by fair means to better their condition; but it was holding and disseminating doctrines subversive of all good governments, that these people rendered themselves obnoxious. They belonged to the Mundas, they chose a Hindu king merely as a matter of fancy and gave to the King the worst half of the country for his maintenance, reserving the best half for themselves; they seemed to have become compact in an everlasting manner, by a charter granted by the King and engraved on a copper plate, which was still in possession of the Bhuinhars, but the charter was of no avail. The Hindus in recent times invaded the best land and turned them into Majhias.[46]

In his report, Rakhal Das Haldar mentions,

> Old obligations were ignored, Majhia's lands, hills, jungles and trees were claimed as a part of Bhuinhari. It was demanded in short, I should make the Bhuinhars quite independent of the Zamindars. Where lands were invariably lost within eight, ten or twelve years, never beyond the period of limitation fixed by law, as if they were in concert with the local officers for depriving the

> Bhuinhars of their lands. For otherwise how could the Bhuinhars have lost so much property so recently without any redress? While Government money was at a stake, it was painful to deal with such claims.[47]

We can very well realise the mental agony of Rakhal Das Haldar on severe trials that he was put to. He rightly[48] apprehended that "when some of the more remote Parganas were visited by the Special Commissioners, serious difficulties might arise". He got appreciation of the Commissioner as well as the Government for his sincerity and rapid survey; but Rev. H. Onsach and 15 others submitted memorandum to the Lieutenant Governor of Bengal in 1876 showing distrust in the Special Commissioner because they remarked "the principal complaints of the people are to the effect that it is through the instrumentality of this Act, and with the alleged sanction of the law, that their *Bhuinhari* land is taken from them. And when asked to whom they accused of not complying with or the frustrating the provisions of the Act, they replied with one voice that it was the Native Special Commissioner who has been entrusted with its execution.[49] It further stated :

> The dissatisfaction entertained by the Kols, as regard the decision of the Special Commissioner's assent their Bhuinhari is based upon their conviction that natives, be they Mussalmans or Hindus never can and never will decide impartially between themselves and *Thekedars*. The Kols between the native Judges are naturally favourably inclined towards the *Thekedars* who are for the most part not only their brothers in faith but also often in caste and his prejudice is especially strongly pronounced against the above named Babu.[50]

The operations under the Act were extended to as many as 2482 villages situated in 35 Parganas of the Lohardaga district. As many as 13,473 claims were disposed of, besides 1,161 applications for commutation of services and 3,544 miscellaneous cases. Of the 13,473 claims, 7423 were contested. The Special Commissioner granted review of their own judgment in 294 cases, and 844 appeals from their decision were preferred to the Divisional Commissioner, 28 in the modification, and 14 in reversal of the orders passed by the Special Commissioners. As many as 68 were summarily rejected and in 98, the cases were remanded for further hearing. The expenditure of these operations under the Chota Nagpur Tenure Act of 1869 amounted to Rs. 2,69,887 besides minor charges for tents and surveying and mathematical instruments. The Registers of lands recorded as privileged tenures under the Act filled 13,720 pages of 69 volumes.

The sanguine expectations of the framers of the Act as to its success in removing all grievances and allaying all disturbances were soon found out to have been illusive. The reasons[51] were not far to seek. Firstly, the Act came too late, it was due as early as 1839 when Dr. Davidson, then Principal-Assistant to the Governor General's Agent urged the necessity of an authoritative investigation into the claims of *Bhuinhars*. Secondly, the cause of the failure of the Act was due to ignorance and stupidity of the aborigines. Instances of managing the situation by the *zamindars* and their men, while proceedings under the Act went on in the villages, were not wanting. Thirdly, the Act left untouched several other classes of tenure and a number of other rights to land or their produce, about which these aborigines had always been keen. Thus no provision was made in the Act for the protection of immemorial rights of these people to cut and appropriate wood from the village jungles for building and repairing their houses, making and mending their agricultural implements, as well as for fuel etc. No provision again was made for securing to the *Bhuinhars* the mango groves and topes of other trees said to have been planted by them or their ancestors on uplands and over which they claim to have been always in possession *Sarna's* and *Korkar* lands, too, were similarly left unrecorded. The most objectionable omission of the Act had been the exclusion of *Khuntkatti* tenures from the scope of the Act. While these failings of the Act of 1869 were obvious, the passing of the Registration Act (Act XVI of 1864) which came into force on 1st January, 1865 and the Registration Act (Act XX of 1866) which came into force on 1st May, 1866 would seem to have given an impetus to such alienation. The Sardars got opportunities to whet up the agitation. This will be discussed in the chapter dealing with Sardari movement. The Christians missionaries also filed several memorials which too have been dealt in separate chapter.

Chota Nagpur Landlord and Tenant Procedure Act (1879)

Ultimately after much consultation with local officials and deliberations in the government, another Act named as Chota Nagpur

Landlord and Tenant Procedure Act (Bengal Act I of 1879) containing 164 sections was passed. To quote Baden-Powell :

> The value of the records made under this Act is to a great extent secured by the existence of another special Act (B) I of 1879 — which regulates the relations of landlord and tenant in Chutiya Nagpur.[52]

Thus it was a device to fix the occupancy right and decree rent suits. The Act did not attempt to draw any theoretical distinction between the tenants and the tenure-holders, but referred to the *taluq*-holders and persons having a permanent and transferable interest in land as well as of the *raiyots*. The possession for 12 years gave a right of occupancy to the *raiyot* in all lands excepting the Majhias lands or the waste lands reclaimed by the landlord (the Khamar of the Permanent Settlement), or in his *nij jot* or home farm, or in lands called *ma'n* lands (held in virtue of office) or as *Saika*, i.e., lands held by contract from years to year, or under a contract containing express stipulations.

Bengal Tenancy Act (1885)

But when the Act of 1879 was implemented it was also found that amendments in certain sections were essential. But not till 1885 when Bengal Tenancy Act (Act VIII of 1885) was passed, a great deal of conflabulation continued between various sets of persons representing local government — provincial and central governments and the landed interests of the Chota Nagpur and other parts of the province. But Act VIII of 1885 was not allowed to be applied in Chota Nagpur till 1892 by the Lieutenant Governor and that too on the understanding that the questions of necessary modifications were to be considered in the Select Committee.

Meanwhile the *raiyots* and their leaders were not sitting idle. The Christian *raiyots* refused *rakumats* and customary demands and German Christian revived old agitation. Sardar were active as usual. Lieutenant Governor Stuart Bailey had to come personally to Ranchi for proper understanding of the situations. The agrarian dispute led British Government to think in terms of new legislative device. It seemed expedient to retain only such portions of Act I of 1874 as were framed with special reference to the existing circumstances. It was also expedient to empower the Government to order such commutation with application when the Lieutenant Governor considered that the adoptation of such a course was calculated to avoid the serious dispute. C. E. Buckland observed "the agrarian disturbances most difficult to deal with new originate in claims to these services (*Bethbegari*, *rakumat* etc.)" which are generally demanded to an extent unwarranted by law, and as often refused when justly due.[53] Evidently an Act was required to remove such kinds of service extorted by the *zamindars* from *raiyots*. Ultimately, the Chota Nagpur Commutation Act (1897) was passed in 1897.

The agrarian discontent, however, was at its *nadir* and tribal wrath found expression in Birsa Bhagwan's Rebellion. Birsa movements in 1895 and 1899 culminated in huge carnage following a direct action by the Mundas. The Act IV of 1897 could not provide a solution to agrarian trouble. The search for proper legal remedies to create suitable land system of Chota Nagpur remained unfulfilled till Chota Nagpur Tenancy Act was passed in 1908 and Survey Settlement Operation of Ranchi district was ordered in 1908 just in the wake of Birsa rising. Commissioner Forbes was worried about the laws of landowners of Chota Nagpur also who in dispute with *Talukdars* and Government and was not in a position to do any thing. He observed :

> Having regard to the nature of disputes to the Zamindars and Raiyots in the district of Ranchi, it seems to me that it is absolutely necessary that the Settlement Officer should be vested with power to decide dispute of the nature referred to the section 106 of Bengal Tenancy Act. In many villages the disputes are of this nature. The landlords alleged that certain holdings considered of 10 *Pawas* and that rent is payable at so many rupees per *Pawas*. The Raiyot says that his holding is say 5 *Pawas* and he also probably contests for the rate of rent.[54]

In so many cases the landlord exaggerated the size of the holdings and the *Raiyots* also underestimated it. Therefore, in such disputed relationship, the preparation of records of rights was not an easy job. The cases of encroachment were not few. Therefore, Forbes wrote :

> It is not certainly necessary that every civil dispute between landlord and tenant or between tenant to tenant should be decided by the Revenue Officer but he should have power to deal adequately those which have agrarian trouble.[55]

The main objection of all Survey Settlement operations undertaken with a view to protect the cultivators was that these operations always were responsible for enhancement of rents and Lieutenant Governor John Woolburn, jealously refrained from proposing the fixation of rents. "He was of the view that rents were very low and there was no occasion for reducing them. There was danger of accumulation of evidence that some rent were so ridiculously low that enormous pressure would be brought to enhance them."[56] He did not think that the process of ascertaining and registering existing rents and of commuting praedial services was to be more difficult than that of fixing them. Therefore, he agreed with the Government of India that the Bills should provide for the fixation of rents but that fixation should not include enhancement. Thus in other words the Settlement Officer would fix rents which would not exceed the rent then paid on the existing holdings. Ultimately a Bill to amend a Chota Nagpur Landlord and Tenant Procedure Act (Act I of Bengal Council of 1897) was placed before the Government of India for sanctioning the introduction of the Bill in Bengal Legislative Council in the December 1902. The amendment proposed by the Bill were designed to meet many objections which were likely to facilitate the acquisition of the occupancy right (clause IX), to prevent exaction more than customary rates of rent from non-occupancy *raiyots* (Clause IV), to restrict the alienation of *raiyots* holdings, to recognise the preparation of records of rights, to simplify the existing procedure for the registration of transfers and succession in tenures (Clauses X, XII, XIII), to improve law for commulation of paraedial conditions and many more such objectives. Ultimately the Bill was enacted by the Bengal Council and became Chota Nagpur Tenancy (Amendment) Act (Act V of Bengal Council) of 1903. The Governor General also assented to it but the Government of India had last minute hitch regarding Section 164 of the Act which provided that an entry in records of rights should be the conclusive evidence as to whether a tenancy was a *Mundari Khuntkatti* or not.[57]

The Government of India point of view was that they have also refused such a provision in case of other provinces where records of rights have been long maintained and elaborately scrutinised at repeated settlements. The Government of India admitted that the circumstances of Mundas were exceptional and that it was possible that the proposal was capable of justification but viewed the provision of the section with such misgivings as could only be dispelled through stronger reasons for its retention and these reasons were to be gathered from the papers and correspondence relating to law. The Government of India directed that the earliest possible opportunity might be taken to amend it so as to provide with the retrospective effect from the date the law might be put into operation, that the entries in records-of-rights were to be merely *prima facie* evidence of the facts recorded.[58] In its reply to it, the Government of Bengal, after discussing fully the system of *Mundari-Khuntkatti* and the nature of the tenancy of Chota Nagpur, wrote to the Government of India,

> As the Government of India are aware, the Munda tract of Chota Nagpur Division is at present the subject of survey and settlement operations, and the opportunity for preparing a complete records-of-rights in respect of Khuntkatti Tenure has, therefore, arrived, Section 164 of Act V (B. C.) of 1903 simply enacted with regard to these tenures what was previously enacted with regard to Bhuinhari tenure by Section 26 of Act II (B. C.) of 1869, it is being considered that finality of proceedings is quite as necessary in the case of the former as in that of latter.[59]

However, a new Act was passed with the object of introducing peace and order into a disturbed tract of the country, and therefore, Government of Bengal requested the Government of India not to press for the purpose of amending the Act in question in the manner proposed by them because that would have a very unsettling effect at that time.[60] On 25th January, 1904, the Government of India accepted the opinion of the Government of Bengal that Section 164 of Chota Nagpur Tenancy (Amendment) Act (Act V of Bengal Council of 1903) should stand as "originally passed".[61] Certainly this was one of the greatest steps taken in solving complicated problem of land tenancy in Chota Nagpur.

But the final Act was only to take place after the real state of affairs was revealed by the final settlement operations. Therefore, in 1908 last of the most important enactment took place and the Chota Nagpur Tenancy and Settlement Bill was brought forward with a view to consolidating in one enactment the provisions of the various laws relating to the landlords and the tenants then existing in Chota Nagpur. The aim of such enactment was to strengthen the land tenures and impart suitable base to land revenue administration. But when the Bill was drafted by Bengal Government and sent to the Government of

India for approval to introduce it in the Bengal Legislative Council, it had its satisfaction because efforts were made in the Bill to recognise the principle of the settled *raiyot*. The Bill had almost received unanimous approval of the representatives of the different interests who had been consulted before hand. After some wrangling ultimately the Bill was placed in the Council and passed. On 21st September, 1908 the Governor General gave his assent and the Bill was enacted as Chota Nagpur Tenancy Act. The passage of this Act was an event of great significance for the tenants of Chota Nagpur.

Thus, in this labyrinthine of legislative steps taken by the Government during the course of almost over a century to relieve the agrarian tensional situation in Chota Nagpur, one thing is clear that the Government had been actuated by the desire to plug the loopholes which might, in future, create some trouble. But more it did the more it failed to the detriment of the tenants of Chota Nagpur. Sometimes this consideration, sometimes that consideration, sometime want of information, sometime lack of knowledge, all contributed to make the situation murky. The result was natural. Every legislative step taken by the Government, however, led to multiply the causes of discontent. The Government and its officials might try to give some solace to the *raiyots* from the grinding machine of *zamindari* oppression and *Thikadari Julam* (the injustice of the contractors) but every time the Government was stupified and these factors continued to serve as the catalytic agent of growing discontent.

But in spite of this great piece of social legislation and Lord Curzon's famous Land Revenue Policy Resolution the harassment of the *raiyot* at the hands of *zamindars* continued between 1902-1910 survey and settlement operation of Ranchi and later on in parts of Singhbhum and Palamau, Hazaribagh, etc., where rents were commuted in cash. A strained relationship between the *raiyots* and landlord continued on many score till *zamindari* was abolished but this did not end the weal and woe of the *raiyots* because various land reform measures, still pending for ruthless implementation, have not been able yet to deliver the goods in the favour of *raiyots*.

But Chota Nagpur and Santal Parganas rich in mineral and other raw materials and also endowed with enormous industrial and urban potentiality, started becoming Ruhr of India after Independence and the launching of Fifth Five Year Plan. With the growing pace of urbanisation and industrialisation, influx of large group of people, establishment of new township, trading centres and growth centres, the

FIG. 3.1: Map of Tenancy Law and Survey of Settlement in Tribal Districts of Bihar

traditional rights of the raiyots of this part of the country started being eroded mercilessly. This erosion of tribal rights in their own land created a great stir and land question of the tribals in sixties and seventies of this century entered in the same disturbed phase which they witnessed hundred years ago. History repeats itself. Matters relating to transfer of tenancy rights by the cultivators are governed by provisions in the different tenancy acts in force in the State of Bihar. There are three Tenancy Acts in all. Chota Nagpur Tenancy Act applies to the districts of Chota Nagpur Division namely Ranchi, Hazaribagh, Giridih, Dhanbad, Singhbhum and Palamau. The Santal

Parganas Tenancy (Supplementary Provisions) Act, 1949 is in force in the district of Santal Parganas. The Bihar Tenancy Act applies to other districts of the State and in so far as the area covered by the sub-plan is concerned, that Act is relevant only for the two blocks, Adhaura and Nauhatta of Rohtas district. The Bihar Scheduled Area Regulation is meant for scheduled area.

Section 46 of the Chota Nagpur Tenancy Act, 1908 places restrictions on the transfer by *raiyots* of their rights. Mortgages or leases can be effected only for a maximum period of five years, except in the case of usufructuary mortgages which can extend to seven years and mortgages in favour of co-operative societies, which can extend to 15 years. A tribal *raiyot* cannot transfer his right by sale, exchange, gift or will, except with the previous sanction of the Deputy Commissioner and such transfer can only be to another tribal who is resident within the limits of the area of the police station within which the holding is situated. However, Section 49 allows transfer, by registered deed and with written consent of the Deputy Commissioner, for "any reasonable and sufficient purposes", which will include the following :

(a) The use of land for charitable, religious or educational purposes or for any other purpose which the State Government may, by general or special order, declare to be a public purpose or for the purpose of manufacture of irrigation, or as building ground for any such purpose, or for access to land used or required for any such purpose; and

(b) The use of land for the purpose of mining or any other purpose which the State Government may by notification declare to be subsidiary thereto or for access to land used or required for any such purpose. Section 45 was, however, amended in 1971 and while other raiyots have now been given the facilities to effect a simple mortgage in favour of financial institutions and co-operative societies, without any restriction. Adivasi raiyots can effect such mortgage only with the previous permission of the Deputy Commissioner.

In creating tensional situation, Chota Nagpur Tenancy Act as discussed above did not in the least make insignificant contribution. With the pace of urbanisation and industrialisation, the value of agricultural waste land called the *tanr* has increased manifold, because that wasteland now became the best land for homestead purposes. But matters relating to the transfer of the tenancy right by the cultivators are governed by the provisions of the local tenancy act, passed long ago like the Chota Nagpur Tenancy Act of 1908 and Santal Parganas Tenancy (Supplementary Provisions)Act of 1949. Section 46 of the Chota Nagpur Tenancy Act places restriction on the transfer by the *raiyots* of their inherent rights of transfer, mortgages of leases which could be effect only for a maximum period of five years.

The provisions of Santal Parganas Tenancy (Supplementary Provisions) Act are much more restrictive than Chota Nagpur Tenancy Act since no *raiyot*, whether tribal or non-tribal, can effect a transfer of his holding, except where such a right has been conceded by the record of rights and only to the extent to which the right has been conferred. Even where the rights of transfer are conceded by the record of rights, an Adivasi *raiyot* can transfer his land only to another Adivasi *raiyot* who is resident in the same *Tappa* or *Pargana*. Simple mortgages cannot be effected. Usufructuary mortgages, not exceeding a period of six years can be effected only by non-Adivasi *raiyots*. Adivasi *raiyot* do not have the right of effecting even usufructuary mortgages. The provisions of this Act have not so far been amended so as to provide, in particular, the facility of effecting simple mortgages in favour of financial institutions. The Government is contemplating to do away with this but it is facing agitations. Proposals of the State Government for such amendments were placed before the Bihar Scheduled Tribes Advisory Council sometimes back and the approval of the council was also obtained. However, the proposed amendments have not been enacted so far. In the last meeting of Chota Nagpur Santal Parganas Autonomous Development Authority held in the month of November, 1975 Seth Hembron and other tribals protested to which the then Chief Minister of Bihar had to concede.

In spite of these provisions, the tribal lands have been alienated by the interested parties and those alienated tribal lands fetches better consideration money from the needy persons than their original holders could get. This has created great frustration and political commotion. Dheber Commission went into the details of such cases of land alienation and recommended detailed study of this phenomenon in 1961 which was ultimately taken up by this author in 1963 under the aegis of Bihar Tribal Welfare Research Institute by this author and the State Government published in 1968 a Special Report on Land Alienation so that a healthy consensus for effective amendment in the tenancy laws of this area could be arrived at and the problem of land alienation of the tribal is solved once for all. Ultimately in 1969, Bihar Scheduled Area Regulation in respect of Scheduled Areas was passed with the main intention of restoring the land to the tribals which has been alienated in an illegal manner. Briefly, the Deputy Commissioner under this regulation has been empowered to enquire *suo motu* into the cases of illegal alienation effected even 30 years earlier in Scheduled Areas and would see that the land is restored to the original owner for he cannot possibly pay the amount, but the illegally alienated tenancy have been abolished. While in Scheduled Area (which comprised all the subdivisions of district of Ranchi District, Sadar and Saraikala subdivisions of Singhbhum District, Latehar subdivision and Bhawbria Block of Palamau and Sadar, Jamtara, Pakur, Raj Mahal subdivisions of Santal Parganas) containing more than 50 per cent of the tribal population, the tribals could get back their land alienated even 30 years earlier. In the non-scheduled area governed by Chota Nagpur Tenancy Act and Santal Parganas (Supplementary Provisions) Act, Similar amendments to these acts were passed which could restore the land alienated but only up to 12 years. This differentiation between the privileged bestowed upon the *raiyots* of scheduled and non-scheduled area in two different manners has created a stir especially in parts of Hazaribagh bordering Ranchi district which is a non-scheduled area. Hilly and tribal areas of Hazaribagh, Giridih, and Dhanbad were so much disaffected that the tribal especially disgruntled established their own Government and named it Sibu Soren Sarkar after their leader Sibu Soren of Jharkhand Mukti Morcha and one of the confederates of Shivaji Samaj Movement and dispossessed those whose land the tribals liked.

However, it looks that interested party instead of ruthlessly implementing this Bihar Scheduled Area Regulation, went into the illegality of the retrospective restoration and curiously enough instead of allowing the litigant to test the various consequences of this retrospective restoration the State Government, on the advice of the Commissioner, South Chota Nagpur Division practically withdrew the Regulation restoration affect so much so that the point of 30 years retrospective limitation has made it operative for only twelve years now. This order was really anti-people, though it had been given the garb of meeting the legal technicalities. The result is that whatever restoration process under this Regulation was working, got a jolt and the regulation stands practically scrapped. It is certainly no use to bolt the stable when the horses have fled. Most of the land alienations were effected between 1955 and 1962 when Heavy Engineering Corporation and other big industrial establishments were put up at Ranchi and thereby enhanced the value of the land. Some protests to this were made and Government is contemplating amendment to the Regulations but presently the ordinary limitation period of twelve years is adhered as desired by the said Government order. There could be only a very few persons to be hauled up now while big sharks would be allowed to slip and dive in deep wealthy sea which they have created by befooling the tribal *raiyots* by offering them a few chips, some drinks and some little consideration and thereby alienated their vast expanse of land. The wives of influential officials utilised their husbands position to acquire large property. Big business houses and resourceful tribal leaders ired with each other in exploiting the poor and ignorant tribals. The judgment of Ranchi Bench of the Patna High Court in 1976 annulling the jurisdiction of Chota Nagpur Tenancy Act from the Municipal areas have also annoyed the Tribals who feel defenceless.

This has created another cause for frustration by the tribals and signs of wilder commotions are sometimes coming on the forefront. Only the juggernaut of police repression keep them in sullen silence, but for how long?

Chota Nagpur Parganas Autonomous Development Authority has been preparing a Sub-plan to content the tribals and developing the areas so that the life of the people living in this zone may be improved. It is learnt that Ranchi District is going to have soon a Survey and Settlement operation (offices have been established in January 1976) it is hoped that will set right practically the problem of the land alienation. The Survey operations have been started throughout Chota Nagpur-Santal Parganas Division. Recent re-study report of this author on the Problem, Extent and Remedies of Land Alienation in Tribal Bihar in 1990 is being considered by the Centre and State Governments for initiating several measures to stop the problem of tribal land alienation once for all. The State shall have to look into allotment of land to the landless and the clandestine interest of the neo-rich and the *mahajans*. But all depends on the ruthless implementation of whatever the tenurial legislations are under operation.

NOTES

1. K. A. Nilkanta Sastri, *A History of South India*, p. 157.
2. *Papers Relating to Agrarian Discontent in Chota Nagpur*, Calcutta, Vol. I (1872).

3. R. K. Mukherjee, *The Dynamics of Rural Society* (Berlin, 1957) p. 21.
4. R. K. Mukherjee, *The Rise and Fall of the East India Company* (Berlin, 1955) pp. 97-110.
5. *Fifth Report from the Select Committee on the Affairs of the East India Company.* p. 80.
6. *Ibid.*, p. 47-48.
7. B. H. Baden-Powell, *The Land System of British India* (Oxford, 1892) pp. 182-218.
8. *Ibid.*, pp. 530-31.
9. K. S. Shelvanker, *The Problem of India*, pp. 77-80.
10. B. B. Mishra, *The Administrative History of India* (Oxford, 1970), pp. 413-14.
11. R. K. Mukherjee, *The Dynamics of Rural Society*, p. 29.
12. *Fifth Report*, *op. cit.*, pp. 18-19.
13. R. C. Dutt, *India Today*. Chapter VIII.
14. B. H. Baden-Powell, *op. cit.*, p. 574.
15. *Foreign Select Committee Proceedings* No. 374 dated Fort William, 14th August 1768.
    Note : Available in National Archives of India.
16. J. Reid, *Survey and Settlement of Ranchi District*, 1902-1910.
17. S. C. Roy, *Munda and their Country* (Calcutta, 1910) p. 188.
18. J. Reid, *op. cit.*, pp. 199-200.
19. J. C. Jha, *Kol Insurrection in Chota Nagpur* (Calcutta, 1964) p. 231.
20. *Ibid.*, p. 242.
21. *Board of Revenue Proceedings* No. 3 Para 4 Dated 30th June 1850.
    Note: Available in West Bengal State Archives
22. *I. O. Revenue Despatch to India* No. II of 31st December 1858 Part I.
23. B. B Mishra, *The Indian Middle Class* (Oxford, 1961) p. 259.
24. I. O. Coll to Revenue Despatch No 14 of 9th July 1862. para 47.
25. B. B. Mishra, *The India Middle Class* pp. 261-62.
26. *Ibid.*, p. 263.
27. *Ibid.*, p. 264
28. *Ibid.*, p. 268
29. *Revenue Progress* No. 529A, Paras 3-4 dated 30th August 1875, Nos. 70 of Chota Nagpur Commissioner dated 1st August, 1859 to Captain E. T. Dalton.
    Note : Available in West Bengal State Archives.
30. *Ibid.*, para 6
31. *Ibid.*, para 9.
32. *Ibid.*, para 7.
33. *Ibid.*, para 8.
34. *Revenue Department Proceedings* from J. Geoghejan, Officiating Secretary, Board of Revenue to the Secretary Government of Bengal, dated 30th August, 1875.
    Note : Available in West Bengal State Archives
35. B. B. Mishra, *The Administrative History of India*, (Oxford), p. 427.
36. *Revenue Department Proceedings* No. 4 dated 27th May 1980 from C. Beadon to W. Grey.
    Note : Available in National Archives of India.
37. *Calcutta Gazette*, 2nd November 1881, Part I p. 196. *India Gazette* Part I, p. 511.
38. *Revenue progress* No. 23, para 3 dated 12th September 1860. E. T. Dalton to A.

Money.
Note: Available in West Bengal State Archives.

39. *Revenue Progress* No. 24, para 3 dated 12th September 1860. W. S. Seton-Kar to Secretary, Government of India.
Note : Available in West Bengal State Archives.
40. *Home (Judicial) Progress* No. 136 dated 20th February, 1879.
Note : Available in National Archives of India.
41. *Papers Relating to Agrarian Discontent* 1872 from Rev. H. Onsach and 15 others to Lieutenant Governor of Bengal. Vol. I p. 69.
42. *Papers Relating to Agrarian Discontent*, Vol. I p. 76.
43. *Lieutenant Governor Revenue Progress* (L. R.) No. 2975, para 5 from E. T. Dalton to H. L. Dampier.
Note : Available in West Bengal State Archives.
44. The Chota Nagpur Tenure Act 1869. Section 5.
45. *Ibid.*, Section 6.
46. *Proceedings Asiatic Society of Bengal*, (Calcutta), August 1869.
47. *Lieutenant Governor Revenue Proceedings*. (L. R.) Lohardaga No. 3, August 1870 from R. D. Haldhar to H. L. Oliphant.
Note : Available in West Bengal State Archives
48. W. W. Hunter, *Statistical Account of Bengal*, Vol. XVI (1877), p. 387.
49. *Papers Relating to Agrarian Discontent*, Vol I, p. 69
50. *Ibid.*
51. S. C. Roy, p. 278.
52. B. H. Baden-Powell, p. 582.
53. *Progress of Revenue and Agriculture Department Government of India*, 24th October 1891, para 5 from C. E. Buckland, Officiating Secretary to the Government of Bengal to the Secretary Revenue and Agriculture Department, Government of Bengal.
Note : Available in National Archives of India.
54. *Lieutenant Governor Revenue Proceedings* Nos. 12, para 43 (Ranchi) dated 13th November 1901 from A. Forbes, Commissioner, Chota Nagpur to the Secretary, Board of Revenue.
55. *Ibid.*
56. *Lieutenant Governor Revenue Progress* No. 88-89 (Darjeeling) dated 11th June, 1902 from W. C. MacPherson to Secretary, Department of Revenue of Agriculture, Government of India.
57. *L. R. Proceedings*, December 1903, No. 5 (L. R. No. 3400) dated 24th November, 1903, Part I from A. Earl to the Secretary, Government of India.
Note : Available in National Archives of India.
58. *Ibid.*
59. *Ibid.*, para 7.
60. *Ibid.*, para 8.
61. *L. R. Progress*. February 1904, No. 5 from L. Robertson to the Secretary, Revenue Department Government of Bengal.
62. Dr. S.P. Sinha : *Final Survey Report on Problems, Extent and Remedies of Land Alienation of Tribal in Chota Nagpur and Santal Parganas (Bihar)*, Vol I & II June (1989). Photocopy submitted to Gram in Vikas Vibhag, Govt. of India.
See also by the same author — *Munda Land System Reading 1984 and Peasant Organisation in Chota Nagpur* (Bihar) (1984).

4

EVANGELICAL ACTIVITIES AS FACTORS OF CONFLICT

EVANGELICAL ACTIVITIES had the blessings of the British Rule in India and flourished under the patronage of the Government to the extent that these came to be associated as one of the causes of 1857 uprising. A constant nibbling at the religious system of the native people piqued the masses so much so that the whole country was converted into a raging torrent. Even Disraeli[1] recognised that Hindus had shown usual spirit of toleration to the favour shown to the Christian missionaries ever since the days of Akbar and Jahangir because there was hardly any race in the world better armed at all points for theological discussion than they (Hindus) were. But when the functionaries of the Company's Government combined their secular duties with their religious zeal to promote Christianity, this caused a pang of pain, and alarm throughout the country because nothing acts so dangerously on the Hindu mind as the persuasion that the authority of the Government is exercised to force him to abandon the religion of his forefathers. To quote Disraeli again :

> What the Hindus does dread . . . what he regards with the utmost jealousy . . . what he looks upon with undying apprehension . . . is the union of missionary enterprise with the political power of the Government. With that power he associates only one idea . . . violence; he remembers the missionary enterprise of the Mussalmans. The *Koran* in one hand and the scimiter in the other. . . ."[2]

Colonel Sykes complained that the Government paid heavy salaries out of Indian revenues to a vast Church establishment in the country. They undertook extensive programme of building new Churches to convert the Indians.[3] In the array of British India, a renegade soldier who gave up his religion easily became a Havildar and a Havildar who forshaken his ancestral faith was promoted to the rank of a Subedar-Major.[4] The top British officials went about with the orderbook in one hand and Bible in the other.[5] Many of them informed Lord Ellenborough[6] in British Parliament of their aggressive efforts. With zeal of a Christian crusader, Lieutenant Colonel Wheeler commanding a regiment of infantry in 1857 claimed for himself the responsibility of converting the *Sipahis* and others for 20 years.[7] Even Lord Dalhousie exclaimed in his famous and celebrated Minutes:

> It is announced as a certain fact of very great significance that the young Prince Maharaja Dhuleep Singh had entered into Christian Community; and it is announced also as a matter of great significance that the daughter of the Raja of Coorg had been baptised and that our gracious sovereign was her God-mother.[8]

This statement gives an inkling of the mind of officials who presided over the destiny of India. But there were men such as Marquess of Lansdowne who stung by overzealous evangelical activities was provoked into saying in the House of Lords that if the fact of Lord Canning's subscription to the Bible Societies and Missionaries Associations was correct he did not deserve to be continued in office.[9] As against this the Christian Missionaries were always keen on conversion so much so that when Canning tried to follow the policy of moderation towards 1857 uprising they described him as a pagan and moved the Secretary of State to recall him.[10] However, Rev. Alexander Duff writing in 1858 did not like to be a party to the call of Canning recall and did not like to join the hue and cry against him because he felt that sufficient allowance had not been made for the unexpected novelty and extraordinary difficulties of his position-difficulties more than enough to try the nerves of a Clive or a Warren Hastings.[11] But he too was a strong critic of the so-called traditional policy which meant in common parlance in those days the indifference to the promotion of conversion into Christianity through educational institutions or other devices.[12] He was also against the policy of concession to native feelings and prejudices and characterised it as policy of conciliation. He also talked of 'open eyed policy' and the 'shut eye policy'. By 'shut eye policy' he meant turning away from and shunning the truth of which he accused the local government whereas 'open eyed policy' was seeking supremely the glory of God and good of men would begin with confession of the past errors of sins, past mistakes and shortcomings etc.[13]

The Government refuted the charges that Christianity was encouraged; but Colonel Sykes in the House of Commons quoted reliable figures to show the ever-increasing employment of Chaplains and Bishops in India from 1836-37 to 1853-56 from the returns laid before the House of Commons and boldly asserted :

> . . . it will be borne in mind that all this outlay, of 2,453,882 pounds in 20 years, for Christian purposes, was from the taxes paid by heathens. . . . why in India the Company proclaimed its Christianity at the Cannon's mouth by saluting the Bishops when they arrive at Military stations. The sepoys necessarily asked the cause of the salute, and were told that it was to do honour to the head of the Christian Church, the Lord *Padree Sahib*.[14]

Even Ross Mangles, Chairman of the Board of Directors was never tired of his optimism when in 1859 he declared in Parliament :

> "Providence has entrusted the extensive Empire of Hindustan to England in order that the banner of Christ should have triumph from one end of India to the other."[15]

Looking at the writings of early Christian missionaries, one can always find that they have tried their level best to pressurise the Government to further the cause of Christianity as an agent of furthering the imperialist designs. To them Pax Britannica was meaningless without the religion of Christ being the major persuasion of the subject people. They professed that morals and religion of some description were absolutely necessary for the organisation and maintenance of free and happy state of society. "That region" remarked Lord Boling Brooke, "is necessary to strengthen, and that it contributes to the support of the Government, cannot be denied without contradicting reason and experience both".[16] Again "to make Government effectual to all the good purpose of it, there must be a religion". The author of *The History of Natural Enthusiasm*,[17] remarked "the obligation we are under, of attempting to convert our erring brethren to the faith of Christ, is not more clear than is the principle under the guidance of which we are to proceed in discharging the part assigned to us". The grand ultimate object we ought increasingly to avow is the intellectual, moral and spiritual regeneration of the universal mind — or, in the speediest and most effectual manner, the reaching and vitally imbuing the entire body of the people with the leaven of Gospel Truth.[18]

The aftermath of the 1857 uprising also witnessed a clear approach in the attitude of Government of India as well as the House of Commons to see that Indians were reduced to such a situation that the possibility of any mass scale rebellion in future was completely decimated. Rev. Alexander Duff from his Calcutta Station wrote a series of 25 letters between 16th May, 1857 and 22nd March, 1858 to Dr. Tweedie, Convenor of the Free Church of Scotland's Foreign Mission Committee, London. He highlighted the disaster of the Indian uprising, "which came in such rapid and bewildering succession, and with such resistless hurricane like force, that many sank almost into the very depths of despair. . . . There is a loud cry for the visitation of retributive justice on the hosts of unpardonable murderers, and a loud and honest wail of sympathy with the agonised friends of the murdered, as well as surviving sufferers. And all this is right — thoroughly right and Christian in its way. By any hope of an accelerated restoration of settled peace and tranquillity, would be vastly enhanced were I to see our people and nation prostracted in the dust before a holy God; and then sincerely and truly — and no feignly, such as the Jews of old, in those hypocritical fastings and humiliations which were an abomination to the Lord — *confessing our past sins of omission and commission towards poor benighted, superstition-ridden India, and resolving that in the amendment of the future, ample reparation shall be made for the crimes and negligence of the past*".[19]

The octogenarian Bishop of Calcutta had also made repeated private-personal applications to the Governor-General entreating him to appoint a special day for humiliation and prayer before God; but in vain. A memorial on the behalf of Christian inhabitants was made to Lord Canning; but in response to this, "Governor-General-in-Council issued a proclamation declining it but at the same time announcing the closing of all Government offices for about ten days in honour of most celebrated of our idolatrous festivals' Durga Puja".[20] Duff was angry that no reference whatever was made in the proclamations to the Christ, Christianity or Christians. On the contrary, the invitation was to "all loyal subjects of the British Crown" to offer "supplication to Almighty God", and "to implore a blessing on all measures taken for the suppression of rebellion and crime", which was taken as the most notable stigma and dishonour on the one living and true God, The

Jehovah of the Bible.

Thus to lower and degrade "the High and Holy one", who is a "jealous God", unto the level of the false Gods of Hinduism, and the heads of Gods bowing to all the other Pagan and Anti-Christianisms of India and that, too, by a professedly Christian Government was considered, and justly considered, by all right-thinking Christians as crowning or consummating sin, instead of being a return to God and righteousness. So that this proclamation, instead of tending to remove guilts, was rather calculated to add to the antecedent guilt, or charge of irreligiousness, which has been often laid at the door of the Indian Government. Duff scolded the administrators for not reaching the true point of humbling themselves as a Christian people and nation before the Great Jehovah. That as a nation we have been negligent in the discharge of our great trust, and as a people we have, in manifold ways grievously sinned against God in this land, was undoubted to the missionaries. He found it to be Lord's mercy that Europeans were not consumed. He wrote "that there have been so many instances of fatuous miscalculation and mistake on the part of the enemy, as well as of their counsels being turned into foolishness". That amidst so many exasperated myriads, having so prodigious a stake at issue as that of life and property and empire, no man of towering genius, such as India has heretofore supplied — no *Sevajee*, no *Hyder Ali*, no *Runjit Singh* — should have arisen, capable of combining and concentrating the scattered elements of rebellion, and bringing them to bear down with a sweeping tornado force on the exposed and all but helpless handfuls of British — is surely something, more than notable. He suggested that the palace of the great Moghuls which recently witnessed the brutal slaughter of European men and women and served for many a days as the burning focus of treason and rebellion to all the disaffected throughout the province to be razed to the ground.[20a] Such was the mental state of powerful missionaries serving in India and they always kept up their pressure through their support of members of upper and lower Houses in London.

Thus these push and pull guided the activities of Government to great extent and the Christian missionaries were determined to carve out a place for themselves in Indian subcontinent at all cost, fair or foul, but they always sanctified any step in this direction by taking the name of Lord Christ. The active interference in the religious life of the native people by the Government supported by the activities of the Christian mission was bound to touch the tender conscience of the people. This has greater relevance to the aborigines who were an inflammatory lot and had very little to be benefited by the spiritual benefits that the Church bestowed on them. It is this light that we have to see the evangelical activities of the Christian missionaries and the ferment created by them in the minds of these people in the plateau of Chota Nagpur and Santal Parganas.

Missionary Activities in Chota Nagpur

With the stationing of certain military cantonments at Ramgarh, Hazaribagh and Doranda came the European military regiments along with their chaplains. In this part of the country, of course, the chaplains were to guide the European soldiers into spiritual religious requirement. First contact with regard to the conversion of indigenous people in this part of the country took place in India in 1835. The Anglican Bishop Milton of Calcutta contemplated as early as 1830 to take certain steps to exercise some kind of superintendence over the concourse. In 1842, a Church for the soldiers was built at Hazaribagh, but the actual effort to establish a missionary in Chota Nagpur in right earnest started in 1845 when a team[21] consisting of Pastor Emile Schatz, Pastor August Brandt, Pastor Frederick Batsch, and Pastor Theodore Janke arrived in Chota Nagpur by chance. The four Pastors were bound for Burma but they were wavering in selecting Tibet, Simla or any other such place for their activities. Left in the lurch, these missionaries while strolling in a narrow street of Calcutta came across some natives with dark skin, the Cols from West Bengal. Chatlerton wrote that the "young missionaries were at once struck by these dark skin, bright, merry-faced people, who presented in every way a marked contrast to the decidedly fairer skinned and indolent Bengali and rather martial looking up-countrymen".[22] The missionaries were moved to hear their pitiable accounts and they began to ponder over the possibilities of going over to Chota Nagpur. Mrs. Hoeberlim also pressed their case upon the brethren, who were pleased with the field open before them.[23] Fortunately for these Pastors, Ranchi had two officers interested in missionary activities. They were Mr. Ouseley and Mr. Hannington, the Agent to Governor General in South-Eastern Frontier Agency and Deputy Commissioner respectively. Hannington was specially desirous that the missionaries should come over to Chota Nagpur and he wrote a letter to Dr. Hoeberlim to send the four missionaries to Ranchi to work among the Oraon and Mundas. On

7th February, 1845, Schatz wrote to Pastor Gossner, "This has been decided where we shall go . . . to the Kols, poor, deserted mountain tribes 40 to 50 Germans miles from Calcutta".[24] The four missionaries reached Ranchi on 2nd November, 1845 and stationed themselves at a place between Ranchi and Doranda and named it Bethseda or the House of Piety. The Raja gave them more than 30 acres of land near the house of English officers and began to construct houses and gardens. They had no fund at their disposal. They had to maintain themselves with the help of money which came from Gossner and also from the gifts from the officers of Ranchi.

The optimism which drove these early missionaries from Calcutta to Ranchi evaporated soon because Ranchi was a very inhospitable place of the hard, barren and rocky ground. Chota Nagpur had been constantly visited by famine, taking heavy toll of life. The orphans rescued from famine starvation were entrusted to these missionaries by the magistrates. The missionaries started bringing them up and educated them. They were baptised in 1846 and Christian names like Thomas (Carpenter), John (Compounder), Prabhudayal, Mashihdas, Mathew and Mary etc. were given to them. These orphans constituted the nucleus of the school which they established. The daily chores of these missionaries were that of selfless sacrifice and devotion to the Divine master, praying and reading the *Bible*, traversing the countryside on foot, seeking to find an entrance in villages from where they were sometimes driven out with stones, they were feared as *Safed Bhuts* (white Devils). "At the close of the day or weary, fruitless toil, they might have been seen again digging in their own little garden plots, to raise up a few vegetables for the supply of common table, or working with hatchet and plane, squaring timber for their dwelling houses or schools with their own hands, raising the walls, or laying on their roof of their goodly church."[25] In 1846, new missionaries arrived from Berlin. They were Hermanon Ansorga, Henry Batsch and Buchwaldt, but Ansorge had to leave Ranchi due to some unavoidable reasons. After the arrival of these persons, Domba station, nine miles south of Ranchi was established and was entrusted to Henry Batsch and Brandt.[26] There was bazar at Domba where people came and took medicines from missionaries, but there was no conversion.

Again in 1847, some more missionaries arrived at Ranchi. They were busy with agricultural and manual labour. Dr. Conrad who was physician, joined the mission by the end of 1848. The climate of Domba did not suit them. They left Domba to establish themselves at

Govindpur in 1850. In 1848, they selected Lohardaga, a place situated higher than Domba and connected with good roads. The Deputy Commissioner (Judicial Commissioner) Hannington financed the starting of this station. He might have donated his bunglow with its compound as a help to start the station at Lohardaga. Lohardaga missionaries were visited by some Lals, Thakurs and some members of the family of Maharaja who were supplied pamphlets and books. They were simply enquirers about Jesus. In 1849, more missionaries from Germany were invited to Ranchi to open new stations. Henry Batsch and Garad visited Raja of Palkot and told him about Jesus and left some religious booklets with him. Rev. Nottrott rightly wrote that it would have been easy to preach the Gospel, had it been accepted in Raja's house.[27] In 1850, another batch of missionaries came and preachings were carried out vigorously which created some impressions in the minds of listeners. Dr. Conrad treated within six months of 1850 not less than 5075 cases.[28]

Missionaries laboured hard for nearly five years in these four stations at Ranchi, Domba, Govindpur and Lohardaga; but without any tangible results. They reported to Gossner "we have laboriously ploughed the earth and sown seeds but no fruit will appear".[29] They, however, complained to him "Kols are not becoming converts. All our works are useless. We wish we should be allowed to select another field where we can work with greater hopes".[30] But Gossner observed in his letter to Ranchi Brothers "whether Kols will be converted or not is the same to you. If they will not receive the word, they must hear it to their condemnation. Your duty is to pray and preach to them. We at home also pray more earnestly".[31]

Perhaps prayer and their tenacity worked well in March, 1850 when four Oraons cultivators, followers of *Kabirpanth* fell a prey to the machinations of *Zamindars*. They came to Ranchi to attend the courts in connection with land disputes. They used to stay in the mission and hear the Gospel. The Oraons wanted to see Jesus. Ultimately after much persuasions the first four enquirers were made to understand that they should see Jesus with eyes of belief and faith only and, therefore, they were given necessary teachings for baptism, not an easy matter those days. There was the difficulty regarding breaking the shackles of casteism. The 9th June, 1850 was an epoch-making day when the first four adult converts were brought within the fold of Christianity. Colonel Dalton took official notice to this and wrote to the Government of Bengal "the mission was established here in 1845 but it was not till 1850, that candidates for baptism appeared".[32] Another adult Nirdosh was baptised on the 17th October, 1850.[33] Similarly on the 26th of October, 1851, two Mundas named Sadhu Munda of Bandeya and Mangta Munda of Balalong were baptised by Rev. Schatz.[34] On the 20th August, 1854 he had baptised Luther Singh[35] who turned out a man of considerable influence in later years.

Thus in a decade they had only seven adults from Oraon and Munda communities as their converts although they (missionaries, used all possible methods of propagating under the circumstances. They used to preach about Jesus in the bazaar, villages and roadside or even in the houses of individual as and when the opportunity was available. They used to distribute medicine free of cost and when the crowd collected, they started preaching. Lohrr at Ranchi and Conrad at Lohardaga were treating 70 patients per day and Conrad's mission house at Lohardaga was changed into a hospital. This was preaching through hospital. They started schools where children congregated in day time. The adults assembled there in the evening. They were taught alphabets and told stories and as such preaching was carried on regularly.

Gossner was overjoyed with the news of baptism of adult members of the tribal communities. He had sent 19 missionaries to Ranchi by 1851. In 1855 there were seven districts with seven elders. For proper supervision of *elakas* different districts were formed. These ecclesiastical districts were placed under elders. Next year their number was doubled. The help of local men was required. Noeman of Hethokota was a very active and sincere worker. In 1856, a Catechist named Prabhudayal Ruchut was selected on a salary of Rs. 4 and Annas 8 (equal to Rs. 450 today) per month and was placed under a missionary.[36] His duty was to pray and to study the *Bible* and he was to go personally from place to place with instructions to live only in non-christian villages to carry out preachings. Another local man Christopal was appointed as *Pracharak* on a remuneration of Rs. 13 and Annas 8 (equal to Rs. 13.50 today) per quarter. These congregations began to swell every year. In 1850, they baptised eleven adults in 1851, 27 in 1852, 32 in 1854, 35 in 1856. Thus till the 1857 uprising, 420 adults were baptised of whom 180 were communicants, and their native Christian community consisted of more than 800 adults, young and old, living in more than 60 villages.

Another assessment is that the number of conversions increased to 700 before the Mutiny.[37] Nottrott in 1874 was pleased to record "we have a picture of the 1st November, 1856. . . . By the end of the year about 200 people took baptism. In the winter of 1856, 40+50+60 people increased by baptism every Sunday. In the same year in April the congregation consisted 266 adults baptised. Two hundred children and 800 adults came into contact". He was of the opinion that "by the year 1856 the Congregation consisted of more than 900 baptised souls and more than 2,000 candidates for baptism".[38] Holsten failed to show the exact strength of Congregation before 1857. He gave the figures of 180 converts till 1854, but Sherring's assertion that the missionaries made loyal offer to raise a force of 10 thousand men, consisting of Christians and heathens over whom they had influence and unbounded confidence and that too was declined by the Government officials made us to ponder whether such statement could be taken with a grain of salt in the face of the fact that the missionaries had only 700 to 800 men in their fold. Rev. Alexander Duff also referred to such an offer of help by the natives christians of Chota Nagpur.[39] There is an official corroboration of these facts from Dalton's correspondence[40] that 25 Christian Kols were recruited and this was commended by the Lieutenant Governor of Bengal. This shows Sherring's claim as sheer exaggeration.

Due to this success, Gossner ordered the construction of a Church whose foundation was laid down on the 18th November, 1851. The construction of Gossner Evangelical Lutheran Church was put incharge of Pastor Hirzog an engineer and popularly known as *Mansion Shaheb* because he was planner, designer and supervisor of all the buildings constructed during the early years of Mission. Although there were only 100 enquirers at that time, a massive building with a capacity to accommodate 800 men was constructed.[41] It took about four years to complete construction. It is in Gothic style and any mission can feel proud of that. Its construction involved an expenditure of Rs.13,000 which had been sent by Gossner for this purpose. The church was consecrated on the Christians day in 1855 and it was given the name of the "Christ Church".

Some new stations were started. Nottrott[42] reported that to "the other station Ranchi-Bathseda — five more daughters have increased. In 1850, 12 hours South of Ranchi, the Gobindpur station was founded. West Lohardaga, East Purulia, North Hazaribagh — between this and Ranchi-Pithoria outstation was founded. In the year 1851 missionaries thought of opening of fifth station (since Domba was abolished) at Chaibasa. Henry Batsch was sent to Santal's of Hazaribagh in 1853.

Harrison reported that missionaries at Lohardaga were mostly Germans supported by German Society. They commenced operation as far back as in 1845. The chief mission station was at Ranchi, but in 1854 they also established a branch at Hazaribagh and very recently another branch at Purulia. Batsch was stationed at a place where now Dublin University Mission stands (formerly where cantonment was stationed (1780-1842). Batsch worked among the Santals who were on Tea gardens also. In 1854 Lohardaga Station was abandoned and Pastor Lohrr was sent to Pithoria in 1855 to build a station there.

The missionaries, after completing the construction of the houses, started schools in which children as well as adults were admitted. By way of encouragement one anna in a week[43] was given to those who attended the school throughout the week regularly. Yet there were absentees as the parents kept them engaged in domestic work. The guardians were always afraid lest their children should get converted to Christianity. They used to beat the children and abuse the missionaries. Apart from schooling them, the missionaries introduced among them festivals like thanks-offering during the harvesting season in which boys and their guardians brought the first produce of their fields for offering to Christ. The missionaries had also emphasised the need of giving up drinking by the converts. Prohibition was the usual subject of the discussion and they wanted the congregation to pass laws to prohibit drinking. The church took serious deterrent action against the drunkards. The tribals had no written language; but the missionaries there tried to learn various tribal languages such as *Oraon, Munda* and *Santali*. They learnt Hindi and Bengali also. Henry Batsch often talked with local people in Oraon. In 1850, the missionaries published something in Oraon.[44] We have got no direct source other than writings of Rev. Sherring regarding the Hindus and Mussalmans putting all hindrances in the work of Christians missionaries. Sherring's accounts run like this,

> "Previous to insurrection, the Christians of Chota Nagpur had been sorely prosecuted and oppressed by the landed proprietors whose tenants they were. Their goods and cattle were taken from them, the houses were burnt, their cloth were torn off their backs. One man's rice-field, ready for the harvest, was maliciously destroyed. Some persons were dragged out from their houses and beaten till they were breathless. Others were driven away from their villages with their children. The servants of Zamindar raided the fields of a

Christian. The same Zamindar (landed proprietor put the parents of one of the Christians into prison without due cause. The wives of the Christians were sometimes abused and the men were occasionally in jeopardy of their life. In short, poor Christians seem to have been treated with great ignomy and cruelty. I am sorry to say, that they did not for some time not until their trials had been forced upon the attention of the Government of India obtained protection from the local European authorities which as Christians and as men they ought to have received. Notwithstanding all these troubles, the faith of the Christians continued steadfast."[45]

The 1857 uprising affected the life of the new converts as well as their missionaries to a great extent. The German missionaries and Indian Christians were the worst sufferers during this rebellion as they were weak in strength and factually defenceless and they entirely depended upon the mercy of the *zamindars*. Sherring thus refers to it, "A general scramble for life was made by the residents". The missionaries too were obliged to fly. Running on foot through a marshy country plunging into water up to neck and exposed to the awful rays of Sun, they at least through Gods' merciful providence after a journey of several days, made good their way into Calcutta in safety. "Regarding the local Christians, he wrote" unaided and undefended, the native Christians were now in a sorry plight. They were completely at the mercy of the oppressors, of the Mutineers and of any rebel that rose up against the Government. "They lost all the property and were obliged to hide themselves in caves and jungles from the wrath of their enemies. But none made shipwreck of his faith."[46] Mahto did not find exaggeration in these statements but talking dispassionately one can find a tinge of exaggeration in these statements, because the persons who knew the tribals can not give them the credit of stubbornness which we find in some of the European Communities in Medieval Europe, facing similar oppression.[47] Any way the problem is not to test the veracity of Sherrings' account, but this gives some idea of the situation prevalent in those days. The so-called mutiny lasted only for few months, peace returned soon and Sherring's wrote that the missionaries reported back to their stations. They found there 140 candidates waiting for baptism and large number besides who were eagerly looking forward to receive the rites when they should be prepared for it.

Accidently we have no official record to prove this fact because by

1855 they were not posing any problem of law and order. It is only during the uprising that the Christian converts were looted for which we might have some direct evidence. But enmity between Christian tribals supported by the missionaries, and the Hindu and Mussalman *zamindars* had started purely on grounds of economy and agrarian reasons rather than on the grounds of religion. Some *zamindars* also represented to the Government that the missionaries were the root cause of the troubles and the Christian tenants were so bitter that they did not obey the Government orders. English residents at Ranchi were with the Christian tribals and they provoked the missionaries if Nottrott is to be believed. It is understood that the *zamindars* held meetings to teach lesson to the Christians along with their missionaries and at one time 30 villages were attacked.[48]

But in spite of this, one very important conversion took place on the 20th August, 1857. Pastor Emile Schatz converted one Maninath Singh renamed Wielhelm Luther Daud Singh. Maninath Singh was a Rajput from Bundelkhand, his father Ganesh Singh came to Kakkargarh, 32 miles from Ranchi to live there permanently, where he died leaving Maninath Singh at the age of 10-12 years. He was brought up by missionary as an orphan and proved to be a pillar of great strength to the GEL and SPG Missions in the later years.

Gossner Evangelical Sutheran Mission

The indifference of the Prussian Church to Mission, the lack of sympathy among his countrymen mortified octagenarian Gossner most who was already 85 years old. Nottrott was also conscious of the lack of sympathy for mission in his own people. Pastor Schatz was recalled from Chota Nagpur and deputed to represent the case before the Church Missionary Society, London with a letter from Gossner dated Berlin, 4 December, 1857 proposing the transfer of the mission to the care of the Missionary society of the Church of England. But London on the insistence of Calcutta Committee declined the offer, but showed its sympathy by the sanction of 1000 pounds for the Chota Nagpur Mission. Consequently, Gossner had the satisfaction to see the establishment of the Society named, 'The Evangelical Mission Society of Berlin, founded by Pastor Gossner' with a committee for its management called the "Kuratorium" under the charge of Buschell before he died on 30th March, 1858. Kuratorium in 1861, after the retirement of Pastor Emile Schatz, selected Sternbergh, the Head of the

Ganges Mission, to be the Head of the Chota Nagpur Mission also, thus wrongfully suppressing the claim of Fredrick Batsch to be "the Senior" who had already laboured for the last 16 years. But the crisis was averted by the wise course adopted by Sternbergh himself who did not accept the headship of the Mission.

But in 1864, new missionaries were sent by Kuratorium and new troubles started. Their salaries fell into arrears by five months. New missionaries carried influence with Kuratorium and they levelled charges against old missionaries and mercilessly criticised their work. Kuratorium sent Rev. Ansorge to Chota Nagpur to enquire into the differences between the younger and the elder missionaries. Ansorge could not do full justice with regard to the elder missionaries who were very popular with people as well as the English officials like Dalton and others who formed "The Ranchi Committee". The elder missionaries preferred an appeal[49] to the Kuratorium and pending the decision they withdrew from all active work. With elder missionaries like Batch, Batsch, Bohn, Herzog, Kruger and Pohlanz there were 7000 local converts,[50] while with the new missionaries 3000 converts sided. The Ranchi Committee and the Calcutta Auxiliary Committee earnestly appealed to Kuratorium to avoid this split, but all the appeals and entreaties fell on deaf ears of Kuratorium who expelled them. On and from 22nd November, 1868, Gossners' Missionaries were at last driven out from Gossners' Mission as observed by Cave-Brown.[51]

Society for the Propagation of Gospel Mission

Colonel Dalton and the elder missionaries invited the Anglican Bishop Milman[52] of Calcutta to accept these expelled missionaries within the fold of the Church of England. Bishop finding unfavourable response from the Secretary of the Church Missionary Society, Calcutta, corresponded with the Society for the Propagation of the Gospel in Foreign Parts, London which had assured him of raising special funds in England, should the contingency arise. The converts also applied to the Bishop for accepting them in the English Church. The Bishop by then had discovered that Dr. Murray Mitchell and Dr. Lang of the Free Church Mission Society had visited Ranchi in January 1869 and had declared their intentions to accept the responsibility of the northern and the Santal portions of the Hazaribagh District of the Chota Nagpur Mission.

Bishop Milman held consultations with Lieutenant Governor of

Bengal[53] as well as Schruder and Pilyram, the German members of the Calcutta Auxiliary Committee. Thereafter Bishop visited Ranchi for the second time in April 1869. On 17 April, 1869, 624 converts representing 7000 persons were received into in English Church, in an improvised temporary church made of bamboo and wooden posts, roofed with straw and palm leaves in order to commemorate the occasion. For this, the Bishop was vehemently criticised for humiliating the Lutheran Church in that manner. The event flashed in the India and German Press.

Holsten wrote "The Bishop did this and the conflict went out of the Church and Missionary framework, and a kind of national consideration came in".[54] It involved German prestige. The matter reached the Archbishop of Canterbury through the superior authority of the Prussian Church. Even Bismark was sounded to put pressure on the English Government. But the schism was complete.

The Roman Catholic Missionaries started visiting Hazaribagh after the 1857 uprising. The Government built a church in Gothic style for the service of the European troops at Hazaribagh. Father Camile was posted in 1859 as military Chaplain on a monthly salary of Rs. 150. In 1859, Pope Pius IX sanctioned the opening of Belgian Mission, but the first Jesuit to land in Chota Nagpur on the 24th November, 1869 was Rev. Father Stockmen. While posted at Midnapur, Stockman was deputed by Mgs. Steins, Vicar Apostolic of Calcutta for reconnaissance on the advice of an English officer regarding the feasibility of a mission at Chota Nagpur. Father Stockman found at Chaibasa two Lutheran ministers with 50 to 60 Christians during Sunday service including the officials like the Deputy Commissioner, the Superintendent of Police, and the Inspector of Police, who welcomed him. They encouraged him to open a station at Chaibasa by offering him a big room in the police lines and Inspector Brown played host to him for several months in the middle of 1869. The land was acquired and the church building began to be constructed.

By the year 1862 we find E. L. Puxley and W. T. Storrs, the two punitive force officers, turning into "*Messiah* for the local people in the Santal Parganas". The Government of Bengal had made it "known that Mission would get sites for its stations on favourable terms", and the Church Missionary Society, London, was quick to utilise this opportunity. Rev. Alexander Duff made an extensive tour of Chota Nagpur with Colonel Dalton. He went around Santal Parganas in 1862-63 and ultimately proposed the opening of a mission. Rev.

Murray Mitchell visited Santal Parganas in the winter of 1868-69. Mr. Verrieux, an Eurasian, toured through Santal villages and finally Pachamba was selected as the headquarters of its Santal Mission towards the end of 1869.[55] Thus by the close of 1870, Chota Nagpur and Santalia had four missions — Gossner Evangelical Lutheran Mission (Berlin), The Society for the Propagation of the Gospel in Foreign Parts Mission (London), The Roman Catholic Mission (Belgium), and The Scottish Church Mission (Scotland) each trying in their own to bring the unsophisticated pre-literate tribal society under the Cross.

Some hold that the schism in Protestant Church was an 'unmixed evil.'[56] The Protestants were here since past 40 years without any disturbance. Their break in 1869 did not stop their progress. Whenever police tyranny and disturbances among agriculturists occurred, they went on making new recruits.[57] Hallet also noted :

> "The good that resulted from the division is exemplified by history of the next forty years. Both Missions have made great progress and there has been but generous rivalry between the members of the two churches."[58]

Holsten characterised this period as the period of struggle for fellowship among the Missionaries in which the organisational pattern had not yet fully emerged.[59] Nottrott gave an altogether new shape to the organisation on the basis of new constitution given to this Mission by Kuratorium after the rift. The work of the congregation was increasing day by day and in 1890 the number of converts rose to nearly 35,000. Stations were started where there was danger from the Society for the Propagation of Gospel or the Jesuits. Patrasburg, Gobindpur, Lohardaga were opened. Rev. Han started a leper asylum[60] at Lohardaga with the help of the Hegenburg Mission in 1884. The station at Takarma was opened in 1873 and at Chainpur in 1892. The station at Hazaribagh had a different story. Started in 1853, it had to close down during the uprising, but was started again in 1861. It was merged with the Society for the Propagation of Gospel in 1869. It was again started in 1873, but ultimately in 1893 it was sold to Dublin University Mission.[61]

After the split of 1869, the Old Gossner Mission was named as a new Mission working under the Society for the Propagation of the Gospel in Foreign Parts, London. Rev. J. C. Whitley was put incharge of the Mission. At this time, this mission had stations at Ranchi, Hazaribagh and Chaibasa. Whitley's main task was to organise and consolidate the church bearing influence over nearly 300 villages and to face the non-Christian gatherings, the members of which were pressing their admission into the church with various motives. Therefore, the entire missionary district was divided into 25 circles, each covering 10 to 15 villages, under the charge of a reader or a teacher.[62] In the year 1873, five tribals were ordained Deacons[63] and were stationed at Itki, Maranghada, Murhu, Tapkara and Ramtolia. The congregation was reorganised into 48 districts under seven pastors. In 1882, there were 14 pastors with Father Butsch as their Superintendent.[64] With increasing number of tribal pastors, the Chota Nagpur Mission went on progressing until 1890 when Chota Nagpur Mandali was raised to the Status of a Bishopric with Whitley as its first Anglican Bishop on 23rd March, 1890.

The early eighties of the last century saw the retirement of Rev. Oscar Flex and Adof Herzog, the architects and the veteran Rev. Fredrick Batsch. When Batsch came to Chota Nagpur in 1845, there was not even a single Christian Adivasi there but he left behind 42,000 Christian converts when he retired in 1886 (the earliest report of the Chota Nagpur Mission 1869-70 reports the number of baptised 6000. This number increased to 12,519 by the year 1890). Dalton, the great patron who always stood by the Mission in times of weal and woe also died in 1880. He left behind 500 pounds for the Chota Nagpur Mission Fund in addition to many large donations. He had contributed regularly 120 pounds a year to its support. On his return to England, he made sufficient provision for the continuance of the work. Dalton and other officials had contributed liberally for the construction of a Central Church at Ranchi. Colonel Dalton, the Commissioner of Chota Nagpur Division, contributed Rs. 3,000; Bishop Milman sent Rs. 2,000; Government of India sanctioned Rs. 3,500; the Building Fund of the Diocese, Calcutta granted Rs. 7,500; the Society for the Propagation of Gospel London granted 1000 pounds. The European ladies at Ranchi, Doranda and Hazaribagh rose up to collect necessary funds. General Rowlatt, the Judicial Commissioner of Chota Nagpur, prepared the design of the Cathedral; Colonel Dalton laid the foundation stone of the Cathedral on the 1st September 1870; and Bishop Milman consecrated it on 9th March, 1873 in the name of St. Paul.

The Roman Catholic Mission

The Roman Catholic Mission joined the Plateau in 1869 when Father Stockman arrived at Chaibasa. By 1880 Father Sapart was at Doranda. But real achievement for this church actually started with the coming of Father Constant Lievens on the 23rd November, 1885. In very short time, he gave such a leadership that whatever we find today in this church can safely be taken as a monument of his apostolic zeal. Of course, he was assisted by Father Van Severen, Father Gardon, Father Dehon and others.

The whole area was divided into five apostolic districts of Torpa, Dorma, Dighia, Karra and Tapkara with outstations at Chaibasa and Hazaribagh. Father Lievens was installed as the Director of the Chota Nagpur Mission by Archbishop Mgr. Goethel. Doranda was the *Deraghar* for the converts and store house for the missionaries who used to serve the Madrasi Catholic soldiers posted there. But Doranda had not the fortune to be the headquarters. On the suggestion of Father Mullender the missionaries moved from Doranda to the present site on Purulia Road where a coffee orchard was purchased for Rs. 8000 (some say that it was taken on lease) and the Central station was built in the year 1886.

In Chaibasa, Father Stockman could baptise six or seven families of Munda charcoal burners. Land was purchased in every village where conversion was expected. A house and a chapel were built and a school was started in these villages. Near Bangaon, Burudih was the first Catholic village and the next was Burma. Archbishop Mgr. Goethel visited on 13th February, 1881 and blessed 41 christians. The plots of land were purchased at Sarwada in 1882 and renamed as Mariadih. In 28 July, 1882 the number of baptised was 557. Dolda was also established. In 1885 there were 1837 Roman Catholics in Chota Nagpur.[65]

Contributions of Father Lievens

Father Decock was working among the Oraons at Jamgain in 1880 and was credited to have begun the conversion by admitting 160 Lutherans in the Roman Catholic church.[66] He worked at Murto, Kudarko and Dighia. But a big leap forward was to made by Father Constant Lievens who had picked up Oraon and Kharia in five months stay at Jamgain. Lievens believed in the fact that "the whole Chota Nagpur

FIG. 4.1 Father Lievens FIG. 4.1 Father Lievens

must be Catholics"[67] Bowen had no doubt that his earlier achievements were on account of the Lutherans; but that great stride in mass conversion was made by Lievens by dint of his own apostolic zeal and indefatigible exertions which *inter alia* is a burning example of the evangelical activity being the factor of conflict and tension among the people of Chota Nagpur.

Father Lievens, popularly known as *Libin Saheb*, settled at Torpa in November 1885, and had soon "Christians in 60 villages".[68] From Torpa he went to Karra when his residence caught fire mysteriously; but due to his zeal he could get the consent of four or five villages to embrace Christianity. From Karra he went to Panari and Nawagarh accompanied by Haghenbeck and baptised 2,888 people mostly children.[69] He then turned to Biru and Barway where 35000 Oraons were living. The Oraons living in Berri village were summoned to Ranchi Court where they met Lievens and ultimately won their cases. They immediately got themselves inscribed. The news of his success spread like wild-fire in the villages of Biru and Barway and thousands of heads of families came to Ranchi and Dighia for baptism. In Father Lievens, the Oraons found a liberator and crowds came to him asking for baptism. Thus within three weeks as many as 13000 people were baptised.[70] Lievens baptised 70 persons of Palamau who had gone to Ranchi Court and were in trouble. He entered *Chechari* and baptised 5000 people who were kept incharge of three or four catechists assisted by *chaprasis*. The visit with Mgr. Grosjeen on 20th April, 1891 gave Lievens the consent of 2603 persons to become Christians in Kansir, 24,301 at Barway and 18,885 at *Chechari*, making a total of 35,789 among whom 23,000 were baptised.[71] In his last journey to Barway in December, 1891, Lievens baptised 1,271 persons.

But his failing health forced him to go to Darjeeling and then to Belgium where he died at Loueven on the 7th November, 1893. But his name will live in Chota Nagpur as the name of Father De Nobili lives in Madura and the name of Father Ricci lives in China for his prodigious achievement. Father Lievens studied law of the land as well as the rights and duties of the *zamindar*. He consulted lawyers and magistrates in this connection and taught the people how to win their cases in the law courts. His legal knowledge and his pull with magistrates and police always proved helpful to the tribals who were in trouble and were summoned to Ranchi Courts. His legal help and other assistance must have weighed heavily in deciding whether or not they should change their faith so that they may live to enjoy the fruits of their labour and land. Thus temporal objects guided the tribals to go to the refuge of church which had stalwart champions like Lievens. There were definite signs of uneasiness in different churches at Lievens methodology of conversion.

The petty police officials at Khunti, Basia, Palkote and other places started reporting against Father Lievens. On 26 April, 1888, Lillingston, the Deputy Commissioner of Lohardaga, forwarded to Father Motet these complaints of missionaries taking active interest in landlord-tenant relationship which was to their mind prejudicial to the public peace. On 21 June, 1888, Lillingston again requested Father Motet to instruct these Fathers not to interfere in the matters of dispute between the landlords and the tenants. Stevens, the Commissioner of Chota Nagpur Division in his letter dated 23 October, 1868 to Father Motet wrote about his concern that Father Lievens was persuading the people not to pay rent to the landlord.

On the other hand Motet justified the work of the missionaries saying that if they only "protect people against tyrannical extortions and illegal vexations, is it not the duty of everyman, *a fortiori*, of a priest, to instruct and help a sufferer". In a letter to Stevens, Motet challenged: "I shall be obliged if the petitioners prove single cases in which just rents and services have not been paid and prove that the refusal is due to us". Stevens, however, still felt certain "that no missionary who was anxious, as I believe the missionaries of your society are, for the benefit of his people would encourage them in opposition to the law of the land", and asked that the Fathers be careful that in defence of their interests of the people. He hoped that "the father" is "not misunderstood by them, and interpreted as an encouragement to do mischief and invade the long established rights of landlords."[71] Lillingston, the Deputy Commissioner of Lohardaga made a tour through Khunti, Torpa, Basia and Palkote lasting from 20 November, 1888 to 23 February, 1889; but there is no evidence that the Government tried to stop the activity of the missionaries even though at times they did make further investigations. This encouraged Father Lievens who in Barway alone baptised more than 13,000 persons.

Thus Lievens displeased and alarmed the sections of *zamindars* most, who naturally would not like their prey, the *raiyots*, to be "misguided" (guided) by Lievens or any body and thereby loose their cases against their *raiyots* in Ranchi Courts. As a matter of fact, a serious gun battle took place between the *zamindar* of Haril and Father Cush on the 24th May 1890.[72] A near rebellion situation was created in

Biru and Barway. Father Motet and Lievens were summoned to see the Commissioner Grimley. In discussion that took place, it transpired that the court rightly and wrongly passed orders on the villagers to pay three-year rentals even if the rents were paid. Institution of false cases was a common phenomenon and the villagers at times retaliated by committing excesses. A rumour was current that Queen Victoria wanted everyone to embrace Christianity and Father Lievens was only communicating this order to the people.[73]

On his return to Ranchi on 17 November, 1889, Lievens found Jesuit Missionaries somewhat excited on account of the reports of the landlords which claimed that the people were in rebellion and as proof added that "they were illegally combining against the landlords by gathering in large numbers carrying battle axes, cutting the rice of these gentlemen, refusing to work for them, preventing others from working, forcing people to become Christians, even rescuing people imprisoned from the hands of the police and beating constables".[74]

Commissioner Grimley in spite of their explanation felt the need of an investigation into the accusations and had already sent Mr. Renny, the Acting Deputy Commissioner of Lohardaga and Mr. Patch, the Superintendent of Police, to investigate. Gardon, the missionary at Tetara tried to explain to Mr. Renny that the outcry was a made up affair and the only work of missionaries was to teach the Christians religion to those who asked for and to explain to the people how and when they would apply in their temporal troubles to the government officials. Renny did not agree with him. At Basia he felt the need of strengthening all the police stations. Later on Lillingston, the Deputy Commissioner of Lohardaga, also joined Renny in his tour of the disturbed area. On their tour of investigation, Renny and Lillingston had tried some Court cases (documents available in Ranchi Bishop Archives). These judgments touch on several points the attitude of the villagers and the Christians, the attitude of the two officials towards the Jesuit Mission and the work of missionaries. The conviction of both the officers was that there was rebellion and revolt.

In Renny's first judgment on 26 November, 1889 we find the usual land disputes between landlord and tenants. The case is against six tenants for looting and carrying away the crops of people who refused to become Christians. Renny claimed that the district was in a disturbed situation due to these disputes. The officials claimed that the Jesuits, simply by cutting off the *Chundies* persuaded the simple people to believe that they had become Christians. The missionaries held out as inducements that the *Maharani* (Queen Empress of India) would not let the landlords treat the converts in respect of rent and forced labour as they had hitherto done (Lievens wrote on margin — this way of treating is worse than slavery in some places and about *Maharani* intervening on behalf of the converts he wrote, "False-nonsense").

One of the evil results of such actions of the Catholic priests, claimed Renny was that the simple people (evidently referring to the converts) imagined themselves to be beyond the reach of all laws. The case in question showed this that the converts had been forcing their fellow villagers, who had not been converted to become Christians by forcefully cutting off their *Chundies* (Lievens' remark - "False"). "The evidence shows", wrote the officials, "that the accused threatened to loot the granaries and carry off the crops of persons who refused to follow their example in becoming Christians". Renny concluded that in the present disturbed state of the country several remedial measures were called for in order to check the present dangerous situation. One of the measures was the sentencing of the six accused, four men to two months and two men to four months imprisonments.

In Jharen case also, Renny gave the similar remarks. Four men in village Jharen had cut what they claimed to be their own rice for which they were being sent to Ranchi hand-cuffed by the police on the complaint of a landlord accusing them of stealing his rice. On the way, these persons were rescued by a group of men. According to Lievens this group consisted of about 30 or 40 persons. Whereas Renny claimed that the rescuers numbered some 2500 Christians and took this as an example of rebellion. In this document, Renny repeated several of the assertions made in the previous documents against the Jesuits missionaries and their method of making converts. Twice he blamed the Jesuit missionaries for the disquiet in the area, saying that it was "owing to the grave misconduct on the part of some Jesuit missionaries, this part of the country was in a regularly disturbed state". He regarded the freeing of prisoners as an open resistance to the servants of the Crown and blamed it on the action of the priests. He wrote : "It will be seen that owing to the action taken by these priests, the country is in a disquieted state and that in such a case as this when open resistance had been offered to the servants of the Crown whilst in the execution of their duty it becomes incumbent on me to punish very severely." He did this in order to show the people that the Raj was not theirs and that they would not be permitted to take law in their own hands. He did not mention what part the priests had in the freeing of the prisoners. Early in the documents he claimed that the missionaries "of whom one Mr. Lievens appears to be the Chief" have been going about the country both personally and through native servants. "On these trips these men proclaimed", he said, "that it was the order of the Queen that everyone was to become Christians. By this action the converts would become friends (*Bhaibands*) and relations of the Queen and no longer have to rend forced labour (*beth begari*). Besides they would pay lower rents. As a result of this disgraceful and deceptive conduct of these Missionaries, "a large number of the tenants have become", reported Renny, "what they call Christians and in consequence they have been doing lawless acts." "As an example of lawless act, "he claimed, was that the Christians had been collecting into gangs and going about saying" that it was now their Raj and that the only *Kutchery* was at Tetara" (Fr. Lieven's usual place of residence). The gangs had been doing more — they have been forcibly cutting the peoples' *Chundies* and making them believe that they are Christians; they have gone further — they have cut and carried off the corps of landlords and tenants who refused to become Christians.

Renny explained also as to how, he thought, the people became Christians. "None of these so-called Christians have been baptised. Nor have they been instructed by the priests. All that was done was that the priests had cut off the *Chundies*. By this action the simple people believed themselves to be Christians. Furthermore, none of the women or children have become Christians and people take offence if asked if their wives have also become Christians." Thus according to Renny disquiet was due to the action of the priests and, therefore, he was obliged to punish the act of open resistance to authority with severity so that in future they do not take law in their own hands and do not propagate that "kingdom is theirs". In the witchcraft case too Renny blamed the Christians. The case was one of ill treatment of two women suspected of being witches. At the trial Renny threw all the blame on the Christians and connected two of Lieven's catechists with it and, therefore, sentenced six men guilty of the crime, among them the two catechists.

When Lillingston resumed charge of the district and continued the investigations begun by Renny, certain cases came up before him for trial. Several of the aspersions against the Christians and the missionaries cast by Renny were repeated by Lillingston. In Palkote case the horse of the Head constable of Palkote was beaten by six men and they were charged with rioting. The Deputy Commissioner found the six men guilty of rioting and sentenced to them two years rigorous imprisonment.

In Tangaratoli case, 20 men were accused of cutting and carrying away paddy belonging to the landlord. In his judgment of 26 December, 1889, Lillingston claimed that the case under consideration "is one of the cases arising out of the present agitation in the Western portion of the district". The cause of this agitation, he wrote, "is a number of Christians or rather persons who have had their hair cut off and call themselves Christians". These people have been going about in gangs and exciting the villagers to various agrarian crimes. Lillingston found the evidence perfectly clear. The complainant, a man named Sita Ram Singh proved his ownership of the land for the past six years. The "misguided Christians" and others wanted him to join them and go against another landlord. Because he refused, the Christians and others came in group and cut his paddy crop. The whole village was involved in the act and a search of the houses of all the villagers revealed paddy which, the people admitted, had been cut from complainant's field. Three of the villagers declared that they had been forced "by the other *Chundi-cut Christians*" to join the paddy cutting. Lillingston found all the accused to be guilty of theft and sentenced the four ring-leaders to three years rigorous imprisonment, and all the others to two years rigorous imprisonment.

On 17 December, 1889, Lillingston issued Camp Toto judgment on two identical cases taken up together. The case in brief was that on 3 November, 1889, a number of Christians, among them two of the accused came from the neighbourhood to village Puto. "They called together", read the judgment, "the villagers and told them that it was the order of the Queen Empress that they become Christians. The visitors made the people Christians by cutting off the *Chundies* of those who had them. The inducement offered to the people of Puto to become Christians was that they would be freed from forced labour (*beth begari*) and would recover the lands they had lost at the time of the Bhuinhari settlement. After cutting off the *Chundies* most of the visitors went away. But the discontented villagers of Puto, who had, as they thought, become Christians, set to work. They went to the place where the landlord of the village stored grain which he had received as rent from one of the accused Naktu Munda and took forcible possession of it and returned it to Naktu. When the police investigated, they found the grain in Naktu's possession. The official gave the inducement of non payment of rent held out to the converts as the reason of the looting."

Two days later the same accused persons, went to the granary of Ghosai Oraon, one of the villagers, and took forcible possession of the paddy which he had reaped off his field. This field was called *Banda Pawa* and the paddy crop was a special kind (*malanga dhan*), sown that year by the owner of *Banda Pawa* alone. "The purpose for the looting", wrote Lillingston, "was that at the time of the Bhuinhari settlement, *Banda Pawa* had been claimed by the villagers as their own but the claim had been rejected and the field had gone to the landlord. Since then, there had been several court cases about the ownership of the land". The official claimed that *Banda Pawa* has been clearly shown to be the privileged land of the proprietor and this land he had given to two others. The two recipients leased it out to the villager from whom the crop had been looted. The Deputy Commissioner accused the missionaries of giving the people the "most pernicious advice", of, "pretending to make converts by themselves cutting off the *Chundies* of some and of causing bodies of these so-called Christians to go about the country. This was done so as to force others to become Christians in the hope of getting what they wanted regarding land and rent. The officials wrote that he could say more; but felt that the judgment was not the place" to animadvert on the conduct of these missionaries. He found the accused were guilty even though the accused denied their being guilty. Lillingston wrote that at the present time it was necessary to treat these cases of rising against authority and looting land and crops with severity.

Needless to say that the missionaries refuted these charges and contended that the landlords and police got away with their false accusations against the Christians and against the missionaries. They held that the display of guns and soldiers made by Renny on his tour terrified their converts. The people were threatened, beaten and fined. About ten petitions were filed in court by the Mission against the landlords and their comrades. The Sub-inspector of Toto Police Station was accused by the missionaries of publicly insulting Father Lievens and two of his servants. They accused him also of publicly insulting Rev. F. Candy while holding service in the chapel at Parria. Police station, Sisai and worried him for several days. Any and every old rancour, hatred and quarrel found now its revenge against the Christians.

After the investigations were completed, the landlords hurried to regain their mastery over the Christians. The landlords no longer seemed afraid of European missionaries. Acts of violence were committed against some of the missionaries and that in an area when otherwise the European even when not a friend, was treated with respect. Hugghe, the Jesuit had to transfer his station from Dorma to Khunti. He was reported to have been seized by beard, beaten and wounded by the order of the landlords. Dehon escaped with difficulty from a band of 50 men, the agents of the landlords, who surrounded him in his hut at Gumla in form of "regular pretty siege".

When the missionaries, the defenders of the tenants, were thus attacked, it could well be imagined that the condition of the Christians deteriorated at the hands of landlord and police. Father Lievens gave instances when the village Panari was attacked by the landlord's men while the menfolk had gone to Ranchi Treasury to deposit their rent under the Act of 1879. The children were tortured and were seized but were released only when the womenfolk scraped together all their money and paid off their rents. There were other cases of similar nature. A landlord went from village to village, beating all the people till his demands were met. In Biru also, the vengeance of landlord was wrecked. The very faith in becoming Christian was shaken. Many of the Christians left the Catholic Mission, disillusioned, at least for the time being. Missionaries no longer felt safe. In his letter to Goethel, Lievens wrote on 27 December, 1889 "our people have been forbidden to teach prayers and gather for divine service on Sunday. . . . It is told them over and over that the Government is against them and their *Padris* have been expelled from the country".

Goethal's Intervention

There was a great crisis. The missionaries began writing to Goethel, the Archbishop of Calcutta to whom, as missionaries they were subject. They had to bring him up to date with the situation in Chota Nagpur as he lived in Calcutta. In almost daily letters, mostly written by Lievens, narration of development of events in the mission could be found. Missionaries tried to get his approval and support. Goethel was a prudent man and just wanted to assess as to whether the missionaries could convince him of necessity of acting in their favour. Goethel was a valuable ally, he was held in high esteem by the Government officials in Calcutta.

The Fathers informed Goethel that there was no rebellion and wanted to substantiate their argument by the argument of Patch, the Superintendent of Police and Commissioner Grimley and others. They told that there was peace all where. Only at Ranchi people had exaggerated the situation. Young, a retired British Army officer who had accompanied Lievens to Burway also disbelieved the reports of rebellion. They found connected with Renny's excitability was his lack of impartiality. Lievens' name was sufficient to raise him in fury. In a letter Lievens reported that Renny had told the people that their missionaries had left them and gone to Europe. He mentions Renny telling that Lievens had 'gone to eat frogs.' Lievens wrote — "what will become of our work, if we do not give an answer to that magistrate. In the contrary if this may be put in his right place we shall be free for a long time. In other letter he asked "can Mr. Renny not made answerable before the Superiors for the blame he puts on us and again?" If Mr. Renny has his wish our Mission will suffer greatly, if justice is done, Chota Nagpur is saved from Paganism, from emigration and bondage. Lawyers suggested to Lievens the appeal in higher Court at Ranchi or to High Court at Calcutta. He advised Goethel to hire a Calcutta lawyer Man Mohan Ghosh, considered terror of the lower Courts. He was known to be fearless in pointing out the illegalities of the British government officials. Lievens hoped that this man "might check Mr. Renny on his quixotic expedition". Lievens sent a detailed letter on forms of oppression by the landlord and their men as the *raiyots* and their helplessness.

Having received all these information from the missionaries in Chota Nagpur Goethel decided to act. Being at Calcutta, he was able to meet the highest British officials. The Archbishop laid the matter before the Viceroy of India, to whom he complained for the unworthy treatment received by the Christians of Chota Nagpur. He wrote to Lieutenant Governor of Bengal and visited him. The respect and esteem in which he was held benefited the Mission at that time. Commissioner Grimley of Chota Nagpur was summoned to Calcutta and was made to discuss with Goethel the points of dispute. Goethel gave the Commissioner papers which he had received from the missionaries. Besides this Goethel decided to go to Ranchi and to make a pastoral visitation of the newly converted districts of Chota Nagpur. He informed the Bengal Government of his intention and the Government responded by asking the Commissioner of Chota Nagpur to give the Prelate every possible help he might need. He intended to confer the Sacrament of Confirmation. He wished, also after the events of the last few months, to "inspire confidence in the down cast and vacillating Christians". He left Calcutta on 19 January, 1890 and reached Ranchi eight days after. He set out for the mission stations at Dighia and them to Tetara. From Tetera they returned to Ranchi on February 15, by way of Torpa, Dorma, Karra every where receiving festive reception. It is claimed that the splendour of the visit stimulated the confidence of the people in *Bara Lat Padri* as Goethel was called by men. The visit thus, had special significance specially to new converted villages. There was a friendly letter from Sir John Edgor, Secretary, Judicial Political and Appointment Department, Calcutta awaiting Archbishop dated 1 February, 1890, enclosing the latest from Commissioner Grimley to which Archbishop replied in an equally friendly way promising to give a long answer to Grimley's letter when he had time and opportunity.

While the Archbishop and Lievens were visiting the Mission stations, the appeal came up before the Tribunal of the Judicial Commissioner of Chota Nagpur, Mr. Cowley. The Mission engaged the services of Man Mohan Ghosh, but he reached a day later. During this day some of the condemnations were upheld by Cowley. Ghosh pleaded for three days, with the result that more than a half of the condemned persons were acquitted and punishment of 25 others considerably reduced. The penalties for common offences against law and property were upheld, the accusation of rebellion was rejected; Renny defamatory remarks and accusations against the mission were turned down as unfounded.

Lawyer Ghosh was not satisfied with the result and neither Goethel nor Lievens who in the meantime had returned to Ranchi. They resolved to pursue the cases of those who were still in the prison and at the same time to defend the mission and the work of the missionaries. The confidence of the people depended to a large extent on the attitude of the Government towards Mission. Any sign of suspicion or of opposition towards the Mission had been and would continue to be, interpreted by the aboriginals in an adverse manner. Therefore, they thought that "unless the criticism of Lillingston and Renny were answered and refuted; the work of missionaries would remain under a cloud".

A defence of the mission was prepared in form of a printed public letter drawn up by the Goethel and Lievens known as 'Open letter' from Lievens to Goethel; dated 19 February 1890. This was used by them to reply to Commissioner Grimley's points. The missionaries took up one by one the statements of the Government officials, often quoting passages from the reports and giving the page and paragraph number. They criticised the method of investigation adopted by Renny and Lillingston, contradicted them and pointed out the discrepancies in their reports. On the other hand they defended the apostolate of the Jesuit Missionaries of Chota Nagpur.

Reaction of The Press

For some weeks prior to the appearance of the 'Open Letter' the Press, urged on by Jesuits, had taken up the defence of the aboriginals. Besides *The Catholic Weekly, The Indo-European Correspondence* and other non-denominational papers such as *The Englishmen, The Statesman, The Indian Daily News* and *The Pioneer* published articles on the conditions of the people. Other papers carried articles on the traditional rights of the aboriginals and on their legitimate grievances. The Press made known the aboriginals the idea of ownership of land and, therefore, their aversion to the payment of rent — something that was introduced only in the 17th century A.D. when the Maharaja invited men from outside Chota Nagpur to be his courtiers and these men also took away the land from the Munda and Oraon.[75] These innovations were shown to be the cause of the dispute between the landlords and the tenants. It was also shown that Chota Nagpur Tenures Act of 1869 was passed to solve these disputes. The press reminded the readers not only of the work done by the Act but also the defects like the further expropriation of the land from the aboriginals. *The Indian Daily News* in January 1890 gave details of the exploitation. In short, the papers said that the people "are robbed" and oppressed. On every side, and in their ignorance and poverty, they have not the means of protecting themselves from their oppressors.[76] It was shown that people become restless. The Government sent troops against them and hence they continued to be discontented. The Press showed that the only ones who exposed the cause of the oppressed were the Christian Missionaries. Large scale conversions followed, first to the Lutheran Mission and later to the Jesuit Mission. A brief history of Sardar Movement was given and the Press justified the legitimate demands of the agitators. A mention is made of the work of the Jesuits in the cause of justice for the aboriginals.

To find a remedy for the grievances of the people, it was necessary the Press held, for the Lieutenant Governor of Bengal to visit Chota

Nagpur and to obtain information from all possible sources. Such a visit was necessary and government should see that justice is done to the people for they wished "to be loyal; but their ignorance lacks voice, and can find expression only in overt violence which seems to put them in the wrong, while they may be actually right in their desires". "The people do not require and do not care for sympathy. But they would appreciate fair treatment, to be assured of the fruits of their labour, and such protection and freedom as they have some right to expect under such a government as that of Great Britain."[77]

Shortly after the return of the Archbishop to Calcutta these suggestions bore fruits. The missionaries and the lawyer wanted to appeal to the High Court; but Lieutenant Governor forestalled such a move by showing his intense desire to go to Chota Nagpur. Knowing the reputation of the lawyer in denouncing the illegal proceedings and mistake of the British officials, the Lieutenant Governor seemed to have feared that this Ranchi subordinates would be severely heckled for their manner of investigation. He promised Goethal that he would intervene in favour of the prisoners. He promised, too, that he was ready to give administration proceedings all the possible satisfaction which the mission could expect from a judicial action. Goethal agreed and gave up the idea of having recourse to the High Court. Lieutenant Governor of Bengal, Sir Stuart Bailey reached Ranchi in early March 1890. He re-examined the cases and mitigated the sentences of 12 out of 25 prisoners; but he criticised the arbitrary and unjust conduct of Lillingston and Renny.[78] Lieutenant Governor's resolution of condemnation was given wide publicity in Press.[79] He tried to lay the foundations for a lasting peace in the area. He had a sense of interviews with representatives of the landlords and of the tenants when Lievens was asked to be present. Before leaving Ranchi, Bayleyshowed his appreciation of the work being done by the mission for the education and uplift of the people.

On the whole it looks that Father Lievens was rehabilitated by Sir Stuart Bayley by publicly making his presence felt either in important interviews with the group of landlords or in some inspection of mission schools. Lievens' rehabilitation and restoration of the prestige of Mission depended much upon the personal influence of Archbishop Goethal, his rapport with Viceroy of India and Lieutenant Governor of Bengal and above all his pull with the contemporary Press. To undo what Deputy Commissioner and Commissioner had done, Lievens and Goethal had to exert much. This also reveals the fact that these ecclesiastics had great influence in matters of administration through their acquaintance with the high-ups in the Government and by the pressure through the Press.

Father Hoffmann

Roman Catholic Mission is credited to have yet one more great missionary in 1893 when Father John Baptist Hoffmann came to work in Chota Nagpur. He remained at Sarwada from 1895 to 1907 and the beautiful church is a monument of his ability and untiring zeal. In 1915 he, being a German, was repatriated to Germany but one of his greatest contributions remains to be the *Encyclopaedia Mundarica.* Father Vendeal built a dome-shaped church at Khunti in 1898 and on 20th May, 1906 the foundation stone of the Ranchi Cathedral was laid which was completed in 1909.

Father Hoffmann made history by experimenting to provide credit needs of his congregation when he started a Cooperative Bank and propagated for its success. He believed that "through cooperative Credits, the Catholics would finally be able to escape the tyranny of the usurers, loans taken from the Bank at moderate rates would enable them to free themselves from debts, contracted on ruinous terms, to cope with some pressing necessity, to redeem the mortgaged fields and so on".[80] Accordingly Lieutenant Governor of Bengal issued a decree establishing 'The Catholic Mission Co-operative Credit Society of Chota Nagpur' reserved for the Roman Catholics. Its main aim was to unite the Roman Catholics in order to improve their economic lot, to encourage thrifty habits and to train them to manage their own affairs. This was unique of its type and Hallet and Macpherson characterised it as "the largest society of the kind in India and practically in the world".[81] Father Hoffmann also took immense interest in administrative reforms specially the tenurial reforms. Survey Settlement Operations in 1902 and the passage of Chota Nagpur Tenancy Act in 1908 are mainly due to his exertion.

The United Free Church of Scotland

This church is credited to have started working with the help of medical missionaries at Pachamba. Rev. Archibold Tempelton reached there on the 15th December, 1871 and he was joined by Dr. Andrew Campbell. In course of time several medical missionaries such as Dr. J.

A. Dyre and Dr. J. M. Macphail joined the Mission. Miss Helty arrived at Pachamba as an agent of the Women's Foreign Mission. In 1872 Miss Mary Gilchrist and Miss Jessie Gilchrist came to do work among the women and also to run the girls school. In 1874 five persons were baptised at Pachamba, one among them was Joseph Sido. In 1881, the headman of Saolapur became a convert. The station at Palganj was opened in 1882. A Christian village was founded at Baritand in 1885 and the Manjhi was appointed a Pastor.

Dr. Andrew Campbell pitched his tent at Pokharia and Gobindpur in Manbhum. Jamdiha was opened in 1881 to counter the influence of *Yogi-Baba.* Similarly the station at Kolhar was opened under the influence of a Christian girl named Parbatia, an orphan who passed from one village to another as *Kali Mai.* The people were anxious for the rains which had failed. Campbell prayed for rains and there it came. Influenced by this feat, 97 persons were baptised in a day by the side of a stream in the village. Dr. Wilson in 1886 dedicated a beautiful church at Pokharia to Dr. Campbell 'Friend, Philosopher and Guide'. In 1889, two beautiful churches were built, one at Giridih and the other at Pachamba known as "The Stephenson Memorial Church".[82]

Dr. Andrew Campbell has affectionately been called the 'Appostle of Santals' for his outstanding services to them. The Government conferred on him the title of *Kaiser-i-Hind* and appointed him as a first class Magistrate. He was nominated as a member of the Legislative Council for the terms when the State of Bihar was created. He was also a member of the Faculty of Arts of Patna University. *Santali-English Dictionary* is his most outstanding contribution. People got a better treatment in Campbell's court. Not even a single pleader was needed to enable people to explain their case or urge their plea. Campbell is attributed to have fined a Brahman Rs. 25 for having tried to rob a poor man of his land. Dr. Campbell died on 8 July, 1919 after rendering a long and distinguished services for 47 years. He lies buried at Pokharia. Dr. J. M. Macphail also died on 15th June 1929 at Bamda after rendering 42 years of services. Pachamba, Bamda, Pokharia and Tisri were the four principal stations of the Mission with outstations at Jhalakdia, Giridih, Baritand, Kolhar, Jamdiha, Bungi, Harodih, Budhawadih, Bashaha-Pokharia and Bartoli. In 1929, in the 23 year of its foundation, its name was changed to Santal Mission of the Church of Scotland.

The Dublin University Mission

In response to the Bishop Whitley's call in 1890 half a dozen unmarried graduates of the Dublin University offered to work in any part of the world. They started on the 10th November, 1891 and occupied the dismantled military cantonment at Hazaribagh at the orders of Government of India secured by Bishop Whitley. They worked under the Society for the Propagation of the Gospel in Foreign Parts, London. Hazaribagh was a military centre since 1780 and there was a church from 1842 for the use of the soldiers. But the real work was started with the arrival of the Dublin Mission Brothers who first of all opened one St. Columbus College in July 1899 with 13 students in the beginning and Rev. J. A. Murray as its first Principal. Raja of Ramgarh donated Rs. 3,000. In 1904, the college was upgraded to the Bachelor of Arts standard. This was the only college in Chota Nagpur affiliated to Calcutta University. In 1912, the Hostel Blocks were constructed with the help of a grant of Rs. 30,000 from the Government. In 1917, science laboratories were set up with the grant of Rs. 50,000.

The Brotherhood was chiefly concerned with preaching in the markets and the *melas*. Lectures were also arranged in literary societies. The first convert was Ganpat who was christianed as Gabriel in March 1896. A Trinidad Brahman convert Edwar Ram Prasad Dubey served the Mission and was utilised for conversion purposes. Rev. P. L. Singh was ordained as priest in 1908. By this time a realisation has dawned upon the European missionaries that the Gospel in India must be preached by the Indians if they wanted any success.

Sir Edward Gait, the Commissioner of Chota Nagpur Division, laid the foundation of a church in 1906 at Kodarma which was completed in 1909. Dr. Hearn was the guiding spirit. He had applied to the Government for a grant of Rs. 500 towards its construction; but the Government of Bengal replied "as grants towards the construction of churches can only be made with the sanction of the Government of India, and as the rules drawn up by the Supreme Government, preclude grants except in case of Church accommodation intended for Government servants, the Lieutenant Governor regrets that he is unable to entertain the Rev. Dr. Hearn's request for a grant towards the creation (construction) of a church at Kodarma". But still we find that King Emperors' Blocks of St. Columbus College were constructed with a grant of Rs. 30,000 from the Government. In the year 1917, the science laboratories were set up with the help of a grant of Rs. 50,000 and Sir Edward Gait the Lieutenant Governor of Bengal inaugurated them.

The Seventh Day Adventist Church

The year 1920 saw this church starting its activity in a rented house in Morhabadi, Ranchi which is now the permanent office of this church since the house has been donated to the church. In 1923, Pastor Burges purchased 23 acres of land at Bargain and a building was constructed which housed the school with Pastor J. E. Sandara as the Principal. A Chapel at Bargain was built in 1950-51; but in 1928 a chapel at Kurgi near Itki was built. This church opened its branch at Khunti in 1929 which Pastor W. B. Votaw turned into a big estate with school, hostel buildings by the year 1944. The church is Puritan and Adventists are very strict in matters of food, drinks and smoking and would not make compromise on these issues. That explains as to why there are few converts to the Adventists.

Thus from the above discussion we find that there are three important churches in this part of the country viz. Anglican, now renamed as Church of North India, second the Lutheran, popularly known as GEL Church, and the third Roman Catholic Church. All the three together claim 600,000 souls as Christians in this part of the country. This will be evident from the Table 4.1 as to how far these churches have travelled so far as their number is concerned.

TABLE 4.1: Number of Christians Baptised by various Church Denominations between 1859-1967

Year	Number of Christians	Source of Information	Remarks
LUTHEREN CHURCH			
1859	1600	Nottrott 1874, p. 209	Whole Chota Nagpur Mission
1862	2689	Nottrott 1874, p. 218	Whole Chota Nagpur Mission
1865	7828	Nottrott 1874, p. 215	Whole Chota Nagpur Mission
1867	9600 (approx)	Nottrott 1874, p. 219	Ranchi District only
1868	11,108	Hunter 1877B p., 424	Whole Chota Nagpur Mission
1871	17,000 (approx)	Nottrott 1874 p., 238	Whole Chota Nagpur Mission
1873	16,742	Nottrott 1874 p., 15	Whole Chota Nagpur Mission

Contd.

Contd.

Year	Number of Christians	Source of Information	Remarks
1874	16,877	Hunter 1877B p., 434	Ranchi District only
1877	over 20,000	SPG Vol. 1503 & Chota Nagpur Mission Report, 1877, p. 2	Whole Chota Nagpur Mission
1880	31,253	Hallet 1917, p. 229	Whole Chota Nagpur Mission
1886	32,659	Nottrott 1877, p. 15	Whole Chota Nagpur Mission
1890	over 35,000	Hallet 1917, p. 229, Hahn 1890	Whole Chota Nagpur Mission
1895	40,000	K. S. Singh 1966, p.14	Whole Chota Nagpur Mission
1967	160,000	Chota Nagpur Survey Report, 1969, p. 30-33	Whole Chota Nagpur Mission
ANGLICAN CHURCH			
1870-71	5,773	Hunter 1877B, p. 426	Whole Chota Nagpur Mission
1873	6,099	SPG Vol. 15025, Chota Nagpur Mission Report for 1872-73, p. 7	Whole Chota Nagpur Mission
1875	7,787	SPG Vol. 15021 Calcutta Diocessan Committee Report for 1875, p. 60	Ranchi District only
1877	9,381	SPG Vol. 15030, Chota Mission Report Nagpur for 1877, p. 28	Ranchi District only
1882	11,154	SPG Vol. 15036, Calcutta Discessan Committee Report for 1882, p.28.	Ranchi District only
1883	11,494	SPG Vol. 15036, Calcutta Discessan Committee Report for 1883, p.28	Ranchi District only
1884	11,630	SPG Vol. 15038, Calcutta Discessan Committee Report for 1884, p.14	Ranchi District only
1885	12,435	SPG Vol. 15040, Calcutta Discessan Committee Report for 1885, p.71	Ranchi District only
1886	12,126	SPG Vol. 15489, Calcutta Discessan Committee Report for 1885-86	Ranchi District only
1887	11,791	SPG Vol. 15043, Calcutta Discessan Committee Report for 1886-87	Ranchi District only

Contd.

Contd.

Year	Number of Christians	Source of Information	Remarks
1888	11,284	SPG Vol. 15046, Calcutta Discessan Committee Report for 1888-89	Ranchi District only
1889	11,455	SPG Vol. 15046, Calcutta Discessan Committee Reprot for 1888-89	Ranchi District only
1890	11,792	SPG Vol. 15049, Calcutta Discessan Committee Report for 1889-90	Ranchi District only
1895	10,739	SPG Report for 1895, p.57	Ranchi District only
1967	80,000	Chota Nagpur Survey Report, 1969, p.32	Chota Nagpur
ROMAN CATHOLIC CHURCH			
1885	2092	S.C. Roy, 1912, p.168	Mundas only in the whole Chota Nagpur Mission
1888	11,291	S.C. Roy, 1912, p.169	Ranchi District only
1897	22,723	S.C. Roy, 1912, p.178	Whole Chota Nagpur Mission
1967	360,000	Chota Nagpur Survey 1969, p. 32	Chota Nagpur and Santal Parganas.

The growth in the numbers of the Lutherens, Anglicans and Roman Catholics is shown in Figs. 4.2 to 4.4 respectively.

Table 4.2 gives the official figures as compiled in decinnial operations about the christians following different denominations of the church.

But we find inter-denominational squabbles going on, not only between the three but in the respective churches also. It is not possible to delve deep into the matter here, but from whatever gathered from personal experiences, discussion with well-informed persons and participant observation, we can highlight some points showing tensional situations in the churches.

We have already seen that GEL Church has a very stormy past. But it looks that such tensional situations has been the fortune of this church. These tensional situations naturally marred the cohesiveness; but nonetheless it gave a greater power of resistance to the fissiporous tendencies just as the vaccine prepared out of the diseased animal brings life-saving opportunities to those actually affected by the disease. It is in this context that the recent controversy between

Kendriya Salahkar Samiti *vs*. Dharma Pradesh in G. E. L. Church has been taken into consideration.

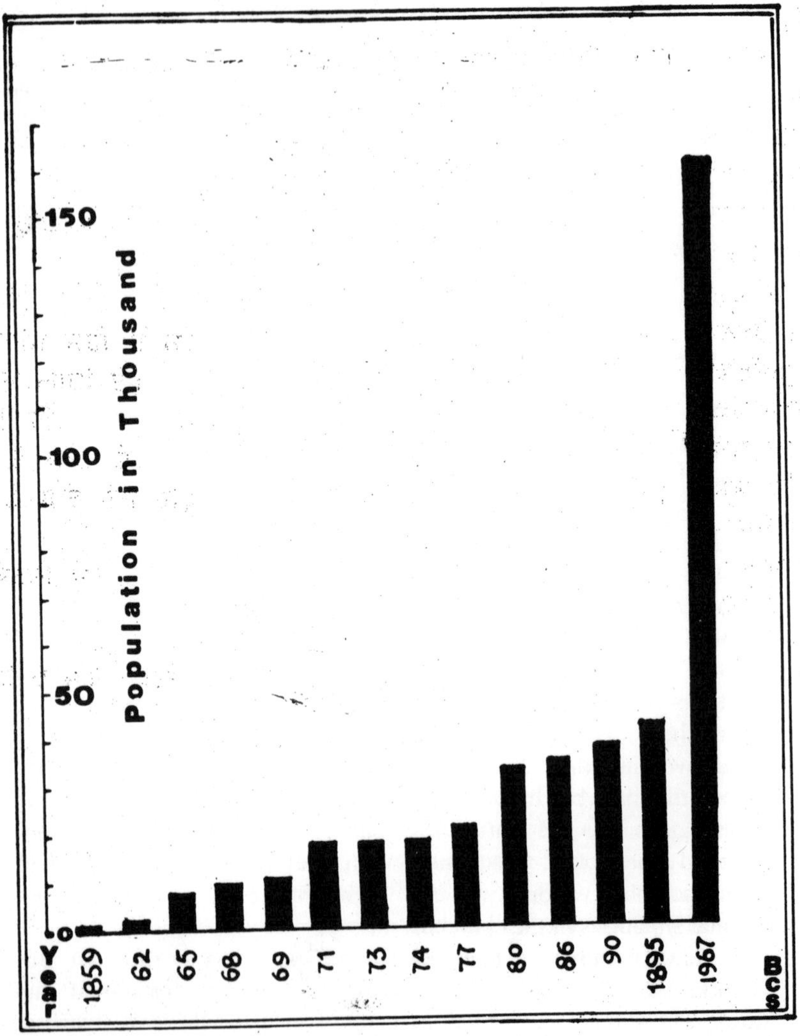

FIG. 4.2: Growth of Lutherans Church

TABLE 4.2: Growth of Christians in Tribal Bihar

Year	Number of Christians				Source of Information	Remarks
	Total	Luthe-rans	Anglic-cans	Catho-lies		
1881	36281	—	—	—	Census 1881, Bengal Vol.II, p.23	All denominations in Lohardaga District
1891	82234	18675	10338	53221	Census 1891, Bengal Vol. V, p.229	All denominations in Lohardaga District
1901	124715	57401	12973	54341	Census 1901, Bengal Part II, p.509	Ranchi District only
1967	600000	160000	80000	360000	Chota Nagpur Survey 1969, p.31-32	Whole Chota-Nagpur

The genesis of the conflict between the two factions of the church lay deeper in the personality and ambition of a few leaders who clashed with each other for their personal aggrandisement. Joel Lakra was one of the earliest tribal Christians to be given foreign university education and was one of the most distinguished personalities. He was made the Principal of the Lutheran School. But the school could not produce good results and, therefore, there was a no-trust motion against Lakra who formed the *Jati Raksha Sabha* and implored Rev. John Topno to flout the Church Central Committee's decision of no confidence. Another factor which got mixed into this was the personal factor of Lakra's, his confrontation with the Central Committee of the Church. This was in the form of the charge of defalcation against J. P. Tigga who was made Headmaster of Lutheran School. The charge was that Tigga did not deposit Rs. 531.76 paise with the treasurer but was alleged to have fabricated the receipt. When Lakra became President of the Church in 1945-46, he could not take any side because he was in minority. There was a feeling that when a top Munda leader defalcated Rs. 22,000; but no charge was instituted against him. Similarly, in World Federation, Mrs. Prabhalata Khess, wife of Mr. Nirmal Minz was sent abroad to Germany for training although the situation was meant for those who were not married and thereby they could be free for service to the Church. There was no satisfactory answers for these charges and Lakra also moved counter no-confidence motion in the Church Council. The Home Board of Germany was obliged to send an

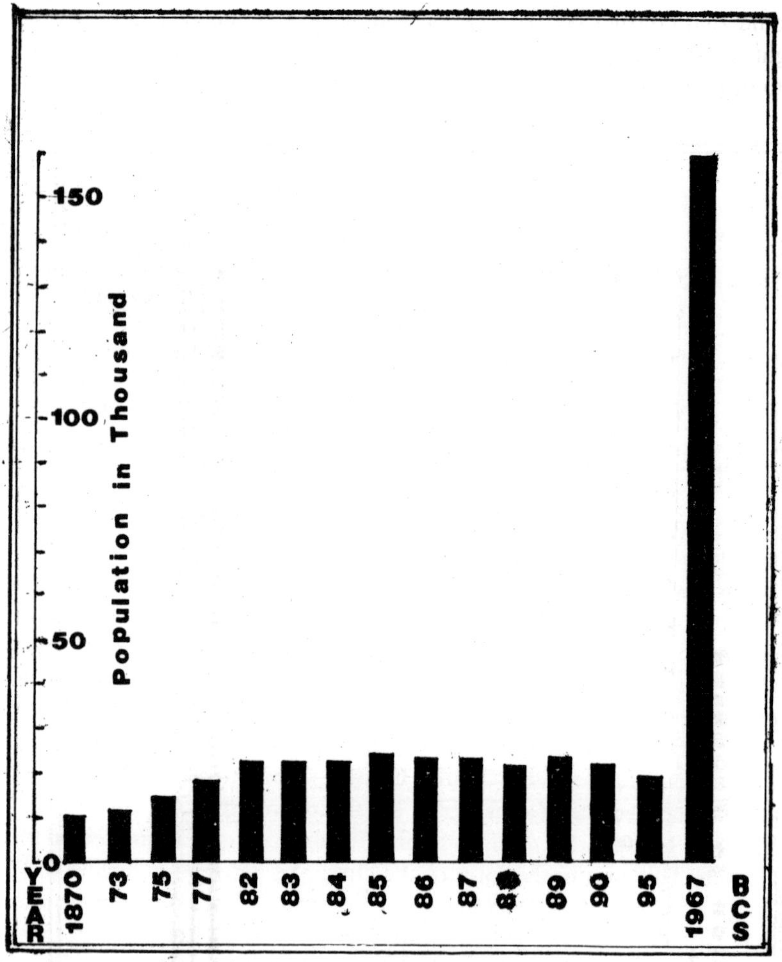

FIG. 4.3: Growth of Anglicans Church

Ecumenical Commission in 1959-60 to go into the whole case of this tensional situation and suggested some changes in the Constitution to suit the ethnic group. Lakra was finally defeated in 1970 and he threw his heart and soul for the creation of separate *Dharma Pradesh*. For this creation of *Dharma Pradesh*, if we take it as a case study, we would find conflict between Oraon and Munda in church matters as a fight for showing their cultural identity. The GEL Church was divided into different Anchals as below (Table 4.3):

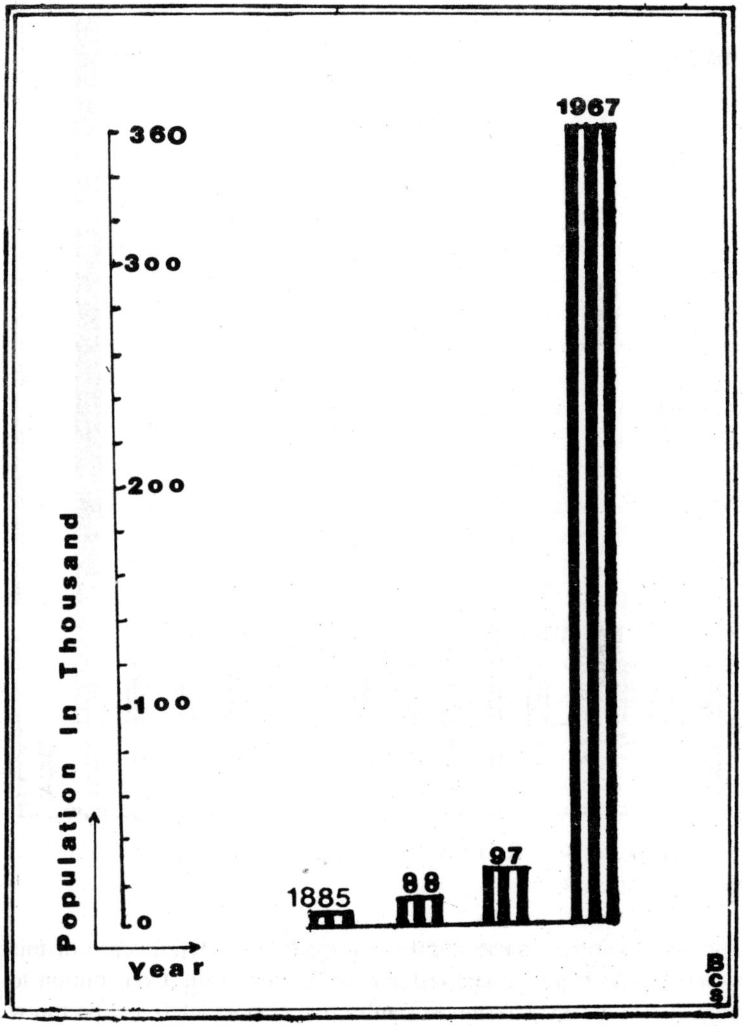

FIG. 4.4: Growth of Roman Catholics

TABLE 4.3: Division of Lutheren Church into Different Anchals

Direction	Area	Population (Approx.)	Dominant Tribe
North West	Duar, Hazaribagh, parts of Ranchi & M.P.	70,000	Oraon
South East	Ranchi, West Bengal, Andaman islands	125,000	Munda
Assam	All parts of Assam, Manipur	25,000	Munda
Orissa	Orissa	45,000	Munda
Madhya	Simdega	11,000	Kharia

Thus it is evident that Oraons are in majority only in the North West. Otherwise the Mundas were numerically superior and the dominant group in the Church. Lakra theorising this situation, pleaded that though he can condemn different *Jatis* in the Church, he cannot ignore it because this diversification has also its Biblical origin. He cited the Parables of Tongues of Babel. He thought in the sense that there were Ganges Christians, Oraon and Munda Christians co-existing since long. But the structure of GEL Church was such that there was need of some change. The *elaka* system of Church Government ensured Munda majority and, therefore, Oraons must clinch the issue of their self-identity, by creating *Dharma Pradesh.* Therefore, several households in Nagri Piska in Ranchi and Lohardaga joined *Dharma Pradesh* but definitely not in large numbers. GEL Church at Lohardaga was divided into four Divisions — KSS, Dharma Pradesh, Old North Anchal and Intermediate.

The fight between the different groups furthered to such a point that the cultural boundaries of the Christians, converted into GEL, was further cut short. Denominational parochialism pervaded though all of them had thematic similarity. The Burial services to the members of the *Dharma Pradesh* were denied by the adherents of KSS and *vice versa.* Not only this, this inter-factional squabble was shown even on petty affairs of celebration of 78th birth anniversary of Joel Lakra. The biographical sketch of Joel Lakra who was decorated with *Padma Shri* was prepared but GEL Mission Church Press refused to print it. It was only after a personal interest was taken by Lakra that this could be printed. Other leaders such as Bage, N. E. Horro and others did not join the anniversary celebration because they thought that by participating in the celebrations they would recognise Lakra's hegemony. For such petty things, sometimes cases were filed between the Dharma Pradesh and KSS at Kinkel in Ranchi District. Section 144 of Indian Penal Code had to be promulgated on 24th April, 1973, as a great scuffle took place between the two groups on the question of Church property.

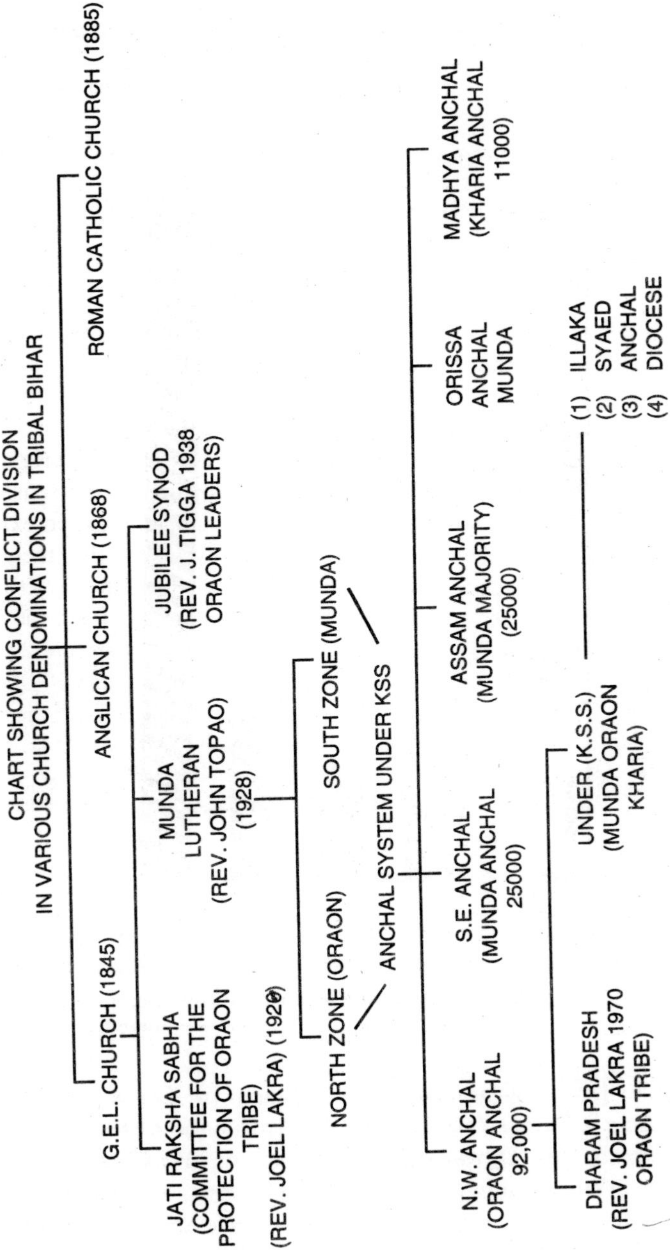

N.B. It is socio-cultural differences rather than religious that caused Conflict in the Church.

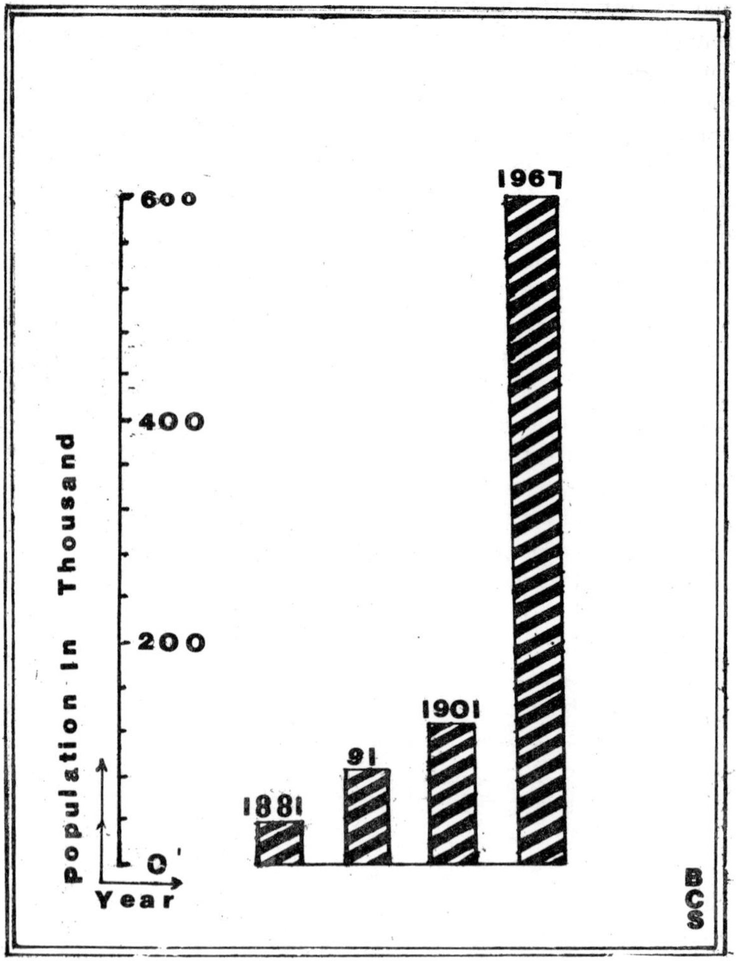

FIG. 4.5: Growth of Christianity in Tribal Bihar

While Lakra spearheaded the creation of Oraon identity by establishing *Dharma Pradesh* exclusively for the Oraons under the GEL Church, Rev. Dilwar Hans, the Bishop of SPG Church sought to start the Munda culture movement by having a College for the superannuate and, therefore, he thought to create a platform on cultural and linguistic affinity so that self-identity of Mundas be established. Initially when this idea was mooted by Hans and a local Munda leader Titus Topno at a general meeting of about 4000 to 5000 Mundas the-then Tribal Welfare Minister of Bihar Muchi Rai Munda also collaborated although he was not a Christian. Perhaps he wanted to make the best use of this cultural platform for his political aggrandisement. Hans had some impact on his electorates and, therefore, the Munda participation might have been for his own political end although he himself is supposed to be an ardent champion of Munda culture and way of life.

Rev. Dilwar Hans and Muchi Rai Munda convened a Seminar on "Munda and Cognate Language" in which they invited Kharia, Ho, Birhor, Munda and Santal etc. belonging to different churches, but speaking Cognate Mundari language. Hans perhaps sought solidarity of the Mundari speaking people or Munda group of language speaking people irrespective of the fact that they belong to different churches. But the response was poor. Only Christians attended the Seminar except one non-Christians Muchi Rai Munda. Initially the Seminar was conducted in Mundari others were allowed to talk in their own tongue. They decided to frame a dictionary of Mundari language and from deliberations it looks that the whole cultural platform of the Mundas was being utilised for the political purpose. Hans also sought the unity of the three churches and there were four joint meetings of Lutherans, Anglicans and Roman Catholics. One such meeting was organised on 21st January, 1973 in Anglican Church compound in which Archbishop Kerketta presided and it was convened by Rev. Hans.

SPJ Church was predominantly Munda, a fact which was evident even from some social and cultural functions. On 24th January, 1972, St. Pauls Church Centenary Celebrations were celebrated in which even in *Prem Bhoj*, few others than the Mundas were present. Similarly when on August, 1973, Gossner College was visited by the Governor of Bihar, to inaugurate Nagpuria Department, the other three church leaders were present. But it was because they wanted to show their united front before the Governor and it was definitely in their own interests to be available there. This congregation never meant unity of either these churches or of the three tribes of Mundas, Oraons and Kharias.

Whether in the celebrations of Easter and Good Friday, the differences between the Lutherens and others have come to the surface. In Easter, the tribal ancestoral worship for Resurrection of Christ has been introduced. Cleaning and white washing of the grave yards and libation before meals are indications of the fact that the Church has compromised with the ancestral worship of the tribals. It was natural because only by agreeable situation, the conversion of these tribes could have been effected. The Roman Catholic Missionaries gave much liberty to the tribals. They even distributed *hanria* (rice beer) to their adherents while the GEL Church strictly forbade them. Different festivals of the tribals have been incorporated in one form or other by the Roman Catholics and have been attached biblical significance.

Thus the churches might have grown to the present proportion but actually they are undergoing great transformation in which the new and old values are at variance and conflict with each other. This is definitely a separate subject of study. But, nonetheless, the tensional situation on account of tinkering with the tribal culture and customs by these churches, they create such a social format that sometimes the churches have to bow down and adopt their wishes. The churches have got deeper in the politics of this area.

NOTES

1. Disraeli in the *House of Commons Debates*, 27th July 1857. p. 452.
2. *Ibid.*, p. 463; Colonel Sykes in the House of Commons Debates; 18th February 1858, pp. 1625-27.
3. Colonel Sykes, *ibid.*, pp. 1623-24. Savarkar p. 59.
4. Causes of Mutiny by a Bengali Hindu quoted by Savarkar, p. 60; Confidential Report on Native Newspapers, Extract from *Kaiser-i-Hind*, 1st July 1883.
5. Kaye and Malleson, I, p. 352.
6. Ellenborough in the *House of Commons Debates*, 9th June 1857, p. 1396.
7. Savarkar, p. 61; Kaye and Malleson, I, p. 352.
8. Disraeli *op cit.*, 11th August 1857, p. 1429.
9. Landsdowne and Malmesbury in the *House of Common Debates*; 9th June 1957, pp. 1399-1400.
10. "The Government of India and Christianity" *Christian Intelligences,* June 1860.
11. Alexander Grey, *Indian Mutiny Causes and Effects*. (Gudson, 1859) Letter no. LXVII, p. 236.
12. *Ibid.*, Letter No. XIX, p. 267.
13. *Ibid.*, Letter No. LXX, p. 302.
14. Colonel Sykes in the *House of Commons Debates*, 18th February 1858, pp. 1620-21.
15. Quoted by Savarkar, p. 55.
16. Alexander Dull, *India and Indian Missions*. 2nd ed. (London, 1840), p. 294.
17. *Ibid*, p. 305.
18. *Ibid*, p. 308.
19. *Ibid*, Letter No. XII p. 141.

20. *Ibid*, p. 114.
20a. *Ibid.*
21. Hunter, 1877, Vol. XVI, p. 423.
22. Chatlerton, 1901, p. 5.
23. Mullens, 1863, p. 40.
24. Nott, 1874, p. 171.
25. Cave, p. 10; Chatlerton, p. 22.
26. Nott, p. 178.
27. *Ibid.*, p. 100.
28. Nott, p. 182.
29. Chatlerton, 1901, p. 22.
30. Nott, p. 183.
31. *Ibid*; Landy, p. 156.
32. Letter No. 510 dated 2nd April 1863 from Colonel Dalton, Commissioner Chota Nagpur Division to A. Eden, Secretary, Government of Bengal.
33. Shital, p. 20.
34. Letter dated 14th December 1857 from Gossner to Christian Mission Society, London.
35. Shital, p. 24; Roy, p. 246.
36. Hul, p. 253.
37. Cave, p. 12, 19.
38. Nott, p. 188, 192.
39. Mullens, 1863, p. 41.
40. Para 3 of Letter No. 65 dated 14th April 1858 from Colonel Dalton, officiating Commissioner, Chota Nagpur Division to A. R. Young, Secretary, Government of West Bengal, published in Judicial Proceedings No. 275 of 13th May 1858.
41. Christ Wuls, p. 21.
42. Nott, p. 138.
43. *Ibid.*, p. 176.
44. Cave, p. 12.
45. Sherring, 1858, pp. 310-11.
46. *Ibid.*, p. 312.
47. Mahto, p. 53.
48. Nott, p. 193.
49. *The Friend of India* dated 13th May and 3rd June 1869.
50. Cave, p. 53.
51. *Ibid*, p. 55.
52. Mitchell, 1871, p. 48. .
53. Letter dated 8th May 1870 from Milmen T. Burge, Private Chaplain to the Bishop of Calcutta to *The Friend of India*.
54. Hul, p. 262.
55. Macphail, p. 12; Campbell, pp. 12-13.
56. A. R. C. N. M., 1869-70, p. 8.
57. Hunter, 1877, vol XVI, p. 245, Joss, Vol I p. 452.
58. *Ranchi Gazetteer*, 1917, p. 425.
59. Hol, p. 263.
60. Para 12 of Letter from W. H. Grimley, Commissioner, Chota Nagpur Division to the Secretary Government of Bengal published in Judicial Proceedings, A, March

1890 (File 3L98).

61. Hol, p. 273.
62. Hunter, 1877, Vol. XVI p. 430, tuck p. 497.
63. Tuck, p. 498, Chaterlton, 1901, p. 77; Hunter, 1877, Vol. XVI, p. 430; Joss Vol. I, p. 453.
64. C. D. C., 1882, p. XI.
65. Joss, Vol. I, p. 417.
66. *Ibid*, p 419.
67. Bowen, p. 86.
68. *Ibid*, p. 78.
69. Schuerren, Vol. I, p. 16; Joss Vol. II, p. 168.
70. Joss, Vol. II, pp. 188-89.
71. Fidelis de Sa, "The Crisis in the Mission of Chota Nagpur and Reaction of the Landlord and Police", *Indian Ecclesiastical Studies*, VIII. 1968, p. 3.
72. Schuerren, Vol. I, p. 8; Joss, Vol. II p. 135.
73. Joss, Vol. II, p. 173.
74. Fidelis de Sa. *op. cit.*
75. *The Pioneer*, dated 21st January, 1890.
76. *The Indian Daily News*, dated 16th January 1890.
77. *Ibid.*, dated 17th January 1890.
78. Judicial Department Resolution dated 15th March 1890.
79. *The Statesman*, dated 18th March 1890; *The Indo-European Correspondence*, dated 29th March 1890.
80. Joss, Vol II, p. 372.
81. *Ranchi Gazetteer*, 1917, p. 165.
82. A. R. D. U. P., 1904, p. 49-53.
82. Letter nos. 1011 T.G. General Dept. from V.S. Mile, Under Secretary to the Govt. of Bengal to the Commissioner Dated Darjeeling the 10th June, 1907, (vide Collection File No. 34 of 1907, 8p.

5

WESTERN EDUCATION AS A FACTOR OF CONFLICT

THE ROLE of education in traditional and simple society is quite difficult as well as significant too for it acts as a catalytic agent of cultural change in its own way. The traditional society, as the one found among the Tribes of Chota Nagpur and Santal Parganas in Bihar, is a simple society in as much as it is preliterate and dependent on oral communication. Not that other simple communities are very much different from them; but the tribals are different so far as mental level, ecology and economic development are concerned.

Education is in essence the transmission of culture from one generation to another and the role of education in a simple society is to strengthen the fabrics of society so that continuity is maintained. The tribal societies in Bihar have their own institutions through which they have been imparting oral instruction and training to their youth for shouldering responsibilities when they turn into adulthood. They had *Dhumkuria* and *Giliora* where apart from other social and cultural activities, community living was practised. They had their *Jatra* festivals and *akhra* where they learnt of the ways and means that make life worth living. The hunters in them trained their youngsters for offensive and defensive use of weapons. This they carried from generation to generation till the Mughals came. The tribal life in general felt little impact except that their economy was faced with the concept of neo-Zamindars and Jagirdars. It was only when the British came use their system of western education for 'civilizing natives' so that they may be weaned away from the habit of resistance to the establishment of the British rule in their part of the country that the real attempt to educate them started. Thus education through British efforts acted as an agent of change, positive and negative and it sometime created ferment. Here in the hills and valleys of Chota Nagpur and Santal Parganas the spread of western education through the direct effort of the British administrative institutions as well as missionary bodies served as a factor of negative change, creating conflict and tension.

Public instruction in eighteenth century was not the business of the State and no one was required to pay any tax for the school. A *Pandit* supported himself by *dakshina* and the *Maulvi* by donations from pious families. When the East India Company began to emerge as a ruling power, it found that teaching in classical languages of Sanskrit and Persian was being imparted through *tols*, *madarssas, maktabs* and *pathasalas*. The new rulers felt that the principles and practices of a Christian government as well as the conduct of its officers should conduce a change of heart and outlook, and as such it thought that something should be done by a revival of the culture which had made India great. The East India Company in its formative years after the grant of *Dewani* did not forget its duty "to improve the morals of their subjects without attacking their religion". One of the very first undertakings Gervas Bellamy,[1] Chaplain at Bengal in A.D. 1731, found himself called upon to promote in Calcutta was that of the charity school. Padro Acquire, a Francisan Mendicant brought up at Goa on the Coast of Malabar, was the first teacher to run the school on Rs. 30 per month. There can be no doubt that the public interest in such an institution was sufficiently stimulated during his first three years to produce means of building a spacious and handsome school house in which eight foundationers and 40 day-scholars were accommodated. They were given books and clothes in the manner of the Blue-coat boys at Christ's Hospital. About 50 years after this charity school, the foundation maintained 20 boys. A wing for the women education was added to the institution under the charge of Mrs. Jane Jarvis at Rs. 35 a month.

But with the establishment of the *Maulvi* in suitable quarters, with 40 stipendary students and a sweeper at Rs. 3 a month, begins the history of educational action in India by the British Government under Warren Hastings in A.D. 1780. Lord Cornwallis in A.D. 1782 was found "supporting the establishment at the cost of government of a Sanskrit college in the sacred city of Benares for the preservation and cultivation of the laws, literature and religion of that nation (the Hindus) at this centre of their faith and common resort of all tribes".[2] But they were not wanted and, being unwanted they were inefficient. The alternative of English had not yet as a practical proposition came into view. John Owen, David Brown etc., authors of famous "Chaplains memorial"[3] made admirable effort to secure Government

English schools for the native population. But the Government faced by a complex of apparently insuperable obstacles, lay low and did nothing possibly less, for they discouraged the work of Christian missionaries whose zeal, they feared, would import more trouble than advantage.

But under the influence of Charles Grant and of Wilberforce, the British Parliament in 1813 included in the regrant of "Company's Charter one lakh rupees in each year which was to be set apart and applied to the revival and improvement of literature and the encouragement of learned natives of India, and for the introduction and promotion of a knowledge of Sciences among the inhabitants of the British territories in India".[4] By this a regular educational policy was initiated. In A.D. 1814, Earl of Moira concerned himself primarily with the village schools and thereby education of the masses. He also proposed to open two experimental schools, one for Hindus and one for Muslims at each district headquarters, and that House of Industry should be set up for the "education, reformation and employment of infant profligates". Moira's proposals, however earnest and moral in tone, were vague and confused and the allotment remained unspent. However a Saptist Mission college was opened at Serampore in A.D. 1818 and a School Book Society was founded in Calcutta, an Oriental College at Agra and so on. *Vidyalaya* or a Hindu College was founded at Calcutta of course with a sum of over a lakh of rupees provided by local subscription.

After Moira's exit in A.D. 1823, the General Committee of Public Instruction was appointed and was put "incharge of the existing government institutions and of one lakh grant and entrusted with the duty of ascertaining the state of public education and of advising from time to time on measures for the better instruction of the people, the introduction among them of useful knowledge, and the improvement of their moral character".[5]

But a New Deal could not be inaugurated till Lord William Bentick was appointed the first Governor-General of United India. He was impressed with a deep conviction of the importance of the subject of education and announced to the Committee that English eventually would be the language of public business throughout the country.

The backwardness of the country, the enormous population to be dealt with, the multiplicity of languages, the lack of qualified teachers, the lack of books, the lack of funds all were combined to render it impossible for the government to attempt to educate the general body of people. The General Committee was evenly divided against itself. Both parties then wanted to educate the natural leaders of the people. Hitherto the action had proceeded in the faith that the proper course was to encourage the Sanskrit system for the Hindus and the Arabic system for the Muslims. Both the systems were religious in their inspiration and content, and the Education Committee deliberated on the controversial points of orientalists and Occidentalists about the best method of imparting education to the 'natives of India'. While orientalists were represented by Horace Haymen Wilson and Prinsep Brothers, the occidentalists had Alexander Duff and Raja Ram Mohun Roy as their supporters. Lord Macaulay, the outside member of the Governor General-in-Council, presided over this deliberation and he decided the issue by his casting vote in favour of occidentialists. Macaulay has been criticised by a number of Indian scholars. Basu saw in it that Macaulay wanted to benefit his own country by this and at the same time to denationalise the people of India. He quoted Macaulay's letter to his father in A.D. 1836:

> "It is my firm belief that if our plans of education are followed there will not be a single idolator among the respectable class in Bengal 30 years hence."[6]

Macaulay's object was to undermine the social and religious institutions of India. Thus it would appear that in all that he did in and for India, Macaulay was not swayed by any consideration or motive of philanthrophy or altruism; he was guided by selfishness — if not quite sordid, at the best enlightened. Basu wrote again that,

> "Macaulay largely contributed, both directly and indirectly to the genesis of the present unrest in this country. He entertained supreme contempt for everything Indian. His Minutes on Education outraged the feelings of the people of India. He, who was not acquainted with any of the languages of the vast peninsula — not cared to know anything of the literature of ancient India — had yet the audacity to pronounce his contemptuous judgement on them."

Out of this acrimonious controversy emerged Macaulay with his announcement on 7th March, 1835 which did at least crow up the dawn. Macaulay's resolution proposed (i) promotion of European literature and science among the natives of India; (ii) the medium to be used was the English language and (iii) that the Education fund should be employed on English education alone. The Committee under Macaulay aimed to have a system of national education in the Vernaculars which should embrace every village in the country. The effect of the resolution was merely to prefer western learning through the medium of English to eastern learning through the media of Sanskrit and Arabic for the limited class with whom they were then concerned. Macaulay's merit lies in the prophecy which he did in Parliament in the following words:

> "It may be that the public mind of India may expand under our system until it has outgrown that system, that by good government we may educate our subjects into a capacity for better government, that having become instructed in European knowledge, they may in some *future age demand European institutions*. Whether such a day will ever come I know not. But never will I attempt to avert it or to retard it. Whenever it comes, it will be the proudest day in English History. To have found a great people sunk in the lowest depths of slavery and superstition, to have so ruled them as to have made them desirous and capable of all the privileges of citizen would indeed add not little to glory all our own. . . ."[7]

Whether Macaulay was a limited Prophet or his prophecy came out more accurate than what he had foreseen is a matter to be discussed today. But Bentinck's, decision on the basis of Macaulay's Minutes in favour of English education has been described as the great landmark in the history of the British Empire.

However, the years that followed Macaulay's Minutes of 1835 were the period of experiment and conflict. "Filtration theory" of education (educate the classes and the masses will take care of themselves) was bogged down in the question as to leaders you were educating. In Bengal, the policy was pursued by establishing an English or Anglo-vernacular school at the headquarters of each district, of developing a few of the more progressive of these to the status of colleges, and of linking school and colleges by a system of scholarships. In 1854, the *Vidyalaya* was taken over by the Government and named as Presidency College at Calcutta which provided the highest instruction. Various mission bodies were energetically at work in the same field establishing and conducting institutions which were to leave their mark on the educational development of the country. The art of printing had been introduced by the Christian missionaries as early as the 16th century and in 19th century when these presses produced books in Indian language as well as in English an extraordinary effect was created. The first newspaper was the *Bengal Gazette* which was started in 1816 by Gangadhar Bhattacharyee which was followed by *Samachar Darpan* in 1818. The time was one of intellectual ferment and unrest, with eager and restless questions about the foundation of religious and social life. Three schools of thought asserted themselves. One indoctrinated with western rationalism was icnoclastic and renounced whole system of Hinduism. The second, stimulated by the new knowledge endeavoured to reform Hinduism from within and to preserve its essential truths. The third consisted of great body of conservative opinion deeply rooted in sentiment and custom and hostile to the infusion of new ideas or adoption of European habits.

But they were the learned gentries belonging to the upper class in the higher seminaries. The education of the masses or primary education was to be conducted through the medium of correct colloquial languages. It need hardly be told that the educational policy of the Government was very widely suspected and its share of responsibility for the Mutiny was great indeed. Leaders, religious and secular, reacted against a system which reduced their pride and influence. The common people saw the old order yielding place to new which ignored their religion and seemed to threaten the foundations of their lives.

In this situation the missionary efforts were responsible for creating great alarm and people definitely became alarmed. The Christian missionaries in the fifties of nineteenth century were considered as 'enchanter' or 'magicians'. Muir's report on Fatehpur Native Schools is a typical depiction of the situation. He wrote:

> "It was rumoured that four Christian Missionaries whom the oriental imagination of the inhabitants invested with the character of magicians, had come from Benares, and that one of them in the garb and appearance of mendicant would visit their houses, and stretch a magic and over the head of their children who smitten with witchcraft, would follow the foreign enchanter, desert their houses and become Christians. However absurd this fiction may appear, it is certain that it spread such alarm abroad, that the schools were in some places deserted and others concealed their

children from very fright: the conjurers were reported to be in every village, and the very *tehseeldaree mohurirs* were transformed into the *moonshies* and *pandits* of the Missionaries, and avoided as their emissaries."[8]

Similar reports from other parts of the country go to prove that general people were, greatly agitated on the role of foreign missionary as enchanter of their children. It would be unwise to think that the tribal societies of Bihar accepted innovation like western educational institutions in their midst without any awe and fearful disposition, rather the situation was alarming there than in other areas, albeit they were inarticulate as a people and they gesticulated within themselves. Of course, they spared nothing when they found it unbearable and rose in rebellion to set right the situation.

Education in Santal Parganas

We have already seen how Chaplains of Calcutta Presidency were forcing the government to allow them to open the mission schools in the areas and wanted government patronage for that. Alexander Duff and others were the leading exponents of the idea that government should introduce Christian teaching into the State Schools. They never reconciled themselves to the Queen's proclamation "changing her officers, on pain of her highest displeasure, to abstain from all interference with the religious belief or worship of any of her Indian subjects". Alexander Duff denounced the working of "traditional policy". He mounted pressure on the Government and wanted that the government be forced to a new Santal Education System as suggested by the Civil Commissioner of Bhagalpur after the suppression of Santal Hul of 1855. The local Committee of the Christian Missionary society came forward and offered the Government to undertake the work on certain reasonable conditions. The leading features of the scheme were that the society would appoint a missionary whose chief business would be to superintend the working of the whole — his salary to be paid by the society, and travelling expenses by the Government, that two inspecting masters chosen by the Home Committee, should be sent from England, and subordinate teachers appointed by the local Committee — their salaries to be paid by Government. The amount of secular instruction was allowed to be fixed by the Director of Education, and the schools were to be open at all times to Government inspection. In short, on condition of the Governments bearing the main part of the pecuniary expenditure, the society undertook the management and direction of comprehensive scheme of religious, secular, and industrial education for the "barbarous Santals".[9]

Lieutenant Governor of Bengal Mr. Halliday fully approved of the scheme and strongly recommended it to the Supreme Government. Lord Canning also took a most liberal view of the case, and recorded his entire approbation of the measure, giving it as judgment that if differed in degree only, not in kind, from grants already made to individual missionaries under the celebrated educational despatch of 19th July, 1854, and that the proposed grants-in-aid to a missionary body for the secular education of an "uncivilised tribe was a wise and legitimate application of the principle of that despatch, seeing that government was in no way to interfere with the religious instructions given".

This approval of the Head of the Indian Government is dated 28th November, 1856. But on the 22nd July, 1857 a despatch was forwarded from the Courts of Directors, formally and decidedly disapproving of the whole scheme. Duff wrote "that despatch is the very embodiment of the 'traditional policy' of the India House". According to the Court, the Santals do not exclusively occupy separate regions or tracts of country, so as to form isolated communities locally separated, as well as socially distinct, from the Hindu and Mussalman populations. They are, on the contrary employed freely by *zamindars*, and speculators in land of all classes, for jungle clearance and for other agricultural purposes, and are thus often located in close vicinity with well inhabited towns and villages, and mix with the general population in many of the relations and concerns of life. The Court, therefore, did not feel that dealing with the Santals, they were exempt from the necessity of maintaining that cautious line of proceeding which they ought always to deem essential in establishments founded or supported by Government for the education of the people of India".[10]

Thus, although they by no means objected to the amount of expenditure proposed for the purpose of 'civilizing and instructing the Santals', they could not approve that part of the scheme which identified the Government with measures prosecuted by the missionaries, and so expose the arrangements to the risk of perverted misconstruction. The Church Missionary was entitled to all confidence, but the Court must "adhere to the conviction that it would be altogether opposed to the rules to take any steps which might have the appearance of uniting the Government with such a society, in measures having the aim of converting any class of the population to Christianity". The Court, therefore, directed that a scheme "should be prepared for affording to the inhabitants of the Santals Districts the means of education through the agency of Government officers, who must be strictly enjoined to abstain from any attempts to introduce religious subjects in any form".

After the receipt of so peremptory an order, the local government had no alternative but to request the Civil Commissioner of the Districts concerned to prepare a new and revised scheme of education for the Santals about which Duff wrote "The Commissioner happened to be a man of singularly independent spirit. And among well informed circle, here, he is understood to have in substance replied that he neither would nor could prepare another scheme — that the present disturbed state of the District rendered the introduction of any scheme utterly impracticable, and that, by the time that peace and order were restored, he hoped a new policy would be inaugurated, which would no longer exhibit us as cowards in the eyes of man and traitors in the eyes of God".

Thus we have seen that neither the missionary pressure nor the official intransigent could browbeat the Court of Directors and they held aloft the promise of positive neutrality so far as religious preaching as a factor of "Operation Civilisation" was concerned. The Court did not for a moment consider the tribals such as Santals as a separate cultural identity. They had positive understanding about them that they constituted a part of the regional and territorial life and their administration should not foster a sense of separatism through patronising missionaries for taking their help in educating them. Even so the local officers had soft corners for the missionaries, but they were moved by the ideology of civilising the tribals at their earliest and they used to give local patronage to the missionaries by providing land for mission centres and recognising the missionaries as their cultural spokesman and the only knowledgeable people locally available for administration. This provided great prestige to the missionaries which indirectly helped the missionary activities.

The discouragement from the Court of Directors, therefore, did not deter the missionaries because by 1860, they were found running 12 boys schools with 350 boys and two girls schools with 20 girls on daily attendance. They were training 25 Santal boys in the art of teaching.

The local government patronised them by granting a lease of 50 *bighas* of land at Heranpur to Church Missionary Society. The Santal Mission set up a school at Bengaria in 1864 to which government granted Rs. 1,000. The main aim of the missionaries was proselytisation, so they did not impart secular education of a high order in their schools".[11] The Secretary of the Santal Mission Rev. Thomas Evans also insisted on the teaching of the *Bible* in the missionary schools. For this he was even ready to forgo the government aid.

In 1873, on the suggestion of the Government, the Education Committee of the Santal Parganas set apart Rs. 430 out of total grant of Rs. 1,200 for the creation of minor and vernacular scholarships for Santal and Paharia boys, out of which three scholarships of the value of Rs. 3 a month tenable for four years were created.[12] By 1879-80, in all there were Christian converts. The Church Missionary Society and Indian Home Missions respectively within the headquarters at Taljhari and Bengoria were the organisation created for these conversions. In 1882, the Church Mission Society maintained 47 *pathsalas* at a yearly cost of Rs. 2,718 and on the recommendation of Education Commission the Government increased the grant to the Society from Rs. 1,000 to Rs. 7,800 a year.[13] Apart from this, the government granted a sum of Rs. 5,000 from the Education Budget for the establishment of *pathsalas* under the supervision of the Santal teachers and inspectors. Under this scheme of 1884 setting up of 100 *pathsalas* was complemented in three years time at a cost of Rs. 5,000 and Rs. 7,500 in the first year, second and third years respectively.[14]

But this scheme was given up for another scheme with a sum of Rs. 7,500 in April 1888 which contemplated to impart instruction to the Santals through their mother-tongue by trained Santal teachers. Table 5.1 shows the extent of education in the whole of Bhagalpur and Santal Pargana Division.[15]

A spurt in the number of students at the turn of the last century was felt because the government embarked upon a new scheme of reorganising the educational system in that region for which Rs. 9,500 was granted in 1902-03. Four Sub-Inspectors and two Inspecting Pandits were appointed. In 1904, the Government, issued orders for imparting instruction through local language.[15]

The teachers were to be trained and there were 11 such schools in Bhagalpur Division. In Santal Parganas the students flocked to these schools because a subsistence allowance @ Rs. 3 per head per month was paid to *Gurus* under training.[16] Taljhari and Bengoria mission also had their training schools which were aided in 1895-96. The Santals and Paharias were admitted as boarders and in 1903-04 their number was 12 in Taljhari. In 1898-99, two more schools were opened at Bengoria, one for male and the other for female teachers. Thirteen students passed from Bengoria training school in 1903-04.

TABLE 5.1: Number of Schools and Students in Bhagalpur and Santal Pargana Division

Year	Number of Schools	No. of Students
1889-90	155	6125
1890-91	155	5947
1891-92	155	4599
1892-93	155	6231
1893-94	155	6197
1894-95	N.A.	N.A.
1895-96	N.A.	N.A.
1896-97	N.A.	7629
1897-98	N.A.	6452
1904-05	N.A.	13401
1905-06	N.A.	25727

Sources: 1. Reports of Progress of Institutions 1898.
2. Report of Education in Bengal, Third Quinquennial Review, 1902-03 to 1906-07.

A few technical schools were opened in Bhagalpur Division on the initiative of Government Survey and their classes were started at Deoghar and Monghyr. Out of Santal Education Grant, Survey Schools were opened at Dumka, Katikund, Taljhari and Sahebganj in November 1889. Each school had a head carpenter and two or three apprentices who were paid a stipend of Rs. 3 a month. Within a year, the Dumka school became self-supporting. The school at Madhupur was the most flourishing. In 1889-90, 75 students were on the roll, the aided school at Pakur had six pupils in 1897-98. Thus industrial instruction also started taking roots in the Bhagalpur Division.[17]

Education in Chota Nagpur

In Chota Nagpur the responsibility of the first ray of western education lay with the two officials. Cuthbert and Neave who made an attempt to establish "College" for the 'Kols' of Ramgarh in 1831; but it had a short life. Captain Bird established a school and in 1834, a school was started at Chaibassa which later on got English classes attached to it on the assurance of the donation and support by the *zamindars* and other gentries. But it was to the credit of German Mission to lay the real foundation of the western education in Chota Nagpur in 1845.

In 1846, the Magistrates entrusted some orphans rescued from famine starvation to the missionaries and these orphans constituted the nucleus of the school.[18] They were baptized in 1846 and were given Christian names. They were brought up to learn some trade and occupation. Half a dozen Chota Nagpuria started their career in the school. They were — Thomas (Carpenter), John (Compounder), Prabhudayal, Mashihdas, Mathew and a girl named Mary. The daily chores of the missionaries were praying, reading and teaching the little orphans, traversing the countryside on foot seeking to find entrance in villages from where they were sometimes driven out with stones.[19] But they were not detered in their attempt. They went on preaching.

One of the earliest methods employed for evangelisation during the early years was starting schools, collecting children in the day time, and in the evening assembling the adult members and teaching them alphabets, and reading Biblical stories etc. In order to encourage the local entrants, one *anna* (six paise now-a-days) a week was given to those who attended the school throughout the week regularly. In spite of this the missionaries had to go to the villages every morning in order to find out boys for their school. Even if the children attended the school in lure of an *anna*, the guardians sometimes abused missionaries because they feared that their children might get converted into Christianity. It was unfortunate that the first ever attempt to bring western education to the Chota Nagpur was tainted with the attempt to convert the children and use the school more for conversion than for anything else. This definitely did not serve the purpose of secular education in Chota Nagpur. To quote Rickets "though an English government school has been established for some years, it has done nothing towards the education of the people of the province. The number borne on the books is 44, and the attendance in the last quarter of the last year (1853) averaged 24. There are but two whose families are connected with the land of Chota Nagpur. The German missionaries established at *Rainchee*, have better success (probably of orphan school). For many years the prejudice against them was strong, but they have now quite overcome it, and their schools are full. The children are those of the lower order".[20]

Role of G.E.L. Church in Progress of Education

There was a temporary set-back during the 1857 uprising but after that the missionaries were again on their work with great zeal. In 1862, the Hazaribagh school had 23 students on the rolls. Ranchi School was under Brother Flex with four classes and 62 children. Muller talking about the state of education at that time noted 'education was very low, scholars were few — but work was expanding, and they needed great wisdom and grace to guide, instruct organise and lead them to the path of spiritual prosperity'.[21] The Government of India set apart a sum of Rs.50 per month with the Commissioner of the Division for these schools. In 1864, there were 11 village schools with 270 students. On 30th January, 1864 The G.E.L. Theological College, affiliated to the Serampore Theological College in West Bengal, was started with 15 students on roll. In 1865, there were eight schools with 115 boys and 35 girls and the Director of Public Instruction recommended that a sum of Rs. 100 per month be granted to the Mission[22] of which two-thirds was sanctioned by the Government of India.

In spite of these, little interest for learning and education was evinced. In 1865, 70 boys and 34 girls were fed, clothed and taught in missionary churches and commodious boarding houses. In addition there were nine village schools in operation where 106 of the Coles and 52 of other denominations were educated in 1867. A branch of Ranchi Lutheran Mission had been established at Chaibasa and school was started there. There was already trouble due to the attitude of *Kuratarium* and the *Grand Schism* was already there to disturb their activities. But the growth of education had problems which were to be reconciled with the main objectives of the education imparted by the G.E.L. Mission.

Problems of Education	*Main objectives of G.E.L. education*
1. Orientation in the *Mandali.*	1. To prepare enquirers for Baptism
2. Separation of the Church from the school.	2. To give directions for Baptism.
3. Governments liking for secular education.	3. To prepare men for service of the *Mandali.*

To reconcile these, the Mission was faced with the main question of the type of education to be imparted, whether secular or eccelesiastical. Holstein wrote "In fact none was opposed to the principal motive that they (the converts) should get strength to accept Christianity and that their social position should also be raised.[23] But at the same time it should not be lost sight of that the Government was bound with the terms of Queen's Proclamation and no amount of emphasis by Alexander Duff and others could convince the Court of Directors in favour of ecclesiastical education, although the local government had a few enthusiasts here and there who always opted to get all the advantages of the Mission for educational purposes which always led to the conversion into Christianity. Dalton and Yule were the great examples in their own respective Divisions to which they were put as Commissioners".

The Director of Public Instruction Report of 1872-73 mentions of three schools at Ranchi and one each at Burju and Boda near Lohardaga. Gossner Mission report for 1874 shows over and above Ranchi school, 62 villages with 1314 students were imparted education. Besides the Government *Pathsalas* were there which were voluntarily supervised by Didlaukis, the G.E.L. Missionary. The missionaries 'levied a fee which was paid by the guardians willingly'.[24] Slack's Report[25] states that "a great deal of work was done by the Anglican and Berlin Mission. During the year 1885-86, the Berlin Mission had been running 52 schools in which 1299 boys and 63 girls were taught at a total expenditure of Rs. 10,053 of which government paid Rs. 2,360".

Purulia had a Boarding School with 112 children under three teachers where they were taught Hindi with Bengali. There was also an Industrial School with 17 children learning carpentry, blacksmithy, tailoring, shoemaking and pottery. Government granted Rs. 2,242 for the assistance of 25 orphans and the Deputy Commissioner Clay contributed Rs. 455.14 *annas* towards the expenses of the schools. By 1874, the number of schools increased to seven and Purulia Boarding School was raised to the Upper Primary standard with five classes. The government grant[26] for this was Rs. 60 and for the remaining six village schools it was Rs. 24 only. Chaibasa also had a Boarding School with 52 boarders and two day scholars under a European Missionary. Hindi was taught. Rev. Nottrott prescribed his *Kolh-Primer*. Four schools had 108 children on rolls which received occasional grant from Deputy Commissioners Hays and Mannock. In

1874, Chaibasa had besides boarding school nine village schools with 266 children.

Lutherans were pioneers in writing books in Oraon, Mundari and Hindi and setting up a printing press in 1882 which was developed out of stone lithographic press at Ranchi in 1873. This press published *Ghar-bandhu*, the first Hindi fortnightly journal ever to be published in Chota Nagpur. Nagpuria was also enriched and Kharia songs by Kushalmay Shital and Santali songs were ready for printing by the year 1890.

Role of Anglican Church in Progress of Education

The Anglican Church started its functioning after the great schism. Roger Dutt was incharge of Ranchi School which had 228 students in 1872-73. Lord Northbrook visited the school in 1874 and granted Rs. 50 together with a portrait of Queen Victoria and praised the school as the "most excellent". In 1880 it had 1209 students out of whom 157 were boarders.[27] Deputy Commissioner Gorden, Lieutenant Governor of Bengal and an Inspector of Schools visited the school in 1892. The Lieutenant Governor gave a cash prize of Rs. 20 to the children. The girls school was separated from the boys in 1887 and in 1890 the number of girls was 86 only. There were 16 students in Teachers Training School and the Industrial school had 12 boys on the roll. The evening school for adults had 60 students who were taught by W.L.D. Singh. An inspecting master supervised 11 rural schools. In 1884, it rose to 38 with 951 children on the roll. The government contributed Rs. 2,252 towards the maintenance of those schools. A theological seminary under Rev. Oscar Flex and Roger Dutt was flourishing in 1887. The Boys Middle English School at Murhu with its 74 boarders and 58 day scholars was doing excellent work among Mundas. Towards the end of 1908, a Lace school was opened for young women and girls who were 20 in number. A female Normal Training class was opened in the year 1909 to prepare female teachers for girls schools. In 1895 a Blind school was started at Ranchi where blind men were taught industrial work in cane and bamboo and blind women in mat-making. Reading and writing were imparted through Braille system.[28]

Role of Roman Catholic Church in Progress of Education

From the very outset Father Lieven's educational policy was to eradicate illiteracy. In 1886 the number of schools were 30 but in October 1883, it was 60 and 1887 it rose to 77 with 2400 children on roll. As early as 25th March, 1887, St. John School with five day scholars was opened with the government help of a few desk and benches. Father Stockman started a girls school at Burudih. At Ranchi the wives of two catechists taught 20 girls in 1889.[29] With the arrival of four Irish Lorreto sisters in 1890, the Ranchi girls school started regular teaching work.

Role of Scottish Free Church in Progress of Education

Through the exertion of great missionary such as Dr. Andrew Campbell, this Mission was successful in spreading education in the part of Manbhum (now Dhanbad District) and Hazaribagh districts of Chota Nagpur.[30] There were training schools for boys and girls. There were 38 village schools with 33 teachers and two inspecting *Gurus* in 1897. The government sanctioned Rs. 2,000 for this Mission. There were industrial schools. In 1894 there were 27 schools for boys and seven for girls and eight for both with total number of boys at 898 and girls 258. In 1915, the number rose to 151 schools with 2747 students on roll. Lace making and spinning were also taught.[31]

Role of Dublin University Mission in the Progress of Education

The missionaries came from Ireland and were unmarried graduates of the Dublin University. They worked under the Society for the Propagation of Gospel in Foreign Parts, London. Hazaribagh became the military headquarters of Chota Nagpur in 1780 and a Church was established as early as 1842 for the benefit of the soldiers. Pandit Laxmi Narayan[32] taught Hindi to the Europeans. But later on, the Church was abandoned and it remained for the Dublin Mission to bring Hazaribagh on the educational map of Bihar. Miss K. Smith was the pioneer of Boarding Girls Schools for Europeans and the Anglo-Indian girls; but it was closed in 1897. In 1903, Miss White opened primary schools among the *Harijans* of Hazaribagh town. The girls school at Korra and the Boys school at Ichak had 25 students each. Apart from primary and Kindergarten schools, night schools and orphan schools were also started. The Dublin Mission was also credited to be the first mission to start a Degree College named after St. Columbus in Chota Nagpur in July 1899.[33] Rev. J.A. Murray was its first Principal with 13 students in the beginning. The Government allotted a rent free accommodation for it in a part of old Post Office building. A donation of Rs. 3,000 came from Raja of Ramgarh. In 1904, the college was raised to degree standard affiliated to Calcutta University. It was the only Missionary college for the non-christians, run by the Society for the Propagation of Gospel or the Christian Mission Society in the province of Bengal. The Government very liberally granted Rs. 30,000 in 1912 to build the King Emperor's Blocks. Science laboratories were set up with the help of a grant of Rs. 50,000 in 1917. The college remained for many decades as the only centre where the people from all over the plateau regions and adjacent area used to come for higher education. Some of the earliest graduates among the tribes/non-tribes of Bihar were from the college.

Significantly enough apart from Christian missionaries, the *zamindars* of Chota Nagpur did not lag behind in patronising education in their own way. Raja of Ramgarh, Raja Mukund Narain of the district of Manbhum, the Rani of Pandra and the Maharaja of Chota Nagpur were notable among such patrons. The Estates in Gajarat Mahal under the direction of Commissioner of Chota Nagpur were also taking action for the spread of education in their respective areas. The administrative reports of the Commissioner state eloquently about their attempts. The Raja of Ramgarh[34] maintained a free school at Ichak where about 96 students were on roll. The Manbazar school founded by Raja of Manbhum made very fair progress.[35] The school established by Rani Hingan Kumari,[36] the Rani of Pandra later on developed into a high school. Sidhnath Singh of Karharbari supported an aided school at Pachamba.

Ranchi Zilla School

The Maharaja of Chota Nagpur donated Rs. 1,000 for the construction of a school building at Ranchi. The local people also started a vernacular school on 1st May, 1868 with 56 students. The school proved to be very popular and received grants-in-aid. In spite of this, the government feeling was that "no great object (was) to be gained by immediately pushing educational operations into these localities".[37] The official documents relating to the opening of Zilla School at Ranchi reveal the intentions of the government as well as the missionaries with regard to the spread of higher education in the area. Whereas the native gentry was keen for the establishment of the colleges, the Deputy Commissioner on 3rd November, 1875 felt that the "District is not yet ready for a high school. The local missionary Fathers discouraged the government from establishing school of high standard as they claimed that the state of education among the Koll tribes is such that the establishment of a High school would be premature and utterly useless as far as they are concerned".[38] H.L.Oliphant, the Deputy Commissioner, Lohardaga concurred with this view and recommended to the Commissioner of Chota Nagpur:

> "There is a little probability of our school supplying a certain numbers of scholars for the High School during the next two or three years because all the boys who are at all promising are trained for our missionary work as Pastors, masters, catechists. But I have no doubt that the Hindu population could gladly avail itself the opportunity to secure higher standard of education towards their children and even contribute a little towards the maintenance of a school of that description eventually that is to say three or four years hence when our present wants are supplied. The missionaries would also find itself at liberty to have the Christian element represented in the High School now proposed."[39]

But as early as 5th January, 1867, the Secretary to the Local Committee of Public Administration submitted to the Commissioner of Chota Nagpur a proposal that the land belonging to the Raja of Panchet be acquired under Act VI of 1857 as this was the only proper site available. The whole area was $12^1/_2$ *bighas* costing Rs. 20 per *bigha* but Raja Nilmani Singh Deo of Panchet granted his *Bagan* as a gift. The school was to be constructed at a cost of Rs. 7,711 and was to cover an area of 57600 square feet; but later on it was reduced to 7360 square feet.[40]

Fate of Secular Education

In the seventies the government policy underwent a change. Without relaxing the rules relating to grants-in-aid, the government granted Rs. 600 a year to the mission schools to meet the cost of establishment and to pay the salary of teachers, if the villagers agreed to pay the other half. The government was even ready to grant Rs. 10 to 15 to schools maintained by the missionaries provided they subordinated religion to education. But the grant was not to exceed Rs. 5 if the schools were meant for Christian converts only. The intention of the government behind this idea was to propagate the spread of secular education, whereas in actual practice it had to make concessions in favour of the missionaries due to the peculiarity of the place.[41] The missionaries were doing plain talking about their object of spreading the education. They always said that "while no branch of secular education shall be neglected, we claim for the missionaries the right of teaching in the school the word of God, and if this be not conceded, we shall feel ourselves compelled to do without government aid, much as it is needed".[42] W.C. Fyfe, successor of Alexandar Duff, the Head of the Mission of the Free Church of Scotland admitted:

> "this is not to be wondered at for the chief object of every mission school is evangelisation of the pupils. There should be no attempt to conceal the truth that Mission schools were established and have been carried out with the object of making converts. . . . The teaching of *Bible* is, therefore, the primary end of Mission schools, while secular instruction is given simply with a view to this end."[43]

And it must be made clear that the share of these missions was great in the education of the Chota Nagpur. The picture of different missions maintaining a number of schools in 1886-87 is shown in Table 5.2.

The break up of tribal students in the different districts of Chota Nagpur in 1889-90 is shown in Table 5.3.

In 1891-92 the number of students in the mission schools in Chota Nagpur division is shown in Table 5.4.

From all these data, it can very well be understood that the missions had a very larger share in educating the people of Chota Nagpur.

Besides the missions and the Government the East India Railway Company also took interest in the promotion of education and it provided Rs. 300 for the maintenance of schools for the children of its labourers under an Inspecting Pandit. In November 1892, the Lieutenant Governor of Bengal visited 19 schools and expressed satisfaction at their working. In 1895 the enrolment in these schools was 1355 students. As a token of its interest in the education of the wards of its labour force. The East India Railway Company not only started "compulsory and free education but subsidised primary education for children of their labourers and colliers".[44] The Kolhan schools in Singhbhum worked by providing free and compulsory education effected ruthlessly by the Manki who compelled all the boys of the villages under them to go to the nearest school.

Table 5.2: Number of Mission Maintained Schools and Their Enrolment in 1886-87

Sl. No.	Name of Mission	Number of Schools	Number of Students		
			Male	Female	Total
1.	G.E.L. (Protestant)	25	558	169	727
2.	S.P.G. (Anglican)	42	896	171	1,067
3.	Free Church of Scotland	46	880	154	1,034
4.	St. Xaviers Mission (Catholic)	10	250	50	300
	TOTAL	123	2,584	544	3,128

Source: Report of Public Instruction, 1886-87, para 137.

TABLE 5.3: Breakup of Tribal Students in Different Districts of Chota Nagpur in 1888-89

District	Number of Tribal Students
Manbhum	2,021
Hazaribagh	1,257
Lohardaga Ranchi	5,692
Singhbhum	7,754
TOTAL	1,7624

Source: Report of Public Instruction, 1888-89, para 137.

TABLE 5.4: Number of Students in Mission Schools in Chota Nagpur Division in 1891-92

Name of Mission	Male	Female	Total
G.E.L.(Protestant)	1,189	279	1,468
S.P.G.(Anglican)	1,361	222	1,583
Free Church of Scotland	867	81	949
St.Xaviers Mission (Catholic)	142	53	195
TOTAL	3,559	635	4,195

Source: *Report of Public Instruction*, 1892-93, p. 201.

The higher education in Chota Nagpur in the last century was mostly confined to the government run Zilla Schools in 1885-86. The first tribal boy passed his entrance examination from Ranchi school and got a scholarship for his studies in Burdwan Maharaja College.[45] In 1887-88 three tribal students matriculated. Two special junior scholarships were created to encourage the tribal boys to join the high schools in large number. In 1891-92, two tribal students one Christian and the other a non-christian passed the entrance examination from the Ranchi and Chaibasa Zilla schools respectively. In pursuance of the recommendation of the Indian Education Commission, 1882 a good deal of emphasis was laid on the training of teachers and the government opened training schools in each district. The classes were held in the morning or evening and on Sundays and other holidays so that teachers might join them without abstaining from their schools. In 1890-91 in Chota Nagpur, the number of these training schools was seven with 107 students; but by the end of 1899 all these schools were closed down. Only the mission training schools flourished.

Industrial Training

The despatch[46] of 1854 laid emphasis on technical education. In Chota Nagpur Division, the Zilla Schools at Hazaribagh and Chaibasa taught the rudiments of surveying. In 1882-83, survey class was opened at Ranchi to train local *amins*. The S.P.G. Mission decided to set up a school at Ranchi to raise a superior class of workmen in the district and to improve the method of work and also the quality of products for which there was ample scope.[47] A sum of Rs. 3,000 was granted to the school for the purchase of machinery and another sum of Rs. 100 per month was also granted to the school and this amount was subsequently raised to Rs. 151 per month.

From 1874 the Ranchi industrial school under the Superintendence of Rev. Herzog, a missionary started functioning. In the beginning only Christian tribal boys took admission who were taught carpentry and other useful arts besides the three R's. The school was equipped with all the necessary machines and equipments and the manufactured goods were by no means bad and they had their great demand in the market. When Rev. Herzog left the school, the school languished. The Government allowed the management to utilise the money of the Ranchi (Chutia) Fair Fund amounting to Rs. 12,000 for revitalising the school and, in 1894, the government took over the management of the school. Some of the students trained in this school managed the newly established industrial schools at Bend, Lohardaga, Hazaribagh, Silli,

Chaibasa, Giridih and a few other places. At Hazaribagh Railway Industrial School the students were trained for the job of fitters in the railways. The Catholic convent at Ranchi taught women shellac making and Roman Catholic Missions at Chaibasa instructed the women in the art of weaving.

Such being the state it is but natural that the tribals of Chota Nagpur and Santal Parganas had a very massive effect on their life due to the exertion of the missionaries, the Government and the local gentries. Apart from the general scheme of things under the direction of different churches in Chota Nagpur and Santal Parganas there were a few lone souls like Traffalgar Douglas who worked among the tribes near about Sooree, the district headquarters of Birbhum which once embraced greater part of Santal Parganas, whose reminiscence have been preserved by W.W. Hunter in Old Missionary[48] which contains a true account of the life of a missionary devoted to his cause and his congregation. This is in the form of a case history to show the conflict in the mind of a true missionary about the impact of Western education in the minds of the people in backward tracts.

The old missionary Traffalgar Douglas had started in all 30 village schools among the Christian population throughout the district as well as in the hilly tracts. The system was self-supporting. The elders of the outlying Christian villages, in which a teacher had been established, levied monthly dole in money and rice for his maintenance. The surplus fee from the central station school supplemented these allowances in the poorer hamlets. The Old Missionary's custom was to plant out a teacher, and to maintain him until he gathered together a group of pupils often under no better shelter than spreading banyan tree. By degrees the villagers began to take pride in watching their children being taught. They set up a thatched hut for a school house and provided for the subsistence of the master. The missionary then withdrew his grant and applied the money to planting out a new school elsewhere. He held that education should not be expected to pay its way at starting, among people who have never known its value and that this was a case in which the supply must create the demand. Perhaps Douglas was successful in influencing Lord Auckland in starting similar schools for backward tracts as well as training classes for teachers.

Douglas laid so much stress on teaching as compared with the preaching which formed the popular idea of a missionary. Douglas once told Hunter in 1890 "The only way that will bring the natives to truer and more enlightened idea is the gradual progress of education. *The attempt to change the faith of the adult population have hitherto failed*, and *will, I am afraid, continue to fail*". "But", Hunter interposed, "is not our state education doing the need work on a far larger scale"? "I greatly fear", replied Douglas, "that it is not your state education that is producing a revolt against three principles which although they were pushed too far in ancient India, represent the deepest wants of human nature — the principle of discipline, the principle of religion, the principle of contentment. The old indigenous schools carried punishment to the verge of torture. Your government schools pride themselves in having almost done away with the rod, and in due time you will have on your hand a race of youngmen who have grown up without discipline. The indigenous schools made the native religions too much the staple of instruction, opening the days work by chanting a long invocation to the Sun or some other deity, while each boy began his exercise by writing the name of a divinity at the top. Your government schools take credit for abstaining from religious teaching of any sort, and in one time you will have on your hands a race of youngmen who have grown up in the public non-recognition of a god. The indigenous schools educated the working and trading classes for the natural business of their lives. Your government schools spur on every clever small boy with scholarships and money allowances to try to get into a bigger school and so through many bigger schools, with the stimulus of bigger scholarships to university degree. In due time you will have on your hands an overgrown clerkly generation whom you have trained in their youth to depend on government allowances and look to government services, but whose adult ambitions not all the offices of the government would satisfy. What are you to do with this great clever class, forced up under a foreign system, without discipline, without contentment and without a God?"

"The day will come" Douglas went on as in a reverie, "when your date educators will be face to face with the results. They will be forced back on the old indigenous schools as the sure foundation of public instruction in India. They will find out that races who for ages have borne a heavy yoke throughout life cannot be trained up without discipline in their youth. They will also discover that the end of national education is not to create one vast clerkly class, but to fit all classes for their natural work. You will then, I suppose, set up technical schools, to do in some manner what the old native system of the hedge-school and the hereditary handicraft did in perhaps on growing up in a discredited faith and it will piece together a moral text-book to take the place of God."

Thus, having charted course of the development of western education in Chota Nagpur and Santal Parganas in particular and the whole eastern India in general, this survey arrives at the threshold of the twentieth century when there were available scores of new literates especially among the Christian missions to take up the leadership of their community and who in their own way rendered yeoman service. Barthelemo was perhaps the first of the tribal literates who thought of the pitiful condition of the people and tried to organise them on the lines of Dacca Students Union at Hazaribagh especially in the St. Columbus College where he was a student. The tribal communities directly in touch with the European masters such as Nottrott, Shekrefured and others, had already created a stir in their own way with *Sardars* who followed the principle of "petition and protest" against various forms of injustice and wanted to pay rent direct to the State instead of paying to the intermediary like the *zamindars* and thereby they had imbibed the German concept of City state, a position which they wanted to attain.

If the *Sardari Larai* is the product of German and Scandinavian teachers, who moulded their political thinking, the Anglican and Roman Catholic teachers in the first decade of the century laid the foundation of the political movement based on party affiliations. Barthelemo, Ignes Beck and others were the product of such a situation. Thus western education and that too under the European missionary teachers prepared stormy petrels among the tribes who clamoured for their self-identity, and also self-rule for themselves. It might be that they were misdirected in their demand for a separate State for the tribals only, this phenomenon has been discussed in the Jharkhand Chapter. The genesis of this separatist movement may be traced to Jaipal Singh, a Munda young man, bred and brought up in England. He donned Oxford Blue, taught in Princes College and ultimately came to lead his people in a mammoth movement to have self-identity under the banner of *Adivasi Mahasabha*. No doubt, Jaipal Singh was considered as the newest pawn of the Christian missionaries to be placed on the political fermament in Chota Nagpur which definitely paled a handful of non-Christian leaders such as Rai Sahib Bandi Ram Oraon and Theble Oraon etc. into insignificance. Might be, they were not the product of the Christian schools; rather they were from secular schools. It is needless to say that *Adivasi Mahasabha* was transformed into the *Jharkhand Party* and for decades together the Christian tribals dominated the political scene and filled the reserved seats of the legislature. They bolstered up a case for separate Jharkhand State so that they could be free from the influence of the *Dikus*.

There was a time when Jharkhand Party under the leadership of Jaipal Singh was the best and most powerful political force; but at the same time the non-Christian tribals who had many reasons to feel aggrieved for being neglected by these Christian leaders, threw up leaders such as Kartik Oraon, Sukru Bhagat, Bhaya Ram Munda, Muchi Rai Munda, Lal Hembrom, Bariar Hembrom and others who were the product of Thakkar Bapa educational institutions. Thakkar Bapa had opened a large number of schools in most interior parts of this area and these schools were run under the supervision of Adim Jati Seva Mandal, Nibaranpur and Santal Paharia Seva Mandal, Deoghar, and they came to challenge the leadership of Jharkhand Party from the platform of Congress Party. For sometimes they were not successful; but slowly and silently they paved the way ultimately for the merger of the Jharkhand Party with the Congress Party in 1963 and now it is the Congress as a Party which sends the largest group of its reserved legislators to the Bihar Legislative Assembly and the splintered Jharkhand groups have been reduced to hopeless minority except the newly formed Jharkhand Mukti Morcha.

The working of various political parties such as Congress, Bhartiya Jan Sangh, Socialist Party, Communist Party of India, Communist Party of India (Marxist-Leninist), Proutist Block and others among the people of this part of the country created a somewhat very good political education of these people and the behaviour of the tribal electorates in the reserved constituencies though not yet free from the tutelege of the christian missionaries, but of late, has started showing signs of maturity. These are indeed the product of the political education and the village schools run under the christian and non-christian organisation.

The western system of education has definitely changed the attitude of the people in this part of the country. They have set new goals for them. The Christian institutions as well as the State owned institutions and Thakkar Bapa organised institutions have been pouring forth such literate persons who are taking up the leadership of the area and filling up the cadre of Jharkhand and different political parties. Therefore, these institutions have created a different types of tension. In 1919. Compulsory Primary Education Act was passed, and it became the responsibility of the various municipalities to open schools and so was the responsibility of the District Board. In 1935, when the Government of India Act was passed, provincial autonomy was granted, and education became the part of Gandhian thinking on national system of education. That was the Basic education. Basic schools, basic training schools and other organisations were opened. In 1946, Primary Education Act, 1919 was amended so as to incorporate basic education in its fold under a Basic Education Board which was given the responsibility of elementary schools up to Class VIII only. Of course, post-basic schools also were there but they were primarily secondary classes. In 1949, a diversified course from Class VIII was started for all groups, Arts, Science and Commerce. This experiment was not found successful. These ad-hocism and various experiments in tribal areas also created a vicious circle and they went a long way in marring the calibre of the non-christian schools and remained stagnant and from that situation they have not yet emerged. When Mudaliar Commission Report, was published in 1952-54, a higher secondary system of education was introduced which meant addition of one more class at the secondary stage of education and the introduction of diversification of courses on all India basis. It was introduced in Bihar first but the same was abolished in 1971. National Education Commission Report, 1964-65 suggested a national pattern of secondary education, 10 years elementary and secondary education plus two years of higher secondary education or Inter-school or Inter-college education plus three years of degree course. There was placed emphasis on Indian Constitution in which there were expressed directions for having compulsory universal and free education imparted within the 10 years from the date of implementation of the Constitution to the age group of 6-14. It was also directed in the Constitution that every child has to be educated through the medium of his own mother-tongue from the elementary school stage from class I to VII. But all these remained pious wishes because we find that the tribal education remained a myth inspite of the fact some primass and reading materials have been claimed to have been prepared. It is general education which is imparted, not in the tribal dialect but in Hindi, perhaps because it is understood well. Except in Santal Parganas, Santali is taught, of course, in Devnagri script because the tribals have no dialect of their own.

There are many tribals such as Lakho Bodra and others who have clamoured for a tribal script of their own and they have prepared the literature in their *ol lipi*; but it is yet to be accepted by a large group of people. At best it could have been done that the teachers should have been made conversant with the tribal languages or the dialect of the area they serve. These teachers shall have to be trained in a special orientation course where the life, culture and aspirations of the people of the area is made known to them and the teachers in the tribal areas learn the tribal language of the area concerned and pass the tribal language examination. The State Government, for better administration, conducts tribal language examination at different district headquarters like Chaibasa for Ho, Ranchi for Mundari, Daltonganj for Oraon, Dumka for Santali for the officers posted in the area but these language examinations are conducted in slip-shod manner and it is only the lure of honorarium and the fear of stoppage of increments that force the Government servants in these areas to sit in the examination than having some understanding of the tribal language, custom and manners. Therefore, the State Government shall have to open a Research Institute at each divisional headquarters level in order to develop and enrich and strengthen different tribal languages. Text-books in different tribal languages are proposed to be published since the Fifth Five Year Plan and subsequently.

Presently (in 1990), there are 107 Ashram schools, 8670 Primary schools, 1889 Middle schools and 523 High schools in the Tribal Sub Plan area of Bihar which has 16506 villages. The tribal Sub-Plan area has about 50 per cent tribal population. As against All India literacy percentage 36.70 per cent as per 1981 Census. All Bihar has 26.11 per cent literacy and in tribal Sub-Plan area has only 16.99 per cent literacy, among Scheduled Tribe females it is 7.75 per cent.[49] The Christian Missions have large number of schools of different grades, many of them run on State grants, have been doing yeoman service to the cause of education; but at the same time they have been epicentre of tribal discontent, a fact which is evident at the time of Birsa Seva Dal Movement in 1968. But one would always like to join the then Vice Chancellor, Dr. A.K. Dhan, of Ranchi University in his bold optimism when he declared in the annual function of Institute of Journalists, Ranchi in December 1975, that the tribals or as a matter of fact Chota Nagpuris, have travelled fast and reached a stage in their life when their self-identity has been fully proliferated and they could be depended to run any avocation to the best of satisfaction. Incidentally, the talker himself was a tribal who had resigned his membership of Union Public Service Commission to run the

University which is situated in the heartland of Tribal Bihar. Tribals of Chota Nagpur and Santal Parganas are marching ahead.

NOTES

1. H.B. Hyde, *Parochial Annals of Bengal*, (Calcutta,1901), pp. 86-87.
2. India, Bureau of Education, *Selections from Educational Records* 1920, Part I, p. 10.
3. H.B. Hyde, *Ibid.*, pp. 215-17.
4. L.S.S. O'Malley, ed., *Modern India and West* (Oxford, 1968), p. 141-42.
5. *Ibid.*
6. D.D. Basu, *Rise of Christian Power in India*, (Calcutta, 1931) p. 803.
7. A.B. Keith, *Speeches and Documents in Indian Policy*, Vol.I, 1922, p. 265.
8. W. Mind, *Report on Native Schools in the Fatehpur District* in Henry Stuart Reid: *Report on Indigeneous Education of Vernacular Schools*. Agra, 1952.
9. Alexander Duff, *The Indian Rebellion : Its Causes and Results* (London, 1858), p. 239-40.
10. *Ibid.*, pp. 241-42.
11. *Selections from Education Department* No. 5 dated 9th March 1868 from the Secretary of State for India, p. 205.
12. Resolution on the *Report on Public Instruction*, 1870-71.
13. *Report on Public Instruction*, 1878-80 p. 222.
14. Letter No. 2199 J dated 29th November 1887 from John Beams, Commissioner Bhagalpur Division and Santal Parganas to the Secretary, Revenue and General Department, Government of Bengal.
15. *Report on Education in Bengal.* 3rd Quinquiennial Review 1902-03 to 1906-07, p. 790.
16. S. Prasad, "Tribal Education in Bihar", *Man in India*, 51 (1971), p. 385.
17. J.S. Jha, "Missionary Education in Chota Nagpur Division in Bihar", *Journal of Historical Research* (Ranchi), May 1961, p. 12.
18. *Ibid.*
19. (i) J.Cave -Brown, *The Chota Nagpur Mission*, London 1870.
    (ii) H.W. Tucker, *Digest of the S.P.G. Records 1701-1892*, p. 10.
20. *Rickets Reports of Chota Nagpur*, 1854 para 139, p. 37.
21. J.Muller, *A Brief Review of Ten years of Missionary Labour in India*, 1805-61, p. 45.
22. Letter No. 1746 dated 9th March 1865 from Junior Secretary Government of India to the Director of Public Instruction, Government of Bengal.
23. W.Holsten, *Johannes Evangelista Gossner, Glaube and Gemeinde* (1949), p. 308
24. *Ibid.*, p. 320.
25. *Slacks Report* 1888, Section VIII, p. 19.
26. A.R.G.M., 1874, pp. 15-16.
27. C.D.C. 1880, p. 10.
28. S.C. Roy, *Munda and Their Country* (Calcutta,1912), p. 265.
29. F.J. Bowen, *Father Constant Lievens Apostle of Chota Nagpur* (St. Levis, 1936), p. 114.
30. Campbell, p. 28.

31. S. Mahto, *Hundred Years of Christian Mission*, (unpublished thesis, Ranchi University) p. 221.
32. Eyre Chatterlon, *A Story of Fifteen Years of Mission Work in Chota Nagpur* (1901), p. 181.
33. F.B. Bradley Bist, *Chota Nagpur: A Little Known Province of Empire* (London, 1903), p. 23.
34. Letter dated 8th July, 1869 from E.T. Dalton, Commissioner of Chota Nagpur Division to H.L. Dampier, Secretary, Government of Bengal.
35. Letter No. 1156 dated 26th June, 1865 from E.T. Dalton, Commissioner Chota Nagpur Division, to H.C. Bayley, Junior Secretary, Government of Bengal.
36. Letter No. 1157 dated July 1865 *Ibid.*
37. S. Prasad, *op. cit.*, p. 369.
38. Letter dated 19th October, 1875 from Rev. J.C. Whitley to Captain Lewis, Secretary, District School Committee, Lohardaga.
39. Letter dated 17th November, 1875 from H.L. Oliphant, Deputy Commissioner, Lohardarga to W.G.F. Robinson, Commissioner, Chota Nagpur Division.
40. Letter No 2711 dated 10th May, 1869 from Colonel J.E.T. Nicholas, R.E. Secretary, Public Works Department, Government of Bengal to the Superintending Engineer, Bihar Circle.
41. S. Prasad, *op. cit.*, p. 369.
42. *Ibid.*, p. 383.
43. Letter No. 2869 dated 7th July, 1865 from W.S. Atkinson, Director Public Instruction to the Secretary, Government of Bengal.
44. *Progress of Education in Bengal*, 4th Quinquennial Review, 1907-08 to 1911-12 Para 279.
45. *Report on Public Instruction*, 1885-86. para 310.
46. Letter No. 7 dated 3rd April, 1876 from Lieutenant J. Rivet Carnac, Secretary, District School Committee, Lohardaga to W.K.F. Robinson, Commissioner of Chota Nagpur.
47. *Report on Public Instruction*, 1876-77. para 246.
48. W.W. Hunter, *The Old Missionary* (Oxford,1896).
49. Dr. Savitri Sinha: A Status Paper on Educationally Disadvantaged Sections: S.C. & S.T. in the Hill Areas of Chota Nagpur and Santal Parganas Tribal in *Educating the preliteratures in Bihar* edited by Dr. S.P. Sinha, Ranchi (1990), pp. 115-126.

PART II

Conflict and Tension in Santal Parganas

6

SANTAL UNREST AGAINST EUROPEAN ZAMINDARS

THE BENGAL system of 1790-93 sought to declare some person to be the landlord or the proprietor and also to secure his position as an effective and influential intermediary between the cultivator and the government. The Permanent Settlement with *Zamindars* as proprietors (1793) with no survey, no record of rights, and no defined method of assessment, was an occasion to provide aristocracy to the subject people because it appeared to have been thought that by it everything else would be provided for itself. It was also thought that this bulwark would prevent rack-renting of *raiyots* as well as the imposition of new *abwabs* etc. In Bengal the farm-system seems to have been "like a plant which, originally introduced for some special purpose, has taken root, and can never afterwards be got rid of, overrunning everything else".[1]

The system involved the presumption that (i) for every local estate or group of lands there must be some person with whom Government should settle, or who should hold the settlement and be vested with a proprietary interest in the land; (ii) that the amount of revenue to be paid by the *Zamindar*, being once ascertained, that amount was fixed for ever under the Law of 1793 and (iii) that the amount was determined not with reference to any area or survey or any other consideration like various fertility or productive powers, of the acres held in each case, or of the influence of proximity to market and facility of communication on the value of produce.[2] Whatever the process, the landlord would certainly become rich and as a class did practically nothing for the tenants, but rack rented them or hand them over to *patnidars* or rent farmers who did so still more. The rapacity of the rent farmer gained so much notoriety soon that he was held in abomination everywhere. The *Zamindars* or his farmers were interested only in squeezing out as much as they could from the *raiyots*, partly because they were under the impression that the *parganas* would be farmed out to them and would be settled with others in the next settlement. Thus they became averse to any kind of improvement in the tenancy. It may be just an accident of history that the same irresponsibility and rapacity which characterises the Indian *Zamindars* and their *Patnidars* also infected their European counterparts in no less measure. This fact has been illustrated here with the help of two case studies. The misdemeanour led to disturbances of the tribal *raiyots* in Santal Parganas against two European farmers of revenue. The first confrontation of 1860-61 against C. H. Barnes, a farmer of Court of Wards Hindwah Estate and the other of 1871 against Thomas Grant, a farmer of Court of Wards Sunkera Estate.

Santal Unrest of 1860-61 against C. H. Barnes

The after-effects of the Santal Hul of 1855 had hardly subsided when the signs of an approaching disturbance among the Santals of the Doomka Division started making themselves manifest. A large body of armed Santals were on the move. In one known instance, the number of such armed men was about one thousand. The twigs of *Sal* tree, a signal among Santals for getting ready for a war, were circulated and the women accompanied the armed bands with large empty baskets for collecting the booty as was evident in the last Santal insurrection. A sense of insecurity prevailed, and many of the inhabitants thought of leaving the neighbourhood of Naya Doomka.[3]

The Lieutenant Governor of Bengal at Parisnath received intelligence regarding the impending Santal rebellion almost daily from Assistant Commissioner Taylor of the Naya Doomka Division. In his letters of 2nd, 4th and 5th May, 1861, the Lieutenant Governor considered it proper that immediate measures be taken to secure the country against the possible rising of the Santals. One hundred troops of the First Police Battalion (Sikhs) under Lieutenant Thompson were despatched from Sooree on the 3rd May, 1861 on the receipt of express message from the Assistant Commissioner just to restore confidence and avert altogether an intended rising. Should a rising of the Santals occur, the Lieutenant Governor[4] wanted an appraisal of the available force made in the whole of Burdwan and Bhagalpur divisions, forming the country, west of the Bhagirathi and south of the Ganges which included the Santal Districts within it. In the former division there were 240 men of the Military Police. A mixed contingent of Sikhs and Gorkhas having a strength of one hundred men was despatched from

Sooree to Naya Doomka. There were 50 men Gorkha of the Military Police at Rajmahal. Besides there were 200 Military Police (Sikhs and Gorkhas) under Captain Baker *en-route* from Darjeeling. The officiating Commissioner of Bhagalpur was instructed to call Captain Baker to Bhagalpur or to send them to Rajmahal as circumstances may require. The difficulty was that the Bengal Military Police had been reduced to such numerical weakness since recruitment was forbidden, and the urgent demand for their services in other divisions, made it impossible to add to the number of men of that force then in and about the Santal country. The Lieutenant Governor had no information of the disposition of the troops in Bengal, but the latest army list showed that in the divisions named, the Bhagalpur Hill Rangers were the only available troops supposed to be quite strong and that too distributed amongst the district of Purnea (North of the Ganges), Bhagalpur and Monghyr. Therefore he recommended[5] that such a disposition of Native Infantry Regiment at Raniganj, a similar force at Sooree, where they could penetrate into the Santal country by the new road via Bowsee a wing at Bhagalpur at the other extremity of the same line, and a wing on the railroad at or near Rajmahal which was recommended by the Government of India in order to secure the country against a possible rising of the Santals.[6]

The Mynpoory Levey and three Troops of Benares Horse had been placed at Monghyr, and a detachment of the Bengal Native Infantry at Bhagalpur, and that a wing of Sikh Infantry had been halted at Purnea in case their march into the Santal country should be needed.

Meanwhile G. Plowden, Officiating Commissioner of Burdwan and an officer of standing and experience was vested with the powers of Commissioner[7] of the Santal Parganas and was rushed to Doomka since Mr. Robinson, the Officiating Commissioner-designate of Santal Parganas was on his way from Purnea to Doomka. Plowden reached Doomka on the night of 5th May, 1861 and took necessary precautions to meet the situation. He wrote demi-official letters almost daily to the Government of Bengal communicating day-to-day developments of the anticipated Santal uprising. No sooner did Plowden reach Doomka than he got the news of the alarming situation through the interception of a letter in Bengali[8] dated 25th Baisakh (i. e. 6th May) written by Pertaub Clunder Race to his father the Rajah of Nulhatty who was then at Doomka. It described an uneasy feeling regarding the Santals in Nulhatty, and the neighbouring country. Plowden was of the opinion that although there was no sufficient cause that he could discover for a

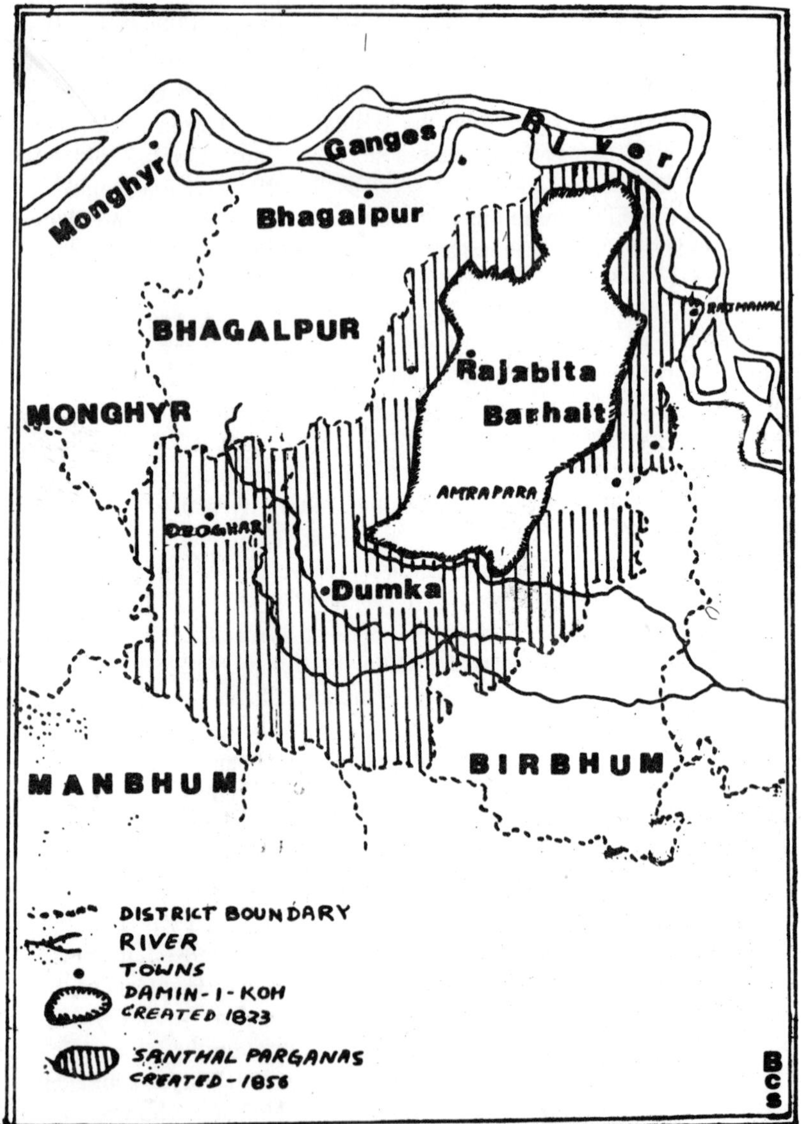

FIG. 6.1: Santhal Parganas 1856

rising and no sufficient indication as yet to warrant the apprehension that a rising was intended, yet it was certain that in some parts, the proceedings of the Santal were not free from suspicion, and that an uneasy feeling, amounting almost to panic, prevailed among the peace-loving section of the population. It was found proper, therefore, to take precautionary measures at once. He wrote of Santal, as a credulous and superstitious race, easily led away, and working out their plans silently and in strict combination. Whatever feeling exists in one part of the Santal tract doubtless extends to every other part though it may not be displayed everywhere to the same extent, or at all in some places. Plowden was of opinion that the Santals were fully informed of the contest that was going on in the Indigo districts, and, no doubt, regarded it as a source of strength to themselves. It was true that the rents had been enhanced only in some Estates, "but all saw that it was the time to make common cause — and his belief founded upon all the facts and indications brought to his knowledge, was that the Santals might be organising, not a rising, but a combination after the example of the agricultural population in the Indigo districts, to resist the enhancement of rents, but, with such a people, such combination might pass at any moment into an insurrection".

H. A. R. Alexander, the Magistrate of Birbhum, wrote about small hunting parties of Santals (of under 100 men) in the Nagore, Khyrasole Thannas in Nulhatty jungles. On the basis of yet another report from the Daroga of Nulhutty Thanna he also wrote that there were from 2,000 to 2,500 Santal *shikaris* hunting with two or three hundred dogs in the Boromesha Hills in the Pakoor Districts, about 14 or 15 miles west of Nulhatty Thanna and that they were going to hunt there till Saturday and that they would again hunt on Sunday and Monday next at Jeypore, six miles North West of Thanna Kurbonah. The party was unusually large and precautions was taken to keep sharp eye on their movement. Therefore, Plowden wanted to take the precaution of having the means of protection and prevention at hand, by Nationing Military Police, as soon as possible, as follows:[9]

Soory	300 men
Rampoor Hat	100 men
Pakoor	50 men
Rajmahal	60 men
Pearpointee	100 men
Bowsee	100 men

Godda	50 men
Deogarh	60 men
Doomka	60 men
	200 men
Total	1080 men

The object and advantage of this disposition were local protection, and the power of advancing, and, if necessary, concentrating a strong force upon any point. At Soory there were only about 100 men available and they were Gorkhas not Sikhs. At Rajmahal there were already, 60 men, and in the Doomka jurisdiction there were 100 Sikhs, of whom 40 were available, under the proposed disposition, for transfer to some other part. Hill Rangers were being sent to Deoghar by Plowden. It was understood they were not to be trusted having a predilection from running away from an enemy. They should, therefore, be posted only at Pearpointee, Bonsee, and Godda but it was better, in his opinion, to post Military Police at all these places. Such swift military and administrative measures were responsible for bringing normalcy in the region but, nonetheless, the Government of India was anxious to know the genesis of this consternation among the Santals which Plowden or his successor was expected to probe in.

One of the foremost causes of the impending disturbance was the enhancement of rent by the *Zamindar*, a natural source of irritation to the tribal tenants in particular. On the basis of the papers it could be found that the real excitement among the Santals was caused principally by the proceedings of C. H. Barnes, an European farmer of an Estate under the Court of Wards. The Estate in question was Pargana Hindwah. It was a hereditary under-tenure not paying revenue direct to Government. Its owner Madho Singh died in 1857 and the Estate was attached. Madho Singh died intestate, having a widow, a minor son Vodit Narain Singh as his heir and a large number of dependents and hangers-on. The property not paying revenue direct to government could not, in a Regulation Province, have been brought under the charge of the Court of Wards, but being in the Santal Parganas. Mr. Yule went by the spirit of the Regulations, and his bringing the estate under the Court of Wards was approved by the then Lieutenant Governor of Bengal, who rejected the appeal made by the widow Sona Kumari against Yule's orders.[10]

Under the new arrangements, the management of the estate was made over to C. H. Barnes who was to hold it as *Surburkar* for the first year on a commission of 15 per cent, and to take it in farm of ten years or until the minor came of age on an annual *jumma* of Rs. 14,000. The farming settlement was not entered into at once on account of the embarrassed state of the property which rendered imminent the probability of a sale being forced. But by the exertions of Mr. Barnes and an advance on his part of half a year's rent, together with cash payments as far as possible to the most pressing creditors, the difficulty was averted, and arrangement made by which the minor on coming of age would find himself in possession of an encumbered and much improved estate. This was the pious wish of the persons concerned with the arrangement, but in actual operation it turned out to be otherwise.

The Hindwah Estate was a *Mokurarree* of Kurrackpur paying to the *Zamindar* a fixed rent of Rs. 2,157 a year. Madho Singh, was a bad tenant and a worse landlord, who never took care of the land or the tenants. He died deeply involved in debt leaving the estate in a wretched condition. The Santal insurrection had swept over the country. Many of the villages were deserted. But the collection papers after the death of Madho Singh showed collection to be about Rs. 16,000 and later on Rs. 19,000 and in Barne's year of *Surburakaree* management showed an actual rent roll of Rs. 21,159 and six annas.

On obtaining the farm next year, Barnes measured the estate, and having laid out a good deal of money in improvements, clearing jungles, making embankments for irrigation, settling new villages etc. he affected a settlement, giving three years leases which raised the annual collections to Rs. 31,000 during the last year. When the settlement expired. Barnes proceeded to make a new settlement which had been the cause of the excitement which lately existed there.

Robinson, the Officiating Commissioner of Santal Parganas, was full of praise for Barnes who spent unlike other *Zamindars* in making improvement in the tenancy. His advocacy for this European *Zamindar* gives an idea of the new experimentation that the top officials preferred to make at times, little knowing that institution of landlordism remained as rapacious as in the Indian hands even if run by an European enlightened gentleman. He wrote that the fact was that the tenants never had a landlord who set to improve their condition, who would advance them money or grain for seed, who would clear jungle, make *bandh* (dam) for irrigation, and set up poor people with cattle plough. "The change was novel and pleasant, and every one was pleased with it, except the retainers of the late *Zamindars*, who did not like to pay rent for lands and villages which they held without a shadow of title rent free."[11] He and Yule were full with praise for Barnes but Plowden's[12] enquiry showed that the tenantry in Hindwah Parganas regarded the increased rents then assessed upon them as excessive, and were consequently dissatisfied. It seemed that the Estate had lately been measured and the out turn of land assessed at greatly increased[13] rates by which the rents had been raised from Rs. 14,000 at which they stood when the lease was given some five years ago to Rs. 60,000. The tenantry objected less to the rates assumed than to the measurement, which, however, fairly and correctly it might have been conducted, they regarded as an innovation to which they were not liable, and they pointed to the enormous increase in the rents, consequent upon the combined operations of a strict measurement and enhanced rates, as palpable evidence of oppressive treatment. The same operations were going on in other farms held by the Europeans. Mr. Plowden enquired into village Elwarra in Pargana Hindwah and "found that rent has been raised to 600 per cent, that is, from Rs. 100 at which it stood up to the end of the past year, on a three year's lease, to Rs. 600, now demanded on a three years' lease from the present year". Plowden[14] commented that Barnes obtained the farm, much too hastily as he thought on a *jumma* of Rs. 14, 000. He first held it one year experimentally as *Subrakar*, and realised Rs. 21,000 in that year. He then clinched the bargain and made the three years settlement which has just expired, yielding a rent roll of Rs. 31,000. And he then proposed a settlement, founded on measurement of every *raiyat*'s holding, for the next three years, which would raise his rent roll to upward of Rs. 60,000. Even if it should remain at that amount for the six years terminating his farms, he would still in the ten years of his lease have realised a profit of Rs. 3,34,000 with very little trouble and outlay to set off against it. He felt that by reduction in length of the measuring rod to the standard length, one *beegah* of old standard had been converted into three of the new, and the rates having at the same time been doubled. These manipulations yielded a six-fold increase. The excessive enhancement of rent is also corroborated by other documents in this series although Robinson and Yule were all apologists for Barne's privilege to enhance the rate of rent.

It was one thing to agree that the *Surburkar* Barnes had legal right to enhance the rent but; it was quite another if such feelings were publicly exhibited before a credulous people like the Santals. When the *raiyots* complained against this excessive enhancement to the Assistant Commissioner Taylor, he met them arguing that under the spirit of the provisions of Act X of 1859 the *Zamindar* and farmers had a right to measure and assess and as such the rates assumed were not too high.[15] Taylor disapproved of the *raiyots* assembling to discuss rent question and he was harsh to them. His Assistant Dr. Gross who was deputed at Nony Hat with a party of the Military Police under Lieutenant Thompson, wrote a letter proposing to commence the disarming of the people the very next day, unless instructed to the contrary. Plowden wrote "such a proceeding at present would have been fatal to the tranquillity of the tract, and moreover could not have been carried out". He was instructed to confine himself strictly to the preservation of the peace, if any disturbance or other unlawful proceedings should be attempted.[16] Plowden after examining of the statements of the various Perganaites of Hindwah came to the conclusion that "whatever disquietude exists among the Santals was owing to Mr. Barne's settlement operations and his implicit confidence and trust in his agents. Had Radachurn (Radhacharan) not left Nony Hat a fortnight or three weeks before the disturbance he would have been attacked".[17]

The tenantry of the Hindwah Pargana and of other lands, either the property of Barnes, or, like Hindwah, held in farm by him were justly dissatisfied with his settlement operations, conducted on his behalf, by his principal Agent, Radhacharan Gangooly. Radhacharan was Barne's confidential Agent, a man he had brought up from childhood. Radhacharan had made the settlement in question of Pargana Hindwah and it was stated[18] that he had resorted to force in taking some of the engagement and had intimidated the *raiyots* by telling them his Master Barnes and the Commissioner Yule[19] were *ek topie* (of one mind), and that there was, therefore, no use in their resisting him or complaining to the local authorities. The *raiyots* were led to believe Radhacharan which they conceived to be borne out by Taylor's inattention to their objections that it was useless to complain to the authorities, Assistant Commissioner Taylor himself narrated the situation saying that "Two Santals came forward to object to the measurements made as unfair, but on an immediate reference to the *Ameen's* papers, it appeared that they had been charged for less first class land than they themselves said was cultivated by them. These men retired abashed amidst a general laugh raised by the other Santals who were present".[20] Again

Taylor narrated one or two *Mostagires* who had taken *pottahs* tendered their resignation, which were accepted at once by Mr. Barne's agent and they were evidently very much disappointed at their resignation being taken and some others who had pressed forward, *Pottahs* in hand, evidently to intimidate the Baboo by making him think they were going to throw up their leases, retired without doing so.

Another cause of dissatisfaction[21] was that Mr. Barnes had some of Santals *Jhyrthans* (place of worship, sacred grove) cut and sent the timber to Colgong. This was done at four places — Gangawara, Photana, Perwannah and Margamma. When the trees were cut from the last place Margamma, the Santals, complained to Taylor who postponed any decision till the arrival of Barnes from Calcutta. Even if when Barnes had come, Taylor could not make any settlement. This incensed the feeling of Santals most.

After Barnes' arrival from Calcutta, several *Pargannaits* and *Mustazirs* went and complained to him. Mr. Barnes said to Gobind Parganite of Sarmee Talook[22] "What use are you Parganites and Mustazirs to me? I do my work. I have no use of you, and will make you level with the *Raiyots*". About these threats to Parganites Plowden wrote:

> "Now, the Pargannaits are an institution of the Santal tract which has existed from time immemorial. They are a body of officers appointed by the villager over circles of villages denominated *Talooks*. Their business is to assist in the settlement and collection of rents, and they are employed by the Authorities on Police duties, being the responsible heads of their respective circles. Their influence with the people, by whom they are much looked up to, is great. Mr. Barnes, a mere farmer has no sort of right to abolish them, and if he had, it might be supposed that he would see the impolicy of losing the services of valuable a body, and enlisting their influence against him, in order to obtain a trifling addition to his rents, but the measure is just such a one as a Bengali Manager (such as his Agent, Radacharan Gangooly, is) might be expected to recommend. To judge of its significance, it is necessary to bear in mind that Pergunnah Hindwah contains an area of about 5,000 square miles and a population of about 1,00,000 souls of whom some 80,000 may be Santals."[23]

Over and above these, the *Mahajans* under the Limitation Law, had instituted a number of suits of late and had also been pressing for payment. Writing about this phenomenon, Plowden wrote "I do not believe that the pressure of the *Mahajans* has been very great or that it has much to do with the present feeling. If it had not been for Mr. Barne's settlement operations nothing would have been heard of the pressure of the *Mahajans.* When a people are smarting under what they consider a grand grievance every little matter is brought it to swell the catalogue".

A possible partial cause of the discontent was assigned to the superstitious belief in a prophecy of one of the leaders of the Santal insurrection of 1848-1855, Kanoo, who just before his execution predicted a rising about this time at which he would reappear as a leader.[24] This is an usual characteristic of the tribal movements everywhere in India when the leader is believed to have resurrected and lived in the people to deliver them the good. This can best be taken as an additional grievance to make their condition as bad as possible. The rumour was that the Deputy Commissioner of Santal Pargana had cancelled all debts incurred previously to the insurrection played the mischief. On coming to Santal Pargana in 1856 Robinson did ask the pressing *Mahajans* to wait until the Santals could pay as they were starving then. Robinson commented:

> "Many of the Santals have, I know, paid those debts, but some refuse to do so, knowing they have more than repaid the amount, but fancying they will not be able to prove it, they think it easier to misquote my order, and say I remitted all the debts, good, bad, or indifferent than to go to court. A few words of explanation soon satisfy them, and if cases of old bonds are carefully enquired into my own experience tells me that very few cases will be decreed against Santals."[25]

The *Mahajans* themselves knew this and hence they put off bringing their suits until the very last moment, in hopes of still getting a little more out of the Santals, and at last fearing the operation of the Limitation Law they went into court. Plowden rightly diagnosed the reason that:

> "Although the tenantry of the Santal Parganas, influenced in some measure, by the contest in the Indigo Districts, might have determined to unite in opposing the excessive enhancement of their

> rents, still he was of opinion that the combination had no other object than to enforce attention to their complaint, and was not of the same character as the combination in the Indigo Districts. They argued that as in the case of the agricultural population in the Indigo Districts, their strength lay in union and that if they objected *en-masse* their objections would be more readily and fully attended to and removed."[26]

One interesting point in this concern was the Income-tax story originated in Bhagalpur owing to the Police making a census which Yule put a stop to, as the rumour at once got abroad that every man was to be taxed on his *lota*, and even for the pumpkin growing on the roof of his house. This spread to the Santals of the Lacchampur estate in Bhagalpore, and so to their brethren in the adjoining Hindwah Pargana, the fact of their not being called upon to pay Income-tax will, with clear explanation which the Officiating Commissioner had taken care to give to all the Santals, be the best remedy for the evil report.[27]

Thus these were the causes of the discontentment bordering on a general rising of Santals. The Santals naturally thought that Taylor sanctioned Barnes' enhancement and that there was no use of complaining further to the local authorities as these officers and Barnes were in league with each other. Had Taylor called Barnes to the spot and insisted on making the settlement in person and in event of not getting the cooperation of Barnes he, as Assistant Commissioner of Doomka could not have allowed such proceeding to go on unless sanctioned by the superior authority. Then the matter could have been taken a different shape. But Taylor instead held the opinion that Barnes was legally entitled to demand such an enormous increase and moreover *Raiyots* could afford to pay it knowing full well that how touchy the Santals were on the rent questions and how general dissatisfaction prevailed on that issue, and that many of the *Raiyots* felt that to pay four annas for each buffalo plough was the only fair and equitable arrangement. Taylor also knew that there was a small party ready to fan any discontent. Knowing all these, it was quite inexcusable on his part not to bring the matter to the notice of Wood, Robinson or Yule as the case might be.

Therefore, the Santals rightly thought that Taylor had given no redress to them. Sunder Manjhi, Parganite of Gaddi Gangwara then residing in Nowadhee was the leader of this discontented group of Santals. According to his statement that when Taylor dilly dallied the complaints and that in the event of Santals being convinced that there was no use complaining to Taylor or Barnes, they discussed the feasibility of going to Calcutta to lay before the Lieutenant Governor the whole case of injustice perpetrated by the British landlord in collusion with British officials. This was agreed in a meeting at Pathoria. One Durga Santal who was formerly at Pathoria and was holding the post of Naik in the Police Battalion at Krishnaghur was also consulted and he agreed to take them to Krishnaghur from where they would go to Calcutta. It was then arranged that Dhunie Parganite of Gurdee, Tulsi Chuckladar of Dhoba, Nungoo Manjhi of Pithoria, Ranghoo Manjhi of Gora Chasser, Bullia Gorait of Gora Chasser, Bhima Parmanik of Moormulla and Sunder Manjhi should accompany Durga Naik to Krishanaghur and thence they would proceed to Calcutta. Some collection for road expenses was also made and Durga Naik got advanced a loan of Rs. 10 from the Santal Sepoys there.

On reaching Calcutta they perchanee came across some Dhangurs at Budluganj where they stayed with them. As their clothes had become very dirty, therefore, they went to a cloth shop to purchase new *dhotis* etc. for Shunie who was to be their spokesman. Kisto Babu was the shopkeeper who persuaded them to meet his uncle Ramababu who was a writer in some Sahib's house. Ramababu wanted Rs. 20 to be paid first then he would take up their case to which they were not agreeable because they wanted to get their work done before they paid. Kisto Babu took them from place to place in Calcutta, showed them Supreme Court, Grand Jury, *Chota Dewanny Adawlat* and other places. Ultimately they had to return to Dumka. They saw Taylor and when he asked them as to what they had done at Calcutta, Dhumie said that they had seen the *Lord Sahib*, that he had spoken very well to them, and that Barnes was not entitled to tax them so heavily as he had done, that Barnes must be satisfied with an increase of two to four *annas* in a rupee. When they had arrived from Calcutta it was their usual time for *Shikar* and they went on *Shikar* as usual where they used to talk over their grievances, and spoke about going to the *Boro Commissioner Sahib* at Bhagalpur, or to *Choto Commissioner Sahib* at Rajmahal.

Sunder Manjhi found a pony at Thanpur which he took to his house and the rumour got spread that *Lord Sahib* had given him a horse. Sunder did not deny that just to show that their errand had not been a fruitless one. Sunder went to Chukhye at the request of Durga Manjhi who sent Goohie Manjhi to ask him to go as the Santals there wanted to know what the deputation had done at Calcutta.[28]

Plowden was confirmed in his belief that no rising was contemplated or was ever intended, and that what had been going on was the organisation of a combination, after the manners and example of the agricultural population in the Indigo Districts, to resist the enhancement of rents. He was not surprised that the deputation was tutored at Kishnaghar by the Agents of the *Raiyots* there and had been by them committed to the care and tutorage of their corresponding Agents in Calcutta.

Commissioner Yule of Bhagalpur[29] commented that it was not usual that a body of *Raiyots* went to Calcutta to lay their grievance before the *Lord Saheb.* In March-April 1857 a man, calling himself *Riyah* of Benares, came to Raniganj and began sending Agents into the Santal Districts with the intent of exciting disturbance. Robinson had him apprehended and he confessed giving many details of the mutiny which broke out soon after. It appeared that he had been in the habit of taking or sending discontented Santals to Calcutta (the feeling caused by the insurrection had not quite subsided then) where they were shown the Supreme Court and the Grand Jury and so on, and crammed with lies as to rents being reduced, debt cleared off etc. which they spread among their brethren on their return. These men came from the Dumka Division and the people then it would seem, remembered their tale.

As a matter of fact the Santals and other inhabitants, too of the Santal Districts had, always since insurrection been accustomed to look upon the Lieutenant Governor of Bengal as their last resort when dissatisfied in a way which the *Raiyots* of the other Districts never had done until they began to throw off the Indigo yoke in Krishnaghur and elsewhere. The Lieutenant Governor of Bengal, Mr. Hallidey, had several interviews with the bodies of Santals soon after the insurrection and he talked freely to them. Recollecting this fact, the Santals for years afterwards addressed him petitions direct, and habit spread to other races in the Santal Districts.[30]

Commissioner Yule had to devote time and energy to explain his settlement of farms with Barnes for which he tried to give great argument. He was agitated and offered the visit of Lieutenant Governor to see things for himself and submit himself to the most searching enquiry of a Commission.[31] Barnes stated that the *Khetowrees* and others, relatives of the late Raja Madho Singh, who had been in his continued opposition for the preceding four years, endeavouring to thwart his every measure, incited some few of the

Santals, who were not Headmen but known to be litigious to go down to Calcutta to represent amongst other things the circumstance of his increase of rent and pray for reversal of the settlement. He alleged that *Khetowrees* financed the deputation.[32]

Robinson, the officiating Commissioner of the Santal Parganas saw that Barnes consented to withdraw his settlement which had occasioned so much discontent and accepted instead an increase of 25 per cent over the whole of estate to which the *Raiyots* readily agreed whereby such litigation, irritation, and agitation were avoided. This was approved by the Lieutenant Governor[33] who put his axe on Taylor for his unsatisfactory dealing with the question by censuring him and removing him to another appointment without loss of rank in the Subordinate Executive Department.

The Governor-General-in-Council concurred with the Lieutenant Governor in thinking that the good judgement and energy with which Plowden had acted deserves commendations.[34] The Governor-General-in-Council had a sigh of relief when the Lieutenant Governor announced that there was no disturbance apprehended and that no active measures of repression were deemed necessary, but the Council wanted some explanation of the circumstances connected with. Barnes and the system under which a farmer, having merely a short lease of an estate, his power to enhance the rents of the tenants to such an extent was to drive the people to the verge of insurrection and alarm the country round.

The Lieutenant Governor also did not think it necessary to follow. Yule throughout in his remarks on the matter of the farming of the Hindwah Estate, and on Robinson's late proceedings in the settlement of the dispute which had arisen and which at one time threatened serious consequences. He would observe, however, that though bringing under the Court of Wards an estate like the Hindwah Estate, which was not paying revenue directly to Government, would not have been supported by law in a Regulation Province. In his opinion, the doing of this in the Santal Parganas was a very expedient measure, and for the interests of all parties concerned. Mr. Yule was perfectly justified in adopting that, but it was found difficult to agree with him in thinking that, considering the absolute ignorance in which the authorities were as to the available assets of the Estate, and so as to the extent of the Farmer's power to increase the rents of land in actual occupation and cultivation, it was prudent in a political point of view to make the arrangement in such a crude and indefinite form.

Lieutenant Governor opined that Yule had taken strong objection to the compromise brought about by Robinson and approved by the Government and in so doing he warmly maintained the Farmer's legal right to raise the rents as he endeavoured to do — a fact which only could be lawfully determined by judicial decree in each case. The Lieutenant Governor found inconsistency in Yule's approach when Yule professed disinclination to permit Barnes' settlement on new principle at the same time Yule's professed irritation on *Raiyots* going to courts or high ups to seek redress. Again Yule in para 13 of his letter considered that "Mr Barnes showed great want of judgment in making at once such an enormous increase and in leaving his *Omlah* to do it unrestrained by his presence" and with seeming inconsistency he found faults with Barnes for consenting to set aside this high and ill-advised settlement, and for accepting the moderate increase of 25 per cent made with his authority by Robinson, on his behalf over the whole estate. Lieutenant Governor was quite unable to concur with Yule's point of view. On the contrary he was of the opinion that Barnes showed not only good feeling and a liberal and benevolent spirit but good judgement in acceding to Robinson's arrangements which at once put an end to all differences between himself and his *Raiyots* and left him with a large profit on his farm, and a quiet and contented tenantry.[35] The Lieutenant Governor could not accept Robinson's allusion to Barnes making extensive improvements in the estate because he felt that would form a small part of the very large sum of money (Rs. 3,34,000) which Plowden in a demi-official letter of seventh ultimo calculated, if the then rates were held, the former would make out of the minor's estate.

The Junior-Secretary to the Government of Bengal J. D. Gordon[36] wrote to the Officiating Commissioner of the Santal Parganas that it was plain, however, that very strong dissatisfaction existed in Parganas and observed the steps taken by the Santals to right themselves as not illegal, violent or improper, rather it was a great matter of 'surprise and regret' to them that the Santals did not make their appeal to the Deputy Commissioner or to the Commissioner. He informed that in this whole affair the Lieutenant Governor was struck with the weak points in the existing administration of the Santal Parganas, particularly such weak points being exactly where it was hoped that this administration was specially strong, viz. the mutual relations of the people and the public officers, the freedom of the intercourse between them, the intimate knowledge by the officers of the feelings of the people and the confidence of the people in the protection of the authorities. This was the point of vital importance as a general question, and the Lieutenant Governor drew the particular attention of the Commissioner, the Deputy Commissioner and every officer in the Santal Parganas to it. No wonder that the Officiating Commissioner Robinson of Santal Parganas and Commissioner Yule of Bhagalpur were also transferred to some different assignments within a year of this event since the Government of Bengal harboured strong feelings about their role and performance in the Santal uprising.

Santal Unrest of 1871 against Thomas Grant

A sudden fall of price of rice from 28 *seers* a rupee to 35 *seers* a rupee in the Dumka division of the Santal Parganas in May 1871 was sufficient to put the administration in alert and what could have been accomplished after major bloodshed was achieved by tactfully, timely and sympathetic handling of the situation. The excitement was over by the end of May 1871; but it left its trail for the administrators at different levels to put the house in order after the silent holocaust of popular feeling against the *Zamindari Zulum* and official tactlessness passed off.

A vague rumour suddenly spread through Dumka and the neighbourhood that the Santals of the entire district were coming into Dumka to complain against the *Zamindar's Zulum* and their avowed object was to obtain redress. This was not confined to only Dumka, rather they intended going to all the district headquarters, and perhaps even to Bhagalpur, with the avowed object of obtaining redress of grievances. They complained that every few year the *Zamindars* are increasing their rents without any rhyme or reason while they are not liable to increase and also that *Mahajans* drive them to despair by the exorbitant rate of interest which they demand and force them to pay. Their main complaints were that many of the *Manjis*, or headmen, had been deprived of the villages because they had not agreed, on the expiry of their leases, to renew them at exorbitant rents, and that the villages had been leased at enhanced rent to strangers (mostly European planters), who had rack-rented them, or their *manjis*, being threatened with being deprived of their villages, had agreed to exorbitant terms and had in consequence been obliged to levy excessive rents from them.[37] The memory of 1855 had hardly become faint and the fears of the people magnified into a serious movement and exodus specially among the Bengali population. In alarm they sold away their stores of grain etc. and hence fall in the price. A report spread that some 500 to 600 Bengalis of the Maheshpur district had left their houses and passed through to Jangipur from dread of the Santals who (they had heard) had risen and were following with the intention of looting the country. The Railway volunteers[38] turned out to meet the danger. The Raja of Maheshpur took active measures to allay this panic by reassuring his remaining *Raiyots* and bringing them back to their villages. Deputy Commissioner Wood, who proceeded to Morarol to ascertain the cause of the panic and tranquillise the people, had an interview with some *parganaites*, or headmen, and gave assurance that the Dumka Santal's complaints were undergoing enquiry, and that just grievances would be redressed.

The Santals were resolute in their earnestness in bringing to the notice of the Deputy Commissioner of Dumka their sad condition in Sunkera, under Court of Wards and other estates. Sunkera estate was in the hands of Thomas Grant. It had been for some years under the Courts of Wards, until Prithi Singh and others were put in possession under a decree from the High Court, but they could not furnish sufficient security and hence the collection of the rents was made over by the Court of Wards to Grant,[39] who deposited the required security, pending an appeal to the Privy Council. Prithi Singh, Sadat Ali and others proprietors, were engaged in making settlement when the estate was wrested from them and passed into the hands of Grant, who immediately raised the rents all round 25 to 30 and even 40 per cent, and also, it is said, levied *salami* from the *Raiyots* at the rate of 10 per cent. They were not asked to agree to the latter, it was simply deducted from their rent when paid in. In addition to these extortionate proceedings, the *Raiyots* complained that Grant deducted from the sum paid in the arrears due for the time when he held the estate in farm previous to Prithi Singh's coming into possession. Since, Grant was simply a *tehsildar* and as such he had no powers to raise the rent his business was solely to collect the rent according to the agreement entered into between the *Zamindars* and *Raiyots*. He had acted illegally throughout, and each one of the *mustajeers* were advised by the Deputy Magistrate H. Rattary to see Thomas Grant which they seemed very much disinclined partly from want of funds and also from fear of Thomas Grant. Rattary recommended to the Commissioner, Bhagalpur that the estate should be taken out of the hands of Mr. Grant. The sooner this done was better.[39]

The complaint in Tuppah Belpata were that Babu Ram Prasad Dass of Monghyr purchased the estate of Maharani Uzirunnisa which was sold in satisfaction of a decree for money and he at once cancelled the nine years' leases given to the *Raiyots* and forced them to take out fresh agreements, of course, on higher rate. The Babu had no right and powers to cancel the earlier *pattas* which were taken from the former proprietor on payment of large sum as *salami*. This came very hard on them and the local officials felt helpless unless these *pattas* were disallowed in court a having been taken by unfair means and with under pressure.

In the Hindwah Pargana of C. H. Barnes and Taluq Singro and Seekhupura and others, the people complained that every few years the *zamindars* raised their rent 25 to 30 per cent and sometimes even by 100 or 200 per cent and that they were unable to meet the demand any longer. The local officers advised the *mustajeer* to allow the *zamindars* to make the settlements with others while *Raiyots* retaining the possession of their lands, and so could the old *mustajeers* of their *Nijjote* land and if the newly set up *mustajeer*'s wished to enhance their rent they would have to see them, and then the court would determine whether they were liable to enhancement. It would be impossible every few years to show sufficient course of enhancement, and the *Zamindar* would soon be brought to terms. This was the only remedy suggested by Rattary.[40] Quoting Smith's diary, Rattary informed that this dissatisfaction has been existing for some years and every now and again a deputation used to wait on him and complain especially from Tuppah Belpata and he recommended necessary measures to be taken to allay this restless feeling of discontent.

Since the Santals were a very clanish people and stuck by one another and keep their plans very secret when they wish to do so, the Deputy Commissioner Brown Wood of Santal Parganas was alarmed.[41] He did not think improbable that the Dumka and Godda Santals might have determined to meet in large numbers at the headquarters of those two divisions, the purpose stated as there had been no doubt good deal of dissatisfaction in those divisions in consequence of the very heavy enhancement of rents, the Santals had been made to pay their *zamindars*, in comparison to those of Hindwah in the Dumka division and Godda, Dhumsyne Amla Mootia and other Parganas in the Godda Subdivisions.

Brown Wood wrote that the Santals held mammoth meetings about these enhancements, but the introduction of the Act of 1859 completely tied the hands of the officers in the Santal Parganas in the same way as was the case with the officers in regulation districts. He brought this fact to the notice of the late Lieutenant Governor Sir William Grey on his visit some two or three years ago. "It is a thousand pity", continued Brown Wood, "that that Act was ever extended to the Lower Provinces as *Zamindars* have not failed to work it to their advantage in every way conducive to their own interests and to the detriment of their ignorant Santal *Raiyots*, and this in no legal a manner too that Santal Officers are helpless to protect the Santals and poorer classes of *Raiyots*. The introduction of *mooktears* had not tended to mend matters, as the *Zamindars* being the richer, were able to secure the best men and hence again the poorer classes suffered . . . in regard to the extortionate rate of interest demanded and taken by *Mahajans*, our hands are also tied, hence the introduction of Act VIII of 1859, before which Yule's Order, prohibiting interest not more than 25 per cent, held good and was strictly enforced, new Santal officers are bound to decree at the rates agreed on by debtors to their creditors". He did not anticipate any trouble from the Santals of either the Godda or Dumka divisions and or of Rajmahal's Santals except as the *Mahajan* grievance as most of them were of *Dameen Raiyots* and as long as they were quiet he had no fear of other Santals in the other district. But he was cautious that the meeting of the Santal was fixed for first Tuesday in June 1871 and he did not wonder that *Bangali* and *Bhojpuri* traders at Dumka might get panicky.

Brown Wood mentioned that he should not at all be surprised to hear that these Santal had been put up to make these complaints by Master Soadiat Ally (Saadat Ali) who was revengeful for the loss of his farms and about him Brown Wood observed, "He is an awfully intriguing fellow. This was the man who, through the Bhangulpore *Mokhtear*, put in that highly objectionable petition against W. Smith, and whom the Commissioner suspended for one year from practising as a *mokhtear* in the lower provinces".[42]

A. W. Cosserat, Deputy Collector and Deputy Magistrate at Godda who was considered very well up in Santali matter, went into the question of *raiyot*'s grievances and laid down the following which gives a very graphic account of the contemporary situation.

> "To the *first* namely — what is the nature of the complaints brought against the Zamindars and the remedy I would suggest? the answer is that — 1st the *Manjees* get short leases, have to pay heavy

salamies in order to get them, and at each renewal there is an enhancement.

2nd — that the leases are not always renewed with the old and time-honoured *Manjee mustajeer* but with strangers, in most cases with the hated *Bhojpuria* or *Bengalee* money-lenders who has managed to make a fortune by endless cheating, and establish himself in the village. In fact that the leases are put up to auction, and the persons paying the highest sum as *salami* and *jamma* got them.

3rd — that the new land jobber always tries, by every means at his command, to obtain possession of the best lands in the village and generally the lands held by the late *Manjhi-Mustajir.*

4th — that he at once commences a new measurement carried on by a dishonest *putwaree*, who always alters the extent of each holding, and cheats the *Raiyots*.

5th — thus unsettling the whole village community and in nine cases out of ten forcing the *Raiyots*, from utter wearings to buy peace at any price.

6th — getting the assistance of the *Zamindar*'s *Emlah* and *Peadahs* who sit *dharna* at the doors of the *Raiyots*, insult their women and make them find "*bootad*" until the demand for a higher rate of rent, or some other unjust or disputed claim is satisfied.

I would not leave you or Mr. Madocks (Officiating Commissioner of Bhagalpur Division) to imagine that this is the general state of affairs, and occurs or has occurred in every *Zamindari* and in a great many villages in each *Zamindari*; in fact, that wherever a village has become worth having or for which there has been competition, it has occurred and that no village is exempt from such a liability, and the minds of the people are unsettled in consequence."[43]

Cosserat became emotional when he wrote "I can give you instances and draw a more elaborate picture of this evil, but it would be writing a great deal which is not desirable, but let me complete this picture by simply asking you what would be the state of the *Damin* and the *Raiyots* resident in it if this system was introduced for one season even, and I leave the subject in your hand".[44]

Cosserat stated that this state of affairs at Godda dates from George Smith's time. "Godda was the only farm that Barnes held and which was not under the control of management of the Court of Wards and under strict application of Act X of 1859 (which was just then in force) by Smith. Barnes succeeded in knocking the old *Manjee-mustajeers* over like nine pins, and was able to do what he pleased and the *Raiyots* being disappointed in the protection they expected from the *hakim* (poorer classes and the Santals in Godda division had greatest confidence in the *hakim*) gradually lost confidence. Also the moral check the officials held the *Zamindars* in up to the introduction of Act X of 1859 kept them within bounds, and they were afraid—in fact ashamed—to do what was then considered such a glaring act of injustice as to turn out an old *manjee mustajeer* from the village for the sake of a small increase in the rent."[45] The matters had changed very considerably first of all by the introduction of Act X of 1859 and secondly by the greater part of the *Zamindari* (Pargana Belputta, Hindwah, Sunkera, Dumka District) which were then under the Courts of Wards passing into the hands of owners. In Dumka, Hindwah and Belpatta Parganas, including Luckmea, were administered under the Court of Wards and the system pursued almost similar to *Damin* system. They comprised one-third or more of Dumka. Barnes held Godda the most important Pargana in this district and though he did much that was wrong he was not altogether beyond officials influence and thus the evils of the present system were not so glaring as they were then.

Grant had introduced indigo largely in the Parganas. The *Zamindars* were following suit. The simple system of collecting rents as found in *Damin* gave place to a system of thoroughly native management with *peadahs*, *putwaries*, and innumerable other harpies, getting about one-rupee or eight *annas* a month from the *Zamindars* and squeezing what they can from the *Raiyots* by threats of insults. Backed by Act X of 1859 every *Zamindar* boldly and fearlessly turned out whatever *Manjee-Mustajeer* he liked. Therefore Cosserat recommended the following remedies:

> "*1st* — that all *manjhee mustajeers* of whatever caste who can prove that village was established by them or their ancestors, shall have a recognised right of occupancy and claims to hold them in the same manner as tenants with occupancy rights under Act X of 1857.
>
> *2nd* — that all *manjhee mustajeers* who have been deprived within 12 years can sue in the courts and recover them.
>
> *3rd* -- that a Special officer or two officials be appointed to

investigate their claims without any charge for stamp fees and confer their rights under the restriction of clause 1 and 2.

4th — that the old system of instituting all complaints *viva voce* whether on criminal, civil or revenue side, be revived with a discretionary power to the presiding officer to accept any written plaints, and to direct that in certain cases written plaints shall be filed."[46]

On 11th June, 1871, H. Rattary, the Deputy Collector of Dumka, wrote that the Santals again collected and he fined a few of them in small sums for persistent assemblage. These men were chiefly from Belpata and the neighbourhood. "Santals", he opined, "seems to imagine that this is the only way in which they can gain redress for any grievance. They seem to think child's play and had I given into them on this occasion, and allowed them to fancy that they were entitled to collect in this manner, they would have given cause for greater annoyance and trouble hereafter".[47] Blumhardt, the Deputy Collector at Deoghar also informed that the Santal were not at all as quiet as they should be. It seemed to him that the two men who were imprisoned by Fraser in 1867 during the *Damin* settlement for inciting Godda Santals to make a row, were at the bottom of the commotion as they were out of the jail.[48]

A. Money, the Member of the Council,[49] did rethinking on the issue of stamp and *mokhtear* laws in force in the Santal Parganas and he did not find them desirale. To him, the introduction of the Civil Code (Act VIII of 1859) was not also of any advantage. As to the Act X of 1859 (Rent Law), all rent questions had been decided in accordance with that even before it was regularly introduced and he was of opinion that extension of any of these Acts had not affected the grounds of the dissatisfaction which was said to exist. The *Manjhee* question was at the bottom of all the rent trouble. He bewailed the lot of Santals who were stupid to consider; and so when *Manjhi* agreed to an exorbitant increase of rent, the Santal *Raiyots* generally allowed him to increase their rents in some proportion. Wood was directed to inquire into the matter and strongly urged that Santals be not led to look to any relief except through the courts. In 1860 or even in 1859 the Government interfered in the Hindwah business and the result ever since has been an impression in the Santal mind, that, in coalition and agitation they could get the Government to interfere again.

Money's memorandum in this regard is a monumental document so far as the willingness of one of the highest officer of the Government to do the rethinking is concerned. This is a fine piece of administrative document showing the anxiety of even Governor-General-in-Council for better administration of tribal areas as well as for the need to rectify past mistakes. He considered the affairs in Santal Parganas really worse than they were represented in papers.

> "I own that I have risen from the perusal of these documents with no other feeling than that of indignation.
>
> It is hardly possible to believe that such things could have taken place under the *very eyes of the series of Commissioners and officiating Commissioners of Bhagalpur*; that they were not brought to the notice of the late Lieutenant-Governor on the spot, and that this system of oppression should be allowed to go on for so many years certainly since 1862 without, as far as I know, it ever having been made known to the Government of India."

The mistake made by Sir Cecil Beadon and his extraordinary conduct, wherein by one stroke of the pen he appeared to have reversed the policy that was laid down for the Santal Parganas after the insurrection, appeared quite inexplicable to Money. He wrote —

> "Can any one, after reading the six causes of complaints stated in Mr. Cosserat letter come to any other conclusion than that there can hardly be found a greater instance of keener and more diabolical oppression having been practised and all this is practised on estates leased by our own Courts of Wards? This state of things which seems to give rise to no surprise or uneasiness or even regret, in the minds of the late or present Commissioners of Bhagalpur. . . . It is almost too horrible to think that the same people who rebelled in 1855 — should be again driven into insurrection, and that there is more than a probability that we shall be obliged to order our troops to go out and shoot poor ignorant savages who have certainly the balance of right on their side."
>
> ". . . . I wish to give no detailed opinion on these papers at present, further than to say that I am prepared to support any proceedings however strong which should be calculated to stop these inequities. I am prepared to separate the Santal Parganas at once from the Division of Bhagalpur. I am prepared, if it be thought advisable, to extend the provisions of the Act of Parliament

of last year to the whole of this District. I am prepared to place the ablest and most determined officers we can find in the Non Regulation Districts of India in charge of the Parganas. I am prepared to break every lease that has been made by the Court of Wards and to place the estates directly under the Court, and if this cannot be done legally to bring them up the Commissioner of the Parganas, having the principal voice in their management. I am prepared to take the strongest precaution to prevent these oppressions from extending into the Damin and the other portions of the Parganas which are now happily free. I am prepared to agree to Mr. Cosserat proposal in his letter of the 4th June, 1871. In short, I am prepared to take any step to prevent these poor honest aboriginals from being destroyed by the neglect of our officers to the concurrent action of Courts of Law, the avarice of European and Native Zamindars and rapacious money lenders who make use of our laws to plunder and destroy the ignorant and the poor."[50]

To this T. F. Stephens,[51] another member of the Council noted:

"I agree with His Excellency, and I have only to add that I regard the Advocate General's opinion on which the proceedings were founded as altogether absurd. If it were correct, the only effect of it would be that we must consent in carrying out the words "except in the Santal Parganas" etc. We should stultify ourselves if we permitted such miserable quibbles to be perverted to such oppressive purposes."

To this another senior member of the Council Sir John Strachey also agreed and was prepared to adopt any measures required to put a stop to these "abominable iniquities".

This anxiety in the highest echeleons of the Government was commensurate with the wind of change that the then supreme government was experiencing. Bengal required arousing and there had been considerable friction between a Conservative Lieutenant Governor and a Supreme Government bent on reforms.[52] Thus contrary to the precedent, the choice of Lieutenant-governorship fell on a non-Bengal officer an avowed reformer for a particular purpose of effecting a period of active reform. The appointment of an avowed reformer as their ruler was not likely to be popular in the conservative circles of Bengal and the new Lieutenant Governor's energy, ability and masterfulness were soon felt throughout the province. Buckland wrote "There has not been before, and there has not been since, such a period of active reform as the 37 months during which he administered the local Government".

The new Lieutenant Governor of Bengal was Sir George Campbell who considered this matter and referred the matter of the effect of the provision of Act XXXVII of 1855 which excluded the territory from the operation of any law subsequently passed in which it is not especially mentioned. But he also considered that officers had large powers which if they exercised under the law should enable them to protect the people from very substantial injustice. He abhorred the idea that if any officer known or had reason to believe or suspect that injustice was being done was justified in waiting till a case was brought into the court. The Santal officers exercise all civil, criminal, and revenue powers under a law which especially relieves them from subordination to the ordinary tribunals and they may well interfere to do justice.[53]

The Lieutenant Governor was surprised to find that Act X of 1859 quoted as tying the hands of the officers and preventing their doing justice to the *Raiyots*, since, if worked as the framers intended, it is generally supposed to give a special protection to all those who have broken up the jungle and occupied the land for more than 12 years, as the Santals have. The Lieutenant Governor did not know that Act VIII of 1859 compelled the Courts to give a rate of interest beyond what may be deemed just and equitable according to the substantive law prevailing, which law, in the Santal Parganas, the Lieutenant Governor took to be "equity and good conscience".

In a similar letter to the Commissioner of Assam, the Lieutenant Governor considered that District officers should not raise and suggest difficulties. It was not for them to pick up legal holes and find legal flaws and to affect a pedantic legality. They should make the best of the situation.[54]

He also referred that some districts had been exempted from the regulations and acts to such a degree as to place the procedure, and even the substantive law, very much within the discretion of local officers, and to enable them to administer a broad equity, and even whether law is more defined, the combination of civil, criminal and revenue powers in the same officers given much opportunity for tempering a too harsh administration of any law. Above and beyond or it may rather be said before law, is the legitimate influence which a good District officer may and should exercise.

Instead of harshly referring a foreign savage to the courts, the Deputy Commissioner might make a suit for the restitution of conjugal rights or a criminal case of adultery, or an action of breach of promise a very simple affair for him, by making out his petition summoning the opposite side promptly, and administering justice, which may be rapid and complete without ceasing to be legal.

The Lieutenant Governor did not think that to be within the law it is necessary to be slow, exacting and unintelligible to simple people on the contrary he believed that if one officer knows how to go the right way about it, he may do much prompt and vigorous justice within the law, especially as has been said above when he combines all powers in his own person. The Lieutenant Governor trusted that there were legal difficulties enough without their being raised by the officers entrusted with the administration of frontier districts and he would not permit them to raise unnecessary legalities.

Thus it was plain that all difficulties of the Santals were due to the change of system of administration in Santal Parganas. After the Santal insurrection of 1855, it had been intended to exclude the Santal Parganas from the operation of the General Acts, but that district had gradually drifted more or less, under the ordinary law and procedure. It appeared to the Lieutenant Governor Campbell that the Santal had good ground for complaint and he earnestly urged a reversion to the non-regulation system of administration. The Government of India agreed that the indiscriminate extension of some Acts to the Santal Parganas had worked much mischief and that a peculiar and simpler form of administration was required. On Campbell's recommendations, a Regulation[55] was passed under the Statute 33 Vic. C 3 for the peace and good government of the Santal Parganas. This regulation gave the Lieutenant Governor full powers to appoint officers, to make a settlement of landed rights, to restore dispossessive *manjis* and others, to settle rents and to record the customs and usages of the people. It also introduced a usury law limiting the accumulation of interest on debts, and it laid down what laws were to be in force in the Parganas, and what were left to the discretion of Government to introduce or withdraw as found desirable from time to time.

NOTES

1. B. H. Baden-Powel, *The Land Systems of British India*. Vol. I (Oxford, 1892), p. 187.

2. *Ibid.*, pp. 286-87.
3. Letter No. 203 dated 7th May 1861 from J. D. Gordon, Junior Secretary, Government of Bengal to W. Grey, Secretary, Government of India.
4. *Ibid.*, para 6.
5. *Ibid.*, para 8.
6. Letter No. 942 dated 10th May 1861 from W. Grey, Secretary, Government of India to J. D. Gordon, Junior Secretary, Government of Bengal.
7. Letter dated 18th May 1861 from W. S. Setton-Karr, Secretary, Home Department, Government of Bengal.
8. Text in English translation

   "A man of mine went yesterday to Guddadhur, who describes his place as well as Nulhuty (from the Darogah of which he has received information) to be in a disturbed state, and warns us to be on our guard. You are therefore requested to set out for this place without a moments delay. The extent to which men's minds are excited cannot be adequately described in a letter. If I have to attend the wedding, no one will remain in the house. I have intelligence as far as source. Similar disorders are rife everywhere. Everyone is selling the grain or rice he has; the same is the state in all places. We cannot do anything unless you come over. The minds of the people of this part of the country are in an unsettled state. Come to us as soon as you receive this. Be on your guard on the way, and tear this note after perusal.

   P. S. Ramdyal being made aware of the contents of this note has reached this place by a force journey."
9. Extract from demi-official letter dated 9th May, 1861 from H. A. R. Alexander, Magistrate of Beerbhum to Plowden, Commissioner, Burdwan District.
10. Letter No. 8 dated 24th May, 1861 from W. Le. F. Robinson, Officiating Commissioner, Santal Parganas to the Secretary, Government of Bengal.
11. List of Bands expenditure Rs. 5,648 -Annas 2-Pie 1 appearing as annexure to the above letter.
12. Demi-official Letter dated 7th May, 1861 from Plowden to W. S. Seton-Karr Secretary, Government of Bengal.
13. Demi-official Letter dated 6th May, 1861 *Ibid.*
14. Same as No. 12 above.
15. Demi-official Letter dated 6th May, 1861 from Plowden (Source : Home (Public) 6th June 1861 No 26-28).
16. Same as No. 12 above.
17. Demi-official Letter dated 9th May, 1861 from Plowden to Secretary, Government of Bengal.
18. Demi-official Letter dated 10th May, 1861 from Plowden to W. S. Seton-Karr, Secretary, Government of Bengal.
19. Same as No. 17 above.
20. Letter No. 180 dated 11th May, 1861 from W. C. Taylor, Assistant Commissioner, Santal Parganas to Brown Wood, Deputy Commissioner, Santal Parganas.
21. Examination of Soonder Manjhee appearing as enclosure with demi-official letter dated 10th May, 1861 from Plowden to W. S. Setton-Karr, Secretary, Government of Bengal.
22. *Ibid.*
23. Same as No. 18 above.
24. Same as No. 3 above.

25. Same as No. 10 above.
26. Same as No. 18 above.
27. Same as No. 10 above.
28. Same as No. 21 above.
29. Letter No. 1 dated 26th July, 1861 from G. N. Yule to J. D. Gordon, Junior Secretary, Government of Bengal.
30. *Ibid.*
31. *Ibid.*, para 4.
32. Letter dated 7th June, 1861 from C. H. Barnes to W. Le. F. Robinson, Officiating Commissioner, Santal Parganas.
33. Letter No. 2887A dated 14th November, 1861 from E. H. Lushington, Secretary, Government of Bengal to the W. Grey, Secretary, Home Department (Judicial) Government of India.
34. Letter No. 1113 dated 8th June, 1861 from W. Grey. Secretary, Home Department (Judicial), Government of India to E. H. Lushington, Secretary, Government of Bengal.
35. *Ibid.*
36. Letter No. 337 dated 20th June, 1861 from J. D. Gordon, Junior Secretary, Government of Bengal to the Officiating Commissioner, Santal Parganas.
37. C. E. Buckland, *Bengal under the Lieutenant Governors*, Calcutta 1901. p. 485.
38. Letter No. 519 dated 22nd June, 1871 from Brown Wood, Deputy Commissioner, Santal Parganas, to the Officiating Under Secretary, Government of Bengal. Enclosed with this was letter as shown at No. 39 below.
39. Letter dated 19th June, 1871 from H. Rattary, Deputy Magistrate, Dumka to Brown Wood, Deputy Commissioner Santal Parganas.
40. *Ibid.*
41. Letter dated 28th May, 1871 from Brown Wood, Deputy Commissioner, Santal Parganas, to H. R. Madock, Commissioner, Bhagalpur Division.
42. Letter dated 3rd June, 1871 *Ibid.*
43. *Ibid.*
44. *Ibid.*
45. *Ibid.*
46. *Ibid.*
47. Letter dated 11th June, 1871 from H. Rattary, Deputy Collector, Dumka to Brown Wood, Deputy Commissioner, Santal Parganas.
48. Letter dated 14th June, 1871 from Blumhardt, Deputy Collector, Deoghar to Deputy Commissioner, Santal Parganas.
49. *Fort William Consultations* dated 21st June, 1871.
50. *Ibid.*, dated 10th July, 1871.
51. *Ibid.*
52. C. E. Buckland, p. 484.
53. Letter dated 28th June 1871 from S.C. Bayley, Officiating Secretary, Judicial Department Government of Bengal to Commissioner of Bhagalpur and Santal Parganas.
54. Letter dated 28th June 1871 from S. C. Bayley, Secretary, Judicial Department, Government of Bengal to Commissioner, Assam.
55. C. E. Buckland, p. 486.

7

KHERWAR MOVEMENT, 1874-1942

THE WORD "*Kherwar*" comes from an old and very well known root "*Khair*", which means "man". The origin of the word "*Khair*" according to Skresfrud may be traced in the names of numerous tribes and places all over India, such as *Khairagar* (an old Santal fort), *Kherias* (of Nagpur), *Kurmis* (of Manbhoom district), *Kharias* (of Singhbhum), *Kharwars* (of Mirzapur district), *Korwas* (of Chota Nagpur), *Karkos* (of Madhya Pradesh), *Kol*, *Kolhe*, *Kodaskili* (of Chota Nagpur), *Hor* (Santals), *Hadi* (a low caste Hindu), *Garos* (of Assam) etc.[1] In addition to this, the word *Kherwar* is also to represent an idea. It is the ancient tribal name of the Santal. To them it is inseparably associated with the golden era of their history when they lived in *Champa* in absolute independence and has no rent or tribute to pay but only a small offering to their leaders by virtue of their office.[2] For the Santals, the Kherwarism is a passionate appeal to the past as well as an ideal to shape the present which in essence always means heavy borrowing from the dominant Hindu culture to improve their position. This is an idea which kept Santals in a state of conflict for a very long period of time. W.B. Oldham, the Deputy Commissioner of the Santal Parganas, at the time of the outburst in 1881 reported to the Government that the name Kherwar involves the necessity of their being in hope and heart the opponent of the Government.[3]

In heart of their hearts the Santals cherished an agrarian dream which was strongly connected with the *Santal Raj.* Skrefarud wrote:

> "The Santals have ever-since their glorious days of Champa in all their wanderings sighed for their lost liberty and this chronic yearning had sometimes, in the presence of foreign power, found expression in an appeal to arms in order to throw off the unbearable yoke. Such was also the case in 1855, when Sidho and Kanu, the ring-leaders of the rebellion, incited their followers by reminding them of the halcyon days of their Kherwar forefathers, and

contrasting it with the grinding tyranny under which their posterity laboured."[4]

Since the golden days in Champa, the Santals felt that they had had no opportunity to act *en bloc*, but the settlement in the *Damin* area and adjoining districts made it possible. During all these years the dream of the *Santal Raj* had been kept alive, and when leaders arose they were ready to act. It must also be added that their knowledge of the mighty power of their rulers was very limited. It was beyond their comprehension to think that their plans to establish their own *Raj* would end in fiasco. The rebellion was quelled, but the unsatiated yearning for freedom continued among the Santals.

Therefore, when after Santal Hul they found that there was left much in the reforms initiated by the Government to satisfy the Santals, they found it obligatory to raise the standard of revolt in 1860 and in 1871. They were quelled and some reforms followed. But Santals could not be fed long on false promises. Hardly had the embers of 1871 commotion in Santal Parganas died down when in the fall of 1874 there was yet another serious outburst of the Kherwar Movement under the leadership of Bhagirath Manjhi of the village Tardiha in the Godda subdivision. He had also taken part in the rebellion of 1855.[5] He had been imprisoned in 1868 for seditious conduct in trying to disturb people's mind by threatening an outbreak.[6]

This outbreak is said to have been partly the outcome of the excitement attending the Settlement Operations and partly from the Kherwar movement. Disaffection manifested itself in resistance to the payment of rent and attempts to form a kind of political organisation. Bhagirath Manjhi and Gyan Parganait were the moving spirit of the rebellion. Fuchs gave a plausible explanation for this outbreak:

> "This tradition of a former purer belief ordinarily does not trouble the Santals, but the dormant memory of God is awakened when anything extraordinary happens, a famine or epidemic, for instance. Then the Santals feel guilty of abandoning their Supreme God and worshipping the spirits, and they vow to reform themselves. This also explains the spasmodic character of the movement. In times of comparative plenty and prosperity very little is heard of it, during times of distress the movement revives."[7]

Bhagirath Manjhi's Movement (1874)

The year 1874 was also the year of great scarcity and famine. The Santals were in great distress. During these critical days, Bhagirath appeared with his Kherwar idea by which he wanted to attract the attention of hungry masses among the Santals. He told the people that he was sent by God to redress their grievances, to fight for them, to mitigate their sufferings and to establish the *Santal Raj* which will be free from scarcity, tyranny and oppression on the Santals. He ordered them to meet at Bowsee, the place where he was anointed as a king. He received rent payments, and issued receipts to the people and asked them not to pay any dues to the Government or the *Zamindar*.

This movement became very popular, and there were at least some followers of Bhagirath in every village of the Rajmahal Damin. Thousands of Santals went to Tardiha, where a shrine had been established with a Santal *Pandit* in charge. Bhagirath ordered his followers to kill their fowls and pigs with a view to purification. He was anointed King of the proposed new *Santal Raj*.[8]

Bhagirath became a *Babaji* (a hermit). In the early morning he gave his audience to the people who came to him each bringing a leaf-cup full of sun dried rice (not the ordinary rice boiled before husking), milk in a *lota,* a bit of betel-nut and one pice. These were placed before Bhagirath who listened to what they had to say, but kept quiet till all had put in their petitions. Bhagirath then would harangue them saying:

> "You have now brought your petition to me, I shall lay them before God (*Chando*). All will be well with anyone whose petition please God, if it does not, he must come again. Come twice, or even oftener, make your petition to me, and I shall pray to Him for you. You must also continue to pray to Him and then you will reap the benefit. If anyone is in serious trouble, he must keep watch throughout the night."[9]

Next morning, before sunrise, Bhagirath would ask the people whether they had kept watch. If they said that they had slept, he scolded them saying that they had come only to eat. If they said they had watched, he asked them whether they had seen *Chando* come down and heard him talk with him. This, of course, was news to them, and they were treated to a new harangue, Bhagirath charging them with lying and telling them that it was their own fault that they got no help. Then he started preaching to them, the subject-matter of his address being very much the same as that of Ten Commandments in Christianity. He charged them to live by his precepts and not to let evil come into their lives otherwise they would remain deprived of God's blessing.

This account is based on Bodding's description of Bhagirath. He noted further that as time went on his style of preaching was somewhat altered, probably because the people did not attain their wishes, and the attendance fell off. He had to find something to explain the one and counteract the other. He said that all evil had to be purged and all should come to him with one heart. "We or our fathers have sinned utterly when our sins are fully atoned for, we shall be the owners of the country." Bodding also wrote that he collected a good deal of money, of which he and his helpers kept most. His account is full of such accusation. To meet famine of 1874 Burma rice was imported. Bhagirath told the people that they could see how God was working for them. The *Sahibs* were afraid. The rice which they brought was rice formerly given by the Santals to the *bongas,* and now brought back under some pretext. It was for the Santals to eat, but they must be very careful not to let fowls or pigs pollute it, and they should bathe daily and then cook their food. Now, if they were only careful, was the time for them to get the land. In the times of Sidho and Kanu it had been God's desire to give the country to the Santals, but they had sinned, especially in having relations with women of other races, and so God had refused to help them. Now they must act otherwise and clean themselves. After this, the people commenced to kill their pigs and fowls, but they were generally wise enough to eat them. From this time the followers of Bhagirath appear to have taken the name of *Kherwar* or *Sapha Hor* (pure men).[10]

Bhagirath's teachings assumed more and more a political slant where he began to proclaim that the land which the Santals cultivated belonged by right to them and that no Government could demand taxes from them. In his meetings Bhagirath used to pass a bowl of rice around asking "who has created this grain"? His disciples answered "God has created it". Then Bhagirath put his second question: "And who has ploughed the ground and sown the seed?" "We did the ploughing and the sowing," was the angry answer of the disciples. Bhagirath then summed up: "If we did the ploughing and sowing and

God let the crops grow, why should we pay taxes to the Government?" Bodding continues to tell that the people who were under Bhagirath's influence thought that the rice imported into the famine-stricken areas was a free gift. They carted it from the distributing centres to their villages. Before they took it into the village street, they sacrificed and ate a black goat at its entrance. After this they took the rice to the *manjhiasthan*, divided it according to their numbers, and commenced cooking in Hindu style. When the time came for paying back the Government advances, they began to disbelieve Bhagirath. He still tried to delude them, but was arrested and imprisoned, and for the time being the movement collapsed. With this also for the time being subsided the Santal urge for complete freedom and an Eldrado on earth of which they had dreamt so fondly. Deprived of their leader, the rebels did not dare strike and a great catastrophe was thus averted.[11]

The Government took strong action to check the movement. Bhagirath was arrested and sentenced to two years' imprisonment. The Deputy Commissioner Boxwell demolished the shrine set up at Taldiha, carried away the image, and took the Santal *Pandit*, Bhagirath's brother Ram Gyan Parganait and an upcountry Hindu Matadin with him to Dumka.[12] An extra detachment of troops from 4th Native Infantry from Bhagalpur was stationed at Dumka and new police posts were established. Ultimately the troops were withdrawn in 1877 when the agitation was thought to have subsided.

Bhagirath had several imitators, who were also called *Babaji* or in some cases *Guru* and worked much as he did. Several of them told the people that they had been commissioned by God to work for a certain time, that is, for five years when the period expired they ceased working. "It is clear", wrote Bodding "that most of them had come into contact with Christianity. They declared that they did not cure people but God did. Only those, who believed were healed, and doubters would not benefit in any way. The people must have clean life and not use filthy language".[13] Some of the *Babajis* started regular meeting with the people on Sunday, and prohibited Sunday labour for them and their cattle. They further directed the people to be kind to their animals, not to strike them on the head or on the bone (otherwise they would cry to God, who would punish the offenders), and to leave pasture grounds for them. Out of them introduced Rama, the Hindu deity, identifying Him with God. At the end of his Sunday meeting harangue he called out with all his might, "*Ram Chando duhai*" and all those present did the same. Some, but only a minority, gave the movement a political aspect by instigating the people to refuse payment of rent for their holdings, on the ground that land which they had reclaimed from waste belonged solely to them. Nearly all these and later *Babajis* appeared first in the vicinity of Godda and thence spread southwards and eastwards.

Bodding noted that little was heard of the movement after the imprisonment of some of its leaders, but Hodne on the testimony of Skresfrud believed that after his release in 1877 Bhagirath, though settled down to become a quiet and peaceful religious reformer, entirely avoiding all political activities, but he continued his work in a secret way. In any case, as it was disclosed later, there did exist a distinct organisation of the Kherwars which was silently spreading and strengthening. Bhagirath died in 1879 about a year before a new outburst took place in connection with the Census of 1881, an outburst which was more violent than any other since the rebellion of 1855.[15]

Dubia Gossain Movement 1880

It is easy to suppress army by superior organisation and force; but it is impossible to kill an army of ideas with any kind of physical force. The invasion of idea is always irresistible and consequently the Kherwar idea could not be eradicated from the Santal mind. Kherwar ideals and the Kherwar movement were kept alive quite imperceptibly by others. A new Bhagirath named Dubia Gossain or *Babaji* appeared among them to preach Kherwarism. As such Fuchs may not be correct when he wrote that with the throwing of Bhagirath and other leaders of Kherwar movement into the jail, the hope of Santals for independence and a paradise on earth of which they had dreamt so fondly died. Rather Oldham, Boxwell's successor (who with his thorough grasp of Santal problem was considered a veritable *Avatar* for the people) as Deputy Commissioner of Santal Parganas had a trying time in quelling this revival of the Kherwar movement. He experienced a great trouble during the preparation for the Census of 1881.

Accidently the new disturbances had its seat outside the Santal Parganas, at Jagesar,[16] in the Hazaribagh District of Chota Nagpur. The new messiah Dubia Gossain had a thorough knowledge of Santal character and their Kherwar hopes. The saint had travelled through several districts in which Santals were located and by austerities which he practised succeeded in attracting the notice of people. He had three Santal agents, one of whom had been employed in the police and could write a little. Those men spread all sorts of rumours in the district and in an excitable people such as Santals and others, it was natural that the wonderful accounts of *Babaji's* supernatural powers were widely disseminated. "These ran their course like wildfire, and caused the utmost consternation among the ignorant. They were followed up and intensified by a perfect avalanche of letters, written on small scraps of papers which were passed on from village to village." These letters contained little else than an order for all to present themselves without delay before the *Babaji* or *Gossain*, but along with each letter came a verbal message ordering slaughtering of all pigs and fowls, the forsaking of the old deities, the giving up of drinking and general conforming to the usages and customs of the Hindus. To enforce obedience it was predicted that calamities such as the deluge of fire, rain, etc., would overtake all those who neglected or refused to conform to the new order of things, and instances were freely quoted where disobedience was followed by immediate retributions. A promise was also given that if all were in readiness by *Dassehra* the *Raj* would then be made over to the followers of *Babaji,* and there would be no more rack-renting or oppression. Rent for as much ground as could be ploughed by a pair of buffaloes would be one rupee, and by a pair of bullocks, eight *annas*. Threats against *Mahajans* were not wanting and the new era held out little prospect of wealth and happiness for them (Mahajans).[17]

In this movement *Kurumbis* or *Kurmis* were also included. They are a semi-Hinduised tribe or caste found in large numbers in some districts of Chota Nagpur. They are evidently of the Kolarian stock, as their name and many of their customs testify, but they have long been merged amongst the low-caste Hindus and their remote connection with the Santals can not have the reason for their now being classed with them. That they keep pigs and fowls, which strict Hindus regard as unclean is more likely to account for it. Be that as it may, under the new arrangement they and the Santals were to intermarry, and thus a new caste would spring into existence.[18]

Campbell also discussed the form of worship of this sect. The Sun was still held in reverence and worshipped daily, but the gods of *Zamindars* (every Zamindar had his own particular deity which was supposed to keep watch and ward over his estate and family) seemed to be unrecognised. Offerings of milk, rice, flour, *ghee*, etc., were to be made, but there was no unanimity as to whom they were to be presented. They regarded Sunday as a day of rest. Hindu rules as to clean and unclean food were vigorously observed. Dancing in the village *ahmelas* and at the shrines of Hindu dieties, beating of certain kinds of drums and intoxicating liquor of all kinds were forbidden and a higher morality inculcated; the fact that evil thoughts as well as evil deeds were sin, was recognised. Brahmins were also employed to perform certain ceremonies.

It was Kherwar idea which attracted his followers to Dubia Gossain and gave him influence. According to Barlow, the Officiating Commissioner of Bhagalpur and Santal Parganas, Dubia Gossain had a large influence among the 18,000 Santals of whole Deoghar and Jamtara jurisdiction and the border of the Dumka subdivision bounding them. Fear and superstition made it easy for the new movement to spread until it filled the whole land.

From Hazaribagh the new Kherwarism travelled to the Santal Parganas and turned violent there. The Sub Divisional Officer of Dumka was besieged in his own tent by a howling mob for a whole night. The subdivisional bungalow at Jamatra was burnt down while the Deputy Commissioner was present. Cosserat, the Officer-in-charge of the Census for the *Damin-i-koh,* was surprised and taken prisoner at Katikhund.[19] Objections were taken to the numbering of the houses and of the people to record their names, while the fact that the final enumeration was to be carried out at night lent colour to the apprehension that government meditated some widespread policy of violence. The census operation was mistaken for yet another occasion when fresh tax would be levied and/or the Santals would be forced to become Christians and/or that their women would be branded and/or that the men would be deported or sent to the Afghan War.[20] Before the final enumeration, set for the night of the 17th February, 1881, the whole Santal Parganas was in a state of unrest and the Government feared a general uprising. In order to overawe the Santals, a body of military police was posted in the district and a field force of 4500 cavalry and infantry was sent up under Colonel Gordon. Troops marched through the district, and these measures proved effective in preventing any further disturbance. In order not to provoke the Santals, the final enumeration was cancelled by the Governor-General.[21] In other districts with a Santal population, the final enumeration in Santal villages was made during the day instead of night. On an enquiry it was found that the old Kherwar idea and Kherwars were responsible for the entire resistance to the census operation. Commissioner Barlow wrote :

> "I think that we must recognise more than we have done, the features of the Santal character, that, whatever may be his outward manner for the movement he is by constitution politically discontented and aiming at a change. Moreover a system has been formulated under the term "Kherwar" which, by mixing up national ideas along with matters connected with social and religious reforms, presents a view thoroughly attractive to the Santal mind, and has created an organisation necessarily opposed to government. This organisation has, in case of the Census, already been once used against government, and is capable of being used again. . . . Without laying any claim to such detailed knowledge of facts concerning it as was subsequently disclosed in Mr. Skrefrud's letters to *the Statesman,* I, from the commencement, myself regarded the movement as dangerous, in the direction and for much the same reason as were indicated in those letters, have the repressive measures were carried out against the leaders in the early stages under my direction."[22]

Barlow also reported that the Kherwars were a closely united community. They had their different head centres, and between these there was a well-organised system of communication so that they could send their message quickly and quietly over great distance.

It was reported that during the Census trouble, the Kherwars gained a host of new followers. They insisted on being listed as Kherwars, and not as Santals. According to the statistics of the Deputy Commissioner, there were 40,960 Kherwars in Santal Parganas in 1881. Of these, 5,000 were new Kherwars, the rest dating back to the Bhagirath movement. Barlow commented that "those who had entered themselves in the census papers as Kherwars would be of course only be of the most pronounced views. There are doubtless many sympathisers who did not enter themselves as Kherwars".[23] Therefore, Barlow suspected that apart from these hard core of 50,960, a large number of sympathisers of Kherwarism were there.

Campbell narrated as to how the influence of Dubia Gossain

waned. He wrote that promoters of Dubia Gossain overshot the mark by fixing the date on which the new order of things was to be inaugurated. The *Babaji's* blessings produced no effect, and another date this time three years in advance, had to be given on which the fields would begin to yield their fruits without labour of ploughing, and plenty would flow into the lap of him who killed his pigs and fowls and gave a handsome donation to *Dub-Babaji*.[24] And to crown it all, the *Babaji* had gone and left the dupes in lurch. Many who had gone to pay their respect to him had returned saying he was not to be found. His has been a rich harvest, as he levied a sum of about one rupee and eight *annas* (Rs.1.50) upon each family who adored him.

With the bitter experience of Santal Rising and Bhagirath's Movement, the government was not to be complacent in dealing with this new upsurge and naturally show of force was made. Commissioner Barlow started rounding up the professed Kherwars under his jurisdiction. He found that those who were shown as prominent members of the faction and as secret converts of Dubia were reluctant to admit the fact. But the Kherwar idea had reached the innermost recesses of their hearts. The *Parganait* of Narayanpur reported to the Commissioner regarding their attitude. He mentioned that the people cried, "We are *Kherwars* and *Rajahs*, and are our own *hakims*. We obey no *hakims' order*.[25] The most noticeable fact ascertained by Commissioner Barlow was, however, that notwithstanding the excitement which the visitors to Dubia Gossain had felt and spread, professed Kherwars were exceedingly few. In the whole Ghati taluq there were only two, one of whom he visited. In Jamtara taluq Pargannah Pabia, the most prominent of them were Gulia whom he arrested and convicted and one another resident of his village.

This meagre number of the professed Kherwars in the jurisdiction of the Commissioner of Bhagalpur Division may be due to the fact that in the face of repressive measures adopted by the government and in the absence of Dubia Gossain, the Kherwars might have found themselves disillusioned and many of them might have willingly gone underground. The Census Reports of 1911 and 1921 and the Sapha Hor movement in 1939 demonstrate that the Kherwar idea continued to prosper and it is not possible to agree that Kherwarism died a natural death with the exit of Dubia Gossain.

Like Bhagirath, Dubia Gossain had his imitators which was noticed by Commissioner Barlow. He found that at the village of Junatpore in the Jartal Taluq some 20 miles west-north of Dumka, a devotee had set up and began his business working his predecessors in the chord, though in most vague and general terms. He had associated with him a scribe, a Bhuinya by caste and had spread through the country numberless "*Patias*" or unsigned letters which allude to the excitement of the time, and exhorted the Santals to be as brothers, and take the deity's name daily. One such document was actually placed by the Santals of one whole taluq as an authority or *perwannah* to resist the Census. However, when coerced by the government, the *Babaji* in alarm to save himself, professed that he was on the side of order, and issued *perwannahs* under his signature enjoining obedience to the authorities.

The name of *Babaji* was Tribhuwan Road in the government record. He was a reputed Santal. His name indicates that he belonged to the Hindus, or Hinduised tribe. His gains were the offerings of a kid and one rupee by each of his visitors. His influence like that of Dubia Gossain had not taken sufficient shape for his adherents to profess themselves Kherwars. As in 1879, the rigid and fanatic members of the sect, who refused to be called by any other name and who adopted in full the forms of the creed, the idea of which was common in its different degrees to all, were found in the greatest numbers in the *Damin-i-koh* of the Pakour Sub-division. The Commissioner noted in the margin that the name of the *Babaji*, the imitator of Dubia Gossain was Karoo Manjhi, and Tribhubhan was one of the *Mohuries*. Karoo was thought by Webnot to be perhaps the man of that name who, in 1865 was sentenced for putting himself forward as *Thakur*. It was also said he was once a sepoy or constable.[26]

The Government took severe punitive action and Dubia Gossain was taken prisoner and was deported to Lucknow far away from Santals as a political prisoner.[27] Other ring-leaders were also arrested during and after the census trouble and sentenced to imprisonment or deportation. The *Manjhis* who had had any connection with the Kherwars were removed from their official position, and the whole question of Santal administration was taken up for reconsideration. In order to break down the clannish feeling of the Santals, the Deputy Commissioner Oldham of Santal Parganas proposed to admit foreigners into the Damin area and introduce the regular police into the whole of Santal Parganas.

The proposal of admitting foreigners into the Damin area was stoutly opposed by Boxwell. The former Deputy Commissioner and famous for his sympathy and understanding of the Santals. He wrote:

> "If we let the Dikus into the Damin we break up the Santal nationality. Then the language will go. Then, without any particular religious change the tribe becomes a low caste of Hindus. They can never rise. In the other districts the same process will go on faster, because there will be no Santal headquarters. In two generation we shall have added one and a half millions to the dregs of Hinduism. . . . If we keep out the Dikus, we declare that we are going to preserve the Santal from absorption. Therefore we should adhere to the old policy of the Damin for the Santal."[28]

This formed the kernel of the government policy. A regular police was introduced in Godda and Pakaur Sub-divisions of Santal Parganas and special reserve of armed police was kept in Santal Parganas till 1893 in order to put down any uprising. The extension of Police system on the model of that existing in Deoghar Subdivision to the *Zamindari* portion of the Sub-divisions of Godda, Pakaur and Rajmahal was proposed which was approved by Commissioner Barlow, Commissioner Munro, the Inspector-general of Police and subsequently the Government of Bengal.[29] Consequently, a police station at Rajmahal with independent outposts at Sahibganj and Barharwa, a police station at Pakaur with independent outposts at Mahagama and Poreyahat were established.

In spite of these measures in day-to-day affairs Deputy Commissioner Oldham and his successor Carstairs remained the true and loyal interpretors of the principles of administration which found expression in Act XXXVII of 1855 and Regulation III of 1872. Their belief and sympathy in non-regulation system grew all the more stronger in years that followed recurrent commotions in Santals Parganas. To quote McPherson :

> "If Mr. Wood and Mr. Boxwell were the makers of Santal system of Mr. Oldham and Mr. Carstairs may well be styled the 'guardians' of the same. Mr. Oldham had Mr. Barlow for his Commissioner throughout his incumbency, but in Mr. Carstairs' time there were frequent changes in the Commissionership and all holders of the office were not permeated with an equal amount of

sympathy for the non-regulation system. Mr. Carstairs had to do many a battle for the principles on which the administration of his district was founded."[30]

Missionary Skresfrud and Kherwarism

As against these sympathetic and proven friends of the Santals, there were a few committed persons among the Santals who wanted to stamp out Kherwarism from their land, from their hearts, Skresfrud's letters and writings throw much light on the working of the minds of the Christian missionaries when Santals in different districts were permeated with Kherwar idea and ideals.

It was simply because the Kherwars took an anti-Christian standpoint from the beginning of Bhagirath's era. At a missionary conference in Calcutta, one of the C. M. S. missionaries told the audience about the Kherwar movement:

> "*Satan* (probably *Matadin*) tried his utmost six years ago to overthrow our work, when a Hindu, who was an ex-convict, converted a Santal to Hinduism and instigated him to do his utmost to influence his people. . . . This led us to open work among the Paharias."[31]

Skresfrud himself took an active part with crusading zeal to check the progress of the Kherwar movement. He wrote articles on the Santals and Kherwarism which were published in *The Englishman, The Statesman* and *The Hindu Patriot* during the year 1874 to 1881. His articles formed the part of Commissioner Barlow's report[32] to the government. The officials more or less depended upon these missionaries for the detailed knowledge regarding the episode and tried to believe them and act up to their advice perhaps without caring that the missionaries reports might be one-sided affair, a personal vendetta against those who opposed Christianity. Skresfrud called for a very strict policy in dealing with the Santals in general and Kherwars in particular because he felt that "especially towards the Seditious Kherwars. . . the reins have been too loose".[33] He was not happy with government resolution to abandon the enumeration on the 17th of February, 1881. He thought of them as "a thorn in the side of the Government" and advising Assistant Deputy Commissioner Smith as how to deal with the Kherwars, he suggested :

"When you have found them (the leaders),

1. Substitute for what I did, a sound *public flogging* the more Santal spectators the better, and have soldiers near if necessary, and let it be clearly known that the men are flogged for libelling the government by setting afloat such absurd and indecent rumours.
2. Tell the people that everyone who propagates this falsehood hereafter will be similarly beaten.
3. Send away the worst of the ring leaders as state prisoners after the flogging.
4. Deal with the Kherwars according to their deserts, and do not treat them any longer as a harmless, if not praiseworthy, socio-religious movement, because the religion is only a means towards an end with them — and that is nothing short of. . . their former Champa autonomy. . . . Only one meeting of all the Manjhis and Parganas of Nankar here at Ebenezar has been sufficient to expel the above rumours and thus preserve perfect peace and normal state of things. I have quieted the people of the Magistrate of Sewry at his request . . . and they were very much excited and first drove away the enumerators."[34]

Skresfrud looked upon Kherwars as a disturbing element. To him Kherwarism as "a rapid, socialistic, political agitation, the religion being only a means towards an end".[35] He regarded the Kherwars also as obstacles to his own personal endeavours in this cause. But mainly, he saw the Kherwars as a threat to the spread of Christianity among the Santals. This animosity against the Kherwar was perhaps responsible for his suggestion that Government should remove the privilege of brewing home-made liquor and libitium, at all seasons, and reduce the liquor shops still more both in order to obviate the main cause of their perpetual poverty . . . and as a punishment for the continual outbreaks against the government.[36] He did not like government decision to free Bhagirath and he proposed the Deputy Commissioner Wood to send him to his headquarters at Benigoria:

"If you would send him to me I would try my best to persuade him

> to leave his evil ways and join us, and through him and Dhoonoo who already is a Christian I think I would be able effectually to check the Sapha Hor movement . . . government would be freed from a great source of nuisance by Bhagirath becoming a Christian. What do you say to my proposal."[37]

Of course, Deputy Commissioner Wood preferred to keep silent on this idea.

When the new outburst of Kherwarism took place Skresfrud arranged a meeting at Benigoria to oppose the Kherwars. Here he claimed to have effectively exposed the Kherwar leader and his absurdities so much so that the Kherwar leader escaped beating by giving a feast the next day.[38] And yet some of the missionaries like Bodding and others would like to see in Kherwarism and Kherwar songs traces of such things which could prove that they were influenced by Christianity. Bodding felt that Bhagirath was either a fallen Christian or had been under Christian influence in a mission school.[39] But neither Stark nor Cole of the C. M. S. mission in whose area Bhagirath lived, in their reports to the government about the Kherwar Movement, mentioned anything about Bhagirath's connection with Christianity. Some stated that the movement was "instigated by the Brahamanical faction of the Hindus, as a countermove to the endeavours of Christian Missionaries to win over Santals to Christianity".[40] The Christian influence had shown a marked increase from 1870 to 1875 in the Santal Parganas. In 1874 a mass movement towards Christianity had taken place, and this progress continued in such a way that in the beginning of 1876, Skresfrud wrote to Sir W. Muir that the great progress had made the missionaries to believe that the whole tribe would come over the Christianity.[41] But Skresfrud found the progress of Christianity checked and this apprehension shattered his hopes. The responsibility for this set back was placed on the anti-Christian stance of Hinduised Kherwar movement. He assumed that religious element in Kherwarism was "only a means towards a political end". But it can be said with equal vehemence that Hinduisation of the Santals has been a long and continuous process which had its genesis in the very first contact between the two people. This started in Champa and since then they have been steadily coming nearer to Hinduism year by year.

The Hindu element was present also in the Kherwar movement of

1855, but it was relatively insignificant.[42] But it was not so at the time of Bhagirath movement in 1874. As a matter of fact, the Hindu influence was so much apparent that G. N. Barlow, the Commissioner of Bhagalpur and Santal Parganas and others even in March 1875 thought of the movement to be of a purely religious origin. Matadin ex-mutineer who was with Bhagirath in the prison, after his release associated himself with Bhagirath by becoming his friend, philosopher and guide. Boxwell wrote regarding him that "I have no doubt that this man's influence has given colour of Hinduism to Bhagirath's movement".[43] When Bhagirath was anointed king of the Santals, Matadin marked him, according to Hindu custom, with a red mark on his forehead. Pilgrimages to holy shrines, sacrificing and killing of certain animals, and adoption of Hindu purification ceremonies and of a *belatika* and the *poita* (the Brahminical holy thread) showed full adherence to Hindu principles and practices. The Hindu influence became still more marked in the movement of 1881 under Dubia Gossain. If we look to census enumerations of different years we will find that pace of Hinduisation increased rather than decreased as shown by Bodding in his researches in 1921.

Subsequently in 1891, the Kherwars did put up their show at the time of census enumeration and were successful in spreading facts believed by them among the Santals.[44] For example, they stated that the British rule was coming to an end; the Kherwars would rule in their place, no taxes would have to be paid, all Santals except Kherwars would be made Christians, the soil of the country being dark belonged to the dark skinned people and not to the whitemen, who would go back to their own country where the soil was white.

Babaji and Kherwarism

In 1897, when a famine visited Santal Parganas a pronounced and widespread recrudescence of the Kherwar movement surfaced up. Several Hindu practices like worship of *Babaji* and addressing everybody as father and mother and becoming vegetarian were found. A number of *Babajis* sprang up in Santal Parganas. People soon began to resort to a *Babaji* who would declare that he had received a command from God that the people were to use earth, *dhubi* grass and cow-dung ashes which would be blessed if they obeyed his commandments. These articles were divided into three parts, which were kept separate. One part had to be either drunk (mixed in water) or applied externally as the case might be. Another part had to be given to the cattle to make them give milk. A third part was to bring prosperity and to be used according to instructions given viz., it was to be mixed in water in a certain way and sprinkled all over the house wherever the inmates had or used or did anything. When taking it home, they had to eat it from clean utensils and after washing. The articles used have a symbolic meaning. The Santals instinctively felt the importance of symbolical action. In 1907 there were a large number of *Babajis* in the South of the Santal Parganas. Their disciples could be seen running, but never walking, from place to place. This was a symbolic action intended to impress the necessity of haste. Similarly in curing a witch the *Babaji* would use symbolic way of spitting and trampling on the figures of *bongas* etc. A *Babaji* was expected to be able to help each and everyone of them as he was taken to be a prophet, an intermediary between the supernatural and the material world.[45]

Bodding noted that becoming *Babaji* in some cases was a lucrative profession. He accused Bhagirath of making money. But he had also the example of *Bariar Babaji* who did not receive money.[46] The people threw it on the ground before him, and when his levee was over, he used to ask whose money had been lost. As no one answered, he said that he had no authority (i.e. no divine command) to take money, called the village policeman and ordered him to give it to the blind and the sick who had come, and also buy them food.

Skresfrud in 1880 wrote that there were already three different sects of the Kherwar movement.[47]

(i) the purist or real *Sapha Hors* worshipping *Singhbahini* (the principal goddess of the *Zamindars*) and the Sun and totally abstaining from drinking and dancing.
(ii) the *Fakirs* or *Babajees* whose profession was to traverse the country and beg.
(iii) the half hearted or *Bhelwaragars*, who, while, joining in all observances of the other Kherwars, retained their old customs also but substituted sweetmeats for animals in sacrificing.

This description conforms to that of Bodding about the three sects of the Kherwars, viz., the *Saphai,* the *Babajee* and the *Samras*, though certain changes might have taken place in the course of time.

Kherwarism and Quit India Movement

Dutta has also mentioned two sections of the Sapha Hors, the *Kherwar Santals* and the *Sadhu Santals*. He found that along with others the Sapha Hors both Santals and Paharias took part in 1942 movement in large number with profound zeal. The Sapha Hors were practising Hinduism by abstaining from drinking and meat-eating and hoisted flags, planted *Tulsi (Basil)* trees and chanted *Ramnam*. They formed a reformed section among the Santals and the Paharias. The so-called process of Hinduisation of Santals had ended in the Sapha Hors leading a purified life by not taking drinks and meat. They placed a white rectangular flag on the top of a bamboo pole much above the top of the house, and at the foot of each pole a platform was raised with a *Tulsi* plant standing on it. They chanted *mantras* to give offerings of sweet, sugar etc., but not animal sacrifice. Kashishwar Chakravarty, a pleader of Dinajpur but spirited Hindu zealot visited Rajmahal frequently about 1930. He found ready hearing from the *Saphas* among whom he preached. Calcutta's Hindu Mission was also brought to carry on spiritual work among the Santals which continued under the local leadership of Lambodar Mukherjee of Dumka.[49] Mukherjee and Sarbanand Misra were the two top-most Forward Block leaders of the District who took part in the political and social activities among Santals and Paharias and were interned at Motihari and Arrah respectively in February 1942. Bhagwan Das of Rajmahal was also associated with this kind of work. They succeeded in gaining adherents in different parts of the district, in spite of the harsh treatment of non-Santal Parganaits in the Damin area. At the village Kadma in Dhanbasa circle, the Santals under the inspiration of Lambodar Mukherjee worshipped an image of *Bharatmata* in December 1940.

Among other local leaders of the Sapha Hor movement, were Charan Murmu and Debu Murmu, both Members of the Legislative Assembly. Chandu Paharia of Chota Basho (Godda subdivision) started a similar movement among the Kuarbhag Paharia. Brijlal Dukania of Pakaur, also member of Legislative Assembly for sometime, had some influence on the Sapha Hors. Their other leaders, working chiefly in Pakaur Damin area, were Samai Santal of Kotaldih (Godda subdivision), Karga Santal and Khaira Santal of Pakaur Damin, and Budhrai Santal of Jethka (Alubera Bunglow in the Pakaur Damin). Lal Hembrom, Paika Murmu, Gopal Hansda, Bariar

Hembrom were the other leaders of the Santals. Bhade Hembrom, father of Lal Hembrom and Bariar Hembrom, died a martyr's death at Bhagalpur Camp Jail serving four years rigorous imprisonment. There was discontent among the Sapha Hors, as also among many other Santals, particularly from 1938 due to various anomalies in the general condition of these people. As the Indian National movement stood not only for political emancipation but also for eradication of such evils, many of them became naturally allied to it, enlisted themselves in the Congress fold, and played an important part in the Quit India Movement of 1942.

On 25th August, 1942 a party of people mostly of Sapha Hor Santals and Paharias under P. C. Patnaik and Shri Krishna Prasad, burnt the Dak Bunglow and the Forest Guard's quarters at Alubera and caused enormous damage. The same party proceeded to Dumarchi and set fire to the Dak Bunglow and the Forest guard's quarters there also. The Deputy Commissioner of the Santal Parganas reported on the 26th August 1942. "It is learnt that some Congressmen and forward Blockists are leading these mobs (Santals and Paharias). It is thus evident that the Sapha Hors in the Damin have started the mischief. They have been joined by some other Santals and Paharias and there is no doubt that in a very short time they will be joined by a large number of others. . . ." Stringent measures were taken against them.

Still the Sapha Hors under Lal Hembrom were found in the night of 30th August, 1942 at Jabardaha to plan the further programme of damaging bridges, culverts and the telegraph line along the Dumka-Rampurhat Road. The telegraph line was cut at the 20th mile on the subsequent day. Mrs. Usa Rani Mukherjee, wife of Lambodar Mukherjee was arrested with four wanted persons. On 1st September, 1942 many of the Sapha Hors under the leadership of Paika Manjhi held a meeting at village Kadma in the Dhanbhora circle in which they took a vow to continue damaging bridges, culverts, telegraph lines and liquor shops. When a military party visited the Sapha Hors, they absconded from their homes. Under the leadership of Lal Hembrom, the Sapha Hors burnt the liquor shops and blocked the roads. While attempting to burn a liquor shop at Palasi in Rajbandh circle the Sapha Hors were confronted with military force which opened fire and killed some persons (two according to Government estimate) and injured many others. The martyrs were Bayeman Tudu, Konka Hansda and Gurma Tudu. Among the injured were Bariar Hembram, Ragda

Murmu, Tumu Tudu, Nandlal Marandi. Lal Hembrom, Paika Murmu and others went underground. The British forces started mopping operations on the Sapha Hors and succeeded in arresting many out of whom several were awarded rigorous imprisonment. Shivu Murmu died in Dumka Jail and Lagu Hembrom died two days after his release from the jail.[50] This continued excitement among the Sapha Hors could be found even in 1943. A police party proceeded against them on the 21st April, 1943 and at Ranga Bunglow arrested one of them. Being already in excitement, the Sapha Hors attacked the police which opened fire injuring many of them. The Sapha Hors liberated their men from the clutches of the police. Naturally they were hunted out and arrested by the police. The renewed activities of Sapha Hors continued till November 1943.[51]

Thus it is evident that the Sapha Hors under the influence of nationalist leaders were no less turbulent than under Bhagirath and Dubia Gossain. Their adherence to Hinduism and abhorrence for Christianity worked well to induce them to continue their fight against the British for self-rule. This time they knew that by self-rule they did not mean establishment of '*Santal Raj*' based on exclusive ethnic group loyalty rather they allowed themselves to be fully integrated with the all-India movement for attainment of national freedom.

Gandhi Ulgulan

While we have seen the Sapha Hors of Santal Parganas carrying the embers of Kherwarism to the field of national struggle, there is yet another case of Bangam Manjhi in Gumia Police Station of Hazaribagh. He started a reform movement among the Santals of Gumia on the line of Dubia Gossain in 1930. Dubia Gossain is said to have established his seat at Jagesor, a place not very far from Gumia and through oral tradition lived in the public memory of the Santals.

With some sort of divine inspiration, Bangam Manjhi of Borobera of Bishungarh Police Station near Bagodar sought to reform his society and followed the usual puritanist method of *Babaji*'s among the Santals. Bengam Manjhi had turned a Sadhu and was known as *Munir Baba* also for his flowing beard, shining face and inspiring and robust personality. The wind of Mahatma Gandhi's non-cooperation movement was blowing hard. Bangam was also swept away by this movement which was termed by him as *Gandhi ulgulan*. He wanted to reform his people. He forbade the use of meat, fish and drinks. He asked his men to take bath daily and be clean by using Khadi cloth in place of mill-made cloth. Soon hundreds and thousands of Santals thronged around him and followed his precept. His teachings were simple and fully in agreement with the tenets of the Sapha Hors of the Kherwar Movement.[52] He started giving *poita* (a sacred thread) to his followers who agreed to follow his path. The Santal women used to be made pure with the help of milk, water, leaves of *Pipal* tree, which were put together in a pot. The Santals from different Parganas such as Jageshwar, Rampur, Gola, Tisri, Palgaju, Barsat, etc., started coming to Bangam in large number and they were purified by offering of *poita*. At times the crowd swelled to thousands. This attracted the Congress workers such as Krishna Ballabh Sahay, Ram Narayan Singh and his brother Sukhlal Singh, Raj Ballabh Singh of Chatra, Badri Singh of Kodamabera etc. They worked amongst them and fanned the movement on the Gandhian line. They became very popular among the followers of Bangam Manjhi. The Government got perturbed over this affair.

This meteoric rise of Bangam Manjhi was mainly due to his own Kherwar appeal but he got a very influential Santal as his great associate. He was Opan Manjhi, son of Kewal Manjhi of village Karmatand of Gumia Police Station of Hazaribagh. Opan Manjhi was the *Pargana Manjhi*. He used to decide cases among the Santals living in the whole Gumia area. His son Lakshman Manjhi,[53] at one time a Member of Legislative Assembly recounted about 50 villages from where Santals would come to his father for justice who was a very influential man. He was intelligent and had smattering of English education up to lower primary stage in Gumia school. He joined Bangam Manjhi and gave him all possible help in reorienting the reformation movement that Bangam wanted to herald.

Opan Manjhi being a *Pargana Manjhi* as well as an influential Santal in whole of Gumia *elaka* was known to Congress workers of the District. He knew Krishna Ballabh Sahay, Ram Narayan Singh and others. They used to see him off and on. With their help, Opan Manjhi started preaching Gandhism among the Santals of course, Bangam was the medium. If Bangam symbolised the revivalistic trends in Santal Culture, Opan Manjhi was there to use this revival movement for the furtherance of Gandhism and Congress movement among the Santals. Brains behind this were certainly Krishna Ballabh Sahay and Ram

Narayan Singh. They had been attracted towards the principles for which Bangam stood which no doubt agreed with some of the important items of the programme of the Congress Party. They used to go to them freely and Opan Manjhi was their spokesman among the Santals. Lakshman Manjhi recollected that these leaders used to stay in their huts and took their food very willingly. Living with them in their huts, partaking their food and sympathising with their lot created a wonderful rapport for these Congress leaders. The Government could know about their involvement with the Santals. The result was that Krishna Ballabh Sahay and Ram Narayan Singh were arrested and sentenced to one year imprisonment each for refusing to furnish security as a guarantee of their remaining aloof from anti-government activities. The prosecution of these two Congressmen gave new impetus to the Kherwar movement among the Santals who were getting ready for any sacrifice.[54]

Bangam Manjhi and Opan Manjhi put their heart and soul in this movement and started their work in full zest. They used to hold meetings in the dead of night and did the *Sudhi* (purification) work among the Santals. The news of this upsurge reached high-ups in Congress party. Leaders such as Sardar Vallabhbhai Patel, Dr. Rajendra Prasad and his inseparable associate Mathura Prasad came to Gumia and attended those secret nocturnal meetings. On the 31st May, 1930, about 210 Santals took the sacred thread, and vowed to follow Bangam Manjhi's creed. Kiran Kumar Sokhe Babu, Sub Inspector of Gumia reported to the higher authorities that the Santals of his area were inducing others to join the movement. The weavers of Gumia had good earnings because Khadi was a must for the followers of Bangam Manjhi.

Ultimately, Opan Manjhi and Bangam Manjhi were arrested and were sentenced to one year simple imprisonment for not furnishing security. They were released on 31st May, 1931. The Sub-Divisional Officer of Hazaribagh sentenced Hopari (Opan) Manjhi under Defence of India Rules to rigorous imprisonment for 14 years and yet Opan remained undisputed political leader among Gumia Santals while Bangam Manjhi relapsed to daily chores of peaceful agriculture. Bangam Manjhi was watched and persuaded not to take interest in politics. He died a natural death in 1947. But Opan remained a turbulent one. He used to be sole Congress leader of Santals of Gumia and was venerated by all. Local leaders from Gumia such as

Rameshwar Choubey, Mathura Ram, Ramdas Chela, Sundar Lal, Timan Lal used to consult him and take guidance from him. He also died a natural death in about 1947.

Thus Fuchs[55] had rightly remarked that every now and then, especially in the years when the crops failed and famine or other calamities threatened new prophets arose who claimed to possess miraculous powers, the power to cure disease, to procure offsprings and prosperity etc. Many Sapha Hors could still be found in Santal country (among Santals as well as the Paharias) wearing their hair in long-matted tresses, who abstained from eating pork, fowls and meat and abhorred liquor. They worshipped Lord Shiva and only killed goats when they performed a sacrifice. Some revivalistic Santals found in Raghunath Murmu a *Guru Gomke* (Esteemed Guru) who founded a cultural organisation known as *Sarna Dharam Semlet*, i.e. Sacred Grove Religious Organisation before 1951. The Semlet was created to show the solidarity of tribals and persuade the Santals and other tribals to return their religion as *Sarna*. Murmu wrote a very long heroic play, *Kherwar Bir* which serves as a Santal equivalent of the *Mahavarta*. Several drama clubs have sprung up to perform *Kherwar Bir*. He is also credited to have created the original Santal Suipt. This movement has been taken by Martin Oraons as a Santals search of a "great tradition".[56]

But it will simply be a travesty of truth to regard Jharkhand movement of Jaipal Singh simply a continuation of Kherwar movement as understood by Fuchs. Similarly Fuchs included Fetal Singh movement as Kherwar movement and attributed in his movement all the features that we have found in Santal areas. As a matter of fact Fetal Singh movement was prevalent among the Chero and Kherwars, the two tribes in Palamau where Santals are very insignificant in number.

But Fuchs is right to say that Santal aspiration was to revert back to Champa days which was the golden age of the Santals and therefore, the Kherwars always lend a willing ear to agitators who promised them independence and a life free from want and oppression.

NOTES

1. Letter dated 8th November, 1880 from Father L. O. Skresfrud to the Editor, *The Statesman and Friend of India.*
2. *Ibid.*

3. Letter dated 25th April 1891 from W. B. Oldham, Deputy Commissioner, Santal Parganas to Commissioner, Santal Parganas.
4. Same as No. 1 above.
5. Olav Hodne, *L. O. Skresfrud Missionary and Social Reformer among the Santals of Santal Parganas,* Oslo, 1966, p 270.
6. Letter dated 7th October 1874 from G. N. Barlow, Officiating Commissioner, Santal Parganas to the Secretary, Political Department, Government of Bengal.
7. Stephens Fuchs, *Rebellious Prophets* (Bombay 1965), p. 53.
8. A. P. Jha, "Nature of the Santal Unrest of 1871-75 and Origin of the Sapha Hor Movement" *Proceedings Indian Historical Records Commission,* Vol XXXV, Part II, February 1960, pp. 103-13.
9. L. S. S O'Malley, *Gazetteer of Santal Parganas.* Rev. ed (Patna, 1938), p. 174.
10. In *O'Malley's Gazetteer,* this whole chapter is said to have been written by Bodding.
11. Stephens Fuchs, p. 55.
12. Letter dated 1st October, 1874 from J. Boxwell, Officiating Deputy Commissioner, Santal Parganas to G. N. Barlow, Officiating Commissioner, Santal Parganas.
13. L. S. S. O'Malley, *District Gazetteers of Santal Parganas,* 2nd ed. (Patna, 1938) p. 177.
14. Olav Hodne, p. 271.
15. *Ibid.*
16. "Santalisthan", *The Hindoo Patriot,* 23rd September 1878, p. 45.
17. S. P. Sinha, "The Kherwar Movement in Hazaribagh District", *Vanyajali,* Vol IX, 1961, p. 99.
18. Letter dated 24th November 1880 from Alexandar Campbell to the Editor, *The Statesman* (Calcutta).
19. *Ibid.*
20. Same as 13 above, p. 68.
21. Letter dated 8th June 1881, from G. N. Barlow, Commissioner, Bhagalpur and Santal Parganas to the Secretary, Judicial Department, Government of Bengal.
22. Letter dated 5th February 1881 from Colman Macaulay, Officiating Secretary, Government of Bengal to the Commissioner, Santal Parganas.
23. Report dated 8th June 1881 from G. N. Barlow, Commissioner of Bhagalpur and Santal Parganas.
24. Letter dated 24th November, 1880 from Alexander Campbell to the Editor, *The Statesman* (Calcutta).
25. Letter dated 10th March 1881 from G. N. Barlow, Commissioner of Bhagalpur and Santal Parganas to Secretary, Judicial Department, Government of Bengal.
26. *Ibid.*
27. "Santal Disturbances", *The Englishman,* 22nd February, 1881.
28. Letter dated 14th November 1881 from J. Boxwell, Magistrate of Darbhanga to Under Secretary, Revenue Department, Government of Bengal.
29. Letter No 2701J, dated 31st July 1882 issued by the Government of Bengal.
30. Quoted in L. S. S. O'Malley, *District Gazetteers of Santal Parganas,* p. 69.
31. *Dicennial Missionary Conference,* Calcutta, 1882-83, p. 311.
32. Same as 27 above.
33. L. O. Skresfrud, "The Santal Parganas", *The Englishman,* 15th February, 1881.
34. Letter dated 8th February 1881 from Father L. O. Skresfrud to Mr. Smith, Assistant Deputy Commissioner, Dumka.

35. Same as 1 above.
36. Same as 33 above.
37. Letter dated 23rd April 1878 from Father L. O. Skresfrud to Mr. Wood, Deputy Commissioner, Santal Parganas.
38. "Santal Disturbances", *The Englishman*, 7th February 1881.
39. P. O. Bodding, "The Kherwar Movement among the Santals", *Man in India*, 1921, p. 231.
40. "The Santals", *The Englishman*, 16th February 1881.
41. Letter dated 6th January 1876 from Father L. O. Skresfrud to Sir W. Muir.
42. K. K. Dutta, *The Santal Insurrection of 1855-57*, p. 166.
43. Letter dated 1st October, 1874 from J. Boxwell, Deputy Commissioner, Santal Parganas to Commissioner of Santal Parganas.
44. Same as 13 above pp. 178-79.
45. *Ibid.*
46. *Ibid.*
47. Same as 1 above.
48. K. K. Dutta, *History of Freedom Movement in Bihar*, Patna (1938), Vol II p. 185.
49. *Ibid.*, pp. 186-87.
50. *Ibid.*, p. 195.
51. *Ibid.*, p. 288.
52. Same as 7 above p. 57.
53. Reminiscences of Lakshman Manjhi, Ex-Member of Legislative Assembly, as related orally to the author.
54. K. K. Dutta, *History of Freedom Movement in Bihar*, Patna (1957), p. 64.
55. Same as 7 above p. 58.
56. Martin Oraon, The Santal : A Tribe in search of a Great Tradition, Detroit (1965), pp. 105-19.

PART III

Conflict and Tension in Chota Nagpur

8

MULKI LARAI, 1859-1895

THE TRIBALS of Chota Nagpur in the eighteenth century were faced with two great challenges — firstly, the agrarian breakdown by the influx of new group of people inducted by the introduction of landlord-tenant system in Chota Nagpur and secondly as flowing from the first the lukewarm trial and error method of introduction of British administrative reforms and the European Missionaries who were prone to bring about calculated change in the life of the tribals so that their rebellious sting be removed. History is witness that the tribals met these challenges valiantly by putting up series of violent uprisings, agrarian agitations and resistance movements. All these confrontations constitute the subject-matter of the *Mulki Larai* which means the fight for the motherland or the country waged by the tribal people under their own indigeneous leadership of Sardars and reformers from 1859-1895, the most fruitful period in the growth of tribal personality or identity.

Before the British rule these tribes lived in fairly self-contained villages in arcadian simplicity and to quote Rakhal Das Haldar they led a life of "old non-Aryan Commune" by practising settled agriculture together with little shifting cultivation, hunting and gathering in the forests. They lived with the Hindus peacefully who came to them at the start of the Christian era or even before and influenced Hindu pantheology in their own way. They in turn absorbed a number of Hindu deities and reciprocally the Hindus absorbed tribal dieties and rituals so much so that it would be difficult to recognise the tribals different from Hindus in many ways. Land was held communally. Villages, and groups of villages had quite democratic, judicial and political autonomous institutions. Even the potters, cowherds, blacksmiths etc. who served and lived in the tribal villages were accepted in tribal political and religious life on more or less unequal terms because in *Mundari Khuntkatti* System these *Praja-horoko* had right to enjoy the fruits of the land only given to them by the *Haturen horoko* or the *Khuntkattidars*. Land in tribal areas was considered as a gift of nature and whoever first reclaimed the land became its owner. *Khuntkattidars* were the original reclaimers of the land and their successors. Ownership of tribal land was hereditary but not commercialised and transferable. Basic pattern was that the paddy land was individual property while the *tanr* and wastelands were community and village property.

The force of circumstance gave birth to a loose monarchy among the tribals when a Phani Mukut Rai, a ward of Madra Munda came to be recognised as the Raja of Mundas by the common consent perhaps the fifth century A.D.[1] We have already seen that the institution of the Raja among the tribe was a workable hypothesis, a natural growth of the social system of the Mundas. Raja in the beginning was protecting the Mundas and others under him and received some *Chanda* (subscription) for his maintenance and, therefore, he was not coercive and displayed no pomp and grandeur and his system of administration was less cumbersome and complex.

After the grant of *Diwani* when the British penetrated in this area they foisted their own concept of land system based on manorial tenancy. According to the English law, the land belonged to the sovereign and the users of land have only tenancy privileges. The right of the sovereign was just transferred to the intermediary on the condition of regular payment of fixed rent. In 1793 when Permanent Settlement was promulgated in Chota Nagpur also the *raiyots* were averse to accept the landlord and the peculiar practices prevailing in Chota Nagpur operated against the delivery and acceptance of *pattas*.[2] The privileges of the *raiyots* were to be recorded according to the express provision of the Permanent Settlement. The *zamindars* were also protected by the fixity of revenue and tenants were assured of fixed rent and security of tenure through preparation of record of right which was their ancestral right. Till Bhuinhari Survey or as a matter of fact Lala Lokesnath *Paimaish* there was no effort made by the government to record the duty and responsibility of the landlord as well as tenancy privileges of the *raiyots* in Chota Nagpur. The neo-landlords had to bring a large number of *amlas* and *patwaris* in their employment and the British Government also brought a large number of persons in their employment, the *Daroga*, the *Karkoons*, *Mokhtears*, *Sokhtears* etc. The British also inducted money-economy in a land where barter system was the means of economic transactions. Therefore, it was no wonder that they preyed upon the simple *raiyots* and soon dispossessed tribals of their land. The traders, money-lenders, adventurers, all came to join in this nefarious game. The lands of the tribals were encroached and their economic exploitation went on soaring. The distant courts at Chatra or Sherghatty were useless for securing justice against these intruders. The destruction of Khuntkatti system and village system just lay in the logic of this situation.

Several violent protests were made against these injustices. The Great Kol rebellion of 1832 is the culmination of the situation and this led the British government to administer the tribal area from Ranchi which was situated in the heart of the Tribal country and follow a much different system of administration under Wilkinson Rule. But they could hardly cure the agrarian ills of the people of the plateau area. Land alienation continued apace, and the newly settled money-lenders, *amlas*, tax-gatherers, police etc. remained in advantageous position. The main interest of the British here in this area was political pacification of the country and peace at any price. It was never their attempt to enforce and implement rules against land sales and other abuses and most of them served the *zamindars* of their area against their *raiyots*. In the Kol rebellion middlemen were terrorised, killed and expelled, but after pacification of the country they returned to avenge themselves on the Mundas. The process of the breakdown of the agrarian order continued apace.[3] The peasant proprietary tenures were greatly disturbed[4] and in that way the insurrection recoiled unfavourably on the aboriginals so much so that many Kols had to leave the country for distant land in Assam. When after some years they returned, the farmers and sub-proprietors objected to their re-entry and refused to return their lands which they claimed. It was this clan of uprooted Bhuinhars who had been gravely hurt and who had seen world by going out to distant lands that constituted the nucleus of the *Sardari* or *Mulki Larai*.

As to the origin of the agrarian disturbances it would be worthwhile to know the views of important civilians who served the area in important, high and responsible positions. Sir Charles Stevens read a paper on "Some Reminiscences of Chutia Nagpore" in February 1901 in the Jehangir Hall of the Imperial Institute, London. He was ex-Commissioner of Chota Nagpur Division and Ex-Lieutenant Governor of Bengal. He spoke in high terms of the self-sacrificing zeal of the Catholic Fathers of Chota Nagpur and by way of illustration he gave long extracts from the diary of his wife during their tours in the interior of the Ranchi District. Sir Charles described the origin of the agrarian disturbances:

"I have found them (the Kol) most tenancious of what they believe to be their rights. Their comparative ignorance and stupidity have attracted oppression at times. Rajas and landlords have called in the help of cleverer and stronger people from outside, and this process is still going on. But oppression is not tolerated beyond a certain point, and in the past has led to rebellion and much bloodshed. At the present day, too, most troubles and difficulties in the administrations arise from the encroachments of the outsiders and the dogged resistance of the people."

W.H. Grimley, another Commissioner who succeeded Sir Charles Stevens also wrote in 1896:

"The result of the enquiries begun by Mr. Renny and continued by Colonel Lillingston is to establish the fact that the unsettled relations of landlords and tenants have been brought about in a great measure by the greed and rapacity of the former. The investigating officers travelled over a large tract of country and wherever they went had to listen to the same story of oppression, in the form of illegal exactions, excessive enhancement of rent, unlimited demands of *beth begari,* and the withholding of receipts of rent."

W. H. Grimley again in his administrative report for the year 1895-96 wrote:

"Primitive people are by nature singularly tenancious of purpose cling to old traditions, and this feeling among the Kols led up to the Agrarian Agitation of 1889, when they made an effort to free themselves from the yoke of middlemen, the tharldom of *beth begari*, and other unpleasant incidents connected with the cultivation of land."

Rev. Hahn wrote in *The Statesman* (Calcutta) 27th May, 1891:

"The wonder is only how the Kols are bearing up with their present position. They do it in this way; they like a good drink and whenever the *Zamindar* requires them to be in good humour, or to forget an injustice done to them he has recourse to giving them pice for drink."

On 14th January, 1890 the Chota Nagpur Reform Association, Ranchi also resolved against "extortion, ill-treatment, torture and forced labour to which ignorant people are subjected, to which we can bear testimony, are shocking to our eyes".

The two Settlement Officers Leister and Reid[5] wrote in altogether different vein in 1902 :

> "It appears to be, however, certain that from the earliest days of Hindu landlords and middlemen had always recognised the right of the descendants of the original clearers of the villages to hold certain lands called Bhuinhari either rent-free or at a quit-rent. The Bhuinhars were obliged to render certain feudal services, such as accompanying the landlord on his journeys, cultivating his *Khas* lands, and repairing his house. Dr. Davidson, in his well-known report, dated the 29th August, 1839, refers to this well-known custom. Among the primitive communities of Mundas and Oraons, it is certain that the reclaimers of a patch of land in the jungle was regarded as its owner. As community progressed, he paid a slight tribute or rendered slight service to the village chief, but his status as *bhuinhar* or pioneer, or descendant of a *bhuinhar* was always regarded as vastly higher than that of the late-comers, who had settled on the land when the village was established. The Hindus no doubt, at first fully recognised this custom. But, as their numbers increased in the first half of the nineteenth century, the pressure on land increased, and they began to demand tribute or rent from the *bhuinhar* as well as from the ordinary *raiyots*. The *bhuinhars* resisted clinging tenanciously to the ancient custom. As the parties became exasperated, extravagant claims were made on both sides. The landlords, while acknowledging the privileged character of *bhuinhari* land, were not willing to admit their existence in any but a few of the oldest villages, while the whole body of *raiyots*, on the other hand, began to advance claims to the privileges of *bhuinhars*. Finally the opposing parties began to dispossess each other by force."

Thus we can form a roughly correct idea regarding the genesis of the agrarian discontent that rocked the Chota Nagpur region for over half a century and even after.

Agrarian question took a new turn when a band of European Christian Missionaries started spreading Christianity among the aborigines and with this question entered upon an intensive phase of agitation directed against the alien *zamindars*. The aboriginal exasperated at the tyranny of the *zamindars* and apathy of the British administrative machinery sought their solace under the protection of Cross just to meet the situation squarely. A Roman Catholic missionary observed:

> "As a general rule religious motive are out of question. They want protection against *zamindari* and police extortions and assistance in the endless litigation forced on them by the *Zamindars*. As a consequence (a) most of the converts came over (after Panchayat) in which villages or in groups of villages, (b) a certain number of isolated families came over either for help against *Zamindars* or police extortion or against the rest of their co-villagers who prosecuted them because they were pointed out by the *sokhas* as wizards or witches and (c) personally I know of some cases where individual come over from religious motives. But these cases are rare."[6]

Hoffmann, a Roman Catholic missionary wrote "tortured beyond all endurance for nearly 50 years they believed that now at last the day of their delivery was dawning".[7] The tribals hoped that the missionaries though of the castes of Alkisun (Captain Wilkinson, the Agent), but not so powerful, would indeed prove a powerful check on the malpractices.

The life of Raulus Pahna Topno[8] illustrated the typical case of Munda Khuntkatti convert who rose to lead his people against the oppressors. Major Hannygton, the Deputy Commissioner at Lohardaga stressed during the visit of H. Rickets in 1854-55 the necessity of protection of these under-tenures which was essential for the permanent tranquillity of the country, but with no results. In 1859, Commissioner Dalton proposed the introduction of Act I of 1859 in Chota Nagpur division with certain modifications, but the Board of Revenue objected to it. However, the existing procedure for disposal of revenue suit was modified in accordance with its spirit and the Commissioner continued to hear appeals. The establishment of the courts for cheap and easy administration of justice led the Kols to believe that Government was getting partial to them. The Kols had learnt by that time the tricks of landlords and they instituted a large number of cases for the restoration of lands with varying results under the impression that government favoured with their claims. Majority of these were utterly false. Armed with decree copies they forcibly took possession of land to which they had not any shadow of right.[9]

During 1855-57, the *zamindars* were reported to be alarmed at the spread of Christianity in a bid to terrorise not only the neophytes out of their allegiance to the G. E. L. Mission but also to the Missionaries out of Chota Nagpur who were reported to have embarrassed the Christian *raiyots*. Missionary Herjog was beaten by a *thicadar* (contractor) in 1855 and in 1856, the *zamindars* cut the paddy of Christians in 20 villages and in those of 30 villages decided to drive out the missionaries. During the early phase of the Mutiny of 1857, the *zamindars* had the upper hand and they came down upon the missionaries and the Christians who fomented agrarian discontent.

But the tide turned in 1859. In the Agrarian movement from 1859 onward one can find the beginnings of the offensive of Christian *raiyots* against the *zamindars*. They soon became a powerful and organised society, and the aboriginal Christians backed by the moral and sometimes by the financial support of the European missionaries, were very different persons whether in the courts or in the villages to the aboriginals of the primitive village community. Colonel Dalton, the Commissioner of Chota Nagpur Division who was well-known as a friend of the aborigines and as a supporter of the Missions personally investigated into German Missionaries allegation of various outrages said to have been perpetrated by many Hindu landlords on the Kol converts, and stated in his report to Government that "the Christians were more frequently aggressors than the aggressed".[10]

Thus during the 50 years which elapsed since the Great Revolt of 1857 the history of the Ranchi District was one of the agrarian discontent, culminating into *Sardari Larai* and the Birsa Rising. It is also the history of the spread of Christianity. An impression rapidly gained ground that to become a Christian was the best way of shaking off the operation of the landlord which resulted in great accession of strength to the rank of nominal Christians. A reasonable desire to be reinstated in *bhuinhari* lands actuated some. A dishonest idea to become one of the favoured family of *bhuinhar* seized others.[11] The next step was to profess Christianity and come to the mission at Ranchi from where they returned with their hair, puritanically, cropped and then ready to assert their rights and defy their landlords. This gave birth to conflict between Christian aboriginals and their landlords which towards the end of 1858 assumed serious dimensions. Troops had to be sent from Ranchi to Gobindpur to preserve order in Basia and Sonpur.

The authorities realised that the only effective method of preventing repetitions of such outbreaks was to remove the grievances that had caused them i.e., the absence of record of right. Accordingly, Lala Lokesnath Sahi, a local *zamindar* and Sub-Assistant Commissioner was deputed in 1858 to prepare a register of all Bhuinhari lands. He began the operations in August 1860 and continued till his death on the 13th August, 1862. His enquiries covered 572 villages only, whereas 143 villages were left incomplete.[12] Although Lala's ability and sincerity in preparation of register were later on applauded by Rakhal Das Haldar, the first Bhuinhari Commissioner, yet the missionaries and their converts criticised him for helping the non-Munda landlords against the aboriginals. The reason, as Reid puts it, was that "the claim to half the lands rent free was evidently capable of indefinite expansion, it was a very convenient theory for adoption by the turbulent *raiyots*, who dreamt of recovering their ancient status through the agency of Christianity".[13] Any way the investigations of Lala did not meet with much success.

In order to settle disputes authoritatively and finally, Act II of 1869 was passed. This has been discussed in the second chapter on land tenurial systems. The Bhuinhari survey revealed how great had been the havoc committed on the *Bhuinhari* lands in the half a century that preceded the passing of the Act. The Mundari villages succumbed to the continual encroachments of the *zamindars* and *Bhuinhari* area shrunk in size and the *Majhas* and *Rajhas* lands increased in direct proportion to the dimunition of the *Bhuinhari* area.

The 'stupidity and ignorance' of the aborigines contributed to the failure of Act. An account says "A great many of them looked with suspicion on the proceedings of the surveyors and the Special Commissioners thinking that nothing but the imposition of a new tax, or something like it, was contemplated, and this superstitious fear of the *Bhuinhars* was turned into account by the landlords and *Thikadars* who tried their utmost to dissuade them from putting forward their claims. In pursuing their objects they had recourse to promises or threats or gifts or money for the sake of spending it in the liquor shops, and last but not the least contrived means to disunite the *Bhoomihars*. Government officials and the missionaries too tried their utmost to enlighten the people on the purpose of the Government in passing the Act. The missionaries even translated it into their language and admonished them to be of one accord and after all the speak the truth, but only the Christian listened to what was told to them and the non-Christian 'Kols' for the most part either omitted to claim their *Bhuinhari* lands in full or in part and in many places combined with the *zamindars* against the Christians and thus against their own cause. It must be admitted that in some instances the Christian put forward exorbitant claims and therefore, made their statement unreliable, thereby loosing instead of gaining something.[14] Rakhal Das Haldar also quoted several instances when the *Bhoomihars* out of their folly lost their rights by allowing themselves to fall in the trap of crafty *zamindars*.

The Act left untouched several other classes of tenures and number of other rights to land and their produce about which these aborigines have always been very keen. Thus no provision was made in the Act for the protection of the immemorial rights of these people to cut and appropriate wood from the village jungles for building and repairing their houses, making and mending their agricultural implements, as well as for fuel and other domestic uses. No provision again, was made for securing to the *Bhuinhars* the mango groves and topes of other trees said to have been planted by them or their ancestors on uplands, and over which they claimed to have been always in possession. *Sarnas* and *Korkar* lands, too, were similarly left out of the record. Another most objectionable omission of the Chota Nagpur Tenure Act of 1869 would appear to have been the exclusion of Khuntkatti tenure from the scope of the Act.[15]

The destruction of Khuntkatti tenancies went on and the discontent, thereby, created brought out the outburst of 1888 of the *Sardars*, the leaders of agrarian disputes, a description of which might be of some interest to the readers.

K. S. Singh wrote that the 40 years of *Sardar* agitation provides the immediate background of Birsa's Revolt, the second in many respects, a continuation of the first.[16] But there is a good deal of difference on this point. Sinha contradicting Singh's assertion remarked that "perhaps they failed to understand the real significance of these two movements".[17] Therefore in view of the controversy an examination of the whole issue here will not be out of point. The examination of this issue will indicate in brief the outline of the two movements which may be reckoned as the two separate movements in the *Mulki Larai* for attainment of *Abua Raj* and *Sona Leka Disum*.

To quote Hoffmann, *Sardari Larai* was a "political agitation of the Mundas in order to recover their ancient rights and to be put under the direct administration of the British officers".[18] The *Sardars* were credited to have taken recourse to legal means of "prayer, protest and petition" to the Government to win back their kingdom. Although Hoffmann considered it as a political agitation of the Mundas but if we look at the list of the *Sardars* we find in it some of the Oraons too, may be there was coincidence of interest of the Oraons Bhuinhars and *Mundari Khuntkattidars* and there was identity of interests. Since Mundas were the dominant group, the agitation came to be known by their name. Among the Oraon Sardars mention can be made of William of Khatanga Sargaon, William of Jhujhari, Mathias of Erchero, Somra Badhura of Magantoli, Keso Bhagat of Chitakundi, Somra of Baghi, Jakariya of Jengi, Samuel Kura of Chalki, Eliazer of Jhanjhori etc.[19] Those prominent among the Mundas were Nikodim of Dehkela, John of Myr, Johan of Champadih, Tenga of Jilingkel, Eliaser of Kasmar, Martin of Nagra, Gideon of Piring etc. These *Sardars* were very much respected. The signatories[20] to the memorials of 1884 appear to have been 36 in number. 1. Samuel Munda, 2. Munmasi Munda, 3. Paulus Munda, 4. Patras Munda, 5. Boas Munda of Pargana Basia, 6. Biswas Munda, 7. Jakaria Munda of Parganas Belsia, 8. Nikodim Munda, 9. Bernabas Munda, 10. Paulus Munda, 11. Manmasi Munda, 12. Nikodim Munda, 13. Doah Munda, 14. Rijha Munda, 15. Mansid Munda, 16. Obed Munda, 17. Lita Munda. 18. Mansid Munda, 19. Gidhone Munda, 20. Samuel Munda, 21. Gopal Munda, 22. Rada Munda and 23. Mani Munda of Pargana Sonepur, 24. Johan Munda and 25. Jhirga Munda of Pargana Belkadi, 26. Daud Munda and 27. Mano Munda of Pargana Lachara, 28. Tingo Munda of Singhbhum, 29. Gidhone Munda of Porahat, 30. Thinga Munda and 31. Singa Munda of Tamar Pargana, 32. Samuel Munda, 33. Asale Munda, 34. Markus Munda and 35. Amus Munda of Pargana Doisa and 36. Joseph Munda of Pargana Khukhra.

Who were these *Sardars*? Many Kols had to leave the country for distant lands in Assam and some of them were intelligent enough to become *arakati* or *coolie* catchers.[21] These uprooted *Bhooenhars* who had seen world and who had been tutored well by the missionaries, constituted the nucleus of the *Sardari Larai*. They represented the Munda and Oraons of all the parts of Chota Nagpur. They were the earliest literates among the tribals schooled by the G. E. L. Mission.

The Missions on Chota Nagpur apart from practising agencies were responsible to some extent for the dawn of education. Through their educational institutions rays of western influences were poured forth. It was made all the more attractive because of the personal contact between the foreign teachers and aboriginal pupils. With the dawn of education came a vivid realisation of the present position as well as their rights and privileges and consequently a class of Tribal intelligentsia came into being, who were made cautious of their rights, privileges and dues.[22] The Christian mission did not think for a moment that the class which they were creating by their untiring endeavour and zeal will be a turbulent class ready to challenge even them (the missionaries). As a matter of fact their schools, churches, hospitals, presses, cooperative societies, workshops, legal assistance in the law courts against the *zamindars* were meant for those tribals who were ready to embrace the Christianity and thereby play a second fiddle for the foreign Christian missionaries. The mission historians interpreted the Munda history in their own way suiting their convenience, an interpretation which was accepted by the then Government. They talked of the Arcadian simplicity of which the Munda lived. To quote Sukumar Haldar:

> "The Kols, Mundaris and Uraons are the aboriginals of the district. In ancient times they had no kings and no chiefs and were divided into families, and kept together by their *Parhas* or conferences. The fields they had cleared and prepared were their own yet the whole land belonged to them. After a time a part of the Uraons and Mundaris in the new so-called *Bhoonihar-patti* of Chota Nagpur chose a King and for his maintenance gave him a grant in land, viz., half of the fields of each village. The better half the Kols kept for themselves as their own land in this they retained their possession without any rent for it till the establishment of the British courts in 1832."[23]

The Mission text-books told how the ancestors of the Mundas reclaimed the jungles and converted the country by their labour into a smiling garden. It told the Munda boy how his forefathers successfully drove away all the wild animals from the country and also how enemies who were worse than wild animals came in as interlopers and robbed them of the fruit of their toil. It further stated that in spite of various laws framed by the English to restrain these foreigners (Hindus) the unhappy Mundas were still being despoiled by the Hindus and Mussalmans. The schools in which these doctrines were inculcated were largely subsidised by our government.[24]

This clearly showed that how well these Christian missionaries made use of the existing agrarian discontent in the country as a temporal means for the attainment of their spiritual end. Such things do happen when religious propaganda gets drifted into the political and economic channels.

The *Sardars* had with Christianity imbibed those ideals of peasant proprietorship which were prevalent in some of the German City States and refused to acknowledge any obligation to any landlord below the State. They induced a large number of Khuntkatti villages to withhold the extremely low rents which were due to the Mankis or other landlords who in consequence sued them for rent and obtained decrees against the Mundas.[25] This was the Leister's description of the situation which according to him was also responsible for the breakdown of the Mundari Khuntkatti tenancy. The *Sardars* emphasising the individual or peasant proprietorship as against the communal character of Khuntkatti system went indeed a good deal in destroying the Khuntkatti system.

Not only the GEL Mission or Missions of any denomination but the Calcutta *Babus* had also something to do in shaping *Sardari* ideas. These Calcutta *Babus* or wire-pullers grafted all kinds of illusory ideas "on their fertile minds". The Mundas were credited to have wasted more than lakh of rupees over these *Babus* who were said to have changed the nature of the agitation.[26] They made believe the *Sardars* that the Great *Sarkar* i.e. Governor-General or Viceroy was on their side but Ranchi local authorities were on the side of the *zamindars* and money-lenders.[27] Calcutta *Babus* also told the *Sardars* of the imaginary decree regarding their rights being issued and also about their cases pending in the High Court and Parliament. These were naturally circulating in the countryside among their people who were made to pay more and more everytime in promise to get the decree from High Court or Parliament. Even Gyanendra Nath Tagore was consulted by the Mundas. Tagore dispelled their doubt regarding 20 years of limitation by quoting from the Institutes of Manu that the Limitation did not affect their claims to *Bhuinhari* Lands. But counsels of moderation and realism were thrown to the winds and the *Sardars* would be satisfied with nothing less than the restoration of the past, the expulsion of all hated *Dikus*. Their demands were considered unreasonable more than once and the authorities blamed that "temperament of Kols which was one of remarkable obstinacy and dogged tenacity of purpose singularly suited for the development of spirit of independence". W.H. Grimley, the Commissioner of Chota

Nagpur Division rightly wrote:

> "Their dwelling on their old tradition and past wrongs was at the root of their most preposterous claims which would never be realised and their claim to hold land as proprietors without intervention of *Rajah, Zamindar* and middlemen of any kind between them and government were attempt to tear out of any kind life's history and to back to the primitive times of their forefathers under a village community."[28]

Hoffmann, the Sarwada missionary, enunciated a theory of stubborness of the Munda of the *Quadrilateral*. The *Quadrilateral* is the centre of Birsa and Sardar Agitations and consisted of villages which had arisen in comparatively recent times throughout these wooded mountains and had been for the greater part inhabited by men who had seen their households or *bhuinhari* lands pass into the hands of the *zamindars* and *Mahajans* by ways, which, however, apparently illegal, seemed to their minds mainly either of open theft or "sharp practice of worse type"[29] by probably the descendants of those who re-treated in wake of Tamar and Kol Insurrection. By far the most outrageous in their demands about lands[30] was their assertion that they would be satisfied with "nothing short of a revolution of a state of things as they existed before the coming of the British and lastly by those who found it impossible to live any longer under landlords not particularly commendable for clemency".[31] These people of the *Quadrilateral* brought with them "the hatred" for the aliens which they not only kept alive but also communicated to such of their tribesman as "might have" suffered little as yet from the Mundas. These people were further susceptible to the agitation and discontent in the *bhuinhari* area which was the first scene of operation of the *Sardar* Agitation. Such was the make-up of the people called the *Sardars* who led the land agitation in their times and proved their stubborness by their claims and tenancity to carry the fight to any level.

Noosh Eleazar and 14000 other Christians moved a petition on 21st September, 1867 complaining that local officials, Commissioner Dalton of Chota Nagpur being one of them, harassed them by unwarrantable extortions and unjust demands and cut their crops on account of their conversion to Christianity. On enquiry it was found that only 20 converts were connected with the petitions. However, a large number of Christians joined the deputation that first proceeded to

Calcutta to obtain a hearing on behalf of all Kols who had claimed to have "certain proprietary rights on the soil as Bhoinhars".[32] Their complaint against Dalton and Maharaja was found without any foundation.

Rev. H. Onasch and 15 others, the GEL Church lost no time in petitioning and causing others to petition against the instrumentality of survey itself and its native Commissioners of whom Mundas were suspicious as well as against the need for abolition of manifold imposts, taxes etc.[33] The Government though sympathised with the motives "that actuated the members of the mission in promoting welfare of the Kols", warned them against entertaining any nation that Kols would gain any "secular advantages by embracing Christianity"[34] and turned down the complaint against the native Commissioners.

The predicament of a conscientious missionary at the sight of manifold disabilities suffered by Chota Nagpur *raiyots* could be very well evident from the writings of A. Nottrott, a contemporary German missionary, then present in the Munda area. His writings in German were published in 1874 and rendered in English by J. MacDougall of Harvard for the writer. Nottrott wrote:

> "In 1864 The English Church Bishop came to Ranchi to see the Kol Mission, and the many Kols assembled for the occasion thought it would be a good opportunity to present him with a petition, containing many signatures, which urged him to help them in their troubles. The Senior Missionary in the Kol Mission then took the paper away and tore it up. Did he want the Bishop not to learn of the true condition of the Kol which would have put the Governor (it must be the Commissioner that is meant) of Chota Nagpur in an embarrassing position? Soon afterwards, a group of about 100 Christian tribals went to Calcutta and made allegations to the General Governor (this must mean the Lieutenant Governor). The same missionary then excommunicated 25 or 30 of the leaders in the most heartless way and even forbade the Christians to eat with them. The Missionaries, seceded from the mission after 1868, do not seem to have cared about their oppression of the Kols. They have not once heard the complaints that spring from their sorely troubled hearts. Two of the Christians are still held in Ranchi Jail on account of their land disputes. Nobody had paid them a pastoral visit, nobody has sent them the books which the Jailer, a heathen, had requested for them. To be sure it is not for a Mission to involve

itself as an arbitrator in its people's worldly disputes. But to bear witness against open oppression, and to act as an advocate and protestor, a mission is certainly pledged before God to do that."[35]

Rakhal Das Haldar, one of the earliest Bhuinhari Commissioner against whom insinuation of favourtism was brought by the G. E. L. Mission and its men, wrote:

> "I have observed to the effect that those who have had the legal status of Bhuinhars have ample reasons to be thankful to the government for the operations, but there is a minority whom neither the government nor the special officers appointed by them could ever satisfy. These men are probably descendants of people who left their villages before the Kol Insurrection of 1832 and it is these men that have always been the most outrageous in their demands about lands. They want nothing short of a revolution of a state of things which has existed in Chota Nagpur certainly since long before the country came under the British Government, and it seems as if they can only be convinced of the good intention of the Government and their officers if the Hindus were totally expelled from the plateau of Chota Nagpur. I have no easily practicable means of ascertaining the total quantities of lands claimed by the people as Bhuinhari within the last eleven years, but from my experience of their claim I cannot be very far from the truth when I say that, if all the lands claimed were added together, the amount would probably exceed the total quantity of the cultivated and culturable lands within the pergunnahs of the estate that were brought under the operations of the Act. It was therefore utterly hopeless task to satisfy all claims."[36]

What Haldar could not put in his official correspondence, he jotted down in his Diary:

> "These missionaries are believed to be wolves in sheeps skin. If they are doing some good one way or other they are doing positive and great mischief. The sublime Christian religion they have managed to bring into disrepute."[37]

As a matter of fact long before the Bhuinhari survey ended an agitation against it was master-minded. Rev. H. Onasch and others in their petition had directly hinted to the Lieutenant Governor of Bengal to the "influence of social (agrarian) pressures" under which the whole masses of the Kols would embrace Christianity and would allow itself to be transformed into a Christian nation. The Missionaries assured the Government of their effort to instil into the hearts of the Mundas, love for their Sovereign and their fatherland, principle of rectitude and justice, obedience to law and all those virtues which tend to advance national prosperity and welfare of the State.[38]

But these missionaries miscalculated it when at the time of Bhuinhari survey, they attempted to throw a suggestion that *Pahnai, Bhutketa, Dalikatari* lands in a particular village should necessarily go to the mission as the villagers had joined Christian Church. The tribals had not expected this from their Church leaders. They might be docile and obedient Christians but they were tribals first. They were shocked at this suggestion. The tribals though simple, honest and unsophisticated, but they were very much attached to their land, the land which they had been ploughing for long, the land which was made cultivable for the first time by cutting the forest by their forefathers. They were not ready to part with that though they had embraced Christianity. This led to the rupture in the adherents of the Church and they revolted openly against them. This was a great betrayal. The whole aboriginal population, Munda and Oraon, lay stunned and stupified at this and were overcome by sense of deep frustration. They had not changed their religion for receiving such a maltreatment at the hands of the Christian Missionaries. They felt that they have been stabbed in their back.[39]

The Missionaries had held out the prospect of Kingdom of Heaven even on the earth of Chota Nagpur. They had also held out vague hopes of emancipation of the *raiyots* from their landlords, but with the passage of time the *raiyots* found that even the *Padris* could not keep their promises and thus they started grumbling. Several of them when they found that the missionaries could do nothing for them, turned round and began to sever their connections with the Mission. Finding that their attempt had misfired, the missionaries approached the authorities and prevailed upon them for formulating more stringent laws concerning *Bhuinhari* survey and actively worked to see that the prominent *Sardars* are arrested and their movement or *Mulki Larai* is suppressed by all means. That also explains the hostile attitude of the Missionaries against the *Birsaits*.

These *Sardars* underwent a different phase of struggle when they started reckoning the Christian missionaries as their enemies along with the *zamindars* and the local party officials who were considered to be the aides of *zamindars*. But not deterred by this infidelity of the Church leaders, the *Sardars* went on pressing their claims, however, extravagant. The missionaries started perpetuating worse tyranny on them. Therefore, the *Sardars* also memorialised against the oppressions practised upon them by the German Lutheran Mission. They narrated those oppressions as, arresting and dragging the Mundas, making them naked, snatching money from their possession, and freeing some of them from wrongful confinement after getting some ransom, of looting the property of the house of their victims and getting *Kabooliats* signed by them and dispossessing them of their land and of cutting those trees which they worshipped.[40]

Birsa-Banda

In spite of these, the *Sardars* never became disloyal to the British Government as such. To the very last, they clung to their hopes that the Viceroy and the Queen would give them redress if they could succeed in placing their case before them. But as against that the volteface of the missionaries brought about unprecedented resentment so much so that particularly the Oraon Sardars started and constructing churches of their own, made of leaves and carried on their worship in their own fashion. Mansidh of Bagru declared himself as *Prabhu Isu Khrist* (Lord Jesus Christ) and for every Christ must there be a John, the Baptist. John of Mahantoli became John, the Baptist. Masidas of Baghi assumed the title of the Raja of Chota Nagpur and in this way they were completely cut off from their original churches. These independent churches called *Jhandia Mission*. They withdrew their children from the schools run by foreign missionaries and began to celebrate rites and festivals separately. Nottrot has drawn a detailed account of this phenomenon.[41]

The Masidas-Mansidh-Johannes Bahadur leadership of new sect had some 20 families of adherants comprising about 100 people. Initially they asked the mission for help in land question for which they were ready to pay for the salary of all the native helpers financial support to schools as well as for the construction of the chapels etc. But when the Church did not oblige, they severed their connections with Church completely. Masidas Birsa was cursed and excommunicated. Masidas took the line that no other system of government was right except the old Munda one, according to which they only attributed authority to local popular assemblies, which were, above all, quite free. He also sought the support of non-Christians apart from the Church members. He claimed the whole country as their property and refused to pay rent to anybody. In his scheme of things, all heathen land-owners and renters were to be driven out and they would only pay rent to Government. He wrote a series of petitions full of absurd demands and threats and got them sent through ten to twenty strong men. So long they avoided violence the government did not care about these demonstrations but it could not remain peaceful. They plundered the barn of a landlord and distributed the rice stored there saying that it belonged to them. They then styled themselves as landlords, asked for the rent and received it. Naturally complaints were made against them. Several of them were sent to jail and thus for several months the movement cooled off. In the face of repression, a good many of them relapsed into heathenism, whereas many others returned to the fold of the Church. In 1878, the mission inspector came to Lohardaga. He found Masidas Birsa, though very much excited, working as the guard of the mission station where the Missionary Didlaukies had appointed him just to remove him from his group and also to keep a continual eye upon him.

Hahn, one of the missionaries, took great pains to win most of them back to an orderly Christian life and to Church. He found that the Birsa people, despite their apostacy from the Church, did not want to abandon Christianity. They claimed to belong to the true house of Israel. Masihdas Birsa was their King. His throne was a big round table that was a holy place. When he renounced the sect, he sold his throne to a missionary for Rs. 10 to provide for his family. Mansidh, the scribe, was a priest. Johannes Bahadur was a herald. Mansidh even claimed to be divine, and gave out that he was the second Adam and the lord of the world. In Bahadur, Moses and John the Baptist were reincarnated. He maintained obstinately that he had baptised Christ. He cried, "You are really seeing me once again. Am I not John the Baptist? Do I not dwell as him in this body"? Adam, they learned, was the first Bhuinhar or inhabitant of the whole world. His children had obtained Chota Nagpur which he had bestowed on them, since the Munda and Oraons are his descendants, nobody else has any right to any property there. The promised time is near. Then the Judgement of the world will come. Already the second Adam (Mansidh) has appeared to destroy all unjust judges (Englishmen), all the hirelings of their sheep (missionaries), all wolves and oppressors (landlords and tenants). He repeatedly made it clear to the missionary Hahn that he would be crushed in his hands, and that only they would be masters of Chota Nagpur. He had a service in his house every Sunday, at which the members of the sect turned up. When the sermon was over, there occasionally took place the baptism of new catecheron and more frequently that of the old Christians who had joined the sect. Water was not used, but a little piece of paper with the candidates name was dipped in water, and stuck on his forehead. Then Mansidh said "I baptise you in the name of God and the Holy Ghost". Christ's name was omitted, since he himself was Christ. Also, Bahadur (or John the Baptist) baptised in the same way. The service consisted of the sermon, baptism, the creed, the our Father, and singing. Near Lohardaga is a mountain with caves. The members of the sect called this mountain Golgatha, and one of these caves is called the Lord's tomb. They often went there on a pilgrimage. It was thought that Jesus had risen from the dead from this grave, in the person of Masidas, just as he had announced that he would soon rise to Heaven. Birsa, the founder, soon left Lohardaga. He wandered here and there. He was also seen in Burju now and then. This was because his two daughters by his first marriage were with a nurse in Nottrott's house. Nottrott took one of them to Germany in 1857, the first girl among the Kols to have gone there. To Nottrott Birsa narrated his life story and revealed something of why he had become a socialist agitator. The cause of it was the many unjust oppressions he had experienced at the hands of the Hindus.

Thus as we have seen that such incidents like setting up of a Raj at Doisagarh, the ancestral *garh* of Chota Nagpur Maharaja, by a band of persons under the leadership of the John Bahadur of Magantoli (John, the Baptist), styling themselves as sons of soil took place in 1881. From other account it was learnt that from Doisagarh they sent threatening letters to the Magistrate of Lohardaga and incited the people to acts of insubordination as if their Raj has been set up. Among the Oraon Sardars, Masih Das of Baghi styled himself as Raja of Chota Nagpur while from amongst the Mundas one Man Masih also declared himself as Raja. Baralal of Palkot, a scion of the ruling Nagbanshi family of Chota Nagpur Maharaja was stopped in his journey by a mob of Christian claiming Raj for themselves.[42] Baralal with great presence of mind, succeeded in making good his escape. Meetings were held by the Mundas at different places in the South and South-west of the district and in Porahat, and it was said that the thirty five *sardars* gave out that as they had filed strong petitions against the thirteen *hakims* of the district, the people should resist the authority of the local officers and seize *Manjhias* land. It was probably owing to the precautions taken by the authorities, the strengthening of police force and the exemplary punishments awarded in few cases that came up to the courts, that there were not many instances of riots or serious disturbances in harvesting season. Only one case of paddy cutting at Tilma, and cases of trespass on the *Manjhias* lands of the Rani of Tamar besides a few cases in the Parganas south and west of Ranchi were reported to have occurred.[43]

Rai Movement

While Oraons *sardars* were completely cut off from their original churches, the Mundas *sardars* turned towards the Roman Catholic Missionaries. Father Lievens had started his work at Torpa, though he refused any connection with the *sardars* but was able to create a great movement of conversions to the Roman Catholic Church. The movement was very soon called *Rai Movement* or the confederation against the *zamindars* and it is probable that this name originated with the *sardars*.[44] This was perhaps in the year 1889-90 when Roman Catholic agitation spread over the police stations of Basia, Palkot, Sisai and Chainpur etc. In November 1889, a petition from certain Zamindari alleged that in Panari Kasil, Nawagarh, Barwe, Aidhar and Korambe a large band of Kol Christians moved from village to village making people Christian by cutting their hair and threatening damage to their crops.[45] The landlords were in hot soup. The Deputy Commissioner of Ranchi received a report dated 10th November, 1889 from the Head Constable of Kurdeg outpost saying that a mob of 2500 Roman Catholics had rescued four persons from the custody of the police as the latter could not oblige them by removing the handcuff of the accused.[46] The Commissioner Grimley made it clear to the Zamindars that "on no account could they be allowed to give trouble to the Christians merely because they were Christians on the other hand he told C. Keufhenkel of Garjan of the cross complaints which had been preferred and pointed out that immigrants into the state, whether Christian or not, must not set up laws and customs of their own".[47] Thus the Government point of view was clear on these issues at least in the official reports. Father Lievens cited instances of a rich landlord of the district offering him on several occasions a sum of Rs. 1,000 on condition of his refusing to admit as Christians the tenants of five of his villages.[48] No wonder that such landlords should have viewed with alarm and indignation the conversion of their tenants and a consequent growth of manly independence in them. Roy wrote:

> "It cannot however be denied that drunk with hope, these excitable aborigines occasionally exceeded the bounds of moderation. Tingling with pulsations of a new life, some of the new converts appear to have attempted to coerce their unconverted brethren into accepting their new faith and sharing in the large life that seemed to open out to them. Like the young hill-streams of the district, after heavy showers of rain heaving and swelling till they overflow their banks, the upheaval amongst these enthusiastic neophytes of an excitable race, appears, occasionally to have led them into reprehensible excesses."[49]

Alarmist reports of the *zamindars* and *darogas* were considered exaggerated, but when the *Indian Daily News* of Calcutta first drew the attention of certain insinuations against the Catholic Mission, then we find Lieutenant Governor Sir Stuart Bayley visiting the District to see things with his own eyes. The Government moved quickly and Father Motet of the Roman Catholic Mission was warned by the Commissioner of the "extreme folly of meddling with the land question".[50] Lievens had to leave Torpa afterwards. About 200 Roman catechists were arrested and then let off.

The *Sardars* found to their great dismay that even Roman Catholics also failed in getting back their lost Raj. They started their agitation against all missions. They arranged themselves against all the three — the *zamindars*, local officials and the missionaries. They accused all missionaries being hand and glove with the *zamindars* and local officials. A saying "*Topi Topi ek Topi*" got currency among the tribals and the *Sardars*' mind boiled at the retalisation that the Europeans *en bloc* organised against their movement. The Christian missionaries prominent among them, Father Nottrott and Father Dedlockes, tried their influence to bring *Sardars* under different terms of imprisonment and they were successful to a great extent in their attempt. This might have put a stop to this interesting legal battle of the Mundas, but this also convinced them that they had to overthrow these missionaries, the *zamindars* and local officials from their country lock, stock and barrel. The Calcutta *Babus* had also let them down and would not help them to recover their rights and lands. There was no alternative to fight unaided their own battle. The prayers, protests and petitions and the legal and constitutional means had not yielded any result. "The imaginary league between the Chota Nagpur *Sahebs* and the Hindus *(Zamindars)* was too powerful to be overturned by the legal agitation which they thought was going on in the High Court of Calcutta and Parliament."[51] Thus dejected at this some of the *sardars* dropped their agitation almost completely though a few of their old "isolated groups" continued engaging Mr. Jacob, a Calcutta Bar-at-Law, to plead their cases in Courts. Hoffmann wrote "At a time I have heard known *Sardars* (leaders of the agitation) and other people say: we have appealed to the *Sarkar* for redress and got nothing. We have turned to the Mission, and they too have not saved us from the *Dikus*. Now there is nothing left us but to look to one of our own men".

But the Government on its part tried to do their best suiting their colonial interest to safeguard the interest of the tribal *raiyots*. The agrarian troubles were to some extent temporarily allayed by the executive action of Grimley announcing scale of services renderable for each holding which purported to be founded on the ancient custom of Lohardaga. The scale was fixed at 14 days against the unlimited demands made by the *zamindars* by abusing their prerogatives. These measures were avowedly meant to meet the emergency, and though partially successful at the time, their effect was transient as a solution of the problem.[52]

In 1897, after several years of discussion, a Bill was introduced and passed in Bengal Council providing for the voluntary commutation of paraedieal conditions and services laying down a procedure for enhancement of rent, and regulating the registration and resumption of intermediate tenures. The system of personal service was a picturesque relic of the feudal era. It was subject to many abuses and it was gravely abused too. As such it had to disappear. All such services were to be commuted by the Settlement Department throughout the District, and with them the conditions *awabs* and *rakumats* which were secondary cause of dispute, and both questions have been finally set at rest.

Between 1893-95, various *Sardars* were prosecuted on charges of extortion and assault on those who did not pay the subscriptions. The operations of the *Sardars* extended throughout the northern Pirs of the Porahat estate in Singhbhum, the whole of the Munda country and the adjoining parganas of present Sadar and Gumla sub-divisions inhabited mainly by Oraons. The ferment in the Munda country and adjoining parganas was entirely distinct from the agrarian agitation in the Oraon country, which again began to take a serious turn in the year 1887-90, though the causes were analogous. The claims of the Mundas were the more extravagant as they demanded a reversion to the state of affairs which prevailed when they were the sole masters of the country. Though Oraons were affected by these ideas and sympathised with them, their special grievances were the heavy exactions of paraedieal dues and services.[53] But the result of the Commutation Act of 1897 met their demands only to some extent and proved that compulsory commutation was essential to the peace of the district. This was done by the Survey and Settlement undertaken by Leister and Reid in 1902 after good deal of deliberation. The settlement operations acted as a sedative of agrarian discontent.

Ulgulan

The *Sardars*' arrest and the suppression of the agrarian disturbances of 1889-90 might have brought peace but, as a matter of fact, the calm was illusory. Beneath that illusory calm was the storm of seething discontent. The atmosphere was highly charged and one spark was needed to incite the whole Munda Country. This was supplied by Birsa Munda (Fig. 8.1) of Chalkad, a lad of about 20, who came to lead a people who had been chafing under the iron heels of the *Jagirdars*, *Thikadars*, Clergymen and an alien government. In him Mundas found embodiment of their aspirations and Birsa fulfilled their expectations by giving them a leadership, a religion and code of life, and held before them a prospect of a *Munda Raj*. But it would be unwise to consider the *Birsa Larai* as the continuation of *Sardari Larai* because the underlying significance and goals of the two movements were quite different. While the *Sardari Larai* was a political agitation of the Mundas and Oraons in order to recover their ancient rights and to be put under the direct administration of British Officers, the *Ulgulan* of Birsa a direct action against government, landlords and missionaries by declaring that Victoria Raj had ended and his Raj has started.[54] Birsa refused to acknowledge any authority superior to himself and declared himself the prophet of *Singhbonga*, the *Dhartiaba* of his people. This was another part of the *Mulki Larai* which Birsa waged under his wonderful leadership. History is witness that Birsa was responsible to a great extent for the restoration of the tenancy rights for which the *Mulki Larai* was started after the Mutiny of 1857. We find *Mulki Larai*

FIG. 8.1: Birsa Bhagwan

revolving round two important movements — firstly, the *Sardari Larai*, a fight of 'prayer, protest and petition' and secondly the *Ulgulan*, the direct action by the Mundas under Birsa Bhagwan. We have seen the first, and now will see the second and try to find that the second was not a continuation of the first.

Persons such as Birsa are immortal even if they are dead. Their character, their ideals, their activities remain as a beaconlight for times to come. Birsa has been a path-finder and his great soul has been a soul of a liberator. His life has been an open book, full of glorious deeds which can be ideal for persons who care to follow him. It was at the close of the last century that he shook the British administration and infused new blood in the hitherto benumbed veins of Munda society and other tribal societies of Chota Nagpur. The Sepoy Mutiny of 1857 failed miserably and the post-mutiny period witnessed the worst demonstration of British oppression which was carried to such an extent that a grave-yard silence prevailed all over. Some people might be stealthily adding faggots to the fire of discontent, but only few could dare protest against an all powerful British Government. But Revolutionary Birsa took upon himself the task of fighting out for the legitimate grievances of his people with a weapon in which we can find the tinge of non-violence and non-cooperation. At the same time he asked the British and their stooges the *zamindars* and the foreign missionaries to quit India. This was his originality. The tenets of his religion gave Birsa a place of honour in the Indian Renaissance Movement. Thus he was placed in the galaxy of the national heroes of India such as Kunwar Singh, Laxmi Bai, Nana Saheb, Tantia Tope, Raja Ram Mohan Roy, Dayanand Saraswati and so on.

Birsa's dream was to reform and revitalise the oppressed communities of Chota Nagpur by giving them a sense of understanding of their own culture and their glorious traditions. He wanted that his followers should oppose injustice perpetrated by a foreign government, governmental system and foreign missionaries. He was dreaming to establish *Abuaraj* (own kingdom) where there would be no tyranny and no oppression but all peace and plenty. The poor, helpless *Adivasis* found themselves pitted against a powerful machinery of oppression constituting the British administration, the missionaries and the *zamindars*. There was a ferment in the minds of men and they were in search of a real liberator. In such a volatile situation Birsa came to them to lead them out of the morass, to give them a code of life and prospect of forlorn *Abuaraj* looked there. He started revitalisation movement. That was only possible if the *Adivasis* built their own character and moral and had some understanding of their old glory and tradition so that they could measure their sword against their natural enemies. At Chalkad he clearly understood that it was very difficult to defeat British Imperialism with violent agitation but nonetheless he propagated to fight with the help of moral strength and character building.[55] Birsa had a wonderful sense of understanding the need of the time and mind of the people and the rightly exhorted his people to fight the monster of British imperialism with moral strength and not by violent means. Therefore, Birsa Movement which is known as *Ulgulan* could be divided into two parts, first the Chalkad Movement of 1895 and the Final Showdown at Sail Rakab in 1899.

In 1895, Birsa started preaching his religion *Birsa Dhoram* from Chalkad which was his headquarters. He analysed the then decadant aspect of Munda society, their loss of land, their loss of freedom and faith. He drew lessons from different rebellions of *Adivasis* and pointed out that an *Adivasi* could never think of success whether it was the Kol rebellion, Santal rebellion or Sepoy Mutiny. Therefore, he propagated the cult of non-violence and non-cooperation. He forbade the use of drinks, non-vegetarian food and sacrifice to different *Bongas*. He emphasised the principle of plain living and high thinking. He asked them to use sacred-thread and abstain from food for a day in a week. He prescribed the worship of *Singh-bonga* and asked them to give up the worship of other *Bongas*. Therefore, he was preaching a monotheism in the land of polytheism. He forbade inter-dining and inter-marriage with the Christians and tried to non-cooperate with the *Jagirdars* in matter of production in the field. He wanted to make his disciples fearless and, therefore, he emphasised that the soul is eternal and it never dies though the body might decay. Hundreds and thousands of Adivasis, Mundas, Oraons and Kharia made bee-line to Chalkad to offer their homage to the new God and have *Darshan* after giving up their cultivation and other avocations. This assemblage and non-cooperation to the common economic activities of the district resulted in wrath of the British authorities who were promptly persuaded by Thakur Jagmohan Singh of Bangaon and Father Lusty of Murhu to put Birsa in chains because to them Birsa was a disturber of peace.

British force swooped down in the dead of the night and gagged Birsa and whisked him away to Ranchi Jail. Hundreds and thousands of his followers were left as dumb-founded a mute spectators of cowardice of their enemies. They did not raise their arms to wrest their *Dhartiaba* because it was the express desire of Birsa that his disciples were not to resort to violent means. This self-restraint shown by inflammable people such as Mundas, Oraons, Kharias etc. demonstrated the deep impact which Birsa as a religious teacher made upon the minds of his people. Once again this non-violent aspect of the movement of the Birsites found expression when Birsa was brought to Khunti to face the trial for waging war against Her majesty's Government. Batches of Birsites came to have a glimpse of their *Dhartiaba* and remonstrated against the delay in the trial before the Deputy Commissioner. They wanted to court arrest so that they may be able to meet their *Bhagwan* in the jail. They offered their neck and wanted to lay down their life. They were arrested but later released. Birsa was also later released after serving a term of two years rigorous imprisonment in jail.

It was hoped that Birsa would be taken to be a false prophet by his people because his prophecy of a deluge and rain of fire etc. never took place, but interestingly enough Birsa had not the least trouble in getting his band of disciples by his side just after his release in 1898 and he re-started his movement for final show-down. Secret meetings were held in the difficult and out-of-way hilly terrain in the darker hours of night. A network of secret groups was spread over throughout the length and breadth of Munda country, the secrecy of deliberation of such could only be compared with those of Irish Secret Societies.

Though Birsa got his band of disciples under him in no time who were ready to do and die for their Master but some of the disciples became restive and they wanted to use force to meet the force of the British imperialism because to them the oppression of their enemies had reached its nadir and they were bent upon to take up arms. Several times Birsa warned his disciples of the pitfalls of violent ways of conducting an agitation but sensing that situation will go out of control if it was not allowed, ultimately, he had to permit his followers to shoot arrows at some of the stations of foreign missionaries without creating any violence so that their genuine wrath was demonstrated and administrative machinery was made to take notice of the situation.

Ultimately on the Christmas night of 1899, the arrows were shot at several stations of foreign missionaries; but the situation went out of the control and there were some killings. The countryside became panicky, the police stations were attacked and burnt. British forces were pressed into action through all the corners to quell this rebellion.

On 9th January, 1900 a final showdown took place on Sail Rakab near Domarihill which resulted in large scale killing of Birsaite men and women. Inhuman atrocities followed and Birsites had to face perilous days. Either they had to change their faith and get converted into Christianity or join the other Birsites in jail at Ranchi. A man-hunt with the help of local intelligence was launched for Birsa Bhagwan. He was detected at Rogode and could be apprehended near Shankra forest in the Porahat area of Singhbhum District.

Birsa was made to stand a trial before W.S. Courtts, a Special Magistrate. On 9th June, he attended the Court as usual but in the evening in the jail he was declared dead due to cholera. His deadbody was disposed of surreptitiously next morning.

The British administration might have disposed of the deadbody of Birsa and might have the sadistic feeling of an accomplishing a feat, but Birsa's death assumed such a wide proportion that there was widespread criticism in important news papers such as the *Pioneer, the Statesman, the English Man* etc. Not only this, jooming of guns at Sail Rakab reverbated in the Council Chamber of Bengal where Sir Surender Nath Banerjee thundered against the British administration for shabby deal to the Nationalist movement of the Birsites. Public opinion gained such a momentum that a general survey and settlement for Ranchi district was ultimately ordered and Lister and Reid were entrusted to this task. The ghost of Birsa dominated the scene and British Masters were obliged to deliberate on a Bill for granting the *Adivasis* special tenancy like Mundari Khuntkatti and others. Ultimately, the Government understood the necessity of regulating landlord-tenants relations which was the most unsettled in Chota Nagpur and therefore, enacted Chota Nagpur Tenancy Act in 1908 which can be very well be said to be the *Magna Charta* of the Tribals of Chota Nagpur. The passing of the Chota Nagpur Tenancy Act was a significant phenomenon which restored to the *raiyots* of Chota Nagpur special privileges and protection, a measure which was unique all over the Indian sub-continent.

Thus with the martyrdom of Birsa Bhagwan, the course of discontent and ethnic deprivation passed off to another channel of political protest made through political platform rather than taking recourse to battle axe and war arrows. This course of the political agitation has been examined in the next chapter which surveys the aftermath of this Great Ulgulan in the shape of various political movements.

NOTES

1. S. C. Roy, *Munda and their Country.* Calcutta (1912), p. 140.
2. R. N. Sinha, *Bihar Tenantry 1783-1833.* Bombay (1968), p. 70.
3. Letter No. 11 dated 22nd May 1880 from R. D. Haldar to Deputy Commissioner, Lohardaga, published in *Papers Relating to Agrarian Discontent.* Vol. I, p. 83.
4. Letter No. 2975 dated 23rd December 1871 from E. T. Dalton, Commissioner Chota Nagpur Division to Secretary, Revenue Department, Government of Bengal.
5. J. Reid, *Survey and Settlement Operations in Ranchi District,* Calcutta (1912), p. 35.
6. L.S.S. O'Malley, *Census of India, 1911* Vol. I, Part I. p. 138.
7. John Hoffman, *Encyclopaedia Mundarica,* Vol. c. p. 1446.
8. A. Nottrott, *The Life of Paulus Pahna Topno : A Good Soldier of Jesus Christ,* p. 3.
9. Same as 3 above.
10. *Supplement to the Calcutta Gazetteer,* October 1868, p. 500.
11. M.G. Hallet, *Ranchi District Gazetteer,* Patna (1917), p. 44.
12. Same as 1 above p. 270.
13. Same as 5 above.
14. Same as 1 above pp. 276-78.
15. F. A. Slacke in *Bengal Legislative Council,* Debates, 18th July 1903.
16. K. S. Singh, *Dust Storm and Hanging Mist,* Calcutta (1966).
17. S. P. Sinha, *Life and Times of Birsa Bhagwan,* Patna (1964) p. 114.
18. Same as 7 above Vol XIII, p. 3843.
19. Manuscripts of Julius Tigga, quoted in 17 above.
20. Same as 1 above p. 288.
21. Same as 7 above pp. 154-164.
22. Same as 17 above p. 39.
23. Letter dated 15th November 1869 from Rev. F. Batsch to Deputy Commissioner, Lohardaga published in Sukumar Haldar: *Jharkhand X-rayed,* p. 3, Also in J. Reid, *Survey and Settlement Operations in Ranchi District,* p. 34.
24. *The Statesman* (Calcutta), 12th May 1916.
25. Same as 5 above p. 84.
26. Letter dated 14th January 1900 from John Hoffmann, S. J. to A. Forbes Commissioner, Chota Nagpur Division enclosed as Annexure 4 with letter No. 5T-B dated 17th January 1900 from A. Forbes, Commissioner Chota Nagpur to Chief Secretary, Government of Bengal. *Proceedings of the Home Department* No. 336 dated August 1900.

    Note : Available in National Archives of India.
27. *Ibid.,* p. 77.
28. *Ibid.,* p. 141.
29. John Hoffmann's letter in 26 above.
30. Same as 3 above, p. 85.
31. Same as 26 above.
32. Letter No. 227 dated 31st January 1868 from E. T. Dalton, Commissioner, Chota Nagpur Division to the Under Secretary, Government of Bengal.
33. *Papers Relating to Agrarian Discontent,* Vol I, pp. 65-72.
34. *Minutes of Lieutenant Governor of Bengal,* 5th July 1876, pp. 65-72.

35. A. Nottrott, *Gossner's Mission to the Kols : Picheres from the life of a Missionary* translated from original German into English by J. Mac Dougall 1874 p. 96. 36. Same as 3 above pp. 84-85.
37. Diary of Babu Rakhal Das Haldar, First Bhuinhari Commissioner See entry for 3rd August 1876.
    Note : available in Santu Lal Library, Ranchi.
38. Same as 33 above, pp, 65-67.
39. Same as 19 above, pp 39-40.
40. Memorials of certain Bhuinhari Mundas dated 10th April 1891 to the Judicial Commissioner, Ranchi District, Lohardaga, Chota Nagpur. Explained and forwarded by Cockril A. Smith, Attorney-at-law. File No. 11/7, Revenue Department L. R. Branch, May 1892, No. 20-22
    Note: Available with S. C. R. O. Patna.
41. Same as 35 above.
42. N. Kumar, *Bihar District Gazetteer,* Ranchi, Patna, 1970, p. 68.
43. Same as 1 above pp 286-87.
44. Same as 7 above Vol. XII (S) p. 3843.
45. Letter No. 558 J dated 13th November 1889 from H. W. Grimley, Officiating Commissioner, Chota Nagpur Division to Deputy Commissioner, Lohardaga, published in Papers Relating to Agrarian Discontent, Vol. I, p. 136.
46. Same as 42 above p. 69.
47. *Administrative Report of the Tributory and Political States of the Chota Nagpur for the year 1888-89*, pp. 137-39.
    Note: Available with National Archives of India.
48. Letter dated 19th February 1889 from Father Lievens to Catholic Archbishop of Calcutta.
49. Same as 1 above pp. 295-96.
50. Same as 33 above p. 135.
51. Letter dated 4th January 1900 from John Hoffman to A. Forbes, Commissioner Chota Nagpur Division. Proceedings Home Department, No. 336, August 1900.
    Note: Available with National Archives of India.
52. Papers Relating to Agrarian Discontent. Vol. II. p. 17.
53. Same as 5 above p. 46.
54. Judgment of W.S. Coutts, Joint Magistrate in Appeal No. 184 of 1901, Paperbook Part II, pp. 124-25, quoted in S.P. Sinha, *Life and Times of Birsa Bhagwan*, p. 114.
55. Same as 17 above pp. 53-66, 72-79.

9

TANA BHAGAT MOVEMENT

APPEARING SUPERFICIALLY as a fall-out of the faulty and unsympathetic survey and settlement operations in Chota Nagpur during 1902-08, the Tana Bhagat Movement mostly among Oraons of Western Chota Nagpur erupted as a direct sequel to the desperation and oppression by the local landlords and police buttressed by equally apathetic British administrators and unmindful local intelligentsia. The Tana Bhagat millenarian[1] cult sprang up in 1914 and swept through the Oraon country claiming some 26,000 adherants at its peak period. Finding their age-old Gods and Goddesses failing in their role of their saviour from manifold troubles, they worked out a new religious cult or movement on the old Bhagat pattern and termed it initially *Kurukh Dharam* or the real or original religion of the Kurukh. From their endless chanting of *Tana Baba Tana* (Pull out, Father, Pull out) in their exorcism hymns, the new cultists came to be nicknamed *Tana Bhagats*.

This movement started actually in April 1914 when a certain Jatra Oraon of Chingri village, close to Bishanpur Circle in Gumla district, refused excessive demands made by the local police on Oraon tenants for their unpaid labour, and he proclaimed that in a vision he had from *Dharmes* or God, he had received a revelation for the Oraons. Soon he commanded a huge and enthusiastic following. Those were the days when the Oraons of present Bishanpur Thana and Chechari in Palamau were subjected to excessive requisition for labour, during the construction of the Summer Residence of the Lieutenant Governor on the Neterhat Plateau. These people were also forced to act as beaters during hunting and as carriers of packages of the local police for mere pittance. This galling situation goaded by the inequitous tenurial situation and unjust British local system forced Jatra to lead his people so that he may bring them out from the then morass. Leaders are not made, but are born. Jatra, having in-born quality of leadership of his people, effective in speech and emulative in behaviour, proclaimed that it was God's order that he and his men should not work as coolies, or labourers under the *zamindars* or men belonging to other castes and non-tribals. He announced that Oraons should adore God alone i.e. *Dharmes,* through prayer and *bhakti* (devotion) and that they should completely abandon the worship of minor spirits or '*bhoot*' and do away with animal sacrifice. It was also God's command, according to him, that they should lead an ascetic life and give up meat-eating, alcoholic drinks and singing of songs and dances and gaudy dresses. He ordained that the Oraons ought, however, to stop ploughing the fields and paying rents to the landlord and refuse themselves as labourers to any non-Oraon police and *zamindars.* Jatra taught his followers that what he proclaimed were divinely inspired prayers and incantations for exorcising spirits, curing diseases and for neutralising evil spells of the witches. He warned them that those who do not follow him would soon perish, that the foreigners would soon be expelled from the country, that the *Oraon Raj* was about to begin and he would be its King.

Because he refused to allow his followers to work for the *zamindars* and for the Government, Jatra and his leading disciples were arrested and produced before the Sub-Divisional Court, tried and sentenced to imprisonment. But they did not allow the movement to die; rather the movement spread like wild fire throughout the Oraon country. It was only because what Jatra preached was the very idea which was agitating the minds of the people. It was Jatra who gave the definite tribal colour to this cult. The idea of non-cooperation and protest was not new to Jatra. His predecessor Birsa did it. Sardars had shown their mettle, but it was Jatra and his followers who gave a definite shape to his cult which is still existing among a large number of Oraons in South Ranchi. The charismatic personality of Jatra had already produced leaders of his movement in every direction of the old Ranchi District. The atmosphere was so much charged with new idea that it was difficult to stop the movement.

Other prophets took over the direction of the movement which received great impetus in 1915, especially when the early German victory was common talk everywhere. The new cultists not only abandoned the worship of '*bhoot*' but they expelled them out of the country with a vast excorcism. They marched across Oraon Country, chanting incantation, making loud invocations with all the beneficient powers known to them i.e., moon, starts and some heroes such as Birsa and the victorious German Kaiser to come to their aid and expel the spirit.[2] The rumours of a coming massacre of the dissenting Oraon by the *Tana Bhagats* frightened the farmers so much so that they fled to towns for safety. But the prompt posting of the police force at the likely trouble spots forstalled any break up of violence.

In 1916, the belief of a coming *Messiah* became quite strong among the *Tana Bhagats*. It was rumoured that very soon either God himself or any envoy of his such as Birsa Munda or the German Kaiser would come to set the Oraons free. In Palamau, this belief became so strong that several of the *Tana Bhagats* removed rows of tiles from the roofs in order to facilitate entry of *Messiah* into their homes. They also took the precaution of killing their dogs, lest their barking should disturb his advent. Some *Tana Bhagats* actually called at the Mahuadanr Thana and demanded from the Police a copy of the *Bahi* or the legal document of the Kaiser, authorising them to rule over the country. Yet other *Tana Bhagats* spread the rumor that the Kaiser had already arrived in Chota Nagpur, bringing with him a cart-load of gold for his Oraons. Peace was finally restored in the Ranchi District by the end of 1917. But the movement now spread among the Oraon labourers of the tea estates of Assam. Insurrection of Oraon was feared there also. In 1918 a rebellion in the native State of Surguja and Mahuadanr by the *Tana Bhagat* had to be suppressed by military force which is discussed in detail elsewhere.

Between 1917-20, the *Tana Bhagat* formulated their new rules of conduct. They became convinced dissenters and gave up the worship of spirits. Thursday was chosen as a *sabbath* day for rest and prayer meetings. They prescribed a very ascetic life for their followers asking them to give up meat-eating, drinking, dancing in the village squares and hunting. Daily bath became a very popular ritual with *Tana Bhagats*. Inter-caste dining as well as inter-caste marriage with non-Bhagats were tabooed.[3]

As already mentioned in the beginning, the *Tana Bhagats* resented the inferiority of their position to dominant caste Hindus and neo Christians very much, and wished to improve their own position in the social ladder. They believed that the only way to improve their condition was to have right relationship with God, and for this they devised certain rituals and prescribed special rules of conduct. They believed that the correct ritual to ensure the right relationship with God was to give up impure things and lead a pure life, and then only they could commune with God, who would deliver them from all troubles.[4] The rules of conduct followed by them are still similar to those of the Oraon *Bhagats* or *Sokhas* who are approached for divining the cause of some calamity to man, cattle or crops and the means of removing it.

The Bhagat communes with God (*Dharmes*) directly for deriving his occult powers. He, therefore, has to lead a pure and active life of devotion to *Dharmes*. Since God reveals Himself, he must purify himself before he worships God. He must give up eating meat because every life is sacred. He must bathe every morning before proceeding to his daily worship and making offerings. He must also not eat anything until he has finished his worship in the morning. In the traditional system of the Oraons, all the religious ceremonies require offerings and sacrifices of animals, food or drink to the deities and spirits. But a Bhagat does not make any sacrifices. Instead, in his *Deokuri* (Temple), he offers flowers and sweets and burns incense or butter as a token of his devotion to Dharmes. For him, religion is not just placating Gods out of fear, but to have an intimate personal relation with the *Dharmes* in his heart. Hence, his devotions are not for conciliation or fear but for love, adoration and reverence. To him, all other spirits except the ancester-spirits are evil spirits and, therefore, must be shunned. He relies only on the supreme deity Dharmes for his powers and uses his beneficient powers for the good of the people. He does not drink nor must he sit down and eat with the people who drink (*madhuas*). He must not eat food cooked by the others.

Just as an Oraon Bhagat can commune with God directly, so the Tana Bhagats believed that they also can commune with God if they lived a life of ceremonial purity. So their rules of conduct are not different from those of the Oraon Bhagats. *Tana Bhagats* are required to give up all kinds of drinks, meat etc. They must not take food cooked by anyone except those who belong to their own faith. They were also required to give up dancing in the *akharas*, holding *Jatras*, engaging themselves in hunting expeditions or becoming members of the *Dhumkuria*. They were not supposed to wear coloured clothes or any kind of jewellery nor decorate their bodies with tatoo marks. They were required to give up practice of witch-craft and the propitiation of old deities as the new creed had no place for them. As the *Tana Bhagats* say *Niti Dharm alarghi nadehum mala Baba, bhutehun mala* (for the followers of good and true religion, there were no spirits or *bhuts*) or *Erapanta ballinta, manal nadan, tana Baba tana* (All the spirits of the house and the house and the door whom we sought to appease so long, do pull them down, O Lord). They believed that God exists within their heart when they say *Baba, Baba, badar, Bhairo, Baba namhai jianu rads* [O Brothers, you call father (God). But the father is really all the time within you]. It is not possible to quote here all the principles of the Tana religion. There is a genuine out-pouring of the people's soul in their songs and prayers. With the new conception of Dharmes as the spirit of Love and Purity and as one who dwells not only throughout the universe but in the hearts of the individuals as well, the *Tana Bhagats* ideal of moral conduct of individual as well as the community has changed in conformity with the new conception. Love and goodwill towards their fellow men, kindness to all living beings, and purity in food and habits have become the principal virtues of the *Tana Bhagats*.[5]

Large gatherings of the followers of this new religion at nights and ghost and witch-hunting campaigns till early dawn caused great panic among the *zamindars*. A large number of Tanas stopped payment of rents to the *zamindars* and money-lenders apprehended rising of the Oraons against themselves and reported the matter to the police and roused suspicion against these religious enthusiasts. The police officers, who neither understood their songs or prayers nor were permitted to witness the proceedings, regarded these people as disloyal and their meetings illegal. The authorities thus prohibited their gatherings and many were sent to the courts as likely threats peace. These measures were adopted with a view to stop the growth of the movement. The movement subsided as soon as the excitement died down and people became more reconciled to changed circumstances and also found that the new faith failed to secure their lost rights in land. Even then it stiffened the backs of the authorities who suppressed it with strong hand. The tribal people began to realise that the religious motive by itself was not sufficient to keep it alive as a popular movement.

How a tribal cult could imbibe the spirit of the realisation of Gandhiji and his enunciation of non-cooperation will be exemplified by assessing the role of *Tana Bhagats* in the non-cooperation movement launched by Mahatma Gandhi? From 1920, most of the Tana Bhagats joined the Indian National Congress and played a prominent part in the non-cooperation movement. When Gandhiji started the non-cooperation movement in the early twenties, Chota Nagpur Division was also stirred by the movement from 1920 onwards. From January 1921, the tribals specially the Oraons and the Mundas responded in large numbers to the appeals made to them by the Congress workers. Predilections of Tana Bhagats also added faggots to the fire as they had also demanded the *Self-rule* for themselves. Under the leadership of Shibhu and Maya, the Tanas, in the year 1919, started a movement which the police authorities wanted to stamp out because "unless the movement received a check" or the followers are made to realise that "their so-called leaders are not *Bhagwan* (God) and incapable of being punished". The Deputy Inspector General of Police feared a serious spread of the movement.[6] Shibu, Maya and other leaders like Sukra, Singhia, and Debia were arrested and convicted. But in spite of their arrest, the "whole movement was not an end".[7] In December 1919, about 400 Tana Bhagats assembled at Tiko Tanr, a place associated with the famous Kol Insurrection of 1831-32 where valiant Budhu Bhagat fought against the British force and sacrificed his life. The new leadership was in the hands of Turia Bhagat and Jitu Bhagat. They passed several resolutions — one of these being for non-payment of *Chaukidari* tax and no rent to the *Zamindars*. This "no-tax no rent campaign" got currency soon on getting support from the Congress Party. A sizeable area of the tribal population accepted this programme of the Congress not because of certain sophistication or emulation and persuasion but because these tribals were on the same track of mind and Mahatma Gandhi's call for non-cooperation fitted in their programme of action. They found a correlation between their aspirations and the programme of Mahatma Gandhi.[8] They started donning Gandhiji cap and carrying Congress tricolour flag as a symbol of their being rebels against the Government and very soon they became non-conformist like the Congressites of those days.

Gandhiji's rapport[9] with Tanas was spread among the tribes of the area specially by a handful of devoted self-sacrificing workers, like Gulab Tiwary, a typist in the Ranchi District Board Office, Moulvi Usman, a follower of Maulana Abul Kalam Azad and Head Maulvi in Anjuman Islamia Madarsha, Ram Tahal Brahamchari, Ramchander Prasad, Nagarmal Modi, etc. Ranchi was frequented by Swami Vishwanand, a famous labour leader of the time who delivered inspiring speeches. Gulab Tiwary had given up his job in the District Board and joined Ranchi Pinjara Pole on Rs. 40 per month, Nagarmal Modi of Ranchi who was doing business in Calcutta and had made fortune took up his abode at Ranchi, Mohammad Yusuf, Mohammad Ishaque, Mohammad Alam and Alizan Saudgar were the devout compatriots of Gulab Tiwary. On 3rd February, 1921, the Superintendent of Police, Ranchi, reported to the Deputy Commissioner of Ranchi. "Till the end of October 1920 Gandhism with its attendant movement such as non-cooperation and anti-drink campaign, etc. had found little support in Ranchi." There was but one respondent Gulab Tiwary who had shown marked activities in endeavouring to spread "pernicious propaganda". He wrote that "On 18th and 19th November, 1920, Ranchi received Padamraj Jain, Bholanath Burman, Mohammed Zakaria, Abdul Rajaque, and Sunder Dutt Seobi from Calcutta in a mighty procession attended by a *Hartal* (strike) in the town from 17th to 21st November, 1920. Between these dates several meetings, public as well as secret, were held which were largely attended — at one place 60,000 people including tribals many Tanas were present". Speeches were for the abstinance from drink and advocated non-cooperation. An arbitration court was established at Doranda and there were strikes in the schools. "Thus non-cooperation movement under the local leadership gained ground slowly at first, but more rapidly as time went on."[10]

The Superintendent of Police, Ranchi, coming to the second stage of his note wrote : "Hitherto, people who concerned themselves with the movement were of the non-aboriginal classes, like *Banias, Marwaris, Gwalas, Kahars*, etc. As long as these persons alone were influenced, the situation would not be said to be serious, but on 31st January, 1921 we find Gulab Tiwary addressing a meeting of Oraons. On the 1st February we have Osman, the newly-appointed Head Maulvi of Anjuman Islamia Madarsha, speaking in a general meeting of Oraons, Mundas, Bhuians, Ghashis, all aboriginal and barbers, Chamars and other non-aboriginal classes. Gulab Tiwary and Ram Tahal Brahamchari also addressed this meeting in which speeches were all on the subjects from non-cooperation and anti-drink to boycott of anything European". The Superintendent of Police informed that they "succeeded in arousing considerable excitement amongst their hearers". But apart from their meetings he was greatly anxious about Mundas and Oraons mostly Tanas which were to be held at Ghaghra and Madhukam where Gulab Tiwary, Maulvi Osman, and Ram Tahal Brahamchari were to address. The Superintendent of Police was frank enough to admit : "in my opinion this meeting ought not to take place". He also wrote, "There is a rumour that the Tana Bhagats have asked Gandhiji to visit them". "Probably, this is but a rumour, nevertheless, it gives an indication as to the trend of affairs. Hitherto, the Non-cooperation Movement have been closely watched. Our informers have obtained access even to their secret meetings. It was hoped that the movement would calm down as I beiieve it would have done, were the Oraons and Mundas were kept free from taint." The Superintendent of Police was convinced that the time for action had arrived and he wrote to the Deputy Inspector General of Police and Criminal Investigation Department, Patna for deputation of an expert stenographer to record the speeches of Gulab Tiwary and others. He was equally bothered about the impending visit of Maulana Abul Kalam Azad at Ranchi. He maintained that he required a corp of stenographers because so many serious and important meetings would go on simultaneously and they shall have to be reported verbatim. He felt that action under section 155 of the Indian Penal Code can only be taken if the alleged objectionable speeches were reproduced word-by-word in the light of several High Courts rulings on this point. He also recommended to the Government to extend Seditious Meetings Act (Act X of 1911) to the Ranchi district so that action under Section 5 of that Act may be taken, if necessary.

According to another report[11] submitted by the Superintendent of Police, Ranchi on the subject of Non-cooperation Movement among the Oraons and other Adivasis of Ranchi from 31st January to 13th February, 1921, it is clear that during the course of 13 days several meetings were held. As many as four to five meetings a day used to be held in different places. Ram Tahal Brahamchari addressing a meeting of aboriginals of Ranchi told his audience that "they were the true rulers of Chota Nagpur". In Lohardaga, Kishun Sahu spoke in the meetings of aboriginals at Village Senha. At Ormanjhi, Gulab Tiwary addressed a meeting of aboriginals coming from 18 to 20 villages and it was here that Maulvi Osman was restrained from speaking by the Government order. Meeting at Itki, Ghanghra, Kokar, Tamar, Bundu, Doranda and Madhum were held in which large number of aboriginals attended. In one large meeting on 12th February, 1921, at Kuru, which is a Tana Bhagat centre, about 8,000 Adivasis attended. Ram Tahal Brahamchari made very inflammatory speeches. He also addressed a meeting of 200 Tana Bhagats at village Sosopa where he was served with a notice under Section 144 of Criminal Procedure Code as a consequence of his speeches at Kuru and Sosopa. Thus, we find about 18 meetings were held during the 13 days period. The Superintendent of Police was worried and he reported that on the anticipated spread or disaffection at the increasingly rapid rate Section 144 of Indian Penal Code was hardly adequate. In his opinion all meetings should be stopped in the district, particularly in the Tana Bhagat area, i.e. Police Stations of Mandar, Kuru, Lohardaga and Bero.

On 19th February, 1921, a meeting was to be held at Lohardaga and this time three other non-cooperation leaders — Imam Ali, Ram Reksh Sharma and Swami Vishwananda — had come to Ranchi. On the 16th March there was a complete *Hartal* as a protest against the settlement of excise shops. Tana Bhagats were attending the meeting organised by the non-cooperation workers and their leaders were in touch with the Non-cooperation Movement at national level. On 9th March, 1921, the Deputy Commissioner of Ranchi had informed the Commissioner of Chota Nagpur, "The Tana Bhagat Movement continues to give trouble and there is ample evidence that the efforts of agitators to associate it with non-cooperation has given the movement a new life".[12]

Dr. Rajendra Prasad, Mazrul Haque and others were touring Dhanbad, Hazaribagh, Ranchi, Jharia and other places. Pandit Motilal Nehru paid a hurried visit on 6th March, 1921, and addressed meetings at Jharia, Dhanbad and Chatra. At Giridih, there was a tremendous enthusiasm for the non-cooperation movement. On 2nd May, 1921, the Commissioner wrote to Inspector General of Police "You are perhaps aware that non-cooperation has probably taken a stronger hold in Giridih than anywhere else in the Division. It is easily accessible to the agitators and there have been a large number of meetings held. It is also quite clear that they have got a pretty thorough organisation of the volunteers and they have started *Panchayat* and very fulfledged system of boycott". At Jamshedpur also, there was considerable enthusiasm and meetings were organised which were addressed by Pandit Hari Shankar Vyashji, a Kathiawari disciple of Mahatma Gandhi. He visited Chakradharpur also where he was served with a notice under Section 144 of Criminal Procedure Code; but nonetheless, Chakradharpur remained undoubtedly a stronghold of Non-cooperation Movement. The anti-liquor campaign and non-cooperation at Chaibassa was a wonderful success because when the Deputy Commissioner held an auction of excise shops on 14th March, 1921, he wrote 'for liquor shops not a single bid was obtained.'[13] Santal Parganas was also influenced by the movement from the very beginning and sale in excise shops was affected throughout the district.

Consequently, Government repression also followed against this unique awakening in Bihar and Government resorted to various means of repression. On 31st January, 1921, G. Rainy, the Chief Secretary to the Government of Bihar and Orissa issued a Circular to all Magistrates and Collectors which went down in the history as a infamous Rainy's Circular. Deoki Prasad Sinha of Daltonganj moved a motion for adjournment in Legislative Council on 28th February, 1921 and characterised this circular "as a Carte Blanke" to the men on the spot to use every means in the power to suppress this movement.[14]

All-India Congress Committee laid a great stress on the constructive activity at its meeting in Bombay in July 1921 and called upon all persons belonging to the Congress to discard the use of foreign cloth from the 1st day of August, 1921. Needless to say that it had also salutary effect on the tribals specially the Tana Bhagats. They completely boycotted foreign cloth and started the use of *Khaddar* and Gandhi cap.[15]

Tana's active participation with Congress was witnessed at Gaya. All top-notch of national horizon were present. Deshbandhu Chitarnjan Das the President-elect of Congress, Hakim Azmal Khan, Motilal Nehru, J.M. Sengupta, Sarojini Naidu, S. Srinivas Iyengar, C. Rajagopalachari, N.C. Kelḳar, Sardar Vallabh Bhai Patel, Kasturba Gandhi and many others came from far and near. For the first time, about 60 Oraons, Tanas and Mundas came from Chota Nagpur to Gaya by 21st December to attend the Congress. After that about 400 aboriginals, men and women, went to Gaya on foot. Many Tana Bhagats came in a lorry under the leadership of Gulab Tiwary. Ranchi district alone sent 800 people to attend the Gaya session of the Congress. Gaya Congress left a profound influence on the minds of the Tana Bhagats and other aboriginals who were for the first time initiated into the wider struggle of national freedom movement and had the occasions to rub their shoulders with the greatest Indians of their times practically on a footing of equality. They, on their return from Gaya held several meetings to draw up programmes for national work. Deoki Nandan Lal took the lead in convening several meetings in town and mufassil areas according to the decisions of the Gaya Congress. Dr. P. C. Mitra, Gulab Tiwary and others held meetings at different places for collection of money for Tilak Swaraj Fund and enlisting volunteers.[16]

In the meantime there was a heroic Satyagraha at Nagpur to defend the honour of India's National Flag which had assumed All India Movement by May 1923. Thousands of people ran to Nagpur to vindicate the national honour and courted imprisonment of various terms. Tana Bhagats from Ranchi were amongst such volunteers and several of them were beaten and put in jail. Hardeo Narayan Singh, a Bihari Martyr sacrificed his life at the Nagpur *Satyagraha.*

Belgaon Congress and Tanas

In Belgaon Congress, the Non-cooperation Movement was suspended, but there was an emphasis on the constructive activities of *Khadi* work. Ram Narayan Singh of Hazaribagh, Krishna Ballabh Sahay, and Jimut Bahan Sen were champions of introduction of spinning and *Khaddar* in schools under their control. A big *Khadi* exhibition was opened in Ranchi Arya Samaj Hall on 5th October, 1926 when Dr. Rajendra Prasad was also present and scores of Tana Bhagats attended. The leaders life Dr. P. C. Mitra, Ram Tahal Brahamchari and Deoki Nandan Lal were indefatigably exerting for the constructive programme of the Congress among the tribals. Large number of Tana Bhagats used to attend occasional meetings and participated in processions. Ram Narayan Singh, President of Hazaribagh Congress Committee was the guiding spirit. A *Charkha* demonstration was organised in front of Durga Mandap where Babu Mahendra Prasad of Chapra, the elder brother of Dr. Rajendra Prasad, delivered a speech appealing for Hindu-Muslim unity and spread of *Khadi* work. Tana Bhagats in large number attended this. Thus, in spite of formally suspension of Non-cooperation Movement constructive activities were vigorously pursued in the province in general and in Chota Nagpur in particular.

Mahatma Gandhi's Bihar Tour, 1925-27

Mahatma Gandhi, in a bid to further the constructive activities among the masses made whirl-wind tour in the interior part of the country. His Bihar trip in September 1925 was not the first. He had come to Patna and then to Ranchi during the Indigo *Satyagraha.* Famous meetings between Mahatma Gandhi and Sir Edward Gait, the Lieutenant Governor of Bihar, took place on 2nd June, 1917 and consequently Sly Committee was appointed on 10th July, 1917 to go into the question of Indigo plantation. Therefore, Bihar, or as matter of fact Chota Nagpur, was practically not a new place for Mahatma Gandhi. But in September, 1925, Mahatma Gandhi came as a national leader who had held out a hope for the amelioration of the people as well as the end of foreign rule in India. Purulia was the venue of Bihar Provincial Conference under Mohammad Zubair. Gandhiji attended this. After that, Mahatma Gandhi visited Jamshedpur at the request of C. F. Andrews who was heading a labour union there. Dr. Rajendra Prasad was also with him. It was at the instance of Mahatma Gandhi that the labour union was recognised by the Tatas. He came to Chakradharpur also and from there to Chaibassa, the heartland of Ho tribe. He met the Mundas at Khunti on his way to Ranchi. He saw a silent reform movement begun by the Congress workers from 1921, going on among them. Gandhiji was favourably impressed by the simplicity and docility of these tribes. He recorded, "among these tribes there is quite a colony of them called *Bhaktas*, literally meaning devotees. They are believers in *Khaddar*. Men as well as women plied *Charkha* regularly. They wear *Khaddar* woven by themselves. Many of them had walked miles with their *Charkha* on their shoulders. I saw nearly 400 of them all plying *Charkha* most assiduously at the meeting I had the privilege of addressing. They have their own *Bhajans* which they sing in chorus.[17] At Ranchi several meetings were arranged for him where he raised money for Desh Bandhu memorial fund.[18] Gandhiji was taken to the village of Golkunda where an experiment in hand-spinning was being made through a cooperative society by Girish Chandra Mazumdar, a *Khaddar* enthusiast. He then motored to Hazaribagh where he addressed students of St. Columbus College.

Gandhi's third tour of Chota Nagpur started from Daltonganj in January 1927 when thousands of villagers of hill sides, such as Korwas, Parahiyas, Bhuiyans, Kherwars, Cheros, etc., from distance of 20 to 30 miles gathered. The contribution there mostly in copper and nickel, amounted to Rs. 526. From Daltonganj Gandhi moved to Mairwa where a mammoth meeting was held in a gathering of 30,000 people. This "was at once a model of orderlines, and the biggest" that Mahatma Gandhi had addressed at that time in Bihar.

Simon Commission at Ranchi

Events took a new turn in 1927-29. On 8th November, 1927, a Statutory Commission on Constitutional Reforms was appointed with Sir John Simon as the Chairman and other six English men as members. The exclusion of the Indians from the personnel of the Commission naturally caused countrywide resentment and universal condemnation. Patna greeted the Commission with black flags. The Commission left Patna for Calcutta via Ranchi and Jharia coalfields. At a meeting of the citizens of Ranchi held on 18th December, 1927 under the Presidentship of S. K. Sahay, a resolution was unanimously passed to boycott the Simon Commission. Deoki Nandan Lal, Dr. P. C.

Mitra and many Tana Bhagats coming from different parts of Chota Nagpur, joined in the demonstration against it and showed black flags. The police report informs that the Tana Bhagats of Mandar, Kuru, Lohardaga and Karra assembled under the leadership of Kohara Pandey of village Navdip, Police Station Patan of Palamau District. Dr. P. C. Mitra and many others along with about 150 Tana Bhagats left Ranchi on 27th December, 1928 to attend the Calcutta Session of the Indian National Congress which discussed resolution on Dominion Status.

Bangam Manjhi Movement

In the meantime, there arose among the Santals of Gomia, a reformer Bangam Manjhi of Borobera who with some sort of a mysterious inspiration like Tanas sought to reform his society and soon gathered around himself thousands of disciples.[20] He exhorted his followers to be clear and pure, and use *Khaddar* exclusively. This attracted the notice of Ram Narayan Singh and Krishna Ballav Sahay who sympathised with them, but they were themselves arrested. Their arrest gave impetus to the movement among the Santals.[21] Meeting of these Santals used to be held in the dead of night on each full moon, and some of these were attended by such prominent leaders as Sardar Vallabh Bhai Patel, Dr. Rajendra Prasad and Babu Mathura Prasad. On 31st May, 1930 about 210 Santal took sacred threads.

Independence Flag at Ranchi

At Ranchi too, there was considerable awakening. On Independence Day, a huge procession consisting of Tana Bhagats and the students of all the local institutions was taken out and Dr. P. C. Mitra hoisted the National flag at the junction of three roads near Sadar Hospital amidst shout of *Bande Mataram, Bharat Mata Ki Jay, Kranti Ki Jai*, etc. On 28th January 1930, a meeting was organised at Silli by P. N. Bose, the local Assistant Station Master who was resident of Jhalda. Besides local leaders Nibaran Chandra Das Gupta and Atul Chandra Ghosh of Purulia, Sri Raghavacharya, editor of paper *Mukti* of Purulia, Ramchandra Adhikari of Deshbandhu Press of Purulia, Mathura Prasad of Sadakat Asram, Patna, etc. addressed other meetings at Ranchi and in its neighbourhood during February and March 1930, which was well attended by Tana Bhagats and others. According to the police report,

1963 Tana Bhagats had enlisted themselves as Congress members and they, under the leadership of Bhuka Bhagat were fully prepared for the impending fight of Civil Disobedience Movement. A meeting to celebrate Political Suffers Day with Jatendra Nath Thakur in chair was held on 30th March, 1930 at Ranchi in which Dr. P. C. Mitra, Gulab Tiwary, Nagar Mal Modi, Charwan Bhagat, Madhu Bhagat and Ramchandra Prasad addressed the audience. Salt *Satyagraha* was in full force in Manbhum under Nibaran Das Gupta.[22]

Bardoli Satyagraha and Tanas

A successful *Satyagraha* Movement and no-rent campaign had been organised by the peasantry of Bardoli Taluka in Surat District under the leadership of Sardar Vallabh Bhai Patel. This had a profound influence on the tribals of Chota Nagpur and specially the Tana Bhagats. They threw themselves heart and soul in the midstream of this *Satyagraha* and were jailed. The table below will give the latest picture (up to 1968) regarding the institution of cases, number of cases disposed of the number of cases pending when the Government of Bihar launched a special drive to benefit the Tanas under Ranchi District Tana Bhagat Land Restoration Act. This will give the idea of magnitude of sacrifice made by Tanas then.

Cases				Area Restored	Number of Family involved
Instituted	Allowed	Rejected	Pending		
Cases 1170	224	760	188	2702.64	224
Appeals 99	47	35	17		

Picketting at country wine shops was very particular programme of the Tanas. Liquor shop at Lohardaga was picketted by the Tanas and they were beaten like any thing. Baldeo Sahu was the wine-king of the area and he had great influence. Police acted at his beck and call. He used to have hired musclemen to belabour these picketteers. But the Tanas never minded this physical torture. As a result, no liquor addict dared to go to the liquor shops in day time. But there was the doubt that in the cover of night helpless drunkard used to go to the liquor shops. In picketting the liquor shops the names of Dukhi Bhagat, Luta Bhagat, Baro Bhagat, Ballia Bhagat at Lohardaga, Sania Bhagat, Bhukhlu

Bhagat at Kisko, Mangra Bhagat, Gounda Bhagat, Jhari Bhagat, Mathia Bhagat, Lakhna Bhagat, Jhirga Bhagat at Bagru are still remembered.

At the liquor shop at Sonsopa, Yetwa Bhagat of Chanho and others used to do picketting. Dasarath Sahu, the distiller, brought the police and got them beaten mercilessly. The Tanas used to go to the *Bhathi* with the tricolour in hands and Gandhi cap on their heads. They used to lie down on the doors of the *Bhatti* and were beaten and sometimes taken to jail, Yetwa Bhagat of Patratu Chanho had gone to Karachi Congress also. Lands of Tanas were auctioned in 1934-35. Kohra Pandey of Palamau, a worker among Tanas used to visit Sonsopa and work among the local Tanas. Dr. Rajendra Prasad also visited those days and was given reception by the Tanas at Mandar, Opa and Kuru. Mahadeo Sonar of Choreya, Nageshwar Prasad, Deoki Nandan Lal, Dr. P. C. Mitra of Ranchi used to visit them off and on an advised them to continue the struggle. Krishna Ballabh Sahay used to visit Tana areas and he was very popular among them. Nageshwar Babu, Akhauri Narayan Sekhar Singh of Gumla and others used to visit the Tanas of Kuru, Opa and Mandar and used to hold nocturnal meetings in out-of-way places. They used to give them directions which they used to get from Dr. P. C. Mitra and Deoki Nandan Lal of Ranchi who were thought by the Tanas as the linkmen between them and the Congress High Command which they called *Oppar*. Four anna membership was the regular feature of Tana Movement. Bhukha Bhagat, Yetwa Bhagat, Gooa Bhagat, Madho Bhagat, Bhual Bhagat were used to collect subscription in their respective areas and deposited it with Bhukha Bhagat at Mandar who was the President of Tana Bhagat of Mandar Police Station. Bisua Bhagat of Cheter alieas Biswamitra Bhagat was highly respected by Tanas. He went to jail in 1936 and 1942. His wife also used to attend meetings of the Tanas. The formation of Congress Ministry in 1937 was welcomed in almost all quarters. It was celebrated as Ministry day all over Bihar. Tanas dream came true and they started thinking of the real *Swarajya*. But when Dr. S. K. Sinha Ministry resigned, the Tanas once again geared up their loins to give a stiff fight.

Ramgarh Congress and Tanas, 1940

The Ramgarh session of Congress met under the Presidentship of Maulana Abul Kalam Azad from 19th to 20th March 1940 in a large and artistically decorated amphitheatre, formed by the natural undulations of the ground on the bank of the river Damodar in the hilly tract of Chota Nagpur. Large number of Tanas under Lalo Bhagat, Yetma Bhagat, Soma Bhagat, Biswamitra Bhagat, Khabia Bhagat from Bishanpur, Chandwa, Kuru, Ghaghra, Opa, Mandar, etc., attended the Congress at Ramgarh. They covered the distance brisk walking on foot in two days resulting in injury to their legs. They presented a purse of Rs. 400 to Gandhiji.[23] Huts in large number were put at Ramgarh where they were to stay; but the excessive rains which continued for all the day and night rendered them useless and they passed their night almost standing. They met national leaders who had special sympathy and affection for them. They were given special treatment by Mahatma Gandhi and Dr. Rajendra Prasad. Gandhiji exhorted them to go on working for their noble cause and all trial and tribulations could be over after they had attained *Swarajya*.

Individual Satyagraha, 1941

Mahatma Gandhi instructed that "in view of the fact that individual Civil Disobedience had already commenced and large number of Congressmen had already been imprisoned all over India, it become the special duty of every Indian to concentrate with redoubled zeal on constructive programme without the fulfilment of which no Civil Disobedience, mass or individual, can help us to win and retain *Swarajya*". A National Week was observed by following Mahatma Gandhi's advice for self-purification by fasting on the 6th and 13th April, 1941 and by more concentrated efforts to increase membership, constructive work and propaganda for *Swadeshi* and *Khadi* goods, communal unity and eradication of untouchability.

Laloo Bhagat and other Tanas of Kuru reported that they used to sell *Khaddar* after they brought it from Shankar Babu Bankar Lal of Ranchi. They used to get *Khadi* from Lohardaga also. Deoki Bhagat and Gondla Bhagat were great *Khadi* enthusiasts and they propagated it. Intensive drive for membership of Congress was done and so also other constructive programmes were followed.

Individual Satyagraha was offered by several leading Tanas — Rati Bhagat narrated that the Tanas used to go to *hat* and bazars and recite —

"Brothers and sisters, in this War any help with men and money is a sin and undesirable. It is proper for us to oppose the War recruitment measures through non-violent *satyagraha*."[24]

So many Tanas offered for courting arrest that they were harassed by not being taken to Police Station under arrest, rather they moved for seven days from one *hat* and bazar to another reciting the pledge given above. At last the Tanas were asked to go to Ranchi on foot and preaching *satyagraha* in the way. They were met with mounted police and were beaten. They were housed in the Congress office. Tanas narrated that Deoki Nandan Lal induced them to take their food in some hotel which they did not agree inspite of the fact that Deoki Nandan Lal admonished them for practising untouchability. They claimed that they had already got exemption from Mahatma Gandhi and at last they cooked their own food. Next day they returned to their respective villages as none was arrested.[25]

Revolution of 1942 and the Tanas

Ranchi had already become a storm-centre of the movement because of the valiant Tanas involvement in Congress nationalist movement. Tanas had by then the tradition of fighting for national cause for more than two decades. On the 17th August, 1942, a large procession was taken out at Ranchi. The Police with a contingent of armed force dispersed it on the Sharadhanand Road near the office of the *Nagrik Rakha Samity* and several persons were arrested. On 19th August, 1942, a batch of Tana Bhagats of the Chainpur, Bishanpur thanas burnt the Bishanpur Police Station. The police arrested some of the Tana Bhagats and beat some of them mercilessly. On 21st August, 1942, some Tana Bhagats broke the lock of Sonchipi Ashram which was sealed by the police earlier because it was considered to be the centre of Tana Bhagat movement. Next day, the railway line between Itki and Tangar Banshili were damaged. Dr. P. C. Mitra was arrested the same day but Chorka Bhagat escaped and played havoc with police till he was arrested after a month in the last week of September at Gumla.

On the 23rd August, 1942 the telegraph line was cut and rails were removed at many places in Tana areas. The same day Tana Bhagats assembled at the Mandar Hat in which Mahadeo Sonar, Chamara Bhagat, and Gaoa Bhagat delivered speeches appealing to the people to push on the movement and exhorted the Government servants to resign. All of them were arrested by the police. On 24th August, four

Tana Bhagats entered the Branch Post Office of Burmu and snatched the *dak* by overpowering the postal staff. They were arrested by the police. Some other Tana Bhagats were also arrested the same day, while they were distributing leaflets at Sons Bazar in the Mandar Police Station. On 28th August, 1942 some Tana Bhagats also tried to occupy the Burmu Police Station but they were arrested. Lalu Bhagat was arrested on 28th August, 1942 alongwith Khabea Bhagat, Lakhan Bhagat, Surju Bhagat and they all were taken to Phulwari Sarif Camp Jail where they underwent two years' rigorous imprisonment.

On 3rd September, 1942, some Tana Bhagats delivered speeches at Tuko Hat in the Bero Police Station advocating non-payment of taxes and they were also arrested.

On 26th September, 1942 many Tana Bhagats assembled at Dasagaon Hat, in the Chainpur police station with the object of asking the Sub Inspector and the Post Master to leave their posts. Two of their leaders were arrested, and their houses were searched. Again on 2nd October, a large number of Tana Bhagats came to Gadah Kujam, in the Bishanpur Police Station with a view to attack Dumarpat Dak Bunglow. Many of them were arrested (only 6 according to a Government report) and their assembly was forcefully dispersed by the Police. On 5th October the telegraph line between Gumla-Lohardaga road was cut. On 16th October, 1942, some Tana Bhagats took out a procession at Bero which was dispersed by the police and several of them were arrested. On 18th November, 1942, some Tana Bhagats alongwith one Anil Kumar Mukherjee were arrested at Mandar for distributing pamphlets of similar nature.

In Palamau Girija Nandan Singh and many Tana Bhagats were arrested at village Tippu, Police Station Latehar on the 31st August, 1942. Next day many Tana Bhagats of Latehar and Garoo Police Stations and from Lohardaga assembled at Latehar and formed a procession there and preached in the *hat*. On the same day liquor shop at Barwadih was raided. On 12th September, 1942, a party of Tana Bhagats zealously engaged in furthering the course of the national movement entered Chandwa Police Station and hoisted the national flag there in front of Sub-Inspector building, but on their attempt to hoist the national flag on the main thana building, they were arrested and sentenced to varying terms of imprisonment and were also fined.

Jail life of the Tanas was also very heroic. At Patna camp jail, stationed at Phulwari Sarif the Tanas used to get Volunteer Training in camp known as *Gandhi Shivir* under the captainship of Lalji Babu.

Ashirbad Bhagat at Kuru narrated that while undergoing training in the said camp in the jail while he was performing the duty of a *Sentri* on the gate of *Gandhi Shivir*, the jailer Mr. Fuller was prevented by him to enter into the *Shivir*. For this, he was put in cell for one month. Puran Bhagat was also trained in camp.

Laloo Bhagat[26] at Kuru narrated that at Phulwari Sarif camp jail he had to bury several of his fellow Tanas because they could not stand the jail life and its rigours. He attributed severe beating and the oily food served to them in the jail as the main cause of their death. Tanas were not used to take so much oil and thus their stomach got upset and they died. In the camp jail the Tanas were respected by their fellow prisoners and top leaders in Jail used to sympathise with them. As many as thirty Tanas of Kuru Police Station were in Phulwari Sharif camp jail, six of them died in jail. Many of them died just after their release. Only a few of them like Lalu Bhagat, Ashirwad Bhagat, Puram Bhagat, etc., are still alive to tell the tale. Lalu Bhagat, Some Bhagat and Ratti Bhagat and others were honoured by the Prime Minister Indira Gandhi at Delhi on the 16th August, 1972 by *Tamapatra* for their heroic role in the national struggle for freedom. The Tanas braved all odds of jail life as well as life outside the jail in a hope that they shall have their *Swarajya* when they would not be pressed for rent, forest dues, rail fare and bus fare and many other concessions which the simple Tana mind could think of. Their land was being cultivated by those who had taken them by auction purchase. This used to rankle in their hearts. Krishna Ballabh Sahay and others emphasised the need of restoration of their land back to them and thus the Ranchi District Tana Bhagat Raiyots Agricultural Land Restoration Act, 1947 was passed with a view to restore their land which were auctioned.

Thus the sequence of events in the Tana Bhagat Movement shows the impact which Mahatma Gandhi and his associates created on the tribals specially the Tana Bhagats. No where we can find that these tribals during these years claimed *separatism* or they were embroideled in fighting the Dikus rather they were involved in greater stakes of life which were before them, the stake of liberating the motherland from the vice clutches of British Imperialism. They made unprecedented sacrifices to attain this much cherished freedom. Their exploits in liberating the country have been the romance of the local as well as national history. They remained in the main stream of country's freedom struggle and history is witness that they have never changed their determination. Their present population is 18,451 in 467 villages.

Tana Land and the Restoration Act always get lapsed and then revived periodically. It is a tragedy that this community of self-sacrificing spreading in different 18 blocks have been forgotten in old Ranchi District.

Of late, we have perceived a tendency among some scholars to read much in separatist movement among the tribals of Chota Nagpur and characterise it as tribal solidarity movement. Some of them believe, that after, Birsa's failure in 1900 (if at all was a failure) there was "sullen silence". When they look back on the relevant events of the first 38 years of this century from the vantage point of 1939, they find that "sullen silence" applies to the rural illiterate Adivasis.[27] It is quite interesting to find that such scholars perhaps deliberately shut up their eyes to the movement of Tana Bhagat which inextricably got itself mixed into Non-cooperation and Civil Disobedience Movement propagated by Mahatma Gandhi and his followers right from 1916. Such scholars do not consider the movement as a relevant event and therefore, they completely skip over these events. But as a student of history, specially who has worked in the project of compilation a History of Freedom Movement in India and Bihar these above mentioned episodes in the history of Tana Bhagats and the great popularity of national and local leaders among them demonstrate the solid fact that tribal community in general have thrown their lot with the lot of the nation and had fully integrated with it. This was achieved by unflinching sympathy and goodwill as ringing sincerity in their heart and, therefore, there was a communion between tribal interest and national interest. The whole community of Tanas and other such communities are Gandhiji's greatest contribution.

NOTES

1. Ekka Philip, "Revivalist Movement Among the Tribals of Chota Nagpur" in *Tribal Situation in India*, Simla, Indian Institute of Advanced Study, 1972, p. 426.
2. *Ibid.*, p. 427.
3. R. O. Dhan, "The Problems of the Tana Bhagats of Ranchi District", *Bulletin, Bihar Tribal Welfare Research Institute* (Ranchi), Vol 2 (1960), pp. 136-38.
4. S. C. Roy, "A Religious Movement among the Oraons" *Man in India* Vol. 1 (1921), pp. 226-321.
5. S. C. Roy "Revival Movement in Oraon Religion" in *Oraon Religion and Custom*, Ranchi, 1928, pp. 312-409.
6. Letter dated 20th April, 1919 from Deputy Inspector General of Police, Chota Nagpur Range to Government of Bihar, Ranchi.

7. Letter dated 15th October, 1919 from Commissioner of Chota Nagpur to Government of Bihar, Ranchi.
8. Same as 3, p. 169.
9. S.P. Sinha, "Gandhi's impact on the Tribals of Chota Nagpur 1920-30" In *Gandhi and Social Sciences*, New Delhi (1970), pp. 151-52.
10. *Ibid.*
11. K. K. Dutta, *History of Freedom Movement in Bihar*, Patna (1957), p. 336.
12. Letter dated 15th April, 1921 from the Commissioner of Chota Nagpur, Ranchi to the Chief Secretary, Government of Bihar and Orissa.
13. *Ibid.*
14. *Proceedings of Bihar and Orissa Legislative Council*, 1921, Vol. 1, pp. 272-87.
15. Same as 9, pp. 155-56.
16. Report dated 2nd January, 1923 of the Superintendent of Police, Ranchi.
17. Same as 9, pp. 157-58.
18. Mahadev Desai, *Gandhiji in Indian Villages*, p. 238.
19. Same as 9 p. 159.
20. *Ibid.*
21. *The Searchlight*, 16th February 1930.
22. Same as 9 p. 160.
23. Oral statement of Rati Bhagat to the author on 30th August 1972.
24. *Ibid.*
25. Oral statement of Lalu Bhagat and other Tanas at Tanti to the author on 30th August 1972.
26. *Ibid.*
27. P. G. Ganguli, *Separatism in the Indian Polity* : A case study in Anthropology and Archaeology, Bombay (1969), pp. 58-107.

10

THE LEGACY OF POLITICAL CONFLICT

THE NINETEENTH century in Chota Nagpur witnessed the holocaust of bitter tribal revolt of Birsa for bringing back the rights of the tribals. It also bequeathed to the new century the yearning for *Abuaraj* (self-rule) so that the land of their forefathers could become *Sona Lekam Disum* (country of gold). If this rebellion of Birsa brought in its train the resolution of the agrarian conflict in shape of Chota Nagpur Tenancy Act, 1980 and survey and settlement operations, the beginning of this century also witnessed the *Abuaraj* clamouring which was the logical conclusion of that agrarian struggle. There are many instances when by launching political campaigns they wanted to wrest the political power too. That is why we find that although the tribals who would have been contented with their *Magna Carta* in the form of Chota Nagpur Tenancy Act and Survey and Settlement Operation in Ranchi District, but history is witness that not for a single day the tribals sat contented. Rather they fought relentlessly for political power also so that their condition is ameliorated in a special sanctuary created for them.

In this political determinism of the tribes of Chota Nagpur and Santal Parganas, one can find them throwing challenges to the British Government in the form of Tana Bhagat Movement in Ranchi, Sapha Hor Movement in Santal Parganas, Phetal Singh Movement in Palamau, Hari Baba Movement in Singhbhum, Bhumij Chatriya Movement in the then Manbhum etc. Apart from these movements, one can find interacting political forces working in this Plateau in the form of missionaries of respective congregations. It is said that they had learnt this lesson that if they have to flourish, they must be by the side of power and create such a cleavage between the people of Chota Nagpur that tribals as a people must be separated from the rest of the population so that they are kept segregated and unaffected by the political upheavels being experienced throughout the length and breadth of the country due to the various forces of nationalism working there. Thakker Bapa and his band of self-less workers were working among the *Adivasis*. Tana Bhagats threw themselves heart and soul in the Gandhi's Non-cooperation Movement. Therefore, it is said that Christian missionaries, imbued with imperialist ideas, had thought that there will be no bishop, no king. Therefore, these missionaries shaped in the initial years the political thinking of the new literates among the Christian groups and groomed them for a role in the political agitation against the dominating Hindu population. With this limited political concept to liberate the tribals from the so-called tutelage of the Hindu-non-tribals, the Christian missionaries bolstered up political propaganda through one committee and society or another and ultimately were successful in paving the way for creation of a mighty political forces of Jharkhand Party under Jaipal Singh. It is quite a different thing that in this politics of Separatism, Muslim League became the major partner of the Christian missionaries. But this definitely paved the way for self-determinism of the non-Christians tribals which were epitomised in the political manuvouring of Theble Oraon and others which ultimately afflorenced in the bright Karticism of Kartick Oraon, a foreign-educated ace Design Engineer, who became the Deputy Chairman of Chota Nagpur and Santal Parganas Autonomous Development Authority and Minister of State in Union Government till he died in 1982. Every action must produce a reaction and this is very well depicted in the brief survey of the different movements in the field of politics of this area. Those movements might differ from each other in tenor and texture, but they definitely are the ruthless mirror of their own time. Wresting of power through ballot and not by battle-axe has been one of the features of this political battle going on which has created at times tensional situations and therefore, a little analysis of various elections conducted in this part of the country especially in reserved constituencies have also been done here so that the role of Jharkhand Party and Kartik Oraon in contrast with other regional and national political parties could well be understood.

Jharkhand and Other Political Movements

Tribal society is based on kinship. The introduction of Christianity had implied secular repercussions which were vital for the tribals in general. Christianity converted some of the tribals spiritually and others secularly. The result of the complex process was that, given the indigenious 'rulers', the immigrants and the relevant British policy, the missionaries had succeeded in producing not only an Adivasi elite-Christian, skilled in new vocations and capable of reading and writing in English — but also a diffused mass of tribals-Christians and also non-Christians — connected with the elite. Ranchi was both symbol of suffering and redemption — the suffering brought to them through the actual working of the power system in which they perceived themselves to be involved; redemption through various repercussions of the impact of Christianity. In the absence of town like Ranchi new Adivasi would have remained localised in the mission stations in different parts of the Plateau. Therefore, the crucial role of Ranchi in drawing the new Adivasis together into a non-traditional 'urban' milieu cannot be over-emphasised. The town centralised the new Adivasis, and provided them with a framework in which they could see their own strength and thus prompted them to undertake concerted action to solve what they perceived as their problems arising from their interaction with the immigrants from the plains. The elite Adivasis, therefore, lived, as it were, in two worlds, both bristling with unsolved problems. After the suppression of Birsa rising and consequent passage of their *Magna Carta*, the Chota Nagpur Tenancy Act in 1908 and introduction of western education, the new Adivasis particularly based in Ranchi or Hazaribagh formed various committees, societies and associations for the improvement of the lot of Adivasis during the twenties, thirties and forties of this century.

The various Christian missionaries who took very active part in the land question were now naturally turned to secure political division of the State of Bihar by bolstering up a movement among the tribes. The tribesmen were reportedly told that they were different people, that they were deprived of their political rights by their *Diku* masters, that they could not prosper unless they are completely alienated from the non-tribals people of their area. Not that the tribal people were getting most favoured treatment from their *Diku* compatriots and the situation was very good, but the source of a generated tension and conflict on the eve of the First World War was also the distribution of what Robert Dehl calls 'divisible benefits'. A class of newly-educated tribal youth was given to think of the maladies and injustices by which they were suffering and, therefore, under the guidance of European teachers they started gesticulating to reform themselves so that they may prosper. But this remained a closed door movement among the Christians students only because the educated class came mostly from among them and they were the persons who were in intimate contact with the European teachers either at St. Columbus College, Hazaribagh or at different mission centres at Ranchi and suburbs and other seminaries of repute run by the missionaries. Therefore, the movement of handful of Christian students under the patronage of their western missionary teachers had in the beginning an innocent urge to improve themselves. It is quite different thing that these movements ultimately served as the nucleus of bigger Jharkhand Movement for the establishment of a separate State for the tribals later.

Jharkhand Movement essentially of socio-political importance was mooted in the beginning for bringing out reformation and prosperity in decadent tribal society. Therefore *Unnati Samaj* was formed under the leadership of western-educated and trained tribal leaders mostly Christians to improve their situation socially and economically. In doing so they were also found propagating the political aspect of the Adivasi question and they were successful to a great extent in projecting an ethnic and separatist identity later on.

Dacca Students Union, 1910-13

In the formative phase a little student organisation was founded in 1910 by J. Bartholmen[1] a young orphan from Chaibassa and a student of St. Columbus College, Hazaribagh. He was brought up by an American Missionary at Chaibassa and as a college student he had the personality of an organiser and had also a strong urge to help a fellow student. He used to go out and organise and address Christian students conferences at different places and thereby try to learn about the problems of poor students. He attended such conferences at Sirampore and Dacca. We need hardly say that Srirampore was the centre of a great missionary activity and Dacca was also the inspirational centre for the neo-Christians who were in search of their new identity. Therefore, it will be in the fitness of the things that J.Bartholmen had his real training in Bengal and therefore, the first leader of the new movement was Bengal-based and Bengal-oriented.

In 1911 and 1912, after return from Dacca Conference he decided to form Dacca Students Union. In such union consisting Christian students, patrons and professors, the missionaries were requested to give religious discourse. A fund for needy Christian students was also raised and it took the shape of monthly subscription and donations from a few German Missionaries. At St. Paul Institute, Ranchi, a drama was staged which fetched an attractive amount. Bartholmen, encouraged by this, held a general conference of Lutheran and Anglican students and a new branch of this union was opened at

Ranchi also and put under the stewardship of Peter Hayward. Bartholmen completed his graduation in 1915 and joined St. Paul High School' Ranchi as Assistant Teacher. Though he remained active in movement for sometime, but it looks that he was not allowed to blossom forth into a great leader of the tribal people. He was philanthropic and was clear in his mind to help his Christians brethren for which he was striving so hard. His era was an era of hardwork and laying the foundation of a mighty edifice which ultimately overthrew Bartholmen and overshadowed him.

The First World War created a great stir in the life of the people and, therefore, we have no knowledge regarding the political movement in this era except that the Christian missionaries of German nationality were interned and later on turned out from the country by the Government. The German Christian missionaries were by that time the real men behind the political scene in the tribal world and with their removal the tribal Christian remained leaderless and friendless. Tana Bhagats used to mutter "the German Baba" and they were delighted at the debacle of the British at the hands of the Germans and, therefore, the whole community of Tana Bhagats was taken as belligerent. This is significant that the twenties and thirties were years of experimentation with the new techniques for concerted action, non-kin voluntary organisation. Tanas and others were then together with the wider national organisations like India National Congress. The new converts under their respective missions formed their own voluntary organisations.

Chota Nagpur Unnati Samaj, 1913

Bartholmen's pioneering effort was followed by others who formed Chota Nagpur Improvement Society or the Chota Nagpur Unnati Samaj in 1913 with Theble Oraon, Rai Saheb Bandi Ram Oraon, Rev. Joel Lakra and Paul Dayal etc. as the leading members. Rev. Joel Lakra as the chief spokesman of the Samaj claimed to have represented before Simon Commission in 1928 for creation of separate state for the Adivasis.[2] Samaj unexpectedly embraced non-christian tribal leaders like Theble Oraon and Bandi Ram Oraon, Ranchi-based enlightened leaders. But this healthy situation was not destined to continue for long and they differed on many issues. Ultimately, this difference led to the formation of Kisan Sabha with Theble Oraon which continued well for sometime, but could not achieve any marked success in the election held in 1935-36.

Chota Nagpur Catholic Sabha

The members of the Dacca Students Union and Chota Nagpur Unnati Samaj were overwhelmingly either from Anglican Mission or Lutheran Mission and a few non-Christian like Theble Oraon and Bandi Ram Oraon. The Roman Catholic Adivasis also wanted their own organisations and thus the Chota Nagpur Catholic Sabha was formed and there was no difficulty in popularising it through the large network of the Catholic Church. Its aims and objects were purely socio-religious and economic, though it also involved itself in the political issues of the day. Within short time the Sabha grew to such a strature that it set up its two candidates for 1935 election who won the contest by routing Kisan Sabha and Unnati Samaj candidates. Catholic Sabha's Ignes Beck represented the area in Parliament during 1935-1940 and he somehow or other fell under the spell of Mohamad Ali Jinnah who entertained a great contempt for Congressmen and the Congress Party. Beck contemplated and visualised that unless the denominational differences among the Adivasis were removed and they stood united for a common cause, the aboriginal mass will not attain salvation from social, economic and political backwardness. Therefore, he worked out a plan for common front and contested Ranchi Municipal elections and won a glorious victory. They now believed in the efficacy of permanent alliance to fight the *Diku Raj* and work for emancipation for the Adivasis by creation of a separate State.

Chota Nagpur Adivasi Mahasabha

In 1938, some of the voluntary organisations, except Tana Bhagats and Congressite tribals, coalesced and their leaders convened the *First Adivasi Mahasabha*, presumably to present united front. This coalescence of the voluntary organisations was amorphous and the new organisation was merely a political forum for leadership with little contact with the masses. The coalescence of Kisan Sabha, Chota Nagpur Unnati Samaj, Munda Sabha and Catholic Sabha came about on 31st May, 1938 under the leadership of Trio, Theodore Surin (President), Rai Saheb Bandi Ram Oraon (Vice-President), and Paul Dayal (Secretary) at Hindpiri convention at Ranchi which was attended by about 400 delegates from all parts of the districts. A Working

Committee consisting of 21 members representing various Christian missions was also formed. Separation of Chota Nagpur was demanded. From the very beginning, it was clear that the organisation was sponsored and backed by the Christian missionaries and loyalist non-Christians like Rai Saheb Bandi Ram and others who were alarmed at the Tana Bhagat movement in Chota Nagpur and their complicity with the national and local leaders and workers of the Congress organisation. Tana Bhagats in a body had already become staunch Congress members by 1936. It is said that for mere self-preservation they (missionaries) conceived the idea of separating Chota Nagpur from the rest of Bihar. In October 1938, a regular office of the Mahasabha was started in the house of Jaikaran Tamoli (Christian) of Ranchi and a Hindi fortnightly paper styled as "Adivasi" was published with Rai Saheb Bandi Ram and Michael Tigga as printer. This continued till the merger of Jharkhand with Congress with Gopal Munjhal as its editor.

The *Second Adivasi Mahasabha* was held on 20 January, 1939 at Ranchi. By the end of 1938, Mr. Jaipal Singh, a new Adivasi towering over all others, returned to the Plateau after two decades. He was immediately accepted by the Adivasis as their *Marang Gomke* (the supreme leader). During his long absence Jaipal Singh was nearly forgotten. A few months before his arrival as the President of the Second Mahasabha, the Ranchi-based new Adivasis had spread the story of the remarkable career of this Christian Munda. Thus the legend of Jaipal Singh developed among the masses almost over-night and to many Adivasis he appeared as a Divine gift. A man of thirty six in 1939, he had his first education at St. Paul's School, Ranchi. He was the son of a *Pahan* at Takra village not very far from Ranchi town. Jaipal Singh's father worked for Anglican Canon Cosgrave. Cosgrave looked after young Jaipal and then helped him to Darlington, England, where he gave him private tuition in 1919-20. During this period Jaipal also studied at St. Augustine's College, Canterbury and excelled in all fields of sport, eventually becoming hockey captain there. From 1922 to 1926 he was at St. John's College, Oxford. He was the hockey captain and also the President of the Junior Common Room. In 1927, he was an Indian Civil Service Probationer, but he eventually failed. Meanwhile, he had obtained a Full Blue in Hockey at Oxford and between 1923 and 1928 he toured France, Belgium, Spain and Germany as a member of the Hockey teams comprising Indian residents in Europe. In 1928, he captained the Indian Hockey team which won the world championship. He earned special congratulations from the Viceroy of India. From 1928 to 1933 he was a Covenanted Mercantile Assistant in the Royal Dutchship Group, Calcutta — the first Indian to hold such a post. From 1934-37, he was Commercial Master at Achimpta College, Accra — an appointment at that time in the Senior Colonial Service. From 1937-38, he was Senior Assistant Master at Rajkumar College, Raipur. In 1938 he was Revenue Commissioner and Acting Colonisations Minister in Bikaner, one of the largest Native Princely States. He married the grand daughter of W.C. Bannerjee and had three children. To the new Adivasis, a man with such a career was the concrete embodiment of their own aspirations, and he exceedingly fitted in the structure of the then new Adivasi politics. He was an outsider in the sense that the was not involved in the Ranchi-based politics for leadership. He was, however, also an insider because he was Munda by birth. They took him as an incarnation of Ranchi himself. In his *Reminiscences*, Anugrah Narain Sinha wrote about Jaipal Singh:

> "Sri Jaipal Singh, a Christian tribal, was working in the Bikaner State on some post. He had to give it up for some reason. He wanted to get some employment in Bihar. A suitable employment for him could have been available only in the Department under the charge of Dr. Sayed Mahmood, but Dr. Mahmood was not inclined to oblige. Later on the Bengali community helped him financially to become the leader of the tribal people. Inspired by anagtonism, Jaipal Singh organised the tribals and became busy in teaching them to keep aloof from the Hindus and oppose Congress."[3]

At this very time where the Congressites failed N.N. Rakshit, a Tata-based businessman-politician won. He was said to have been let down by Congress leaders in his election to the Legislative Council of State and he found in Jaipal a suitable person who could be used against Congress for vendetta. When in February 1939, Jaipal Singh with Theble Oraon went to Jamshedpur, Rakshit was their host. He alleged to have received some money from Rakshit which he assured him was to be spent in good cause. It was here then they gave birth to Chota Nagpur Separation League, Jaipal informed that he kicked off the offer of a place in Bihar Ministry. But Singh soon fell with Theble and there was the parting of the ways.

A few living persons corroborated the claim that Second Adivasi

Mahasabha was one of the biggest draw of Adivasi and non-Adivasis that Ranchi ever saw. On 21st January,1939 at about 11 A.M. a crowd of about a hundred thousand Adivasis gathered at the place where the Main Road joins the Railway Station Road and the vast concourse of human heads extended up to Lutheran Church. Jaipal Singh in his presidential address declared :

> "This is one of the most momentous occasions in my life. I have been separated from your midst nearly twenty years and you are now asking me to be your leader in the tremendous struggle ahead of us for our economic and political freedom . . . One of the last wishes of my Guru the late Canon Cosgrave, was that I should come back to Chota Nagpur and lead my people to enable them to take their station in the national life of India. I solemnly dedicate myself to the work you are committing to me. . . . The Adivasi Movement stands primarily for the moral and material advancement of Chota Nagpur and the Santal Parganas, for the economic and political freedom of the aboriginal tracts and, in sum, for the creation of a separate Governor's province comprising roughly Chota Nagpur and Santal Parganas, with a government and administration appropriate to its need. It is conceded everywhere that Chota Nagpur suffered by being tagged on to Bihar. In separation alone lies the salvation of Chota Nagpur (audience roared-Victory to Chota Nagpur). We will be content with nothing less than an existence of our own, a separate province, a separate government, a separate administration. Then and then only can we ever hope to shape and mould our great destiny. We have waited patiently and silently long enough for others to help us, we have trusted others in vain to help us march forward along the path of progress and improvement. Thank God, we have learnt our lesson in time. We must help ourselves. Our great future is in our own hands. The Adivasi movement has recently amalgamated into a united organisation of all the many aboriginals (groups). . . . All the past divisions and distressing dissensions have completely disappeared and the Adivasis are now all one in their struggle for freedom from the tyranny of mere number. We offer united front and amazing fact in the annals of the aborigines. All the missionary institutions working here are with us, another remarkable achievement. Even the Bengalis are crying for separation, the European and Anglo-Indians are openly showing us their

sympathy. You have not to go far to find the explanation for all this bewildering changes."[4]

Jaipal Singh delivered a lengthy address and was greatly applauded. He enkindled in the hearts of the teeming millions of Adivasi a hope of emancipation and showed to the Government the reasonableness of accepting the reality. Rakshit was present at the conference and he presented a motor car and sum of Rs. 250 to the Adivasi Sabha. The Mahasabha at Ranchi was an epoch-making event in the history of the Plateau because for the first time the demand of Chota Nagpur and Santal Parganas as separate State, proliferated from the simple way of a few disgruntled Adivasi leaders. Separatism as a cult was first preached ably by Marang Gomke and it remained a powerful voice drawing in Chota Nagpur and Santal Pargana for years together and it still remains a great force.

In January 1939, there sprang up another aboriginal organisation known as Munda Santal Sabha with Prof. J.C. Heyward of St. Columbus College, Hazaribagh as President and John Senai Nag as Secretary to protect the interests of aboriginal tribes by starting unions in villages and helping them in getting remission of rents and other facilities in the matter of education and preventing litigation etc. Formation of this Sabha, it is said, was not liked by Jaipal Singh and his supporters and they made vigorous propaganda against Heyward. The Sabha itself was said to have been sponsored by Congress as a counter blast to the Adivasi Sabha. Heyward could not withstand the opposition of Jaipal Singh and others and ultimately in June 1939 condenscended to merge the organisation with the Adivasi Maha Sabha and himself became the President of the Hazaribagh Committee. Heyward, though a good scholar and fluent speaker, was destined to play a second fiddle to Jaipal.

About July 1939, the non-Christian aboriginal started separate organisation called The Sanatan Adivasi Sabha as they were smarting under a feeling that they were being neglected and exploited by Christian adivasis. Theble Oraon who had broken away from Jaipal's Adivasi Sabha was one of the sponsors of this movement. Thus it was the destiny of Jaipal Singh and his party that non-Christian Adivasis remained alienated from him for a lurking suspicion entertained by them that they are being exploited by the Christian leadership, a fact which ultimately paved the way for emergence of Kartik Oraon as the embodiment of non-Christian tribal aspirations in 1962. This remained a direct danger on the secular posture that Jaipal Singh from time to time tried to make. Ultimately he could not convince them.

According to a secret West Bengal police report, Jaipal Singh is reported to have met Subhash Chandra Bose in August 1939. He made overtures to Bose to enlist his support for the separation movement, but he failed in his attempt. In December 1939 while addressing an Adivasis meeting presided over by Jaipal Singh, Subhash Chandra Bose advised the Adivasis to become Congress members and capture the Congress machinery instead of nurturing grievances and demanding separation.

As soon as the Second World War broke out in September 1939, Jaipal Singh lost no time in "offering services of Adivasis in the cause of democratic rights" and became "ready to supply man power to British for the struggle" which was loudly proclaimed in the Annual Adivasi Mahasabha Conference held on 15th March, 1940. He visited Santal Parganas also for propaganda work. Congress Ministry resigned and with this automatically was lost the importance of any such Adivasis agitation and Jaipal Singh found it more profitable to carry on war recruitment among Adivasis. All subsequent Adivasi meetings held in Chota Nagpur were turned into war propaganda meetings. Some people say that the movement of Jaipal Singh was a clever strategem of the British and the missionaries who wanted to stem the tide of integrationist movement that was launched among the tribals by the Congress leaders and workers in shape of Tana Bhagat and other such movements. Jaipal Singh's attempt to keep Adivasis labourers out of the Unions organised at Tata by Prof. Abdul Bari and his war recruitment anxieties proved his retrograde role that he was playing in the national life. All criticism of government and grievances of Adivasis put forth by Jaipal Singh were probably meant for Congress government which was in power for only a couple of years. With its exit Jaipal Singh became silent as if the British Government running the administration was going all out for the Tribal amelioration programme. His political activities started again when the independence of India was in sight. Therefore, it is said that the loyalist image of Jaipal Singh was disliked by many. As far back as June 1939 it was noticed that the "Star of India", a Muslim League daily of Calcutta was giving publicity to Jaipal Singh's activities. Some Muslim volunteers had pledged to work for the separation of Chota Nagpur. In 1941 Annual conference of Adivasi Mahasabha, many Muslim leaguers were invited to attend. Jaffar Imam of Bihar Muslim

League was also requested by Baghib Ahsan of Calcutta Corporation to attend the conference when the tribals were to demand their *Adivasi Pakistan*.[5]

Adivasi Mahasabha, 1941

The Annual Adivasi Conference was held at Ranchi on the 8th and 9th March, 1941 and representatives of Depressed Class Association and Bengal Muslim League were present at the Conference. In his presidential speech Jaipal Singh repeated his demand for the separation of Chota Nagpur and pledged full support of Adivasis to Government in war efforts. His target of attack were the caste Hindus for which they should start a resistance movement. On the other hand his drift towards Muslim League could very well be found in his words – "I have been invited by the Muslim League of Bengal and the Adivasis there to make a tour of that province. I have been invited to address a protest meeting at Calcutta Town Hall tomorrow when all the Ministers and eminent leaders of Bengal will be present. I mention this to let the British Government know that we are not alone in our grievances. . . Let them (Hindus) think that Muslims and Adivasis are not going to tolerate *Hindu Raj* for one second. We will fight for our religious integrity and our racial *izzat*". The Muslim League leaders including S. M. Usman, Member of the Legislative Assembly and Baghib Ahsan addressed a meeting of a Adivasis women at Ranchi on 10th March, 1941.[5]

This greater complicity of Jaipal Singh with Muslim League annoyed Rakshit, his patron and there was rupture between them in April 1941. Muslim League fully utilised Jaipal Singh and his platform of Adivasi Mahasabha for its sinister game to prevent tribals being enumerated as Hindus and, thereby reduce the numerical strength of Hindus so that their political influence ends. As a matter of fact it was clear to many that Jaipal Singh was, for sometime, alleged to have played a stooge of Muslim League, for his invectives against Hindus were not in the least going to improve the Adivasi's lot.

Baghib Ahsan of Calcutta Corporation and a very prominent Muslim Leaguer also prompted Jaipal Singh to go to Santal Parganas and organise the Santals in the manner as he had done at Ranchi. He was alarmed at the large number of Santals on the either side of Bengal-Bihar Borders were "falling victims of Congress deception and fraud" and were being pitted against government forces resulting in their killing and ruin. He wrote that there could not be greater tragedy than their falling prey to Congress bid to establish *Hindu Raj*. He exhorted Jaipal Singh to work in a concerted way and consolidate and strengthen the Adivasi National movement. He promised to defray the expenses of one or two Santal Preachers as well as the co-operation of the Muslims of Santal Parganas. He wrote "unless the Adivasis and the Santals organise as a separate national entity ready to cooperate with others (like the League) on equal terms, they may become a casualty in the Congress War for *Hindu Raj*. He also wrote to Maulvi Umar Ali, Merchant and Zamindar of Bankura, for engaging two Santals, on Rs. 30 per month to work under the direction of a League leader and propagate in the following way so that "message of Pakistan and Adivasisthan was carried to every home of Santal":

1. They will have to preach that the Santals must boycott Congress Mahasabha and keep aloof from their moves.
2. They will have to preach that the Santals are not Hindus but a separate nation and the original rulers and masters of India who were ruined and enslaved by the foreign Aryans.
3. They will have to preach that the Santals and Adivasis should combine and reunite with the Muslims and the League for obtaining their freedom and rights because both of them are beef eaters and as minorities opposed to Hindu domination and both of them demand separation and freedom of Chota Nagpur and Santal Parganas just as they demand separation of Pakistan.

Baghib Ahsan also sent letter to Sir Kwaja Nazimuddin, H. S. Shuhrawardy and other members of the Bengal Pradesh Muslim League in which he made the suggestion that there should be a confederacy of Bengsman (East Pakistan and Adivasisthan). In *Adivasis* – than he wanted to include Chota Nagpur, the Santal Parganas and neighbouring areas inhabited by the Adivasis and other aboriginal tribes. The confederacy intended would appear to be a kind of "Zoliverin" in which each area would have a separate legislature but there would be joint management of the railways, communications, customs, defence, foreign policy, currency, postal services etc. He envisaged "peaceful penetration of Islam and Islami culture amongst the inhabitants". His idea was to make the area Muslim dominated as wide as possible and had calculated that in the confederacy mentioned above there would be Muslim majority of about 52 per cent which would be just sufficient to give that community the whiphand. He also wrote, "It would be realised that Pakistan depends on the agreement of the British, the rulers of India, and that they will wholly favour Adivasisthan-Pakistan Confederacy because it would give free scope to Christian Missions in Chota Nagpur".

A Conference of Jharkhand-Chota Nagpur-Pakistan was held at Ranchi from 30th December, 1945 to 1st January, 1946 in which prominent Muslim Leaguers like H. S. Shuhrawardy, Latifur Rahman and others attributed the miserable condition of Momins, Adivasis and scheduled castes to the maladministration by Congress Government and promised full support to the demand of Adivasis for a separate Jharkhand Province. They exhorted the audience to vote for Adivasi and League candidates.

The annual Adivasis Conference was held at Ranchi on the 2nd and 3rd February, 1946 with the Jaipal Singh in chair. In his presidential address, he said that the Adivasis movement had gained great momentum and Adivasis were determined to fight the election on separation issue. The Muslims, he said, had given unqualified support to their demand and the President of the Hindu Mahasabha had also recognised that our demand for separation was just. One of the speakers Nisar Hussain, a Muslim Leaguer assured the Adivasis of full support of the Muslim League and expected in return similar help from them. With the help of Muslim League, Adivasis resorted to violence during the elections and achieved partial success at the Polls. They gained seats in Ranchi and Singhbhum, but Jaipal Singh received greatest shock of his life when he was defeated by a Congress candidate.

Jaipal Singh is said to have been heavily financed by the Bengal Muslim League whose plan was to incorporate the much coveted Plateau of Chota Nagpur into the Eastern Pakistan. He was present in Calcutta on 16th August, 1946, the *Direct Action Day* of the Muslim League and was one of the speakers at the League's meeting held near the Ochterlony Monument. He is reported[7] to have said that 100 million Adivasis were with the Muslims. They (Adivasis) had enough of *Ram Raj*. They were ready to fight against Congress with the Muslim and were ready to face bullets in the help of Muslims. But the ghastly scenes of murder, rape and arson committed by Leaguers following the *Direct Action Day* greatly shocked the conscience of Jaipal Singh and that made him sadder but not wiser. Riots in Calcutta were organised by the Muslim League and Suhrahwardy tried to secure an assurance from Jaipal Singh that in the event of trouble spreading he must be sure of Adivasi's support to the fullest extent. Jaipal Singh's intention was to exploit the League for funds but it appeared that he was not prepared to involve Adivasis in riots for the League. At Ranchi Jaipal was approached by local Muslim Leaguers who tried to secure guarantee of full support from him and requested him to find some clever Adivasis blacksmiths to work for the Muslim League (evidently for manufacturing weapons). But he gave them an evasive reply.

About this time Jaipal Singh was elected to the Constituent Assembly and was mostly engaged in Assembly work at Delhi and practically he had little time to engage himself in his League and Adivasis Movement work. Perhaps his association with the top notch of Indian Leadership in the Constituent Assembly opened his eyes and turbulence which was in his breath had to be forshaken for some time. Mr. Jaipal Singh was reported to have been inclined towards Congress then and is said to have admitted Jawaharlal Nehru to be the only able leader of India. He accordingly invited Jawaharlal Nehru, Vijay Laxmi Pandit and Jagjivan Ram to attend the Adivasis Mahasabha.

In March, 1947 at Chaibassa Adivasis Kisan Samaj was formed by Satish Chandra Korha and Mukund Ram Tanti, teachers of Jaganathpur Higher Educational School with an obvious object of propagating against government paddy procurement drive. Adivasi Labour Federation was formed with Jaipal Singh as president and Brajo Mohan Bari as Secretary in a meeting at Jorapokur, Kolhan-Jhinkpani, Singhbhum on 16th March, 1947 with a hope to organise themselves in all possible ways before the transfer of power by June 1948. In his presidential speech at the Annual Conference of Adivasi Mahasabha held at Ranchi on the 13th April, 1947 he was reported to have said that although Muslims League was supporting the Jharkhand separation movement, Adivasis will not allow themselves to be misled by the League. He was not in favour of Pakistan and did not like to boycott the Assembly. He, however, reiterated his demand for separation of Chota Nagpur and hoped the movement would continue till success was achieved.

Amin Ahmad, Member of Legislative Assembly of Chaibassa and other Muslim Leaguers of Jamshedpur were found contacting Ranchi Muslim Leaguers of Jamshedpur such as Khan Bahadur Mahiuddin and others for movement of a separate Chota Nagpur as Jharkhand for common interest. On 18th March, 1947, Muslim Leaguers met at

Ranchi under the chairmanship of Syeda Akhtar Khatoon of Bangalore and resolved that in future all efforts for inter-marriage between Muslims and Adivasis should be made and large scale conversion of Adivasis to Islam should be launched by the National Guards so that Chota Nagpur may be brought under Pakistan. They expected to get 43 per cent population in event of separation and suggested to hold a Chota Nagpur Conference at Jamshedpur which should be addressed by Mohammad Ali Jinnah.

Moreover, partition of Punjab and Bengal as the basis of transfer of power changed the situation. This greatly dashed the hopes of Muslim Leaguers residing in Chota Nagpur and Santal Parganas but nonetheless they allegedly continued their overtures unabated by "fraternising" Adivasis and instigating them to take law in their own hands. Amin Ahmad an Ex. I. C. S. was at Chaibassa and said to have maintained his contacts with some of the prominent Adivasi leaders like Lacham-Purti, Mukund Ram Tanti and others. He threw a suggestion that Adivasis should lay their grievances before Mohammad Ali Jinnah. Amin Ahmad and Faqruddin Razi were behind the cases of violence that happened in Chakulia and Kolehan in which police had to open fire in self-defence.

Jharkhand-Separation League

Jharkhand Separation League met on 22nd March, 1947 under the Chairmanship of Habibur Rahman M. L. A. (Centre) and attended by Amin Ahmad (Ex. I. C. S.), W. S. Hitchcock, (Retired Inspector General of Police of Hatia), Ramacker (Planter Daladali), Rahmat Khan of Muslim League and Mohamad Hanif, sub-Inspector of Police, Ranchi (under suspension), Rai Saheb Bandi Ram Oraon (Poornia Ranchi) and Ignes Kujur (Pathalkudwa) etc. It was resolved to raise a fund of Rs. 1,00,000 to finance the movement. They elected the following office bearers — Julius Tigga as President, Nisar Ahmad, Mr. Ramacker and Kirchu Ram as Vice-President, Ignes Kujur as Secretary, J. C. Heyward as General Secretary. Other known Muslim Leaguers and their sympathisers, some of the important members of Rantu Raj family and some of the traders of Ranchi were also coopted as members.

In Santal Parganas Christian Santal and Muslim Leaguers conjointly held a number of meetings in the month of June 1947. There was a move to boycott and non-cooperate with Hindus so that they do not get Adivasi labourers to work on their fields. In District Board elections, Muslims joined hands with Adivasis in creating disturbances. On 21st June, 1947 about 250 delegates from Bhagalpur, Monghyr, Hazaribagh, Purnea, Manbhum, Birbhum and Maldah had assembled at Dumka to hold a Jharkhand conference under the presidentship of Debi Soren. In all about 3, 000 Santals and about 150 Muslims were present. Abdur Razak of Mohespur was one of the speakers. Resolutions demanding separation of Jharkhand, condemning police firing at Sarath on 5th June, 1947 and on Adivasi in Singhbhum and claiming restoration of powers of Damin Pargainaits were passed. Mohamad Ali Jinnah was said to have assured that Santal Parganas would be included in Eastern Pakistan and that had raised false hopes among credulous Santals.

The creation of West Bengal activised Bengali Association of Manbhum. W. N. Nag, and Adivasi leader from Ranchi toured Manbhum to enlist support for separate Jharkhand but he found the Bengali leaders preferring amalgamation of Bihar districts with Bengal to the creation of separate Jharkhand provinces.

In Hazaribagh during the District Board Election of 1947, the Congress Party candidates were faced with clear combination of all reactionary elements. Raja of Ramgarh was extended full support by Jaipal Singh by placing 200 Adivasis volunteers at his disposal. Raja reciprocated this gesture by promising financial assistance to Heyward for bringing out his old paper *Jharkhand News*. North and West Bengal Provincial Committee under the Keshab Chandra Chakravarty (Resident of 58, Cornwallis Street, Calcutta) wanted to create a new province for the Bengal Nationalists comprising Burdwan Division, Presidency Division and four districts of Rajashahi Division viz. Darjeeling, Jalpaiguri, Dinajpur, Maldha and Bengali speaking portion of Bihar viz., Santal Parganas, Manbhum, Singhbhum.

In an open session of the Division of Bihar Conference held at Gaya on 19th April, 1947, under the presidentship of Chaudhury Abid Hussain, Member of Legislative Assembly which was attended by important Muslim Leaguers from all parts of Bihar, the Conference demanded that province of Bihar be forthwith partitioned into Hindu and non-Hindu autonomous province. It also supported the demand of the Adivasis for a separate autonomous province of Jharkhand. In Santal Parganas a meeting was also held at Dumka on 21st June, 1947 which was attended by 700 to 800 persons of which 10 per cent were Muslims and the rest were armed Santals. Earlier Santals had organised themselves under an organisation named *Hor Malto Maran Sabha* in September 1932 at Kathikund Board U. P. School under the Chairmanship of Late Parganait Sangram Hembrom, Order of British Empire, and a Member of Legislative Council in 1932. Devi Soren was leading the Dumka meeting which criticised Sarath firing and the Congress government officials. It was pointed out that Muslims got Pakistan by fighting and the Santals must win Jharkhand in the same manner. It was expressed that when the Congress could fight the British for independence, the Santals could also fight the Congress Government for Jharkhand. Mohemad Razak declared that the Muslims were solidly behind the Adivasis with men and money and they are ready to shed blood for them also.

Thus we have seen that till 1947 Jharkhand movement remained confined among the Muslim Leaguers and the Christian Adivasis and a section of Bengalis who wanted to effect annexation of Santal Parganas, Dhanbad and Singhbhum in West Bengal. It is evident that Jaipal Singh was with Muslim League or the Bengali faction for financial support. The retrograde steps taken by him from time to time had nothing to do with Adivasi welfare. Rather, it appears that he was set up by interested quarters to bolster up against the functioning of national government. It is also evident that Jaipal Singh was not a very serious separatist and his slogan for separate Chota Nagpur was considered by many simply slogan-mongering. Facts are not too far to be seen. Firstly, Jaipal Singh could not establish rapport with other non-league bodies which also wanted separation of Chota Nagpur. As for example, non-adivasi residents[8] of Chota Nagpur established a Separate Association at Daltonganj in order to voice their demand for a separate state of Chota Nagpur with Deoki Nandan Sinha as their leader. Secondly, Jaipal Singh himself stated on the 16th August, 1947 – "Creations of separate province is a matter outside the scope of our enquiry and we do not find that this is, in fact, necessary for the satisfactory administration of the tribals".[9] But, nonetheless, it was in full knowledge of national leaders that there was restlessness among the Adivasis and at least Dr. Rajendra Prasad, Professor Abdul Bari etc. were greatly concerned about it. Perception of economic injustice, real or imaginary might have induced extreme regional patriotism.

The Chota Nagpur region, the abode of 80 per cent of the scheduled tribes had the least political representation either in important organs of the Bihar Pradesh Congress Committee or in the Bihar Ministry. This ignoring by the High Command of Congress led some of the Adivasi leaders like Harman Lakra and others to say that all non-Adivasis inhabiting in Chota Nagpur-Santal Parganas region were *Dikus* who are there to rule over them and exploit them and therefore, demanded the creation of separate state in which they thought lay their salvation. Lakra wrote to Dr. Rajendra Prasad—

> "All *Diku* (foreigners) who came from outside had been improving their outlook, acquisitive and exploiting in their economic casty (*sic*) and hierarchical in their social structures. Adivasi always found themselves at a disadvantage and this has resulted their exploitation and which means the cause of aboriginal declared Adivasis now stand weary and strained and they cannot rest secure unless and until the right to take full responsibility in planning the scheme of existence is recognised by constituting an autonomous separate Governor's province."[10]

Despite the realisation that something tangible should be done to stem the tide of growing tribal separatism, the Congress did not do anything to mollify tribal sentiment. The claim of Chota Nagpur region for representation on the Cabinet was recognised as early as 1937, but the person included in the Cabinet was not a tribal but a Hindu.[11]

Even at the time of the formation of Congress Ministry in Bihar in 1946 it was insisted that a genuine inhabitant of Chota Nagpur should be taken on the Cabinet. On these lines a memorandum were placed before Mahatma Gandhi, Sardar Patel and Maulana Azad.[12]

The gravity of situation was realised by persons like Dr. Rajendra Prasad, Professor Abdul Bari and others. Dr. Rajendra Prasad sent three emissaries in 1947 to talk to the Adivasi leaders with the purpose to dissuade them from the demand of Jharkhand but all in vain.[13] The cry of Jharkhand was heard by other leaders like Binodanand Jha who warned the authorities about the movement gaining momentum. If and when it did, those in authority would have not Jaipal Singh, the Adivasi leader, to thank but themselves owing to their indifferent and neglect of the problem of Chota Nagpur despite their promises.[14]

General Elections and the Tribals

The heat of the separatism in Chota Nagpur was at its highest in the first General Election[15] in 1952 and again when the States Reorganisation Commission under Sir Fazl Ali visited this area. In its

General Election, Jharkhand bagged 21 seats in Chota Nagpur-Santal Parganas belt and secured 33.4 per cent of the votes as against the Congress who could muster 25 seats by having 31.3 per cent of the votes while the total votes polled was 56.17 per cent. This phenomenal success of a new regional party over Congress, an India national party boosted the morale of Jharkhand leaders. When Pandit Hriday Nath Kunjru, Sardar K. M. Panicker headed by Sir Fazl Ali visited Chota Nagpur and Santal Parganas, battle royal was fought between the protagonists of the Congress and the Jharkhand. It was really the contest between two lions. Bihar Kesari Sri Krishna Singh, backed by his unlimited resources and Morang Gomke Jaipal Singh, supported by all separatist forces who wanted to secede this geographical area from the state of Bihar. This was a magnificent show of the great conflict going on in the minds of the people of Santal Oraon-Munda belt. It is common knowledge that Jaipal Singh could be persuaded by fair or foul means not to press the issue of separatism to the last logical conclusion and his contemporaries brand him as greatest exploiter of Adivasis for his own personal aggrandisement. Jaipal in fact used Jharkhand demand more as a slogan and weapon of horse-trading than as a party. As a dynamic leader, of many parts, he wielded a magic wand with his very presence. He could sway the tribal electorate in whatever way he liked. The election results were a witness to this fact.

Besides the magnetic personality of Jaipal, there were important luminaries such as Sri Krishna Ballabh Sahay and Raja of Ramgarh Kamakhya Narain Singh looming large on the political horizon of Chota Nagpur. The role of these three great men is indeed the history of Chota Nagpur in fifties. Weakness of one was the strength of the other and horse-trading went on through this period without bringing any appreciable amelioration in the condition of the tribals. Exploitation of tribals by tribal on large scale became a new factor of conflict in this area. Number of rich non-tribals, ambitious to become Members of Parliament or the Legislative Assembly, hovered around Jaipal Singh with their fat purse for getting his blessings in the shape of nomination as Jharkhand Party candidates. Thus some of the Parliamentary and Legislative Assembly seats practically came to be turned into a *rotten borough* for an Oberai, a Massani, or a Prasad. This was definitely due to Jaipal's magic wand because as hitherto these were filled wand to win elections. Table 10.1 shows the comparative position of the different political parties.

TABLE 10.1: Comparative Position of Political Parties in Terms of Parliamentary and Legislative Assembly Seats in Chota Nagpur-Santal Parganas

Name of the party	1952		1957		1962		1967		1970	
	Legislative	Parliament	Legislative	Parliament	Legislative	Parliament	Legislative	Parliament	Legislative	Parliament
Congress	25	2	14	—	13	—	30	—	—	3
Swatantra	—	—	—	—	29	—	3	—	—	—
C.P.I.	—	—	1	—	—	—	—	—	—	—
C.P.I. (Ma)	—	—	—	—	—	—	1	—	—	—
Bharatiya Jan Sangh	—	—	—	—	—	—	7	—	—	—
Jan Kranti Dal or Janta Party	11	—	16	—	14	—	—	—	—	—
Jharkhand Party	21	1	21	3	12	1	3	—	—	1
S.S.P.	1	—	—	—	—	—	3	—	—	—

Jaipal Singh may be condemned for his horse-trading; but it would appear that he never allowed himself to be utilised by the Church, rather he utilised the Church for his own political aggrandisement. He threw the ball of politics into a secular court and did his best to keep religion off the ambit of politics.

Merger of Jharkhand with Congress

The turning point in the career of Jaipal Singh and his Jharkhand Party came actually in 1962 elections when he had to share the loaf with Jan Kranti Dal. Out of 41.12 per cent valid votes in 1962, Congress got 23.8 per cent, Jharkhand 36.7 per cent and Jan Kranti Dal 30.3 per cent. In 1957, Jharkhand had secured 45.89 per cent. This was really a shock to Jaipal Singh and a great realism dawned upon him when he allowed himself to succumb to the overtures of Binodanand Jha to join his cabinet after agreeing to the merger of his Jharkhand Party with the Congress Party, a feat unrivalled in the political history of Chota Nagpur. What could not be done by powerful Krishna Ballabh Sahay, the arch enemy of Jharkhand, was done magnificently by clever and foresighted Binodanand Jha. The result was Congress-Jharkhand merger in 1963 in grandiose manner when Congress President Kamaraj, Atul Ghosh, Biju Patnaik etc. came to Ranchi to attend East Zone Congress, as if to ratify the appropriation of Jharkhand by the Congress. What an irony of history – Binodanand Jha fell a victim to the notorious Kamaraj Plan and with this the one month old career of Jaipal Singh as Congress Minister ended most ingloriously.

Krishna Ballabh Sahay stepped in the shoes of Binodanand Jha as the Chief Minister of Bihar and he patronised S. K. Bage, as against Jaipal Singh and thereby subdivided the last vestiges of Jharkhand

Party which stood merged into the Congress perhaps as a "river lost in a desert". S. K. Bage was declared the *de facto* Chief Minister so far as Chota Nagpur affairs were concerned and soon Chota Nagpur Regional Board was formed in 1964 amidst great fanfare and with this Jaipal Singh's eclipse was complete. The terms of merger were that Jharkhandis would get (i) creation of Regional Congress for Chota Nagpur and Santal Parganas, (ii) proportionate representation of Jharkhand Party in the Provincial Congress bodies, and (iii) creation of Regional Board for development of the Chota Nagpur and Santal Parganas.

Sensing that he is being bypassed and ignored by the power that be in the Congress, Jaipal Singh was constrained to write to the Congress President, D. Sanjivaya:

> "Under the terms of condition of merger which were jointly signed by us, I submitted the matter of the Jharkhand Party for the various Congress Committees. Since then at the election of Chief Minister of Bihar, some of the Jharkhand Party Legislators have defected for the sake of office and other allurements. In fact the new Chief Minister has rewarded perfidy, indiscipline and disloyalty. It is, therefore, only right that I should withdraw the nomination and submit the new list of Jharkhand Nominees.
>
> What I saw at the time of the election of the new Chief Minister, Bihar has distressed me deeply. It is a serious reflection on the prestige of Congress. It is a sad commentary on Congress ethics that soon after the merger someone else should be proclaimed as the leader of Jharkhand Party. I have to take the challenge firmly and squarely."

He also wrote to Atul Ghosh, Treasurer of The All India Congress Committee and other important members of the Syndicate regarding the group representation in the Congress 'as colleagues, not as suspects'.

The General Election of 1967 and later the 1969 mid-term election witnessed a bewildering confusion among the electorate of this part of the country free from the strangulating grip of the powerful Jharkhand Party, which was no more the tribal electorate scene. In 1967, all the more in 1964, the tribal electorate was faced with the maze of political parties trying to woo the electorate with their own programmes and manifestoes. The people of Chota Nagpur, who were considered the most backward, most illiterate and most unworthy of exercising the franchise, became enlightened and conscious when they came in contact with other national political parties and their ideologies. Thus the dominance of Church over the tribal electorate started diminishing.

Jaipal Singh as Congressman

Though Jaipal Singh by his own dynamic personalities had always his own way at New Delhi, yet in local party politics at Chota Nagpur he never attained his former self as the sole leader of Jharkhand Party. Political authority for Chota Nagpur, Jaipal Singh and Maharaja Chintamani Nath Sahdeo were entrusted with the task of scrutiny of candidates on behalf of the Congress Party. Thus, for the first time the tribal leaders came out from their own cocoon to work with a national party. In this process he came to realise that the nomination of a candidate was a difficult affair altogether. Bhaiya Ram Munda was also made a member of the Election Committee of the State Congress Party.

In 1967, it was the first occasion that the Congress was fighting in Chota Nagpur and other tribal areas on some significant stake as the successor of its own former enemy, the Jharkhand Party, to whom it had assimilated by merging it with itself. Again, the old Jharkhand in new Congress garb were constrained to talk in terms of the various economic programmes of development, eradication of poverty and backwardness of the people rather than passionately arousing the passion of "hate Diku" campaigns among the tribal electorate and also singing the song of creation of separate State for the tribals. Still there was no dearth of people from this party to harp on the old tune and vomit the same old venom. The general manifesto of the Congress party had little attraction in the areas where Kartik Oraon, though a Congress candidate was fighting on his own manifesto of liberating his own non-Christian brethren from the tutelage of chronic Christian tribal leaders. It need hardly be told that Bhartiya Jan Sangh also bagged a few seats due to the wind of *Kartikism*, a sort of ideological force, couched in terms of political self-determination. The politics of Chota Nagpur and Santal Parganas got a severe jolt when there were more than half a dozen Jharkhand parties of different denominations clamouring for the old election symbol of Cock. On the eve of 1967 General Election, the Election Commission of India freezed that symbol. Thus the protogonists of Jharkhand Parties were left without their traditional symbol of cock and the purity of other symbols made the electorate mind somewhat murky leading to indecision.

The efflorence of the Jharkhand-Congress merger soon started becoming stinky with a few disgruntled leaders of the erstwhile Jharkhand Party started clamouring for the continuance of Jharkhand Party. Harihar Nath Sahdeo, an Advocate of Ranchi became the President of anti-Jaipal Singh Group comprising of Jinus Surin, Chani Singh Munda. John Hore, J. C. Nag etc. They got in touch with the Election Commission for the reservation of the symbol of cock for them under the name of Sahdeo Jharkhand Party. In 1965 in the famous Shilbhadrayaji *vs*. Jain election case, a few erstwhile Jharkhand Members of Legislative Assembly were charged and held guilty of corruption. They were alleged to have taken money from one Jain and voted for him in the Rajya Sabha election ignoring the Party whip. When the probe exposed them and they were in eminent danger of being punished by the party, they changed their side and declared that they belonged to the All India Jharkhand Party under the Presidentship of Paul Dayal, M.L.A. Those M.L.A.'s who were merged with the Congress and enjoyed the fruits of merger, again started talking that they had not actually merged.

In 1966, the Election Commissioner visited Ranchi and the Sahdeo Party and Paul Dayal party represented that they were the actual Jharkhand Party and they had never merged to any party. Sensing the situation correctly, the Election Commission rejected their claims and reserved the frozen cock symbol. In April 1966, a joint meeting of the above two Jharkhand parties was convened and they were merged into one party known as the All India Jharkhand Mahasabha. P. K. Lakra, District President of the Jharkhand Party, Jamshedpur, was elected as the Chairman of the new party. In this election, Sahdeo group remained loyal but it is said Paul Dayal resented Lakra's nomination and he nominated himself as the President of the All India Jharkhand Party. His argument was that since Jaipal Singh, the accredited leader of the Adivasis having not joined the Mahasabha and, therefore, he had nominated himself as the official president of the All India Jharkhand Party in his absence. He also organised its branch at other places. He was allotted the symbol of 'Lion'. In the meantime Harihar Nath Sahdeo also formed his splinter group and tried to establish a foothold in the Santal Parganas and got the symbol of the *Rising Sun*. Jetha Kisku and others of the Santal Parganas and others supported him and his nephew Lal Ran Vijoy filed nomination for Member of Parliament which he withdrew at the last moment much to the great annoyance of the Santali Jharkhandis. Justin Richard joined Paul Dayal party. Thus in Singhbhum also Begum Sumbrai and others were said to have remained vaccilating between the Rungta and Thakur Prasad sphere of influence and ultimately joined Paul Dayal. Thus, at the time of General Election there were several Jharkhand parties viz. Lakra group, Paul Dayal group, Sahdeo group and other splinter groups of Jharkhandis with the result that they were treated as independents by the Election Commission and none was given the symbol of 'Cock'.

From the records of General Election, 1967, it does not become very clear as to who belonged to which group. But on the whole, it looks that Paul Dayal and Lakra both set up rival candidates in Ranchi and Singhbhum and consequently votes were divided. Not only this, in a few constituencies there were seven independent contestants beside other recognised political parties, with the result that persons getting a minimum of three thousand votes could win. The final picture that emerged showed the Congress as the sole party which bagged more than 25 per cent of the votes. Jharkhand Party was wiped out from amongst its strongholds of the tribal communities of Bihar where Jharkhand appeal hitherto had, a mass following. Paul Dayal's Jharkhand Group secured 7.63 per cent of the votes and the Lakra Jharkhand Group secured 3.42 per cent. Therefore, this rejection of Jharkhand concept, so violently preached among them was one step towards the attainment of political maturity that the tribal electorate was gaining day by day.

The national level parties carried weight in the polls. But there was still much ground left for them to cover because 32.66 per cent of the votes were still in the hands of the independents. Those who voted for the independents were non-committed electors. If the voting pattern is seen on Christian and Non-christian lines, the Non-christian candidates in all secured 75.91 per cent the Christian candidates securing 24.08 per cent of the votes. Accidentally the Census of 1961 showed the return of about 75 per cent tribals as Hindus.

The conglomeration of parties claiming votes in the reserved constituencies has been responsible for unsuitable governance after 1967 General Election in its own way. This plurality of parties created worst confusion because no sooner the chance of forming Government loomed large than the personal ambition of the elected candidates led them to defect most unceremoniously to join a party which afforded prospect of some berth in the cabinet. The party to which the electorate voted remained inconsequential. The candidates felt free to go against the banner of the party which they had carried all through their career. The result was that among the Scheduled tribe candidates, all except Philman Toppo changed sides and a few others, mostly of the Jharkhand Party changed sides according to circumstances and the party as a whole remained in quest of suitable opportunities. Of course, a few of them got seats in the Cabinet, but others who could not, remained grumbling. Therefore, Jharkhand politics had to suffer most and it is only through Birsa Seva Dal and Chattra Parishad, Chota Nagpur Plateau Parishad, very recently through Hul Jharkhand, the Jharkhand Party wanted to come up before the electorate. David Munjani's Jharkhand Group with the active support of the lower class Muslim leaders wants to play the role of Paul Dayal of pre-1967 election by setting up a number of candidates. S. K. Bage, a Congress defector to the Jharkhand Party broke away from David Munjani who expelled him from his party. He had also set up several candidates and himself contested from three places, Khijri, Kolebira and Latehar. N. E. Horo, who was said responsible for the discomfiture of Bage in 1967 election, compromised with Bage and shifted himself to Torpa leaving free field to Bage in Kolebira. Jhaman Singh (Congress) was said to be a dummy candidate for Bage because of his earlier contacts with him when Bage was a Congress Minister in K. B. Sahay cabinet. There was a good deal of canvassing for Jharkhand which was wholly repudiated in 1967 General Election when most of the Jharkhand leaders were trounced. But this time it looked that the wave of anti-Jharkhand feeling subsided to a great deal because of two factors. Firstly, it is said that all the Churches in a bid to save their existence combined together to see that the Jharkhand leaders come out victorious in the election and secondly, for this they pooled in all their resources. The importance of Church and its fat-purse in terms of resources, donations and grants from PL480 is a fact of common knowledge.

Kartikism

The revival of old Parha System by Kartik Oraon, Bhikharam Bhagat, Ratti Bhagat and others was of high political significance. Bhikharam Bhagat was designated as *Raji Dewan of Parha Samaj* with large hierarchy of institutional leaders from different Parha organisations. Kartik Oraon was also instrumental in organising Akhil Bhartiya Vikas Parishad, an ace organisation of non-christian leadership in different

States such as Madhya Pradesh, Orissa, West Bengal, Nagaland, Gujarat, Maharashtra etc. The stimulation of anti-Christian feeling could well be realised by going through the press report of mammoth demonstrations staged before the Parliamentary Committee on the Scheduled Caste and Scheduled Tribe (Amendment Bill), 1967 popularly known as Chanda Committee on 16th October, 1968 at the Circuit House, Ranchi, and later on at its annual conference which was inaugurated by Prime Minister Indira Gandhi. She also formally opened the Parishad office at R. I. T. Building in Ranchi. Dr. Ram Subhag Singh, the then Union Railway Minister, Jagjiwan Ram, the then Union Food Minister and Congress President and Dr. Karan Singh, the then Union Minister of Tourism and Civil Aviation and Bhagwat Jha Azad etc. addressed the gatherings from its platform from time to time. The feeling of non-Christian leadership against the hegemony of the Christian leadership came to be best illustrated in the speeches of Kartik Oraon in Lok Sabha on 15th April, 1969 and the memorandum submitted to the Prime Minister Indira Gandhi by Kartik Oraon and 347 others Members of Parliament. These documents give an idea of the conflict that the non-Christian tribals had in their mind.

But nonetheless, anti-Christian feeling was very high in the areas concerned and the parties did not count much among themselves when the matters of election came up before the people. It was the religion and personality of the candidates which mattered more. Of course, Singhbhum presented a different picture where Christian and non-Christian relationship did not matter because Begum Sumbrai, the stormy-petrel of the Jharkhand movement in Ho area of Singhbhum had combined with the inevitable Justin Richard and started Hul Jharkhand movement. The only elected member on the SSP ticket Ratnakar Nayak who defeated Justin Richard in 1967 General Election from Monoharpur Constituency joined hands with him. Similar was the condition with Haricharan Soe who was defeated in 1967 General Election as a Congress parliamentary candidate.

In Santal Parganas, the Jharkhand had been the most disunited. Except a few meetings addressed by Bage and others in Ranchi and Santal Parganas, no attempt was made to forge unity. The Lals of the Jharkhand Movement were not able to organise themselves as before. This time, they were more under the influence of Swatantra Party. But among the Santal Parganas Jharkhandis, a few won on personal grounds, but the Jan Sangh was neck-to-neck with the Jharkhandis and this time they made another heavy dent in the Jharkhand Party. The chance of Satrughan Besra, the only symbol of leftist force in tribal area as the choice from Jamtara Constituency was not bad either.

The Janta Party which had gird up its loins to bag a few seats because the veteran Raja of Ramgarh still had connections among the Lals and others in the rural areas, but as a party it could not show its own mettle because the days were gone when people venerated the royal family. However, the election bait by the Raja saying that the forest land would be distributed and land revenue would be abolished and aspirations of the Adivasis would be respected might have worked. It was still to be seen as to whether the people were going to accept these. But the Raja spent lot over the Election propaganda and himself moved in a helicopter.

The wooing of the tribal electorate was not easy and political parties vied with each other in placating the sentiment of the Adivasi youths trying to show their support for whatever the tribal youths on the main roads of Ranchi demand, including creation of a separate State of Jharkhand. But every tribal understood these pranks and some of them atleast tried to exploit these easy promise-makers. Ultimately, it looked that Christian and non-Christian leadership clashed in the interior and the party ultimately had very little significance in that sense. The Church by itself, would support any candidate likely to give a stiff opposition to the Jan Singh and Congress's Kartik Oraon because they knew that Jan Sangh and Oraon were out and out against them. As it is, the Congress, the Jan Sangh and the Independents including the Jharkhandis of different types commanded respectability (irrespective of their parties manifestoes) of the electorate, as the Swatantra, Jan Kranti Dal, SSP and Communist Party went into oblivion and perhaps there was no chance for them to secure even a single seat. Thus, the pre-election scene of 1969 gives a somewhat different picture than that we found in 1967.

The 1969 Elections

The elections in 1969 presented a fascinating picture of electoral alliances. The tribal electorate was the only segment which did not give any hint of its voting behaviour with any degree of certainty. The simple cut-and-dry personal manifestoes worked. Neither the tribal aspirations, nor the greater Congress prestige, nor the Jan Sangh's All-India image, nor the Communist international position for the emancipation of the workers of the world worked. It was the purely local and most immediate needs and problems from which they were suffering mattered well. Party-wise performance of different political parties would help to know the real situation and at the same time would give an idea of various comparative position of the regional parties working here in contrast with the national parties.

Of the local parties, the Janta Party can very well be taken to be a consistent party which has tried to keep its stranglehold on large number of tribal electorate by contesting all the 29 reserved seats except Barhait. In 1967, the leader of the Janta Party had joined Swatantra Party and contested all the seats in Ranchi district and all except Shikaripara in Santal Parganas, but none in Singhbhum. In 1967, the Janta Party under the banner of Swatantra Party had secured 7.25 per cent of the vote polled and 2.28 per cent of the total electorate but, in 1969, mid-term Poll, the revived Janta Party falling back on its own resources secured 5.31 per cent of the vote polled and 1.90 per cent of the total electorate. In 1969, Swatantra Party contested only 4 seats of Borio, Kharsawa, Kolebira, Simdega and secured 0. 97 per cent of the vote polled and 0. 35 per cent of the total electorate. Thus, the Swatantra Party, independent of Janata Party, had a very miserable position in 1969 mid-term Poll. Therefore, it has to be accepted that of all the local parties the Janata Party had been the most consistent in keeping its grip over tribal electorate.

Next to the Janata Party, Prantiya Hool Jharkhand Party remains the next recognised regional party which contested six reserved seats of Borio, Barhait, Litipara, Maheshpur, Poraihat in Santal Parganas, Majgawan in Singhbhum. Of the six seats, the Hool Jharkhand Party got five and secured 5.14 per cent of vote polled and 1.24 per cent of the total electorate. The entrance of Prantiya Hool Jharkhand Party and getting recognised as the regional party was a miracle. A large number of contestants were there as one or the other splinter group of Jharkhand Party. But it is said, on a hint of Election Commission the Hool Jharkhand party leaders utilised the same opportunity and preferred to have two leaves as their symbol to have a separate identity than to be counted as independents. Although in 1969, the Jharkhand candidates were reckoned as a force and in performances no less better than other regional and national parties, but technically they remained independents in the eyes of the Election Commission. There was no unanimity between the Jharkhand leaders and, therefore, its different factions were given different symbols. The Shoshit Dal in one such other regional party which deserves mention here. It secured 0.37 per cent of the vote polled and 0.13 per cent of the total electorate in 1969 without getting any seat.

The Congress Party was never popular in tribal areas and the Janata Party and Jharkhand Party used to have an edge over the Congress in the previous general elections. The Congress-Jharkhand merger in 1964 created a different situation. But in 1967, Congress Party made its appearance in tribal electorate as the senior partner of Jharkhand Party. It contested all the seats and secured 27.44 per cent of the total valid vote and 8.62 per cent of the total electorate. Certainly this was the most impressive of the Congress success after the merger but in 1969 mid-term poll, the Congress Party though contested all the seats yet could gain only 22.63 per cent of the valid votes and 7.66 per cent of the total electorate. This shortfall of about five per cent votes was because of withdrawal of support of some of the Jharkhandi leaders who found their existence under the Congress umbrella irksome. A number of Jharkhand parties came into being and they started challenging the validity of the Congress-Jharkhand merger because it was not approved by the General Body of the All-India Jharkhand Party. So many All-India Jharkhand parties contested the election and as independent candidates they definitely had a share of the Congress votes. But yet another significant factor was the ascendency of Bharatiya Jan Sangh which improved its performance in the mid-term poll. Though Congress manifesto was there but nobody had any time to give any serious thought to it and in tribal areas the question of forging ahead the tribal development of their areas and small considerations weighed heavily with the lower level of vote-catchers. The Congress Party being the top national party had vast resources which could be profitably used by these tribal candidates contesting on the Congress tickets. But in Oraon Belt (South Ranchi and Latehar) Karticism, i.e., "the non-Christian tribals should be represented by their non-Christian leader for their struggle against the Christian" had some set-back. In 1967 General Election, Kartik Oraon and his partners in Oraon Belt of Ranchi, i.e., Gumla, Sisai, Bero, Mandar, Lohardaga and Latehar fought the election on purely Christian and non-Christian basis and they were victorious. There was no difference between the personal manifesto of Kartik Oraon and his partners under Bharatiya Jan Sangh banner. As a matter of fact, it was reported that the electorate was told by Jan Sangh candidates that in Sisai, Bero, Mandar, Lohardaga, Latehar constituencies the symbol of Kartik Oraon was a pair of oxen with plough and it was said that it was canvassed that symbol of Kartic

Babu in Gumla was a lamp. We do not know whether Kartik Oraon and his men willingly acquiesced in such propaganda, but this undeclared alliance with Jan Sangh got snapped when Sisai seat was lost by Sukru Bhagat, a Congress candidate and trusted lieutenant of Kartik Oraon to a Jan Sangh candidate.

In Santal Parganas, new Congress men after Jharkhand merger had to face severe defeat by Prantiya Hool Jharkhand which wrested many seats from them. In Santal Parganas practically, the question was not voting of Christian and non-Christian candidate, but the real problem before them was to send such candidates to the Legislature who are more vociferous for the tribal interests. The Congressmen were always considered as men of "establishment" and this was the greatest disadvantage to which Congress men had to face. They liked dynamic leaders.

The typical Santal way of thinking all these years had been that they shall have to drive away all the Dikus and it was said they had always considered Congress Party as the party of the Dikus and the Jharkhand Party as the party of the tribals. If Congress had some seats in 1967, it was an indication of the fact that the Santals were coming round and they were having a different political consciousness from what they had in the past, but it was a mistaken conclusion. The Jharkhand idea firmly engrained in the mind could easily be roused by fiery demogogues among them, Justin Richard, who himself came from Manoharpur of Singhbhum, had little difficulty in rallying round himself old Jharkhandis and wresting seats from those Jharkhandis who had joined Congress after the merger.

In Singhbhum, there was a different picture altogether in 1967 General Election after the merger. The Congress had Ghatshila, Jugsalai, Jagarnathpur, but in 1969 mid-term poll they all lost to independent candidates from the Bagum and Horo branch of All-India Jharkhand Party. The Congress was routed in Scheduled Tribe reserved constituencies of the district when all seats went to independents. In Palamau, the only Scheduled Tribe seat was wrested from Congress when Jan Sangh gave a crushing defeat to Congress candidate. Thus, the 1969 mid-term poll brought out a pertinent lesson that only Kartik Oraon could anyhow maintain his position in Oraon Belt otherwise Congress on its own remained "a traitor party". S. K. Bage had to leave Congress Party and Simon Tigga had to go to political wilderness.

Bharatiya Jan Sangh, recorded an improvement of five per cent votes from 17.88 per cent of valid votes in 1967 to 22.67 per cent in

1969. In Santal Parganas, Dumka and Burhait were annexed by Jan Sangh in 1967, but Munshi Murmu and Gopal Morandi did not contest these two seats in 1969. Dumka was taken away by Paika Murmu and Buraihat was taken away by Edward Murandi of Prantiya Hool Jharkhand Party. With this ended the story of the expected ascendency of Jan Sangh among the Santals. In Singhbhum, Chakradharpur was bagged by Jan Sangh in 1967 with a very large margin of vote, but in 1969, it was lost to Hari Charan Soi of Horo faction of Jharkhand who equally gave a crushing defeat to Jan Sangh by securing 46.43 per cent votes against 26.73 per cent secured by Bhartiya Jan Sangh. Manjhia Manjhi contested as Shoshit Dal candidate and secured 26 votes only against 13,249 votes in 1967 when he was a Jan Sangh candidate. From this, it is clear that Jan Sangh in Chakradharpur had its impact. The vote it secured then was not due to any person, but due to its party respectability. Kharsawa seat was taken by Jan Sangh in 1967, but it lost it to Horo faction of Jharkhand Party in a miserable way in 1969. There was a heavy erosion in the position of Jan Sangh in Kharsawa-Chakradharpur belt. Saraikela though not Scheduled Tribe Constituency belonged to Rudra Pratap Sarangi in 1967, but in 1969 he lost it to Jharkhand independent candidate Ban Bihari Mahto. Thus, the whole belt-Saraikela, Kharsawa and Chakradharpur was lost to Jan Sangh in 1969 although in all three constituencies it remained the second party to secured highest number of votes. It was in Ranchi district that Jan Sangh position had improved from what it was in 1967. When it had only Gumla seat, but in 1969 it took Tamar, Khijri, Simdega, Gumla, Sisai seats. This was over and above Ranchi and Kanke, which were non-reserved seats. At least a large portion of Ranchi reserved electorate opted to Jan Sangh in 1969. It also wrested adjacent Latehar seat from Jhamman Singh of Congress.

The Communist Party of India had secured 2.26 per cent of valid votes in 1967 as against 2.45 per cent in 1969. In Santal Parganas, it contested only 3 seats and in 1967 Satrughan Besra of Communist Party had taken Jamtara seat, just on the periphery of reserved constituencies of Dumka and Jama. Therefore, in 1969, the Communist Party had grown stronger in Santal Parganas. This might be due to leadership of Satrughan Besra and others who had penetrated in tribal belt in Santal Parganas. Dumka and Litipara have greater propensity of going red. In Singhbhum, Chaibassa and Jagarnathpur were the two constituencies which were contested by the Communist Party where they got about 1,000 votes each. In Ranchi district, they did not contest at all. The Communist Party in 1967 had secured 0.90 per cent of the valid vote, but in 1969 it dropped down to 0.53 per cent. It contested only Khijri seat in Ranchi district and secured 24,278 votes in all.

The Socialist Party of India was a party of some significance in tribal areas. In 1967 when it had secured 3.08 per cent of the valid votes which dwindled to 2.66 per cent in 1969. In 1967, SSP did not contest a single seat in Santal Parganas but in 1967 it contested Borio, Maheshpur and Poraihat where in all it secured 10,080 votes. In Singhbhum, SSP had contested all the seats except Ghatshila and Jugsalai and secured 20,774 votes in all and bagged Manoharpur seat by Ratnakar Naik. But in 1969 it dwindled to 5589 votes in different constituencies of Chaibassa, Majhgaon, Manoharpur, Jagarnathpur. The reason of this debacle was Ratnakar Naik who won Manoharpur constituency in 1967 as Socialist candidate defected to Jharkhand Party under the influence of Horo faction. This time Ratnakar Naik again won Manoharpur constituency and this shows that in Saranda Forest Zone of Manoharpur Jharkhand had a greater appeal than the high sounding political manifesto of SSP in 1969. In Sisai in Ranchi and Latehar in Palamau districts, SSP got 770 votes and 1090 votes respectively.

Revolutionary Communist Party got 722 votes in Khijri, the only constituency it contested. In 1967, Revolutionary Communist Party did not contest anywhere. Bharatiya Kranti Dal secured in all 345 votes in Litipara and Dumka constituency which it contested. Jan Kranti Dal had secured total 6.405 in Poraihat, Tamar and Khijri constituencies which comes to 0.89 per cent of the valid vote but in 1969 it did not contest a single seat.

Lok Tantrik Dal in 1969 secured 2.59 per cent of the valid votes by contesting 15 seats out of 29 Reserved Constituencies and Jugasalai it had secured 7648 votes. Lok Kranti Dal being splinter of the Congress came before the tribal electorate as remnant of the former Congress and it failed to rouse any interest.

Proutist Block of India secured 905 votes in Torpa, the only seat it contested. Ranchi is the international headquarters of Anand Marg to which PBI is said to be the main prop, but it failed to be of any object of notice.

Coming to the independent candidates, we have got bewildering experience either in General Election of 1967 or in mid-term poll of 1969. It was because that the Jharkhand Party had merged with the Congress Party and its dissolution was responsible for the rise of a number of Jharkhand Parties and the freezing of its 'Cock' symbol by the Election Commission. Therefore, those who preferred to fight election on Jharkhand slogan had to contest the election as independent candidates. Prantiya Hul Jharkhand had secured a separate identity by a clever strategem of changing the name of the Jharkhand Party and contesting with the symbol of 'Two Leaves', but all the Jharkhand leaders were left with the option of contesting as independents. N. E. Horo, S. K. Bage and Bagum Sumbrai and other Jharkhand leaders contested as independents. Therefore, no independent category could be made for Jharkhandis in Ranchi and Singhbhum districts. With these Jharkhandis leaders who contested as independents, we find other independent candidates also contesting, at places more than half a dozen independents contested in the same constituency. Finding this, the Election Commission in reporting the result of votes polled, have lumped them together and if we total it, it comes to 32.61 per cent of the votes polled. This means that largest number of votes were secured by independents or such independent candidates who professed to all themselves as of one or the other brand of Jharkhand Party, and these votes may be taken as the choice of tribal electorate. Even total electoratewise, the independents got 11.02 per cent votes. This means also that tribal electorate was non-committed to any political party as yet and they could be successfully won over by the different political parties and brought in their ambit.

This greater success of independents was obvious because the political scene of Chota Nagpur on the eve of 1969 mid-term poll was confused to a great extent. Birsa Sewa Dal known for its electoral and 'reactionary programme' of driving away the *diku* is alleged to be supported by Church Council of Chota Nagpur and was having favourable rapport with almost all the Jharkhand Leaders. Dal was injecting a new hope of wresting powers even through the use of ballot boxes. Although the leaders of Birsa Sewa Dal believed in fiery slogans-raising and attitude of divisive policies even by the use of bows and arrows, but necessity compelled them to enter arena of electoral battle also. But it could not come as independent political unit. It remained "a militant face" of Jharkhand politicians only and when it was said that such and such candidate was supported by the Birsa Sewa Dal it had practically no meaning. Superficially Birsa Sewa Dal slogans and manouvering always received with greater attention by masses, but when it came to brass-tacks, that is, counting of election ballots they were as miserable as others defeated candidates from different regional and national parties were. Ranchi district specially the constituencies of Kolebira, Torpa, Chainpur were bagged by Independents such as S. K. Bage, N. E. Horo and Jai Rani Oraon. While the first two were known Jharkhand leaders, the last one was a newly converted Tana Bhagat into Christianity and had something to do with Birsa Sewa Dal. He won the election at Chainpur not because he was a candidate supported by the Birsa Sewa Dal, but it was said that he was an agreed candidate of the Church Council.

It was alleged that the Church had a great say in the political manouvering in Chota Nagpur. This was accentuated because Kartik Oraon and other leaders under the Congress banner and Jan Sangh had entered in tribal electorate to unseat the tribal Christian leaders hitherto in power. But this also could not be authentically said that Church had the same say in the matter relating to election in 1969 which it once had in earlier times. It is quite a different thing that sometimes it is alleged that rostrums and pulpits of the Church were utilised for canvassing purposes and by the Christian Father's efforts that the voters were taken to election booths in a row in most orderly manner with dependable knowledge of casting of votes for a particular candidate agreed by the Church leadership. But this had never been the sole reason for the victory of the Jharkhand candidates because sometimes we have found that different candidates of Church had a conflicting candidates of their own and in this manner the electorate was always confused. In 1969, in Ranchi district three seats won by three Independent Christian Tribals such as Bage, Horo and Jairam Oraon (James Terom Tigga), makes one believe that it depended upon the demographic pattern of electoral constituency. Torpa and Chainpur are predominantly Christian constituencies and it was said that it was only the Christian who could win Kolebira because there were large Christian voters. But the real cause of the victory of S. K. Bage was, as it is said, his adjustment with N. E. Horo who had defeated him in 1967 General Election. The Christian leaders understood well that there was no point in fighting among themselves and they had patched up their own differences to give a fight to the forces of Karticism and Jan Sangh. This has worked well in there three constituencies.

In Singhbhum also, there was a large number of independents becoming victorious, but the pattern of independents here was quite different. Here the independent candidates were the old Jharkhand veterans such as Sanatan Manjhi, Puran Chand Birua, Hari Charan Soy etc. and hitherto relatively unknown persons like Bhagwa Kandeyan who secured only 127 votes in 1969 election. In Kharsawa Scheduled Tribe Constituencies, as many as six independents contested the Election. In Majgaon, five independents also fought. Hardly there was any constituency where less than two independents contested the election. Therefore, all independents do not necessarily mean Jharkhandis, but that also does not take away the credit of such Jharkhandis who registered their victory as an independent candidate. All the scheduled tribe seats in the district of Singhbhum were captured by independents, some of whom were old and tried Jharkhandis, and some had defected from other parties. In Santal Parganas, the majority of the seats were taken away by Prantiya Hool Jharkhand Party, but there were Independents who secured some votes. Out of 1,93,099 valid votes, Independents received 18,851 (9.76 per cent). No independents could come out victorious.

Thus on the whole, the Independents had taken eight seats out of 29 seats and one can find that it was a projection of the defunct Jharkhand Party once more trying to make a passionate appeal to the past promises and slogans. "Hate Diku" campaign, one of the main planks of the Jharkhand Party worked well in Singhbhum and Santal Parganas presumably because of the presence of some valiant Jharkhand leaders who exploited the situation created by the so-called Diku population in matters of money lending and creating other galling situation. But in Ranchi district Jharkhand block voting manifested itself in the determination of Christian tribal electorate to return their own candidates for the purpose of canvassing their own grievances against Kartik Oraon or other. This greater adjustment with old Jharkhand slogans in Singhbhum and Santal Parganas bespeaks of a situation in which one can say that the different political parties had not done their home tasks well in these areas. The Hos or the Santals are turbulent and inflammable people. They could be swayed by demogogues and could easily be led to the polling booths, most of them without understanding the significance of the things and registered their votes in favour of their own agreed candidate. Here instinct works well among the Santals and Hos. In Santal Parganas and in Hos area, people still felt that Congress and other parties are Diku Parties and Jharkhand Party is the tribal party. This is perhaps the real cause of the success of the candidates. Congress-Jharkhand merger could have been popular, but it is said that new Jharkhandi Congress leaders because of their sloth and disinterestedness allowed the initiative to pass in the hands of those who were determined to undo the merger. Such disgruntled tribal leaders supported by powerful clique and money houses found easy to hold aloft the banner of separation once again and trounce those who had been contesting 1969 election in Singhbhum or Santal Parganas on Congress ticket after merger of Congress and Jharkhand Parties. The chance of liberal political set up in the tribal areas was once for all for the time being lost.

NOTES

1. L. P. Vidyarthi, "Aspects of Tribal Leadership in Chota Nagpur" in *Leadership in India*, Bombay (1967), p. 131.
2. Oral Statement of Rev. Joel Lakra to the author.
3. Anugrah Narain Sinha, *Mere Sansmaran*. Patna, Kusum Prakashan (1961), pp. 282-83.
4. P.G. Ganguly, "Separatism in the Indian Polity" in *Archaeology and Anthropology*, Bombay (1969), p. 83.
5. Secret West Bengal Police Report.
6. *Ibid.*
7. *Ibid.*
8. Same as 1. p. 136.
9. Constituent Assembly of India, Excluded and Partially Excluded Areas Sub-committee. *Report*. p. 9. Quoted by Kartik Oraon, Member of Parliament in Loksabha on 5th April 1969.
10. Letter dated 4th August 1947 from Harman Lakra, District President Adivasi Sabha, Ranchi to Dr. Rajendra Prasad. Quoted in Ramashray Ray. *The Congress Party in Bihar*. Manuscript p. 232.
11. Rajendra Prasad, *Autobiography* Hindi Version. pp. 477-78.
12. Memorandum dated 18th April, 1946 Submitted by Adivasi Congressmen of Chota Nagpur to Mahatma Gandhi.
13. *The Indian Nation*, 28th February, 1953.
14. Letter dated 8th March 1946 from Professor Abdul Bari to Dr. Rajendra Prasad.
15. S. P. Sinha, "Election Studies in Tribal Constituencies of Bihar", *Bulletin, Institute of Public Administration, Patna University*, 1972.

PART IV

Conflict and Tension in Gujarat Mahal (Tributary States)

11

BHUIYAN REBELLION OF KEONJHAR, 1867-1893

THE AFFAIRS of Keonjhar, one of the Tributary Mahals under the Commissioner of Orissa and on the border of Singhbhum district of Bihar, at one time gave cause for considerable anxiety to the government. There was dispute over succession to the throne. The Raja of Keonjhar died in 1860, leaving behind childless Rani and an illegitimate son by Phoolbai, a concubine and large number of his subjects to mourn his death. That son by Phoolbai, a concubine was named Dhananjay Bhunj. The British Government recognised him as Raja, but as he was minor his succession was put off for such time till he came of age in September 1867. The government was determined to make over to him the management of his estate. Dhananjay's right to succession was disputed by the childless Rani of the late Raja who supported the claims of Brindaban Chunder Bhunj, a scion of the Mayurbhunj family, whom it was pretended the late Raja, her husband, had adopted. "That no such adoption had ever taken place was amply proved and affirmed by all the courts in India before whom the matter came and if it did not appear to Government necessary to suspend making over charge of the estates until the result of Brindaban Bhunj's appeal to the Privy Council was known." [1]

The announcement of Dhananjay's succession in September 1867 was the signal for a strong outbreak of opposition on the part of the Rani and the hill tribes subordinate to Keonjhar who were devotedly attached to her. Deputations were sent to Calcutta to represent their case to the Lieutenant-Governor, but all in vain. The deputationists were explained the causes of not recognising Brindaban Chunder Bhunj and they were sent back. But they were assured that no oppression would be permitted to be practised on them by the young Raja or his advisers. The matters continued in a very unsettled state during December 1867 and January 1868. Revenshaw, the Superintendent of the Tributary Mahals of Cuttack had to camp personally in Keonjhar and it was only when aided by the presence of Dalton, the Commissioner of Chota Nagpur who brought with him the Seraikela Chief, the brother of the widow Rani of Keonjhar that the negotiation assumed a somewhat favourable turn and the large gatherings of hill men in the forests began to listen to reason. Rani consented to withdraw her "factious opposition", a proper settlement was made for her support and the hill tribes, the Bhuias or Bhunyas, united with the rest of the Keonjhar people in formally recognising Dhananjay as their Raja.

But this settlement and attendant calm were illusory. The peaceable conclusion of the Keonjhar Disturbance proved not to be lasting. On the 28th April, 1868, the whole Bhunyapirs and other parts of Keonjhar were rocked by an insurrection of Bhuiyas under the leadership of Ratna Naik, Nunda Pradhan and Nundoo Deorie breaking the three months of uneasy truce. The causes of sudden outbreak were obscure. Commissioner Dalton of Chota Nagpur, attributed it to some treacherous and impolitic action of Bewartha or Chief Minister of the State, while Revenshaw, Superintendent of the Cuttack Tributary Mahals suspected the Rani, and the Raja of Mayurbhunj, a brother of Brindaban Chandra Bhunj, of secretly fomenting the trouble. Ratna Naik, the leader of the hill tracts of Keonjhar organised a combination among his own and the other hill tribes in opposition to the Raja's authority. Large assemblage took place and State policemen who went to chastise them were themselves arrested by the rebels. The Bhuiyas sacked the Keonjhar Bazar, carried off the Chief Minister, intimidated the well-disposed Raiyots and burnt village of the loyalists. The Raja became alarmed for his own safety and applied to the government for the aid of police, declaring his own *paiks* to be untrustworthy.[2]

Deputy Commissioner Hayes of Singhbhum was ordered to the spot with a force of police and the reinforcement was held in readiness at Balasore. Superintendent Ravenshaw addressed a *Parwana* to the Bhuias, and another to dowager Rani and the Raja of Mayurbhunj Kishun Chunder Bhunj (the nephew of Mohurbhunj Raja who died on November 1867 was recognised by the government)[3] calling upon the former to disperse and reminding them of their promises to the Raja and warning the latter against encouraging or assisting the trouble-makers. Brindaban Chunder Bhunj, the claimant of Keonjhar Raj was the younger brother of Kishun Chunder Bhunj the newly declared Raja of Mayurbhunj, but the Raja by his disposition and action was a loyalist and he loyally assisted in the settlement of

Keonjhar by treacherously handing over the messenger of Bhuiyas to the Superintendent which ultimately proved the Rani's complicity in the matter.[4]

Deputy Commissioner Hayes on arriving at Jaintghad on the border of Keonjhar found an extensive opposition against Raja, but believed it to be directly against Bewartha, the chief instigator against the Bhuiyas. The Deputy Commissioner learnt that Bewartha along with 50 men had been carried off to the hills, with the object of detaining them as hostages until the installation of Brindaban Chander Bhunj. The 20,000 insurgents had disarmed the police of Garh and dismounted the guns. The entire country was disorganised, and plundering was rife. Bhuiyas were joined by the wild clans like Juangs and Kols. Both Dhananjoy and the Rani were at the Garh, but Rani's authority alone prevailed. The combination appeared most serious, and a considerable force was deemed necessary to suppress it. But Dr. Hayes with small guards of Singhbhum Kols reached Keonjhar on 7th May, 1868 unopposed. He disarmed the wild tribes who had besieged the Raja and turned them out of the Garh and the people were reassured by his arrival. He sent a written demand for the release of Bewartha and other prisoners and summoned the heads of villages, and was hopeful that force would not be necessary. He was also joined by a body of police from Chaibasa.

On the 9th May, 1868 finding that the Bhuiyas had not released the captives Deputy Commissioner Hayes made an expedition into the Bhuiya country to gain information, but people fled at his approach. Tarpur, the village where Ratna Naik lived, was deserted and he could not obtain any news of the captives. At Betheapada, he met with some of the leading men who asked for six days time to consult the headman of the other *dandpats* with regard to the delivery of the captives, and engaged to meet him at Keonjhar if he would return there.

Hayes wishing to succeed in conciliation acceded to their request. On return to Keonjhar he found the malcontents collected in large numbers around the Garh in an important position at Jonardhanpur about three miles away commanding the road to Chaibasa. After some resistance but without recourse to firing, they were dislodged and a great number of them were disarmed. The chief failed to appear on the appointed day and there were news of their meditated attack on the party at Garh. Considering hostilities inevitable, Hayes applied for 300 troops.

The rains had set in heavily causing sickness and supplies were getting scarce. On the arrival of supplies and reinforcements, police and native infantry, Hayes directed his efforts towards breaking up the combination between the hill Bhuiyas and the people of the plains and inducing the latter to return to their homes and cultivate their fields. Several posts at the foot of hills were occupied partly by strong guards of police and partly by armed *paiks*. But affairs in the neighbourhood of Keonjhar had assumed a grave proportion and serious character. At Tara some of the policemen were surprised by the rebels and taken prisoners. Richie's patrol of 50 police were attacked and surrounded by 2000 Bhuiyas at a place 6 or 7 miles away from Keonjhar on 21st May, 1868. Richie opened fire and dispersed the assailants. The communications of Keonjhar were cut off from either Cuttack or Chaibasa, the dak plundered and the Bhuiyas attacked the camp thrice without success.

Commissioner Dalton of Chota Nagpur sent an expedition into the north-eastern division of Keonjhar presumably under Lieutenant Johnstone to compel the submission of the chiefs and bring in all the principal men who ultimately surrendered. A detachment under Lieutenant Hunter succeeded in finding and rescuing a party of constables from the confinement in a village which had for sometime been the headquarters of Ratna Naik. On 7th July, 1868 Superintendent Revenshaw arrived and assumed the charge of affairs with Colonel Dalton. Expeditions were sent out in various directions. The insurgent took themselves to hiding places in the hills, and no opposition was anywhere encountered. Herds of cattle and stores of grains were brought away and villages which had sided with the insurrection were burnt. The Bhuiyas petitioned for fifteen days time to arrange for submission. They were encouraged to come in, but were informed that no suspension of hostility would in the meantime be granted.

Army despatches of 10th Madras Native Infantry and 37th Grenadiers were pressed into action. Lieutenant Johnstone, the Special Assistant for Keonjhar, was sent into the Bhunyapir with a police force of 100 strong, and Pergunait Jagdar Singh of Pethoria (near Ranchi) and his 40 *paiks*. Besides Rajah Bindessurree Prasad Singh Deo Bahadur of Surguja, Chuckerdhur Singh, Zamindar of Pallhera, Baboo Pooroosutum Deo of Bonaie and others rushed to help the Government in quelling the disturbance for which they earned the gratitude of the Governor-General-in-Council. The Governor-General-in-Council was convinced of the fact that it was by the exertions of Commissioner Dalton and Superintendent Ravenshaw, that the result of pacification was achieved.[5]

Dalton and Ravenshaw, used to jointly send dispatches to the Lieutenant Governor of Bengal and according to them Lieutenant Johnstone, Special Assistant for Keonjhar, fulfilled his mission successfully and satisfactorily by destroying the property of those headmen of certain villages who had not surrendered. For the time being a standing camp in a central position at Banspal was established to encourage the people of all villages, the headmen of which had surrendered, to withdraw their families from the forests and hills and revert to their usual habitations.

On 17th August, 1868, Lieutenant Johnstone sent in the remains of Bewarthas headless corpse but found with a cloth which was identified by the friends of the deceased as a portion of the raiment he had worn when carried off. The chopped off head is reported to have been taken to Ratna's headquarters, and treated by the Chief as a sacrificial offering. Runia Koke Sirdar who surrendered, was made to capture Rutna and Nundo Pardhan while his family was kept in hostages. On the same day from Baitarni Rajah Bindessuree Prasad Singh Deo Bahadur of Surguja and Oodepur, sent in upwards 50 Bhooyas of Kowar and other villages of that very refractory Pir, including most of the headmen, amongst them Nundia Mullick, the chief of the Pir and leader in the affair with Poole at Melan and in several other actions. The Rajah discovered in that man's possession a quantity of property plundered from Poole and from the Rajah of Keonjhar and the arms and accountrements and property of the nine constables captured by the Bhooyas at Tarra, all of which he sent in to the camp of Lieutenant Johnstone. On subsequent dates, the Rajah sent in more men who had been captured or had surrendered to him, and finally on the 26th August, 1868 on the submission of the headmen of Tapalda, the last to surrender, he was informed that the tale of "Pardhans" from the Jharkhand Pir, in which he had been operating was complete. The people were to be permitted to reoccupy their villages without fear of further molestation, and the Rajah and his contingent and the detachment of Police at Baitarni were to return to headquarters.

Ratna, Nundo Pradhan, and his brothers, Sokera, and equally notorious rebels" were hiding in the hills between the outpost at Tomakaut held by the Pallehra contingent, the outpost of Banspal held by the Bonaie contingent, and Rajah Bindessure at Baitarni and Runia Sardar with his Koles were also on their track. "The great prize, **Rutna,** fell to the Pallehra Zamindar on 23rd August, 1868 and next day **the**

Zamindar appeared in camp with Rutna, two other leading rebels, Chemta Pardhan and Dhurni Deorie of Gundola as prisoners; Chuckerdhur Singh of Pallehra had performed a very important service in securing the person of the great fomentor of the Keonjhur insurrection, a chief whose appearance stamped him as a man of mark, of great bodily strength and with features indicative of firmness, boldness and intelligence."[6] Ratna had wielded an extraordinary, almost a mysterious power in Keonjhar for the preceeding seven years, treating with contempt the authority calling for his attendance and evading every order of his arrest. During the present disturbances, though he was seldom seen by the people, yet was implicitly obeyed by them because he had heroically led them on every occasion. On the same day Babu Pooroostum Deo of Bonaie, appeared at the camp bringing in as prisoners Nundo Pradhan and his brother Sokera, and some other chiefs, Bonaie contingent rendered good services culminating in capture of important rebels. Whilst Ratna himself kept in the background, accessible only to his most intimate friends, Nundo Pradhan openly took the lead in the insurrection, and his brother, Sokera, was one of the Ratna's most energetic and unscrupulous agents. The arrest and submission of the Sirdars then reported on complete the full tale of the 60 Pardhans of the hill Bhunyapattar and included a great many additional leaders claiming to belong to the oligarchy or subordinate to them.

Since Sirdars were all under strict surveillance and carefully guarded, "the hill country was declared to be subjugated and the inhabitants of the numerous villages that had been destroyed were glad to be permitted to return to the sides, and to be left unmolested, to reconstruct shelters for their families, and to attend to their cultivation. There had been little bloodshed, but they had suffered greatly from the raids made on them in so inclement a season, and no doubt, they would long remember the lesson they had given them. Another rebel Nundo Deorie took refuge in Sambalpur District.

Major F. S. Hawks, commanding the Keonjhar Field Force was requested to gradually break up the force. Commissioners Dalton and Ravenshaw also wrote to Major Hawkes that they had deemed it necessary to require that the widow of late Rajah of Keonjhar shall leave Keonjhar and proceed to Cuttack, and he was requested to take charge of her enroute. "Her influence in the country is considerable, and to avoid all possibility of any manifestation in her favour, it was expedient that she proceeded under military escort."[7]

The Commissioners took a seigh of relief that the operations undertaken against the insurgents in Keonjhar resulted in the capture and surrender of the headmen of all the villages that were hostile to the Rajah a Dhananjay Bhunj. One hundred and 83 prisoners were convicted. Rutna Naik with four others were sent to gallows while 27 got transportation for life and rest to different terms of imprisonment.

W. S. Seton-Karr, Secretary, Foreign Department, Government of India informed the Government of Bengal of the thankfulness of Governor-General-in Council to various Rajas and British Officers who took part in apprehension of Rutna Naik and asked to present suitable *Khelluts* and rewards to the Rajas so that "it serve as an incentive to other chiefs and influential persons who might be called on in similar emergencies". As to the rebels the Governor-General-in-Council held that the "right and just policy was to offer a complete amnesty to the mass of misguided or excitable inhabitants, and to evince towards the ring-leaders, or to those who have been guilty of acts of violence and barbarity, such a measure of wholesome but not excessive severity as might deter others from like courses in future".[8]

Pacificatory measures were taken and Captain Johnstone, Special Assistant for Keonjhar, was left at Keonjhar as a civilian officer and adviser to Raja. Steps were taken to improve the administration. Captain Johnstone did much "to unite the Rajah and his people, and it was reported that Keonjhar was as quiet and peaceable as could be wished during 1869-70".[9] The Report added, "The Rajah under Captain Johnstone's judicious guidance and advice, took an apparent interest in the duties of his position and in his people. During the year he disposed of nearly all the civil cases and the majority of the criminal ones and the hill people learnt to go to him direct and not through his *amlah*, for advice. He has moved much about the country and seems to have been everywhere well received".

In May 1869, Captain Johnstone carried out a census of the whole Keonjhar, which showed a total population of 1,51,295 people with the following break up:

Anundpore	71,152
Upper Keonjhar	66,343
Bhooyapir	18,800
Total	1,51,295

This shows that Johnstone was successful in his mission so much so that he could take even the census. He really displayed a marked capacity for governing rude and uncivilised tribes.[10] He was subsequently knighted for his service in Manipur. In subsequent years also, the hill people remained peaceful. The report said "Convincing proof of allegiance that they collected Rs. 40,000 towards Rajah's marriage expenses. After negotiations extended over two years, this marriage, took place with the daughter of the Chief of Barkhimedi in Ganjam (Rani is a lady of full caste). It would have been impossible, according to strict caste rules and prejudices, to have found a more suitable alliance, or one more likely to carry weight with the people of Keonjhar". "No doubt, too, the marriage" the report hoped, "will have a good effect on the question of the Rajah's admission to full caste, to obtain which end the Superintendent has been steadily working throughout the year. That there were symptoms of a disposition on the part of members of the family to see matters in different light to what they did formerly, and that the Rajah's position to gradually and surely acquiring stability".[11] But these were simple pious wishes only. The calm was illusory and Johnstone's work was not to last long. After all these episodes of recurrent rebellions of Bhuiyas it was perhaps not be expected that the Maharaja Dhananjay should regard the Bhuiyas with friendly eye and at any rate he treated them with severity.[12] This led to another outbreak in 1891-92 and another suppression, at the close of which C.S. Wylly reported generally on the situation.[13] He recommended that the Maharaja should be permanently removed from power as having shown himself unfit for rule and the state tarren under British management.

Sir Elliott, however, took a different view of the state of things brought to light in Wylly's report. He considered that the oppressions and exactions "may not seem very grievous compared to what has often been recorded of the rulers of native States in other parts of India". He did not, therefore, take so serious a view of the Maharaja's conduct as had been taken by local authorities. The Maharaja, therefore, was allowed to return to Keonjhar in his normal position "accompanied by an agent whose advice he had promised to follow". This Agent was Rai Nand Kishore Das Bahadur, and it should be noted that he was not only a *persona gratissimo* to the Bhuiyas but "the persons whom the leaders of Bhuiyas declared they would wish for next after Mr. Wylly who could not be appointed". The Bhuiyas still revolted during the six month leave period of Sir Elliott. Sir A.

Macdonnell, who was officiating as Lieutenant Governor, issued a menacing proclamation and time was given within which Bhuiyas should surrender at discretion.

As a matter of fact this "menancing proclamation" expressly provided that "your former general misconduct, so far as it affects the State and the Ruling Chief, will be condoned and forgiven, but that any acts of violence or oppression constituting offences against the Penal Code will be enquired into and the offenders dealt with according to law".

But Bhuiyas did not come in and expedition was sent on foot against them. The British police launched vigorous manhunting operations in the hills of Keonjhar burning homes and huts. Officiating Superintendent of Tributary Mahal, drew a vivid picture of the situation as how the first overt act of hostility of the Bhuiyas consisted of the capture by them of a Sirdar and a State Constable, how at Patuli an attack was made by them on a police officer named McMillan which was repelled, how a few days afterwards Babu Durga Charan Das Mukherjee was attacked by 300 Bhuiyas, attack repelled, how a constable escorting baggage was captured by Bhuiyas and disarmed, how the Bhuiyas attacked Chamakpur and sustained assault for five hours, how 2000 Bhuiyas besieged the Unkote outpost, how a party of Bhuiyas looted a village but absconded, how a party of police was attacked by 3000 Bhuiyas and forced to retreat, how the Bhuiyas burnt the Kuar outpost, and subsequently attacked the police there, how they attacked Kushurta etc.[15] However, the Government of Bengal recommended a change in its methods. In order that the hostilities may cease, Maharaja was deposed for 3 to 5 years but not removed from Keonjhar and maintained on state revenue. The state administration was passed on to Wylly as Superintendent. A. Williams commenting on the merit of the proposal wrote — "I think the general opinion would be that a scheme which, while on the one hand it removes the Maharaja from power, on the other hand leaves him in State to intrigue against his *locum tenens*, is in nine cases out of ten predestined to failure, and it may perhaps be observed that if an exactly similar attempt to conciliate the Bhuiyas after their suppression in 1891 was a failure, it is hardly likely to be successful now that they have 'arms in their hands, and the military police have been called off'.[16]

There is a reference to an account of Police attack on Jampani, a hideout of Bhuiyas from where Bhuiyas were forced to retire with loss of some men. Next day a harassing party, which was sent, came across a party of Bhuiyas who were collecting the fallen to bury. The police fired on them, killing one, wounding two and capturing four. Sir A. Macdonell was very severe on these operations. He considered "that it ought to be no difficult matter to establish authority without using their weapon".

Sir Mortimer Durand, Member in the Viceroy-Council, was at his wit's end in deciding the issue because it was not clear to him that the local officials have misconducted themselves or the rising was due to fault of the Maharaja. He wanted that Wylly be sent to Keonjhar to bring about settlement but Maharaja must not be touched without further evidence of his conduct. He called for stringent submission of Bhuiyas.[17]

Finally Simla decided the issue by declaring Sir A. Macdonell's orders as hasty and calculated to demoralise the local officers. It in a way justified hunting of Bhuiyas because of their recalcitrant attitude. But the Government of India accepted that attack on the party busy in funeral rites was a great mistake and it maintained that hostilities must be conducted in a very different manner if these tribals are to be put down effectively. Viceroy-in-Council decision was as follows :

> "We take note of the officiating Lieutenant Governor's opinion that the policy pursued in dealing with the Bhuiyas has been attended with unsatisfactory results and that a "change of method in dealing with the matter is desirable". The paper submitted have, we think, shown that partly owing to the nature of the country and the character of the rebel tribesmen the attempt to put them down has been made ineffectual, although it has involved a considerable amount of suffering and loss of life. We are not satisfied that the operations have been conducted in a manner calculated to ensure success, and we agree with the Lieutenant Governor in considering that the attack on the burying party, which was, we hope inadvertently made, was greatly to be regretted. We believe that there have been faults on both sides, and we should welcome any new departure which might result in bringing about the submission of Bhuiyas, and the redress of their grievances. We share the Lt. Governor's opinion that the consideration which Mr. Cooke would impose are not suitable and should not be insisted upon. . . . In view of these facts, we agree that before further hostilities are resorted to Mr. Wylly may be deputed for the purpose of endeavouring to bring about the submission of the Bhuiyas on the line proposed, but

the terms should not be decided until Mr. Wylly has reported."[18]

The Governor-General-in-Council also reserved his decision on the Maharaja until Mr. Wylly had advised upon this point. It occurred to His Excellency that there might be some time allowing him (Raja) to remain in residence within the State. On the other hand, his virtual deposition and removal from the State, in view of the fact that the measures taken with the consent of Government to put down a rebellion against him have the appearance of inconsistency, and probably render it impossible to restore him hereafter. The Government of India noted that it would be glad if Mr. Wylly were to find it possible to effect arrangements under which the Maharaja would be allowed to exercise a nominal sovereignty over his state under the advice of a British Officer, and subject to conditions which could guard effectually against the misgovernment of his aboriginal subjects. The Council noted :

> "We can say at the end that we have given our careful attentions to the instructions issued by the officiating Lieutenant Governor on the 21st June, that while as we have said, we regret with him the suffering and loss of life which these operations have involved it should remembered that they were undertaken by the orders of the local government and with the concurrence of the Governor-General-in-Council. That with an enemy as numerous as the Bhuiyas an enemy described as "high spirited though badly armed, and aided by the conditions of country and climate under which the operations were carried on, it was idle to suppose that no loss of life and no suffering would occur and that, although we regret the tone of some of the local officer's report, we do not see how they could have been expected with due regard to their duty towards the force under their orders, to restore order by merely by 'show of force' and without using it. The Governor-General-in-Council thought that the officiating Lt. Governor showed a very proper appreciation of the situation when he hesitated to depart from the Government of India, and it because His-Excellency-in-Council held the same view that he made these comments upon the abruptness with which His Honour seemed to have ordered a completely new departure in dealing with the Bhuiya outbreak."

A telegram was sent to Bengal Government approving of Mr. Wylly's deputation and explaining that the Council reserved its decision as to the treatment of the Maharaja, and the terms to be offered to the Bhuiyas, until the Lieutenant-Governor had had an opportunity of considering Mr. Wylly's recommendations.

Thus ended the Bhuiyas rebellion, because we find that the country which was in unsettled condition in the beginning of 1893-94 was gradually reduced to peace and order, and the Bhuiyas tendered complete submission to their chief. The settlement operations in connection with the Bhuiyas and Juang Pirs were concluded on terms agreeable to, and accepted by both parties and leases were granted. The difficult question of personal services claimed by the Raja under the head of porterage, roof-thatching and dragging the car of the family God, out of which the rebellion had mainly sprung, was decided in a manner which it was hoped would be satisfactory and lasting, the nature and extent of the services to be claimed being defined with precision, or else commuted into an enhancement of the ordinary rent.

NOTES

1. *Administrative Report of Bengal for 1865-66 and 1867-68* (available in National Archieves of India).
2. C. E. Buckland, *Bengal under Lieutenant Governors.* Calcutta, 1901 pp. 420-21.
3. *Administrative Report of Bengal for 1867-68*, p. 257.
4. C. E. Buckland, p. 424.
5. Letter No. 1083 dated 22nd September 1868 from W. S. Seton-Karr, Secretary to the Government of India (Foreign Department) to H. L. Dampiers, Officiating Secretary to the Government of Bengal.
6. Letter No 1261 dated 30th August 1868 from Colonel E. T. Dalton of Chota Nagpur and Superintendent T. E. Ravenshaw of Cuttack to H. L Dampiers, Officiating Secretary to the Government of Bengal.
7. Letter No 1207 dated 27th August 1868 from Commissioner E. T. Dalton of Chota Nagpur and Commissioner T. E. Ravenshaw of Cuttack to Major F. S. Hawks, Commander of Keonjhar Field Force.
8. Letter No 1083 dated 22nd September, 1868 from W. S. Seton, Karr, Secretary Foreign Department, Government of India to H. L. Dampier, Officiating Secretary to the Government of West Bengal.
9. *Administration Report of Bengal for the year 1869-70.*
10. C.E. Buckland, *op. cit.*, p. 426.
11. *Administrative Report of Bengal for the year 1871-72*, p. 38.
12. 1893 Foreign Department, Internal A proceedings, September 1893, No. 121-124.
13. 1892 Foreign Department, Internal A Proceedings, June 1892, No. 227-234.
14. Letter No. 792P dated 1st March 1892 from Mr. Cotton, para 4.
15. Letter No. 1075 dated 23rd/26th May 1893 from the Officiating Superintendent of Tributary Mahal, Orissa.

16. 1893 Foreign Deptt., *op. cit.*, Para 8.
17. Sir Mortimer Diwand on the same file as 12 above dated 17th July 1893.
18. Governor-General-in-Council Proceedings dated 9th July, 1893. Paras 9, 10, 11 and 12.

12

UPSURGE IN BAMANGHATTI PARGANAS IN 1866-67

THE TRIBAL upsurge led by Boorda Bhoomiz and Bhagwan Dass in 1866-67 in Bamanghatti Parganas is a typical offensive against the Establishment to express their annoyance with several causes of irritation. The Bamanghatti Raja's men and other non-tribals had to fly away seeing the tribal furry. A State resurgency prevailed which was calmed down by the tactful handling of situation by the Deputy Commissioner of Singhbhum who marched with a strong police force.

The upsurge in Bamanghatti Parganas was the result of distinct universal discontent prevailing in the area against the Raja's rule so much so that was assessed by the T. E. Ravenshaw, Officiating Superintendent of Tributary Mahals, Cuttack, and Dr. Hayes, Deputy Commissioner, Singhbhum that it was "impossible in the then state of feeling of the people of the Rajah to exercise any authority in Bamanghatti until such time as a settlement of rents was made and confidence restored".[1] After the Sambalpur rebellion in 1861, the Raja of Bamanghatti attempted to introduce a settlement and measurement of lands which were "eminently distasteful to the indigenous population who adhered to the old custom of payment as so much per *hal* of 40 or about 40 *Bighas* of land". Had the measurement been carried out with anything like fairness the people might possibly have yielded, but the Raja's *amins* falsified their measurements, and his *amlahs* and *tehsildars* did not give receipts in full for rents paid. When objections and complaints were made, the people were put off with excuses, and no attempt was made to adjust or settle their real or forced grievances. The Raja's subordinates, moreover, committed numberless oppressions and exactions and made themselves otherwise obnoxious to the common populace. These *amins* used to be accompanied by their servants and friends *paiks*, *mugdees*, *choubers*, pole bearers and followers who had lived on the people and committed endless oppressions. Moreover, having been only nominally paid by the prince, they had in many instances to secure their own profits by measuring lands at double their actual areas. Repeated additions had been made to their rents and the *abwabs* and miscellaneous demands had been levied to such an extent as to leave the cultivators only a bare subsistence. No system of accounts existed and seldom were any receipts granted for payments made.

To make confusion worse confounded no regular system of collection was followed. *Tunkees* or assignments of revenue were given by the Raja and his *amlah* and the village headmen sometimes made payments to one person and occasionally to another. Syces, tailors, merchants, servants etc. received these *tunkees* and were left to collect the amount from the unfortunate *raiyots*. Occasionally an elephant was quartered in village, and the demand for gratuitous supplies for all the Raja's *amlahs* on the spot were constant and heavy and were extracted without moderation or mercy. There was no protection offered to the raiyots and they were harassed. Under these circumstance the people were reduced to desperation.[2]

The apparent cause of the rising was that four of the Sirdars were seized, bound to an elephant and carried off to Baripada for refusing to supply provisions to the Raja's local agents. *Sirdars* were the heads of peers or divisions into which a Pargana was divided. The freedom-loving people passed their mirthful days in commune like village or *patti* system and the bond of allegiance to the Raja was very slight. They were a splendid fighting race and the Rajas made full use of them as pawns in a game in their quarrels with each other. They were ready to follow the local Rajas when they led them out to battle, perhaps because of the lure of booty than anything else. Thus, with such loose bond of allegiance, the persistent attempt of superior landlord to reduce them to obedience was bound to be galling and obnoxious. They priced their liberty more than their life and they respected their heads (*Sirdars*) and their rule, because they had the backing of tradition and their obedience to such system was habitual. The *Sirdars* administered the *peers* in arcadian simplicity without becoming tyrants, and they were the most respected guardians of the tribals. There had been some jealousy between the Coles and other sections of the Sudras who acquired lands or property in their village. An idea appears to have prevailed that the Coles, Santals and Bhoomiz should retain exclusive possession of the country.

When the four sirdars were seized and carried off to Baripada tucked to an elephant, it became intolerable to the people. It appears that they were much incensed at their headmen having been bound and carried off and retaliated by driving the Raja's police and every one belonging to him out of Bahalda. The Raja took no measures either to conciliate the people or to maintain his authority. Dacoities commenced at night and were succeeded by day plunderings which continued for nearly a month, during which time the Raja afforded no information whatever on the subject. The first intelligence of the disorganised State of Bamanghatti was received through the Deputy Commissioner of Singhbhum.

As these dacoities and plunderings continued, the entire Sudra population left the country. The plunderers organised themselves under the leadership of Boorda Bhoomiz, a man of no previous notoriety, but who appeared to have taken advantage of the opportunity to bring himself to power. Boorda Bhoomiz, Bhagwan Dass, Kartika Cole, Tolkar Santal and Chikra Cole were the chief ring-leaders and instigators of the rising. They assumed the command of the country. Meetings were held at first by all the Ooperbhag *Sirdars* of *peers* and also those of Bamanghatti from whence a deputation was sent to Ooperbhag and Bhagwan and several of the *Sirdars* crossed the ghats and went over to Bamanghatti.[3]

It was not precisely known as to what transpired at the Bamanghatti conference, but it was generally stated that it was agreed to reinstate the old *Sirdars* or *Zamindars* of Bamanghatti Parganas, Ooperbhag, Juspore and its subordinate five *peers* and to coerce the Raja into measures which might be productive of less misery and oppression. A large number of persons took part in the meeting and attempts were made to negotiate with the Raja's nephew Babu Kishun Chander Bhunje who was at the time in Bamanghatti. He appears to have offered concessions, but he acted somewhat injudiciously in causing the arrest of two or three of Bamanghatti *Sirdars* who had wounded his servants. Those *Sirdars* were later released at Baripada, but they retaliated by turning out the Raja's people.

The Pargana was divided into several *peers* of groups of villages and each *peer* was presided over by a *Sirdars* or headman. These headmen were originally either *Boorahu* or Santals who, as aboriginal inhabitants of the country, claimed a sort of undefined and hereditary right in the soil, and had always objected to, if not resisted, the introduction of Hindu *hattoahs*, *gwalas*, *chassas*, *machantees* etc. The Raja had at various times and for various causes, whether on good grounds or otherwise, gradually introduced and favoured the settlement of Hindu castes and cultivators and had made grants of lands to Brahmins and temples, which though not resisted, or perhaps openly objected to, had been very distasteful to the *deslog*, *boorah* and Santals. The local names of the classes were *hatooahs* and *deslog*. The former including all Hindu Gwalas, Chassas and Sudras, and the latter Boorahus, Coles, Bhoomiz and the indigenous population.

For sometimes before open plundering commenced in Ooperbhag, dacoities were night occurrences. The victims being invariably *hatooahs*. It was rumoured that *hatooahs* would be openly plundered and molested and the *deslog* would be spared. At this *hatooahs* commenced to remove large quantities of their grain in the houses of their former servants belonging to *deslog* castes for safe custody. Complete panic prevailed and people sent deputations to Bhagwan's son and agent at Bunkatti offering to pay black money in consideration of their houses being spared. In some cases payment was voluntary, but in others it was exacted by Bhagwan's sons and agents. In every instance where protection on payment[4] was promised, an arrow and string with three knots were given to the person to be protected with instructions to be hung up in front of their houses. At the same time a bamboo with a bundle of straw tied at the top was to be planted infront of the door. Similar tokens were used in Bamanghatti also. They had started a government of their own; they issued written orders to the headmen of villages and directed plundering operations. A state of great consternation prevailed. The houses of *deslog* were not disturbed and in a very few cases the houses of Coles, Santals and Bhoomiz were plundered. The distinguishing marks of a pole or bundle of paddy were placed before the houses of *deslog* and thus their houses were spared.

Boorda Bhoomiz, it appears, had no particular headquarters. He carried a large broad arrow to which *puja* was offered, and this was the standard around which the malcontents rallied. The offering of *pujah* to the broad arrow of Bhoomiz gave this leader a charismatic personality. Through this system of worship he not only secured the allegiance of the tribal people under his banner but was also successful in cementing his adherents together by evoking a feeling that his followers were the *deslog* and other were *hatooah* — a sense of "we-group" and "they-group". Other instances of use of religion as a vehicle of separation have not been wanting in the annals of the tribals.

In the whole rebellion, personality of Bhagwan Dass, considered to be the descendant of the head Boorahu family of the Pargana, is interesting. His ancestors were said to have held the Zamindari of

Bamanghatti Pargana. When they were deposed, they settled in Ooperbhag, where the grandfather of Bhagwan Dass obtained the post of *suberakar* or manager of Parganas. This continued in the family till his father was turned out with the consent of the Superintendent of Tributary Mahal for misconduct, open resistance to the Raja, embezzlement of revenue etc. Bhagwan Dass, however, succeeded in obtaining from the then Raja a few villages as his maintenance and jagir and amassed some property. He was a shrewd and an intelligent man. As the Raja's oppression increased, Bhagwan Dass availed himself of the opportunity to intrigue and foster the prevailing discontent with a view to induce a crisis, so that he might again obtain the position he had formerly occupied, as not only the head of the clan but as the *Zamindar* of Parganas.

The ambition of Bhagwan Dass was inextricably mixed up with the whole proceeding of plundering and dacoities and he took advantage of the situation created due to general discontent. The result was that Boorda Bhoomiz remained a cipher, getting worship and adoration in the assemblage of his adherents while the whole movement was skillfully operated by Bhagwan Dass, his sons and his agents for the satisfaction of their selfish ends.

Kashi Sardar of Kusumbund, as head of peers commenced an investigation and succeeded in arresting a number of so called dacoits and recovered from them considerable portion of the plunder. Those dacoits confessed to Kashi Sardar that they had orders to plunder from Bhagwan Dass and implicated two of his sons and several of his adherents. Kashi Sardar prepared a report of the case and as was his duty, proceeded to take his prisoners to the Raja at Bariparda. But Bhagwan Dass's sons and adherents waylaid Kashi Sardar, rescued prisoners and forcibly carried off the whole of his papers. Bhagwan Dass from Bamanghatti sent armed *paiks* under his son Muddun Babu to arrest Kashi Sardar. Kashi managed to escape, but the *paiks* kept guard over the premises until later in the day when a party of some 400 or 500 of Bamanghatti plunderers headed by two notorious dacoits known as Nouru and Deeba Coles and Bhagwan's *gomasta* arrived, having plundered another village on the way. Kashi Sardar's house and those of the *hatooahs* in his village of Kusumbund were completely plundered. The Bamanghatti plunderers were joined by a large number of the *deslog* in Ooperbhag, and the party for some days laid waste some of the most prosperous villages in the Parganas. During the time these plunderings were going on, most of the *hatooah* either fled or hid in the jungle and in their absence all the property that had previously concealed was hunted up and carried off, the major portion finding its way to Bhagwan's house at Bunkatti.

Babu Kishan Chunder Bhunje was sent by the Raja with a good number of *paiks.* They came upon the plunderers at Mouzah Moonda Kotta. Seeing his party approaching there was a general panic among the plunderers, who fled in all directions. The ring-leaders escaped; only a few of the rebels including women and children to the number of 70 were arrested and sent captives to Baripada on 30th March, 1866. The Raja also reached Ooperbhag, but had no courage to go to Bamanghatti. Having heard of the trouble Dr. Hayes, the Deputy Commissioner of Singhbhum, entered Bamanghatti on 17th April, 1866. He found that all Sudra population, i.e., other than the Santals, Coles and Bhoomiz were in a state of greatest consternation, having been plundered and turned out of their homes and villages. The only course open to Dr. Hayes was to take effective steps to allay the fears which had seized the Sudra population and make them return quietly to their villages. The next thing was to attempt to procure restoration of the plundered property. This was carried out in a great measure with the assistance of the Santals, Coles and Bhoomiz themselves. At last Dr. Hayes was successful in seizing Bhagwan Dass, Kartika, Cole, Boorda Bhoomiz, Tolka Santal and Chirka Cole and other leaders of the revolt, and they were removed to Chaibasa jail to face trial.

Seeing their leaders removed, most of the people gave valuable information and assistance in recovering plundered property and in many instances readily disgorged their share in the spoil. Dr. Hayes dealt with the situation very tactfully for which he earned the Lieutenant Governor's appreciation. But T. E. Ravenshaw had a different experience in Ooperbhag Parganas where he laboured under considerable difficulty owing to the great influence possessed by Bhagwan Dass and his partisans and the utter and entire absence of the smallest appearance of authority on the part of the Raja. Even the bitter hatred of his oppressive *amlah* did not suffice to induce the people to give any information as they dreaded vengeance to follow after they left the place. The losses assessed amounted to Rs. 12,267 annas 13 pices 10.

In consultation with Dr. Hayes a new scheme in the territory was initiated. The Raja's authority in Bamanghatti was suspended and Dr. Hayes was vested with the same civil and criminal powers in Bamanghatti as those exercised by him in Singhbhum.

Under section 15 of Act V of 1861, a force of one Sub-Inspector and eight constables was quartered in Bamanghatti and the cost of their maintenance was to come from Raja of Mayurbhanj. The *Sirdar* of each *peer* was permitted to exercise police powers under the guidance of Dr. Hayes. An enquiry was instituted. All the *Sirdars* of *peers* and hereditary heads of villages were to be maintained in their position' where they had been improperly ousted in near past they were to be reinstated.

Settlement for all villages was to be made under written agreements with the village headmen, who were to be responsible to the *Sirdars* of their respective *peers* for rents. It was also decided to discontinue the attempt to assess lands by measurements and the old system of *halbondi* was reverted. A fair inquiry was to be made where necessary as to the number and extent of *hals* held by individual cultivators. The standard of measurement was fixed at Rs. 54 per *hal*. All *awabs* and *mangan* were abolished. It was agreed that the Raja should give an undertaking not to demand any levy for cess whatever beyond the fixed and proper rents before the estate was made over to him.[5]

In Ooperbhag Pargana also the management was entrusted to Babu Kishan Chunder Bhunje, the Raja's nephew. Land was to be properly classified and assessed and rates of rent of first, second and third quality of rice land were fixed at one rupee, twelve annas and eight annas per *bigha* respectively. It was also decided to conclude a lease for 10 years on the above rates with the *Sirdars* of *peers*, who were to be responsible for the collection of rents in their respective peers and also were to perform all police duties. The *Sirdars* were to forward the *kisht* instalment of payments of revenue direct to the Raja's treasury. The system of *tunkees* or assignments of revenue was discontinued and so also the demand of *awabs*. A party of police with one head-constable and six constables was posted at Bunkatti for preservation of peace.

Thus this upsurge was an attempt to change the prevailing system of administration perpetrated by the Raja's unjust officials. There was a pervasive phenomenon of prejudice, tension and discrimination between groups on ethnic and racial grounds. The elements of religion and ethnic backgrounds were used between *deslog* and *hattoahs* successfully in this upsurge. Because of these circumstances, this rebellion falls in the category of other tribal rebellions such as the Great Cole Rising, Santal Hul, Kherwar Movement etc. Religion was used in the revitalisation of the movement in the same manner as in the

Birsa Movement. The leadership is charismatic as we find Boorda Bhoomiz getting the *deslog* worship his bow and arrow. In Bhagwan Dass one finds a shrewed politician trying to utilise every opportunity for self aggrandisement. What is astonishing is that in this duality of leadership, the followers got easily disillusioned at the slightest show of strength, all the rebels melted away at the very sight of the Raja's army under his nephew. But nonetheless this rebellion abounds in many administrative lessons which can hardly be ignored otherwise.

NOTES

1. Letter dated 28th April 1866 from T. E. Ravenshaw, Officiating Superintendent, Tributary Mahals, Cuttack from his Camp Office in Deodang, Mayurbhanj to the Secretary, Government of Bengal, Fort William.
2. *Ibid.*
3. *Ibid.*
4. Letter dated 31st May 1865 from T. E. Ravenshaw, Officiating Superintendent, Tributory Mahal, Cuttack to the Secretary, Government of Bengal.
5. Same as 1 above.

13

WILD KORWAS DISTURBANCES (1881-82)

KORWAS ARE one of the least known tribes of Bihar so much so that scholars have held different opinions about them from the very beginning. Dalton,[1] Russel,[2] Thakkar[3] called them a 'kolarian tribe and whereas Risley,[4] Allen,[5] Sunder,[6] and Crook[7] consider them as 'Dravidian'. Mazumdar[8] found hardly any difference between Korwas of Mirzapur and Palamau so far as their primitive and savage condition was concerned. Some researches have recently been conducted on Korwas by Hari Mohan[9] and A.N. Sandwar[10] which go to prove the backwardness and primitiveness of this tribe in Palamau. Although they have been given a new nomenclature of *Dih* or *Danr* Korwa (settled Korwa) to counter-distinguish them from *Pahari* or *Benwari* (hill or wild) Korwas of Jashpur and Surguja in Madhya Pradesh who have been recently studied by Victor Rosner[11] which go to point out that former and later once belonged to the same stock of little known tribe of hunters and food-gatherers or jungle nomads. Dalton was inclined to remark that the "genuine unreclaimed Korwas, glorying rather in the wild-life of the hunter than in the tame pursuits of the agriculturists, have from the remotest antiquity lived by choice as highlanders, thoroughly despising the lowlanders, who indeed appear to have been too much in dread of them ever to have disturbed them".

Once during the nineties of the past century they posed a great law and order problem due to heavy depredations that they carried on in 21 villages of the borders of Palamau and Surguja State. Surguja with an area of 6,103 square miles and a population of 270,366 people had very turbulent people like the Korwas, Kodkus, Kishans and Oraons who posed a great law and order problem from time to time. Korwas rebelled in 1878, but were quelled in 1881-82. The rebellion of Korwas was very difficult. The disturbances assumed wide proportion and was ultimately curbed when large number of armed forces from different places under Commissioner of Chota Nagpur Division were deployed.

The Korwa trouble is linked with the death of Raja Bindeshwari Prasad Singh of Oodeypore, the uncle of the Surguja Raja, who had managed the estate during his nephew's minority.[12] He had managed to keep the Korwas quite repressing them with severity when they attempted to return to their hereditary occupation of highway robbery, but generally treating them justly and fairly. After his death, his cousin, Lal Maheswari Prasad of Lukhunpore, was put in-charge of the State. No sooner he took the charge, the Korwa resumed their predatory habits, and in 1878 it was found necessary to take special measures to put a stop to the dacoities committed by them. The Surguja police used means of dealing with the prisoners which were utterly unjustifiable and must have led to irreconciable enmity between the two parties. Henceforth Mahto Korwa and his brothers, who were then the leaders of the Korwas on the Lahsunpat, declared themselves to be at open enmity with the Surguja authorities, when Andi Korwa, one of the prisoners who had agreed to submit and, therefore, was deputed by Lal Maheswari Prasad to bring over his fellow tribesmen to follow his example, but Mahto and Deo Sahai and his brothers, murdered him.

The Korwas kept quiet for two years till 1881. It might be due to the repressive measures taken by Surguja authorities or due to this trial and conviction of Korwas by Commissioner Taylor who found them guilty in the cases arising out of dacoities in 1877-78. But towards the end of 1881-82 several violent dacoities were committed by the Korwas, and the protection of roads through the State became a great worry of the government. None could be apprehended and as such they were emboldened. After a great concern shown by the government the Surguja authorities sent the Zamindars of Ram Kola and Jhilmilli to inquire into the causes and to arrest the offenders. A special police was put to guard the pass from Chunderpore to Chalguli to the West of the Lahsunpat, while the Zamindar of Kendri who was the aunt to the Raja of Surguja opened negotiations with the Korwas of the Surup Jogi Pahar of the Jamerapat (who had committed most of the dacoities during 1881-82) overlooking the road across the Chaitanya Ghat, which passes along the banks of the Kunhar river between the Jamira and Lahsunpat. Ramna, the Chief of the Korwas, agreed to commit no more dacoities and Bhakua, a member of the of the band was appointed Chowkidar to guard the Chaitanya Ghat.

Kurtha and Puraon, brothers of Rama, however, did not accept the arrangement. They were advocates of violent and extremist measures and of the continuance of their predatory habits. Therefore, they first murdered Bhakua, and later on Rama and his Mahra in a quarrel over the distribution of Rs. 30 and large supply of liquor sent to them by the

Zamindar of Kendri.[13] After murdering them, Kurtha and Puraon and other three of the band fled. They began to commit fresh dacoities in conjunction with the Lahsunpat Korwas.

Instead of arresting the Korwa leaders, the Surguja authorities persuaded Gopal Korwa and Bhowana, Kuthra and Puaron's elder brother, who was one of murderers of Ramna to come down to Chunderpore and settle there, in the hope that by their influence they might put a stop to the dacoities. Commissioner Hewitt of Chota Nagpur on return from his long leave in November 1882, found the predatory raids of Korwas unabated and there was no record in his office to show that any action whatsoever worth the name was ever reported to him. The Commissioner addressed a strong letter to the Surguja Manager pointing out the necessity for taking some effectual measures to protect the resident people and travellers passing through the state from Korwa depredations. This resulted in the arrest of Gopal and Bhowna, who had been ring-leaders in many dacoities, but had done nothing since they came down from the hills in July and had got land near Chanderpore. Korwas were greatly incensed at this betrayal because they regarded that these leaders were entitled to protection from further arrest in consequence of their submission.

This worsened the situation all the more. Kurthra and Puraon were furious at their brother's arrest. Boocha, one of the leaders of 1878 who had been released from jail, was equally indignant at the arrest of Bhowana, who was his near relation. The Korwas had, hitherto, chiefly confined their depredations to stealing rice from villages and property from travellers and had rarely resorted to violence unless those they attacked should fight; but from that time they began attacking, plundering and burning villages, killing cattle, and in some cases wantonly and without any provocation murdering the inhabitants.

The Korwas began with attacking Kotpali, Khujoori, Beyojaoum Baunkapi, and Sauni, large and flourishing villages lying just below Deoghur on the north-east of the Lahsunpat in the valley of Kunhar and they burnt and utterly destroyed all these villages. At last, inhabitants of the Kunhar valley had some relief when Korwas met with rigorous resistance when they attacked Poatsura, four of their men being killed. This resulted in their withdrawal from Kunhar valley and they started attacking the villages on the north. But when there also they met with resistance, they turned towards the north-east towards Chunderpore. Altogether they destroyed 21 one villages.

By this time, the minor Raja of Surguja, Raghunath Saran Singh

Deo attained his majority and Lal Maheswari Prasad (the late Manager) as Zamindar of Mahri, the *purgunnah* where most dåcoities took place, were asked to take measures to protect his territory under his charge and were insisted upon taking action against the Korwas. The Commissioner threatened the Zamindar Lal Maheswari Prasad with fine when he found him not going down to Mahri till June 1881. Reluctantly, he and his men arrived there in June frightened by the prospect of loosing their lives. They were themselves in defensive and they did not dare attacking or attempting to arrest them. Shortly, after the Lal's arrival at Mahri, the Korwas attacked his thana, but were beaten off and, consequently, Lal asked the Commissioner for reinforcements. The Commissioner ordered Mr. Bachman, Inspector of Police in Palamau, to go to Chunderpore with a body of police and to give active assistance to Lal. Raja's Dewan Jaffir Ali Khan came down with the young Raja and the Zamindars of Ramkola, Palka, and Jhilmilli also sent men to help him.

The police force arrived at Chunderpore on the 24th June, 1881, and on the 2nd July expedition was undertaken into the Korwa hills but this expedition was badly organised; was not accompanied by the Inspector of Police, who should have been in command, or by any superior officer. The attack instead of being made on Deoghar on Sumnudri, the village of the Lahsunpat where the Korwa leaders and malcontents lived, was directed against Hutor, where Choran Byga and Udo Korwa, the two men who, as afterwards appeared were ready to come to terms, were Chiefs. The expedition was utterly unsuccessful; the Korwas disappeared into the jungles as the Police appeared, and they did not succeed in arresting any of the men.

The European Inspector of Police of Palamau, Mr. Bachman, wrote such an alarming account of the Korwas that the Commissioner of Chota Nagpur considered it necessary to take vigorous measures to protect the country against men who were determined on active war. The Korwas were utterly unscrupulous and knew that they could do whatever they liked with the Surguja people as it was found that they (Korwas) attacked and burnt three villages and murdered Lal's servants on the day of the expedition of Police to Hutar, besides disarming a body of Surguja Police a few days afterwards. Accordingly, the Commissioner directed District Superintendent of Police Mr. Harries and Assistant Commissioner of Palamau Mr. Renny to proceed with a police force to Chunderpore to take the necessary measures for arresting the leaders and putting a stop to Korwa depredations and to make a thorough enquiry into the origin and extent of the disturbances.[14]

Renny and Harries, accompanied by Assistant Superintendent of Police Mr. Tucker who went because Mr. Harries was ill, and might probably be unable to remain with the expedition, arrived at Chunderpore with a reinforcement of police on the 19th July, 1881. They succeeded in arresting three of the leaders, Hiraman, the Chief of Deoghar and brother-in-law of Kurtha; Deo Sahai, the murderer of Andi; and Birsa who had been one of the most active leaders of Korwa rebels, Boocha who was with Kurtha, the leading instigator of the late depredations, was shot dead while attempting to escape. Rainy season prevented the police from pursuing men who could easily elude pursuit in the dense jungles of Lahsunpat. It was also thought prudent to attack such formidable positions as those occupied on the plateau by the Korwa with half-disciplined police.

The officials, accordingly, left Inspector Hakim Singh with eight head-constables and 48 constables to guard the passes. These men were posted in four stations on the chief passes descending from Lahsunpat, the men of each station being required to keep up a constant patrol round that part of the range committed to their care while Inspector Hakim Singh was to visit each post at frequent intervals. He and the police under him were directed to take care that any man who attempted to descend the hill to commit dacoities were arrested, and that every effort should be made to induce the more peaceably disposed Korwas to come to terms, and to assist in the arrest of the ring-leaders for whose arrest rewards were offered.

The Government of Bengal approved the arrangement. Although no dacoities were committed in villages below the hills after Renny and Harries expedition still Inspector Hakim Singh and the police under him utterly failed in inducing any of the Korwas to come to terms.[15] Willing Korwas were afraid of their lives and so were the leaders, they were determined to resist trusting the inaccessibility to the Lahsunpat which afforded a safe haven for them in the difficult rocks and forests. They were determined to have whole of Lahsunpat for themselves as they thought to turn it into an impregnable fortress by virtue of geographical terrain of the area. Hooter, Deoghar, Lahsun, Sumundri and Jonka were the five villages on Lahsunpat. The Korwas were the main inhabitants of the first four villages but in Jonka a considerable body of Hindu *raiyots* used to live. In 1878, the Korwas invaded Jonka and drove all the Hindu *raiyots* out of it. They wanted to do it again in

1881 with the support of Hurria, Rugsai and Tecko but in vain. The Jonka Korwa leaders preferred to remain faithful and loyal to the Raja. Therefore, the Korwas of Samundri headed by Keso and Jhato, brothers of Mahto and Deo Sahai and the murderer of Andi and Bundren Korwa, guilty of several previous murders, attacked Hurria and his two brothers and murdered them. Police came and occupied Jonka and with the local assistance arrested two of the murderers.

But it was practically impossible to do anything against the other villages or to secure the arrest of the leaders owing to the topographical situation. The whole country with an area of about 120 square miles was under a dense forest, covered with high grass and was totally without any road. In addition to it, the rainy season prevented the authorities to do anything with the Korwas.

Therefore, in October 1881 after the rains, Commissioner Hewitt sent Janki Prasad Tewari, a Sub-Inspector of Lohardaga Police, who had gone to Lahsunpat with Harris and who knew Korwa people and country well. He was asked to go down to Inspector Hakim Singh and to report after consulting and viewing the country with him, whether any additional police from the reserve would be wanted for the task. They reported that further requisition was necessary as the Korwas were determined to fight. Accordingly, the Commissioner asked the Government in October 1881 for a body of reserve police. Consequently, 50 reserve police from Dumka under Inspector Luker, 30 men from Patna were dispatched while Inspector Peters from Dacca was sent to assist in the operations. They all reached Satwarwa in Palamau and Commissioner Hewitt alongwith Renny and Tucker marched with them into Surguja. At Burkol, after consultation with Inspector Hakim Singh, they decided on a plan to sweep simultaneously the whole extent of Lahsunpat.[16]

Luker and Hakim Singh, with majority of the armed force, started from Jonka on the South and marched through Sumundri and Lahsun to Deoghar. Messrs Tucker and Peters started from the east side and marched through Hutar to Deoghar. Renny took to outlying spur of the part above Sauni, and the Commissioner Hewitt with Raja of Surguja and Oodeypore marched from Ketali to Deoghar. The marches were so arranged that the parties under Luker, Tucker and the Commissioner were to meet at Deoghar at 9 A. M. on 19th November, 1881.

But these marches proved abortive because the guide with the party of Luker and Hakim Singh lost heart and fled away before they reached Jonka. His substitute was unacquainted with the latest movement of the Korwas and their whereabouts. Consequently, the police stumbled unexpectedly on the new huts, and unfortunately a child cried in the first hut they came to. This roused the men who escaped. But at Lahsun, the next village they succeeded in securing Choran Byga and his family, a capture which proved ultimately to be most valuable.

Deoghar, the headquarters of the Korwa leader Kuthra was found to be deserted. All its inhabitants fled to Sumundri as soon as they heard that the Commissioner was camping at Kitpali with force. But on descending the hill from Deoghar arrows were fired at the Commissioner's party by a group of Korwas who had followed the police from Sumundri.[17] These arrows were replied with some shots but nothing was visible. The prisoners were called to address them and try to speak to them. They answered but kept themselves out of sight among the rocks till the police party got a part of the pass which was clear of trees up to the foot of the rocks which crowned the height of Deoghar. Three or four of the Korwas who shot arrows appeared above the rocks and when they were told to come down and surrender, they said that they would do so when the police released the prisoners that they had taken. When the Commissioner told them that they were determined to capture them, Kuthra, the leader of Korwas said "you may do what you like but, whatever you do, I will still be king of the Lahsunpat". The hot pursuits of the *boulders men* was proved a wild goose chase. The police party returned to the camp. The Korwas could climb these high boulders like monkey. Thus the whole operation that day proved useless. The government accepted the defeat.[18]

However the police embarked upon a policy of burning the villages which they visited and destroyed the crops in which men of Surguja Zamindars also joined. They were also put as Special Guards at the foot of the passes so as to stop the fugitives flying to Surup Jogi Pahar and the Jamirapat, the near probable line of escape. They found a large party of the Korwas into some precipitous hills overlooking the Kunhar from whence they were trying to escape to the Jamirpat. This flight of the Korwas to some different part convinced Tucker that there was no more fight left in them and, therefore, there was no necessity of keeping the reserve police to do the working of following up through the jungle fugitive, who were without food for more than a few days, and, therefore, brought them back, leaving a strong guard of district police on the top of the *pat*, and a large number of Raja's men along Kunhur valley to take care that they did not escape to the Jamerpat. But inspite of this, the Korwas managed to elude the Raja's guards in the Kunhu valley and reached Surup Jogi Pahar were they were supplied with food by some of their relations, and the subsequent attempts to arrest them failed owing to the supply of provisions for the force engaged not being sufficient.

Although the leaders with families fled away Inspector Hakim Singh with the help of Charan Baiga was successful in bringing in a large number of willing Korwas to submission. In December 1881, when the Commissioner went there, he met Hakim Singh and Charan Baya and a number of other Korwas who promised to live in peace in future and to settle in the villages assigned to them below the Lahsunpat. A large number of loyal Korwas from Pal, Chalguli and Lerna came to settle and since then no further difficulties were experienced. On the 20th December, 1881, 97 Korwas with their families amounting to over 200 persons, appeared before the Raja at Lahsun and were allotted land in villages below the Pat, provision being made for their maintenance till the first crop was reaped. The Commissioner ordered that none of the Korwas belonging to the families of the dacoits would be allowed to live on the *Pat.* A permanent police post was created at Lahsun, on the top of the *Pat*, and two other posts were placed at Sumersotie on the western road leading from Chunderpore to Chalgulli, and another at Chainpur on the Chaitanya Ghat to safeguard these trade routes from Palamau to Surguja.

On the 7th January, 1882, Kuthra and Puran, leaders of Korwa rebellion were arrested. They as well as Doondey, Bundon, Thetho, and Ladra were presented before the Raja who committed them for trial. The Commissioner tried them at Ranchi and they were finally sentenced to death on 14th February, 1882.

Thus with these 'exemplary punishments' the Korwas depredations were brought to an end. It is useless to say that Raja had become powerless to restrain the powerful Korwas who caused great devastation and disorder throughout the Korwa country. They were finally quelled when the Commissioner of Chota Nagpur with large force under experienced European and Indian Inspectors remained engaged in the operation for about six months. The popular nature of the rebellion can be judged by the ready help these Korwas used to get in the place wherever they went in hiding. Therefore, the Commissioner Hewitt issued order that in future none of the Korwas belonging to the families of dacoits would be allowed to live on the *pat* and he wanted to segregate them for times to come. The result is that in popular parlance the Korwas are still taken to be the thieves and robbers' although others have now been leading a life of settled agriculturists, *Kamia* worker and landless labourers.

NOTES

1. E.T. Dalton, *Descriptive Ethnology of Bengal*, Calcutta 1872, pp. 221-30.
2. R.V. Russel, *The Tribe and Caste of Central Province of India*, Vol. III, London, 1916 p. 577.
3. A.V. Thakkar, *Tribes of India*, Delhi, 1950 p. 104.
4. H.H. Risley, *Tribes and Castes of Bengal*, Calcutta, 1891 p. 511.
5. B.C. Allen, *Census of India*, Vol. IV Assam, Shillong 1902 p. 135.
6. D.H.E. Sunder, *Survey and Settlement Report of the District of Palamau*. Calcutta 1896, p. ccxxxi.
7. W. Crook, *Tribe and Caste of North Western Province of Oudh*, Vol. III, Calcutta, 1896, p. 322-34.
8. D.N. Mazumdar, 'The Korwas of United Province', *Man in India*, 9, 1922, p. 237.
9. Hari Mohan, Korwa Way of Life, Unpublished Ph. D. Thesis, Ranchi University, 1961.
10. A.N. Sandwar, The Korwa of Palamau: A Study of their Society and Economy. Unpublished Ph. D. Thesis, Ranchi University, 1972.
11. Victor Rosner, "Leadership Among the Korwas of Jashpore" in *Leadership in India*, Bombay, Asia 1967.
12. 1884, Foreign Department, Internal A Proceedings, pp. 264-66.
13. *Ibid.*, Para 53.
14. *Ibid.*, Para 55.
15. *Ibid.*, Para 61.
16. *Ibid.*, Para 64.
17. *Ibid.*, Para 66.
18. *Ibid.*, Para 69.

14

GOND REBELLION, 1888

GONDS OF Bonai State, a Tributary Mahal of Chota Nagpur and contiguous of Singhbhum's Kolehan, raised a banner of rebellion in 1888 against the unjust and enhanced rate of settlement of the estate mostly in favour of Raja of Bonai levied by Mr. Hewitt, the Commissioner of Chota Nagpur. Though no bodily harm was done but depredation such as looting the *Gountias* and others took place which ultimately brought R. H. Renny, the Deputy Commissioner of Singhbhum with armed forces along with large contingent under Seraikela Chief and others to the Gond country.

The genesis of this rebellion of the Gonds under Judhistir Mahapatur and Saban Dondpat could be found in the long charter of demands placed before C. C. Stevens, the Commissioner of Chota Nagpur who undertook a tour of the State in the winter of 1888-89 under the orders of Lieutenant-Governor of Bengal. This charter of demands[1] was as follows:

"We beg to represent ourselves before your Honour with the humble request that your Honour may do justice by reinstating us in our respective rights, and also by excusing our faults, we will accept whatever rent may be fixed at the present measurement.

1. We, the Mahapatra and Dondpat, used each to hold two "*hal*" of rent free lands, and we pray that these may be restored to us together with any lands which may have been added to them since the last settlement. Moreover, we used to pay the Rajah Rs. 50 each out of the collections made by us, and to keep the rest for ourselves. We now hope that whatever rent may be fixed by your Honour, we may receive an allowance in proportion to the profits which we have been enjoying. Moreover, the Naiks and priests have been in possession of certain lands, and we pray that these holdings may be restored to them.

2. Our forefathers granted some *debottor* lands for the worship of the Gonds *Banshidher* and *Baneswar*, and we pray that these may be maintained.
3. We are ancient zamindars of Bonnai but the *raiyots* have treated us as *Ticcadars* and has ousted us from our zamindaris. We request that the title of zamindar may be given us as before.
4. As a matter of custom, the property of any of our caste fellows dying intestate used to be divided into two shares, of which one used to be appropriated by the head of the caste (Dondpat), and the rest consumed by the members of his caste. We pray that this custom may be maintained. We also pray that orders may be given that all disputes connected with our caste or religion may be settled by the head of the caste.
5. We have planted date trees and the Rajah now demands rent for them, which we have never paid before. We pray that we may be exempted from this demand.
6. We have hitherto been collecting the dues from weavers and others (non-agricultural classes) at the rate of four annas each, but the Raja now demands more than usual.
7. The Raja has no right to the collections made by us on account of cesses from cattle grazers, potters, Uraons, people who sell parched rice, etc.
8. If excessive dues are demanded for the cultivation of cocoons in our *pergunnah*, it is likely that this cultivation will be entirely stopped.
9. The Raja has been in the habit of taking fees from us whenever we had occasion to hunt in our jungles. In default be used to realise a fine of Rs. 5 from us. We pray that this custom may be abolished. "

This charter gives an idea about the situation prevailing at the time. But the Raja of Bonai was himself a very greedy as well as a very needy man. Raja had three unmarried daughters all of whom he wanted, naturally, to dispose off by marrying them with appropriate bridegrooms of his status and society. Deputy Commissioner Renny knew that marriage of one of the daughters of Raja with the son of a Chief in Central Provinces fell through for the want of funds. It was quite possible that the Raja, imagining his end to be near, being desirous of averting from himself the stigma of leaving unmarried daughters behind, was putting forth strenuous efforts to raise funds and being on bad terms with the heir-apparent was indifferent what becomes of the State so long as he got the money.[2]

Deputy Commissioner Renny, who went to quell the disturbance learnt, that "beyond all doubt it was Mr. Hewitt's settlement as well as the action taken by the Raja in trying to enforce it that had given rise to the Gond revolt. He found the Raja was perfectly impracticable in controlling the Gonds and Raja was convinced that the Gonds would never pay the new rents and notwithstanding that he was determined to coerce them to the last degree, trusting for supports from the British authorities. He found all reports of Raja grossly exaggerated with a avowed object of ousting the Gonds out of the country in order to resettle it with outsiders like *Tossas* from Naira in Cuttack from whom he would receive large amount as *Salamies*".[3]

Gond never accepted Hewitt's settlement. Deputy Commissioner Renny was convinced of this fact because rent then was demanded from these Gonds and this was over six times the amount paid by them under Colonel Dalton. Besides a police cess had also been imposed upon them. According to Sabban Dondpat and Judhistir Mahapatur, they used to pay under Colonel Dalton's settlement an annual rental of Rs. 49 annas 8 each (Raja's records showed Rs. 58 annas 8 each); whereas under Mr. Hewitt's Settlement they were required to pay Rs. 322 annas 5 pices 10 and Rs. 303 annas 2 pices 9 rent and Rs. 70 annas 4 pices 10 and Rs. 66 annas 4 pices 4 police cess respectively. The Deputy Commissioner felt that these rates were in excess to those paid by the tenants in Government estate of Kolehan in Singhbhum.

Harsh measures were adopted by the Raja for realising rents according to Hewitt's settlement, knowing fully well that the Gonds would not pay them. From the statements of *Mahapatur, Dondpat*, and several other subordinate *Naiks* it was found that Raja not only made wholesale attachment of property, irrespective of the amounts due to him, but also summarily ejected the *Mahapatur, Dondpat*, and most of the *Naiks*. Raja deputed persons to make attachment and effect the ejectments who harassed and insulted the people in the grossest manner. One Bissesswar Deo, a near relative of the Raja on several occasions carried off all the cattle he could lay hands on, notwithstanding that the amounts he was sent to realise were small. Again a certain Bikram Baboo carried off the timber collected for the building of a temple at Puigaon and further insulted the Gonds by saying that the Raja would marry their women to the Pans (a scavenger caste) unless they paid the rents demanded from them without further demur. The Raja himself made no attempts to deny that cattle had been seized or that he had attempted to supplant the Gond naiks by Tossas. "Whatever may be the truth, we are convinced," wrote Renny, "that the Raja's action produced a violent panic amongst the Gonds who were persuaded that he intended to stop at nothing short of rooting them out of the country, the Gonds themselves having been deprived of their lands, and their cattle were reduced to a condition verging on famine".

Another object in view was to bring down a British officer to hold local enquiries on the spot. Beerjo Dondpat mentioned in his statement that the Gonds, finding petitioning at Ranchi useless had entered on a course of violence, knowing that a British Officer would come down to put a stop to the disturbances and with the full knowledge that they were rendering themselves liable to the severest punishment at Deputy Commissioner's hands. This was borne out by the fact that several leading *Naiks* went to Koira in the anticipation of Deputy Commissioner's arrival. That they all immediately presented themselves to the Deputy Commissioner as soon as they heard of his arrival showed that their main object was at all risks to get a British Officer down to the spot, who would make an impartial local investigation into their grievances.

Last but not the least the previous year (1887-1888) failure of crop had worsened the situation and goaded the Gonds to start depredations. In assessing the actual amount of mischief it would appear that looting was chiefly directed to obtaining food, for according to the lists filed the value of *dhan* and other edibles is stated to be of Rs. 6428 annas 2 out of an aggregate value of Rs. 7,704 annas 11 pices 6 of property alleged to have been stolen. Renny compared the list furnished by Raja with that of the list of the Gonds supplied to District Superintendent of Police, Mr. Stock who accompanied the Deputy Commissioner to Gond country. He found that in aggregate the difference was very small, yet individually they were very marked and existence of these discrepancies inclined the Deputy Commissioner to suspect very seriously the truthfulness of the Raja's lists. *Gomtias* reported that *dhan* was looted from them, but it was not given in the list of Raja. Gonds denied that they carried off any cash or jewellery. It appeared that in some few instances they no doubt roughly handled some of the *Gomtias* and carried of their cooking pots and pans. This, however, only happened in those cases where resistance was offered or food was not given to them on demand. In one or two cases, too, where the resistance was obstinate, the *Gomtias* were made to pay a fine or a small amount before they were released.

The Gond *naiks* stated that they were instigated by no one, but were actuated by a common impulse and held meeting at the first of which they decided on resorting to "looting" for food. At subsequent meetings the particular stores to be looted were fixed upon. Renny opined that the Judhister Mahapatur and Sabban Dondpat were pulling the strings from behind the scene.

Looking at the list we find that the persons "looted" were the Chassas, Pradhan, Teli, Mahto, Tatee, Oraon, Gomtia, Soha, Mahanti, Dey etc. in all 30 persons. The list will show the following :

List	Dhan and Edibles	Cash Rs.	Other Articles	Total Rs.
1. Raja's List	-	184-6-0	1081-12-6	1266-2-6
2. Gond's Leaf Memoranda	6457-6-0	200-2-0	1076-7-6	7733-15-6
3. Difference as compared with Raja's List	-	-	-	6467-13-0

Castewise distribution of the people suffered in these affrays were following:

Chasas 8, Teli 4, Goutias 5, Uraon 3, Mahto 3, Pradhan 1, Tatee 1, Mahanti 1, Saha Dey Das 3, Rajput 1,

These data speak for itself that Gonds did not come into clash with Bhuiyans and any other caste groups who were the functional class like the Kumhars Lohars, Ghasis etc. Even if the above castes were interferred, they lost only a few items of daily use like the following:

Items	Judhister	Mahapatur Valued at	Sabban Dondpat's	Valued at
1. Brass cups (*Kotara* or *Dhuba*)	18		14	
2. Grass *Tasala*	3	Rs. 22	4	Rs. 12
3. Brass *Lota*	2	annas 7		annas 2
4. *Sari*	4	pices 6	2	
5. Bambo *Petora*				

These were delivered up by the Gonds of Bonai to the Deputy Commissioner Renny on being asked by the Commissioner, Chota Nagpur Division to proceed to quell the Bonai disturbances and make arrangements for pacification of the country at once dispatched a force of one Sub-Inspector, two head-constables and 30 constables for the protection of Gurh of Raja at Bonai. The second detachment consisting of two head-constables and 20 constables started with orders to await the Deputy Commissioner at Jamda, place on the borders of Keonjhur and 244 miles from Cheybassa. Deputy Commissioner Renny was informed that detachments for Lohardaga, Manbhoom and the Bhaugalpore Special Reserve Police were to form part of the expedition; but it was found that heavy reinforcement was unnecessary. Two contingents, one from Seraikela consisting of fifty men and the other from Nagra in Gangpore consisting of sixty men also rushed to Bonai. The rains were playing havoc with the roads and rivers did not have bridges. Only by "*hathgori*" the Deputy Commissioner Renny and District Superintendent of Police Stack could reach Jamda. Marching in a mountainous country through which there was no road; the only semblance of a path lay along mountain water course and through dense forests. The officers at times had to ascend close on 3,000 feet. They camped for the night in a malarious gorge by the side of a large roaring mountain torrent between two high mountains. There was no difficulty for these officers in understanding that throughout the country, the Gonds had revolted because of the enormous enhancement of their rents by the Raja of Bonai. Gonds started coming to the Deputy Commissioner's camp when they heard about their (officer) coming and started complaining about Raja's deeds against them.[4]

Before the officers had arrived Bhugwan Serdar of Koira and Tekait (eldest son of Raja of Bonai having strained relation with his father) moved in Gond area and persuaded the Gond chiefs to return to their villages and be normal. Bhugwan Sirdar of Koira was loyal to the British Government and was inclined to help Bonai Raja to a point where there was no serious law and order problem. Tekait loved his Gonds and was popular among them and was heard with respect.

Alongwith DSP Stack, Bhugwan Sirdar also went to Kuntgaon, the bastion of Judhistir Mahapatur. Bhugwan Sirdar opened negotiations with the rebel chiefs and Mr. Stack and Sirdar rode to Haldikuda a place of their hiding and were successful in persuading them to submit. These Gonds leaders were the fief holders on terms of military service to the Government and Raja when there was an exigency.[5]

Mahapatur and Dondpat had two active advisers in Basu Bar Naik and Ghundo Lalo who were active movers of the revolt. They called themselves *Mukhtears* of Mahapatur and Dondpat. They were also taken into safe custody with their client. Deputy Commissioner Renny thought to take Tekait with himself to Cheybassa because he found that he was having a "deadly feud" with his father, the Raja of Bonai and he was very popular among the Gonds and his sympathies were with the Gonds. Besides, a police force consisting of one head-constable and twelve constables was posted in Bonai for the purpose of restoring confidence in the Raja of Bonai and the disaffected Gonds. The head-constable was instructed to keep a watch on the actions of both Raja and the Gonds and see that either side did not molest the other. Some guards were also left at Kuntgaon, the heart of Gond country. The Deputy Commissioner also asked the Raja to keep in abeyance the enforcement of Hewitt settlement for the time being until the Commissioner's impending visit. Great many of the outsiders such as the *Toshas* by whom the Raja had begun to supplant the Gond *Naik* had fled away and consequently the Deputy Commissioner had no one to turn out in order to reinstate the Gond *naiks*.

Gonds were not the only people who were dissatisfied with Hewitt's settlement. The other inhabitants, residing in the Brahmini Valley, were also affected by it, but mercifully they had not revolted. Yet they were very dissatisfied with it and they had hardly anything left with them to eke the existence. Raja complained that not a single tenant helped him with *rusud* provisions for the several contingents and they openly refused.

The Commissioner opined that "it is clear that the Raja, thinking himself divested of responsibility and replying on the support of the Government had acted badly; but at the same time the Gonds in taking to robbery and mischief had deprived themselves of the sympathy to which their grievances to some extent entitled them".[6] He thought that the whole episode was a strategem to compel the interference. Government of behalf of the Gonds, who were or thought themselves oppressed and harassed by Hewitt's land settlement of Bonai and Raja's uncompromising method of enforcing it. He, by and large, supported the action taken by Renny in pacification of the Bonai country.

But one very interesting thing could be found in the correspondence and it was that J. A. Hopkins was critical of his predecessor C. C.

Stevens and he felt that since "he (Stevens) was guided by his predecessor's policy and desire to support the Raja, and the result has been general combination of Gonds to resist the demands made by him". He "found himself bound by the policy of his predecessors but he felt that he sometimes found himself extremely embarrassed as to the means of carrying it out, for one cannot but feel that families which have been settled on lands for generations, which brought these lands originally into cultivation, ought not to be ejected because they decline to agree to a settlement involving demands of six or seven times their former rent. He recommended the settlement should be held in abeyance for a few months until the Commissioner of Chota Nagpur Division visited Bonai. He also recommended to keep *Tekait* and Judhistir Mahapatur and Sabban Dondpat with the two *Mokhtears* tc be away from Bonai and be quartered at Cheybassa or Ranchi."[7]

C. C. Stevens, Permanent Commissioner of the Chota Nagpur Division when joined his post wrote to the Government condemning the officiating Commissioner Hopkins and the officiating Deputy Commissioner R. H. Renny for taking such a view of the situation which was to his mind totally unwarranted as he thought that the settlement was completely successful in the greater part of the State. He was surprised that apart from other cases Renny did not recognise the assistance rendered by Guman Sawant, chief of the Bhuiyas to the Raja of Bonai in his trouble with Gonds. (Gonds were against Bhuiyas in the Bhuiya disturbances.) He discussed the whole disturbance and anologus matter in 44 paragraphs with an exhaustive notes on the Bonai Raja. In the end he wrote in a mood to reconcile himself with the orders of Lieutenant Governor already passed. "I think the time has come when it is desirable that both Raja and subjects should learn that there is a power beyond the Commissioner, and that, though the Government may place a generous confidence in that officer's discretion, he is nevertheless only a part of a great system of administration."[8]

The Lieutenant-Governor approved the action taken by Deputy Commissioner Renny and endorsed by officiating Commissioner Hopkins and asked the permanent Commissioner C. C. Stevens who returned from his furlough to undertake a tour of Bonai and examine the suitability of revising or scrapping Hewitt's settlement. Lieutenant Governor also directed the Commissioner to inquire and ascertain at Bonai who were their ring-leaders in the late disturbances with a view to inflict appropriate punishment. "Although the Lieutenant-

Governor", wrote the Chief Secretary, is prepared to redress grievances when properly represented, it is intolerable that an attempt should be made to force Government to receive grievances, whether real or imaginary, by resort to violence. Whatever the motive of the Gonds may have been in committing the robberies, admitted by themselves, they must be taught that such behaviour cannot be allowed to pass unpunished."[9]

Lieutenant-Governor Sir Stuart Bayley, noted the happy remarks made by officiating Commissioner Hopkins regarding Renny and his officers and men who took part in the expedition to Bonai under him. He desired that an expression of satisfaction may be conveyed to Bhugwan Sirdar for his excellent services and the Lieutenant-Governor thanked the Raja Bahadur of Seraikella, the Mahapatur of Nagra and Maharajah of Keonjhur for the willing assistance rendered by them to the expedition.

NOTES

1. 1888, Foreign Department, Internal, A Proceedings, Nos. 84-85.
   Contains "Memorials of Gonds submitted to C. C. Stevens, Commissioner of Chota Nagpur Division at Gaully in course of his Winter tour of Bonai State in 1888-89".
   (Available with National Archives of India)
2. 1888, Foreign Department, Internal, A Proceedings Nos. 84-85.
   Contains Letter No 271 R dated 11th August 1888 from R. H. Renny, Deputy Commissioner of Singhbhum to Commissioner of Chota Nagpur Division.
   (Available with National Archives of India)
3. *Ibid.*
4. 1888, Foreign Department, Internal, A Book No. 84-85.
   Contains Letter No. 288V dated 19th July 1888 from J. A. Hopkins Officiating Commissioner of Chota Nagpur Division to R. H. Renny, Deputy Commissioner Singhbhum.
   (Available National Archives of India).
5. Same as 2 above.
6. 1888, Foreign Department, Internal; A Proceedings, No. 84-85.
   Contains Letter No. 124P dated 27th August 1888 from J. A. Hopkins, officiating Commissioner of Chota Nagpur Division to Chief Secretary, Government of Bengal
   (Available in National Archives of India).
7. *Ibid.*
8. 1888, Foreign Department, Internal A Proceedings, No 84-85.
   Contains Letter No. 257T dated 8th March 1889 from C. C. Stevens, Commissioner of Chota Nagpur Division to the Chief Secretary, Government of West Bengal.
   (Available with National Archives of India).
9. 1888, Foreign Department Internal, A Proceedings, No. 84-85.
   Contains Letter No. nil dated 20th October 1888 from J. W. Edgar, Chief Secretary, Government of Bengal to C. C. Stevens, Commissioner of Chota Nagpur Division.

15

KHOND REBELLION (1893) AND KISAN TANA RISING (1918)

Khond Rebellion of 1893

THERE WERE recurrent disturbances among the Khonds and the Oriyas in Nayagarh, a Tributary Mahal in Orissa. The first occurrence took place in May 1893 and is said to have been instigated by Nityanand Khetrober Singh, the ex-Dewan of the State. It appears to have been quelled without bloodshed so much so that the matter was not even reported to the Government of India at that time.

But an outbreak of more serious nature took place in January 1894 when in a melee in Kuruda Zilla a police constable Ramjan Khan, was killed by Balia Pardhan Khond and Bhajia Pradhan Khond. One Sub-Inspector Bankandihi Patnaik, was axed to death in the presence of strong guards who remained silent spectators. Altogether seven murders were committed and the murderers escaped detection and punishment. Of the seven victims six were State servants, of whom five were policemen. The genesis of such incidents lay deep in the exploitative administrative machinery and the Khonds that times were no exception. Introspecting on the incident the British officials used to come to some clear conclusion but they were themselves prisoners of their own circumstances. Officiating Superintendent Cooke wrote about the fate of the six victims of Khond wrath and communicated his unhappiness with the system of administration. The seventh man was the Mahajan of Mohipur who, according to Cooke, was murdered, because he was suspected to be an informer. It is also not improbable that the Mahajan was put out of the way by his creditors in order that they might escape payment of their debts.[1]

Nityanand Khetrober Singh and the Raja of Khondpara, another Tributary Chief of Orissa, who had unsuccessfully contested the last succession to the Nayagarh Gadi, were suspected of fomenting the disturbances but the evidence against them was not sufficiently strong to secure their conviction. Chaukidar's version was that Khond Raja had sent money to the Khonds with the object that "If there arise a *golmal*, the Superintendent will send the Nayagarh Raja to *Tapu*, (Andaman Isle) and Khetrober Singh will be the Dewan and the Khondpara Raja will be the Raja of Nayagarh".

The Manager Gopal Santra was, however, found guilty of extreme harshness, rapacity and abuse of power in his dealing with the Raj subjects. Levying of fine as *Kapurchandan* was obtensibly accepted as a sort of peace-offering to the Raja, and it was asserted to be a voluntary payment. A sum of Rs. 1,000 for Raja, Rs. 25,000 for *raiyot* and Rs. 6,000 for the Assistant Superintendent was the distribution of booty. This was available from the levy of Rs. 8 per *raiyot* who had cultivated the strip of land 26 miles long which was destined to become a road but did not. To particularise, he had levied heavy and unnecessary fines and imprisoned suspected persons without investigation or trial, thus causing a great sense of irritation and discontentment. Moreover, in 1890 when the then-Raja ascended the Gadi, the same Manager, finding the State heavily encumbered with debt secured a "crushing enhancement" of the rent, instead of getting the Raja to adopt more equitable means for replenishing the State Exchequer. He was then dismissed and Babu Darpan Narain Das, Sheristedar of the Superintendent Office, was appointed Manager on Rs. 200 per mensem subject to the condition that when things had settled down, he would be withdrawn if the Raja so desired. The expediency of this proviso seemed questionable, but the then Bengal Government had not commented on the point.

An amnesty was declared in the case of all persons not concerned in serious crimes. The terms of the accommodation with Melias was brought into writing which practically put an end to the disturbances. The Bengal Government issued the order approving the appointment of a new Manager, urging more frequent and protracted tours on the part of the Superintendent and Assistant Superintendent and insisted on the murderers being followed up and punished. No report to Secretary of State for India was preferred. But quick came the comment of A. Williams, a Member of Viceroy's Council, "The Bengal Government seemed to acquiesce rather readily in a state of things which involves the murder of seven men to attract the attention of the authorities to the State and Mr. Cook's surmise that six out of seven murdered men may have deserved their fate is not altogether satisfactory".

Kisan Tana Rising 1918

For a fortnight between April and May 1918, the area adjacent to the Feudatory State of Sirguja and Pargana Chechari in Palamau district of Chota Nagpur Division remained the scene of loot, arson, and murder by the turbulent tribes such as the Kishan, Oraon, Korwas etc., in which more than 50 persons including a Sirguja Magistrate and his retinue were killed. The avowed object of this rising was to establish a *Kishan Raj*, after removing the Sirguja Maharaja and exterminating the male folk among the Ahir, Rajput, Bania, Mohamedan etc. living in that area. Political-Agent, Chattisgrah Feudatories, armed forces of Central Province Government, the Maharaja's retainers and a large number of troops from Ranchi and Bhagalpur were rushed to quell the rising. High officials from Bihar and Orissa and Central Provincial governments conducted the raid on the rebel's hideouts and strongholds. Regular encounters and engagements culminated into hundreds of the rebels as dead and large number of them were apprehended and then hanged or transported for life. The rising was quelled mercilessly but with a lesson to the administrators.

The rebels invariably selected out-of-way places where they raised the standard of their rebellion in the *Tappas* of Madguri, otherwise known as Khando, and Mandeva in the North-eastern comer of the then Sirguja State and border of the districts of Palamau and Ranchi and the then-feudatory State of Jashpore. In the heart of these *Tappas* is situated the Jamirpat, a long winding ridge, rising to a height of about 3,500 feet with an extensive magnificent plateau on the top, about 16 miles long and 6 miles broad. It could be reached from Mahuadanr in Palamau via Hamichatakpur and then via Orsa-Pat recently opened for fair weather traffic due to exertions of Forest Department of Bihar and its Contractors. On this plateau are situated about 20 villages of Sirguja and seven of Palamau, the boundary between the then State of Sirguja and the Palamau district running over the hill from North to South. The area is fully hilly and with its difficult terrain is practically inaccessible even today during rainy season.

Such a difficult area was peopled by much more difficult people also. This was the land of the Korwas and Kodkus who were said to be notorious for their predatory habits. Besides them the Kisan the inhabitants of part of Sirguja State of the neighbouring villages of Palamau and Ranchi and the Oraon are homogenous to each other in their manners and customs of living. Their principal occupation is cultivation. Among the other castes and tribes who formed a part of the population of Mandeva and Madguri are the Korwas, Kodkus, Burgahs, Rajwars, Kherwars and Ghansis etc. the Oraon and Kishan population numbered nearly 5,000 in 1918 representing more than half of the entire population in these two *tappas*.

Jamirpat was the scene of this rebellion which broke out mainly among the Kishan and Oraons of the Madguri and Mandeva *Tappas* and the Chechari (Palamau), Barwe (Ranchi) and Khuria (Jushpore). People from a few other castes also participated in the rising. This unprecedented movement among these people was full of mysteries and curiosities. Some say that it was the product of a well organised propaganda, having its origin in the year 1915. Towards the end of that year a mysterious movement found its way into Sirguja State and naturally it affected the Oraon and Kishan sections of the aboriginal population. Enquiries showed that it had started from somewhere near Gangpur border at the South-West of the Ranchi district and spread in the district of Palamau and Feudatory States of Sirguja, Udaipur, Jashpur and Korea. It was known then to be movement confined only to social and religious reformation of the Nagesia Kishan-Oraon communities, but it came to have political significance also. Under the denomination of Tana Bhagatism it became widely popular in all the villages among the Oraons and Kishans who called themselves Tana Bhagats. Meetings were held in villages at which leaders preached the advisability of abstinence from drinking of alchohol and keeping and eating of pigs and fowls. These domestic birds and animals were then either turned out of their houses or killed in large numbers. In almost every village, a white goat was kept for the purpose of worship. The males and females of the Oraons, used to give the goat-god a very hearty reception by washing its feet and feeding it with rice whenever it happened to visit their houses. It was their common belief that after practising *Tana* for three years, they would reach the perfection when the goat would become immortal and they would escape all worldly evils and misfortunes.[2]

The village folks after taking bath in the evening used to collect in a sacred and secluded place in the village to sing *Tana* song in chorus. The songs varied significantly in meaning and composition in different circles. They appeared to be the product of the brainwave of a literate man among them, having contained the names of Hindu mythological gods such as *Rama, Lakshman, Varun, Indra, Agni* etc. perhaps not intimately known to the aborigines. Besides singing they used to scribble on a slate mysterious writings which no expert could decipher. They were advised by the preachers to give up tilling of lands, being given to believe that the output of crops of a single plot of land, by the force of *Tana* reading, would become quite sufficient for the whole mass of the Oraon and Kishan population. Each Oraon used to keep a pointed iron stick as a guard against evils, misfortunes and diseases in his family.

It was, however, suspected that the movement had much to do with the pro-German propaganda, and in view of the probable troubles and dangers which it apparently involved repressive measures were taken to break the tribal unity of these people and the solidarity of the movements as far as possible. Steps were taken to confiscate the iron-rods, goat-gods and slates and they were bound down under the procedure prescribed in the Indian Penal Code to refrain from participating in the movement and continue to follow the ancestoral family customs and usages of their castes. The Feudatory Chief of Sirguja wrote that

> "the measures so taken seemed to have the desired effect, and it appeared that the movement had been successfully checked. There was no sign of any more under-current of the mysterious propaganda until the third week of April 1918 when it suddenly broke out again on the Jamirapat in the form of a rebellion with horrible murders and depredations."[3]

It appeared that the movement apparently seemed to have stopped in 1916. But it was a miscalculation as it actually had not been entirely rooted out. The Tana Bhagatism carefully fostered precautions among its followers against the disclosure to the public and the authorities particularly. Several leaders, in the meantime, had established themselves prominently and maintained communications throughout among the *Tana* readers within and outside Sirguja State. About the end of March, 1918 their *Dak*, scribbled on Sal leaves began to run from village to village conveying orders of the leaders to all the followers to concentrate on a hill on Jamirapat called *Darapahari* from where the rebellion actually started. Ramanuj Saran Singh Das, the Feudatory Chief of Sirguja commented regarding the implicity of German missionary in this rising:

"The superstitious ideas of mischievous and poisonous character infectiously spread among the Oraon and Kishan classes of peoples of this state by their unavoidable contamination with their caste fellows of Jashpur, Palamau or Ranchi in whom the poison must have been originally injected by some vile and mean-hearted German missionaries, of whom there were possibly lots in these places in the pre-war days and, perhaps, also for sometime after the war began. Fortunately, my State was always free from these obnoxious pests, and I can, therefore, safely say that the cause of the unrest is not indigeneous but imported. These treacherous missionaries, who misused their mission and instead of teaching and spreading religion played unpardonable mischiefs are surely primarily responsible for the loss of lives of so many simple, innocent and peaceful men, and I am confident the consequence of this unpardonable sin is awaiting them."

Thus in discussing the genesis of this rising two ideas came before the officials:

(i) That the Tana Bhagat movement is in any way connected with the Lutheran Mission, and
(ii) That the use of the German name by these aboriginal people necessarily involves some connection with the German missionaries. In the files of the Government any one can more across several correspondence between the Government of Bihar and Orissa and that the ultimate responsibility for the outbreak of the rising lay not with indigenous sources in Sirguja but this disaffection was imported from the Tanaism of Palamau and Ranchi districts which was considered a German-oriented movement by many.

Sir, Benjamin Robertson, the Chief Commissioner of Central Provinces trying to convince Sir Edward A. Gait, the Lieutenant-Governor of Bihar and Orissa fully quoted from the reports supporting that the outbreak of rising was due to Tanaism and German missionaries from Bihar border.[4] He quoted the report of Pandit Gopal Rao, the Magistrate who was killed by the mob at Jhaljali. The Magistrate wrote,

"It is said that last year when there was Oraon movement in

Ranchi, Jashpur, Sirguja the Kishans and Binjhias also took part in it. Most of these Kishans and Binjhias were arrested by the police on the information given by some of the influential residents of that locality. The Kishans have since then borne a grudge against those who assisted the state authorities in suppressing the movement and bringing the culprits to book."[5]

Robertson placing his reliance on the dispatches of Mr. Scott quoted him that Mr. Scott had written to the Chief Secretary of Central Province expressing "the desirability of crushing the rising at once otherwise it was likely to become worse and continue indefinitely as the movement was not agrarian nor directed against the State but was social and religious". Mr. Scott also mentioned about Tana Bhagatism of Palamau and believed that Kishans of Chechari (Palamau) who had been affected by the movement must have spread the movement among the Sirguja Kishans. He also reported that the rebels considered themselves as the allies of the Germans and the word 'German' was freely employed by them and used as their battle cry at the attack on the Kusmi Thana. He added that there was little doubt that the rising was stimulated by the Tana Bhagat movement started by the German Missionaries in Ranchi in the year of 1916.

Robertson also quoted the report of Crawford, the Political Agent in Chattisgarh Feudatory States saying that the trouble was due to the "*German Baba*" on the testimony of the headmen of the Korwa tribe in Chalgali Tappa. Crawford's source of information was Bilas Sao, son of Biju Sao, one of the leader of the rising that the rebels were receiving assistance from Germans. Crawford also believed a priest of the Roman Catholic Mission who told him in 1916 that the "German Missionaries were not unconnected with the Tana Bhagat movement. Robertson found several references to the Germans in appeals against conviction of the rebels". In one of the proclamation sent out at the commencement of the rising in which the people were called upon to join the "German" and overthrow the Maharaja and gain possession of the Sirguja State. He felt that it had a real bearing on the trouble that took place. Sir Edward A. Gait did not like to agree with Robertson. He wrote back:

"In this province at last the Tana Bhagat movement was confined entirely to the Oraons, and in spite of most careful enquiries, we fail to find any evidence that the German Missionaries had anything to do with it. It originated among the heathen Oraons and was in fact anti-Christian. The invocation of the Germans by the Sirguja Kishans simply shows that they knew the Germans were at war with us and, therefore, regarded them as allies. The same thing occurred in the Mayurbhunj rising and the Shahbad disturbances, where no one ever thought of connecting it with the German Missionaries. The few men from Chota Nagpur, who took part in the Sirguja rising, all came from Tappa Chechari in Palamau, which was formerly a part of the Sirguja State and is inhabited by a kindred population with whom free social intercourse still take place. There is nothing to show that any British subject outside this limited area had any connection with the rising, or even knew of it uptil after it had occurred. . . . Certainly apart from the probabilities of Tanasim and German Missionaries, economic reasons must have contributed a lot in goading in people to rebellion, regarding which we have copious references in the records of the Government."[6]

F.L. Crawford, the Political Agent of Chattisgarh Feudatory States, laid stress on this aspect.[7] The murders committed at Mauzas Datram and Dumarkhoti were due to a private dispute or enemity brought about by Gaontias harassing the Kishans and demanding from them exhorbitant rates of interests on money and grain loans. This had been given as a reason by more than one person questioned by him. He had reasons to believe that the subordinate state officials immediately responsible for the administration of this part of the State and the welfare of the people had not listened to complaints, but had allowed Gaontias and Ahirs to down the Kishan. One Kishan who admittedly had taken part in the rebellion told Crawford that he had made a complaint against a Gaontia to Jagat Sahai, Tehsildar, a day or so before he was murdered but Jagat Sahai, instead of enquiring into the complaints, had taken Rs. 40 from the Gaontia in order not to take any action. Crawford wanted to believe this because he felt that such actions would certainly goad ignorant jungly people, some day or other, into taking the law into their own hands.

Gait also maintained on the basis of his officers report that the rising was mainly due to the misgovernment and oppression by the Raj Amlas and money lenders.[8] Mr. Scott, Superintendent of Police, Bilaspur who held informal enquiries into the causes of the rising with the help of his Reader Sub-Inspector, attributed the disturbance to the failure of the State officials to redress the grievances of the Kishans, who being incensed at the treatment they were receiving from their more wealthy and influential Hindu and Muhamadan neighbours, finally rose in a body with the object of exterminating the later and establishing a Kishan kingdom. The movement was mainly, he wrote, directed against Ahirs and Banias, against the former because they were never particular as to where they allowed their cattle to graze and against the latter because of the exorbitant rate of interest they charged on loans and the high prices they demanded for cloth, salt and other commodities. Mr. Scott thought that the Kishans must have already reached a state of ferment by the time the Tana Bhagat movement took hold of the tribe and that sooner or later they would have arisen there without the influence of the Bhagats even. W. B. Bretts noted that if Mr. Scotts's information was correct the condition of the Kishans had a bearing on tribal movements in the West of Chota Nagpur also.[9] Information was received that certain Bihar and Orissa men sympathised actively or passively with the rising. As a matter of fact "the whole country round is in sympathy".[10] B. Folley, Commissioner of Chota Nagpur wrote, "The rising is apparently a Bhagat one, probably helped like the others by oppression of the aborigines, stealing their crops, unlimited *bethbegari*, Ahirs grazing their cattle everywhere, extortion by Banias, seems to have started by a quarrel over the cloth with a Baniya". He mentioned elsewhere that "one perennial grievance of the Kishan was the presence of Ahirs on the *pats*. There Ahirs paid some amount per head of cattle to the State of Sirguja for grazing, and the cattle often commit great havoc with the Kishan's crops. Another complaint was the oppression of Raj Amla judging from what he saw he should imagine these people treated the Kishans with the utmost brutality. The exactions of the money-lenders probably constituted a third reason. Enormous amount of *Bethbegari* was exacted."[11]

Thus we have seen that at the bottom of the causes of this rising lay the economic, administrative, social and political factors — economic in the sense of the stark exploitation of the Kishan by the Banias, Ahirs (Gaontias) and Raj Amlas and administrative for the gross mismanagement of affairs by Raj officials. However, Tanasim and German propaganda supplied social and political base respectively to this rising. All factors conglomerated and in their turn produced a great stir and goaded the Kishan to the path of rebellion. One factor was contributory to other. But the situation was such that Kishan would have risen in rebellion in spite of the Tanaism and German propaganda.

Leaders of Rebellion

Labur Kishan, Bigu Sao, Belas Sao, Khikhir Kishan and Bekram Kishans were the leaders of this movement who were the resident of Sirguja State, but there were other leaders too. Rupna Baiga and Budhia Kishan hailed from village Gaguri of Khuria Zamindari in the Jashpur State. Bhairo Kishan from village Orsa and Janbe Kishan from village Sarwat in the Palamau District led their men in their respective area.

The peculiar motions and activities of these leaders are of great interest. Labur and Janbe were said to be regular vagabonds. Bigu Sao, a Jonpuri Bania, whose family came to Sirguja State in the seventies of the nineteenth century, was a man of well-to-do status, and he was himself the *Gaontia* of the village Serangdag. These three were the principal leaders of the *Tana* movement in that part of the country since the year 1916. If Maharaja of Sirguja is to be believed, they used to boast before the ignorant villagers of being persons endowed with supernatural powers and pretended occasionally to come under the influence of providential mercy. Under a State of pretended delirium they used to foretell the coming events and changes of the future and issue commands to their followers. They used to say that shortly a great resurrection was to occur, the German would reign in this part of the country, the present Maharaja of the State was not destined to rule and the Raj would be theirs. Bigu Sao would become the king of Tappa Mandeva and Labur Kishan of Tappa Madguri. They were to fight with the present Maharaja whose arms would become quite ineffective. The bullets would melt into water in the barrels. The swords would twist in the hands of the soldiers. All the non-Kishan and non-Oraon classes such as Chhatris, Brahmins, Mohammadans would all be killed. Other castes, who are resident of the State such as Rajwars, Kharwars, Ghansis, Korwas, Kodkus, Borghis and who would join them, might be spared. No female would be touched but males of their castes, even a child in cradle, would be killed. The Germans would send them arms from heaven. The battle was not between men and men but between gods and men and (the German representing Gods) the rebels would regain their lives if at all killed in battle and so on.[12]

The leaders further explained to their followers that they were in regular communications with the Germans, who travel in *Udankhatola* (air-ship) and that at the time of battle they would descend to assist them. Labur showed to his followers a wonderful weapon, a glass tube about six inches long and half inch in diameter – an article quite new to the aborigines and surprised them greatly. It was said that with that weapon he could kill enemies from a distance of ten miles. They further threatened the residents that those who would not be participants in the battle would be killed and those taking part would be allowed to enjoy land free of rent, besides many advantages. Khikhir Kishan who had been to Assam in 1917 to work as a coolie in a tea garden returned to his house and explained to the rebels that he had been to Germany and had come back from there with orders to carry on the battle on the Jamirpat which was divided half and half between Begu Sao, and Labur Kishan who proclaimed themselves as Kings of Madguri Tappa and Mandevari Tappa respectively. Meetings were occasionally held in different places presided over by these kings-designate and simple and ignorant people listened to their lectures with great interest and showed their faith firmly to them. One king was invited to the *Darbar* of the other and marched to attend the same in procession. In this they carried their affair most skilfully and secretly. The other leaders became the king's principal courtiers, ministers and officials, possessed of more or less with similar qualifications, thoughts and ideas. People had a great reverence for them.

The Uprising

By the end of March 1918, *Daks*, peculiar marks drawn on *Sal* leaves indicating orders of the leaders, were dispatched from village to village intimating to the Oraons and Kishans the probable time by which the battle would begin on the Jamirpat and spread gradually in different directions. On 16th April, 1918, formal orders were sent and by 19th April 23 rebels from ten of the villages of Sirguja State and eight of Palamau collected on the *Darpahari* hill on the Jamirpat where after performing necessary worship they shifted their camp the following day to another hill called *Panchpahari*. On 21st April, 1918 under the leadership of Labur Kishan of Sirguja and Bhairo of Palamau they started the rebellion and marched to village Datram where they murdered two boys, one a Kahar's son and other an Ahir's son, and wounded one Ahir who managed to escape. The next day the party returned to Dumarkholi where seven murders were committed and the village was looted. On 22nd April, 1918 Labur left for Khuria, it is said, to consult personally the Zamindar there and get assistance from him. Till 24th, more rebels from different places began to concentrate and Labur returned from Khuria with some rebels in all they numbered about three hundred.

Pandit Gopala Rao, the Magistrate of the Sirguja State arrested seven men from Dumarkholi and five from Jaljali. The Magistrate and his party consisting of Tahsildar Munshi Jagat Sahai and State overseer Radhashaim Das, Sub-Inspector of Kushmi and others etc., reached Jaljali on 24th April, 1918. There was some long standing boundary dispute between the Sirguja State and Chechari Zamindari and the Magistrate's visited the disputed boundary where they met the Palamau representatives, Kanungo and the Sub-Inspector of Mahuadanr (Palamau). The magistrate's party returned to Jaljali where they were camping. While resting, they learnt that the rebels intended to attack them but they attached no importance to this. Soon after the rebels in large number were seen advancing towards the camp with their war cries, displaying their weapons, running wildly and stumbling fanatically. Palamau officials ran away at the sight of the mob. The Magistrate Gopal Rao tried in vain to bring the mob to reason, but finding it a hopeless task he with Tahsildar wanted to run away on elephant. The mob followed the elephants with their volley of arrow shooting. The elephant, being hit by arrows, shook off the riders who fell on the ground and were mercilessly hacked to pieces. The elephant ran away riderless and four subordinate servants were also reported killed that very day. Tahsildar's Martini-Henri musket and ammunitions fell in the hands of rebels. Camp boxes were broken and papers and records were torn and thrown away.

This gave an initial advantage to the rebels who were now convinced of the supernatural effect of the *Tana* reading and got naturally much encouraged to fight on till a final victory. The news soon spread far and wide and the party swelled up soon considerably, being joined by men from all directions. Serious panic spread among the people who were threatened. They fled to the hills and jungles and distant places with their families to save their lives. Officials serving in the *Elakas* also ran away. Those who did not care to run away were killed. Even babies from the arms of mothers were not spared. Lives of females folk were spared on the belief that the effect of *Tana* reading would be injured if women were killed. The rebels organised their government. Villages were looted and grains were collected and stored in different centres in charge of persons called *Munshis*. Blacksmiths were caught and forced to manufacture *arrows*, *tabbales* and *balwas* and potters to supply earthen pots for cooking. Gopahatu was made the capital and renamed Patpur where a flag was hoisted as an emblem of victory.

What happened in Chechari valley is evident from a contemporary account of Father Dehon who had pitched his headquarters at Mahuadanr after traversing Kurund ghati. He preserved the account of this rebellion in his diary written in English.[13] This is important because it gives an idea into the excitement and nervousness felt in Chechari valley due to this rebellion. Some extracts from this valuable diary covering a period of nine days from 21st to 29th April 1918 are reproduced below:

21st to 24th April, 1918

Big *Panchayat* at Kurund for the Mundas of the *path*. Father Bodren comes from his district to join. Monday morning *Panchait* till breakfast. In the afternoon a big hunt, a wild boar and deer are killed. Tuesday *Panchait* in the morning and hunt in the afternoon in Sohar forest. Two small deer are killed and bear mortally wounded but cannot be found. Wednesday morning came back to Mahuadanr. In the afternoon, I hear the first news that the *bhagats* of the Sirguja are in open revolt. The Daroga comes to see me. He is still very excited and trembling. He tells me that he had gone to Sirguja to see the native magistrate and that while going thither he found the whole country in revolt. The Magistrate, his *tehsildar* and *morasi* had been killed and the daroga had been fired at by their arrows. It seems that the magistrate was trying to calm the *bhagats*, but they instead of listening to him fired some arrows at the elephant on which the magistrate was seated. The elephant fell down and the bhagats killed the magistrate and his men, the mahaut managed to escape.

25th April, 1918

The wildest news flies about the country. Every one says that *bhagats* are coming to attack the Mahuadanr Thana and the bunglows. People are flying in every directions. The Zamindar with his family is off to the Barway, thither are fleeing towards the East. The *bhagats* of Chechari have gone to join those of the Sirguja at least of certain number as delegates. In the afternoon, a man came running to the bunglow saying that the bhagats are coming. I do not believe him and in fact it turn out that what they had seen mere people running away from their villages. They all went to the nearest river or jungle land passed the night there. As far as me barricades ourselves in the bunglow with corrugated iron sheets on the west have all over guns ready-loaded and 4 men watch by turns on the terrace. The boys of the school have gathered a heap of stones in the largest room and received orders to throw them with all their force at the assailants if they dare to come. . . (Mss Torn)

26th April, 1918

We are told they are going to come to-night, 26th April 1918. Some Mohemmedans of Mahuadanr came to see me, fear is written on their countenance. I ask them if they also went to pass the night at the river. Yes, saheb what could we do, there was no one keeping them at house so we had to go as well. I lent them an old sword and told them not to be afraid. To the people of Burkole I counsel to gather stones in every house and be ready to throw them at the bhagats, hide behind walls and doors and if they come hit them wherever you'are. If they are killed so much the better, they deserve it. Do not be afraid and they will not be able to be appreciated? Encouraged they go home prepared to fight. . . . Boys bring stone and make pillets.

27th April, 1918

At night we act as the preceding. Less excitement, the bhagats seems to have heard that we are preparing a warrior reception for them. Up to now every thing has run away before them. We hear that they will come on Sunday or Monday so we keep no watch on the terrace.

28th April, 1918

More insistent rumours that they are going to come today. The boys go for a short walk as they cause the greatest excitement at Mahundanr from a distance they are mistaken for *bhagats* and there is nearly a panic. Luckily a Chowkidar having run a short distance recognises the boys and all becomes quiet for the moment. Watch and barricades resumed.

29th April, 1918

No market today. There are neither buyers nor sellers in the evening. The Superintendent of Police, and Deputy Commissioner arrive with some 30 sepoys.

Farewell to the barricades, no chance of getting the V. C. (Victoria Cross)

From 21st April to 4th May 1918 as many as 51 persons including Sirguja State servants were killed by the rebels in the village of Datram, Dumarkholi, Jaljali, Rajdog, Amtahi, Saraidih, Sarjum, Gophatu, Tatajharia, Garis, Jamtoli, Kanchanatoli, Jamira, Kerapat, Dharhia, which were also looted. The rebels contemplated to advance on Ambikapore, but the rising was knocked at the head in the beginning. When the news reached the Maharaja of Sirguja, he hurriedly collected a force of one hundred armed men with Martini-Henri muskets and license holders with sporting rifles and country guns under Sadar Tahsildar Munshi Niranjan Lal. They started on 28th April, 1918. The Commissioner of Chota Nagpur Division and the Political Agent Chattisgarh Feudatory States were only informed of the disturbances by express wires. Deputy Commissioners of Palamau and Ranchi and the Feudatory Chief of Jashpur were informed of the rising and requested by wire to cooperate with the State force to suppress the movement. Men were deputed to all such places from where the Kishan and Oraon would join the rebels of Jamirpat so that the spread of the movement could be checked. Tahsildar Niranjan Lal reached Kushumi on the 1st May, 1918 with his men and he found on his way to Kushmi that all the inhabitants of almost all the villages had either gone away to join the rebels or had gone to jungles to hide. There was unprecedented panic and terror.

On 2nd May, 1918 some three thousand rebels were sighted advancing on the plains of Kushmi from the east. After some time another party of about same number advanced from the West from behind a hill. Niranjan Lal lost no time in ordering his forces to break up into two and engage them on both sides. The rebels in the east made a fire or two to which Raj men replied hitting one of the rebels at a distance of one fourth of a mile. The shot had an excellent effect and topped the march of rebels from the eastern side. The rebels on the n side began to advance with tremendous wild cries and dancing displaying their war play with their arms. Volleys of arrows e Raj forces, but with no effect as they were at some distance. When the rebels came in good range, Raj forces opened fire hitting many. They rebels realised that the bullets did not turn into water and they started dispersing, leaving a few dead in the field and carrying away a few wounded with them. They were crying "Victory to German". The battle of Kushmi was, however, not a decisive one and it was ascertained that the rebels were ready on Jamirpat with defensive measures.

In the darkness of midnight B. Folley, Commissioner of Chota Nagpur Division, Kilby, Deputy Commissioner of Palamau, Tonnerre, Superintendent of Police (Palamau), Brett, Personal Assistant Inspector General of Police Bihar and Orissa, Scott, Superintendent of Police (Bilaspur) with 74 men marched for the scene of rebellion and by the day break reached Orsa where Kilby in consultation with Niranjan Lal, who was at Kushmi, wanted to break the main backbone of the rebels. There at about 10 A. M. at Orsa, Maharaja of Sirguja and the Political Agent Crawford arrived with the elephants on which were mounted various dependents of Maharaja, *Tamasha Wallas*, *Shikaris, Chaprasis* etc.[14] They complained that they were attacked by 300 (80 according prisoners taken) Kishans. In firing three Kishans were killed and several were injured. Under Crawford's orders one village Jamira of the Kishans was burnt. They proceeded to Gopathu to have it out with the rebels and to raise their strongholds to ground once for all. In the way, they passed through Amtahi, a deserted Kishan village. One section under Brett reached Budha or Budi Nadi where a Gurkha grappled three Kishans and all the four fell in eight feet deep water. As neither the Gurkha nor Kishan would swim, two Kishans were drowned and the Gurkha was pulled out. His eyes were glazed and he was pretty gone, but Brett found that his heart was beating and therefore, applied artificial respiration and restored his breath and handed him over to the doctor who had come up.

However, they reached Gupathu which was completely deserted. Under Crawford's direction, the village was burnt, but stocks of grains were not destroyed. When they were going to burn another tola of Gupathu they could see a Kishan taking a refuge in a piece of jungle. The Gurukhas were advancing in extended order towards the jungle but without any signals. Several Raj sawars pushed on ahead and several of Raj servants got down from their elephants on the fronts of the Gurkhas into the jungle. Raj servants started shooting at the Kishan which made Commissioner Folley very angry.

"It was impertinence on the part of the Raj servants to go in front of the Gurkhas without orders and to fire without orders; the whole thing was disgusting since they were snapping at a man moving about in a jungle as if he was an animal to kill one solitary man seems senseless piece of butchery since it would not have any effect and putting down the rising generally."[15]

Had Mr. Wayfarer not ably handled the Gurkhas one or more of the Raj men would probably have been shot had one of the Gurkhas been hit and the consequences would have been mass scale killing of Raj men. Folley remonstrated strongly with Crawford who was himself ready for shot and he straight away said that if he allowed such thing to happen he would withdraw his men. Crawford was respectful to Folley who was senior to him in rank but he quarrelled with him on the futility of the use of Folley's armed force.

The party returned to Orsa while Crawford proceeded with Maharaja to Kushmi. From Orsa, Bihar and Orissa forces and officers returned to Mahuadanr. There was controversy on the use of force, Crawford wanted the Bihar and Orissa force be kept under his charge so that its proper use was made in quelling the rising. Folley's annoyance with Crawford and Raj men were communicated to the Government of India and Central Provinces. Folley remarked,

"If the enquiry proves that there is serious mis-government, it is for consideration whether the Sirguja State would not be retransferred from Central Provinces to Bihar and Orissa, since it is clear that in the case of rising the Central Provinces government is dependent on Bihar and Orissa for taking the independent steps. Necessary communication in between Sirguja and the Central Provinces are so bad that the Centralsufficient force in the State to deal with the rising immediately and I understand that arising of aboriginals, unless dealt with immediately, generally spread like into fire and attains huge proportions."[16]

State of Bihar and Orissa took great exertions in rushing the adequate force to meet the situation by train and then by cars to Netarhat and Mahuadanr. The Bhagalpur police had to be sent to Palamau and the government incurred an expenditure of Rs. 5,226 and annas 9 which was an object of great correspondence between Sir Benjamin Robertson, Chief Commissioner of Central Provinces and Sir

Edward A. Gait, Lieutenant Governor, Bihar and Orissa. Robertson did not like that Sirguja State be charged for the expenses because the causes of the uprising had trickled from the side of Ranchi and Palamau districts which were the cradle of *Tana Bhagatism*. But Gait argued that it was due to the mismanagement of the State and exploitation by the *Gauntias* and *Ahirs* that the tribals were goaded to rebellion. Ultimately, Gait showed the magnanimity of dropping the matter and earned the thanks of Robertson.

On a tour of this area by the author in 1974, he could find that people are still reminiscent of that great risings of the Kisan Tanas and the names of Labur and Bigu have passed down to generations who remember them as their national heroes in their *akhras* were they sing their folk song and dance to perpetuate their glory. Kusmi is now faintly remembered as a place where hundreds of Kishan heads were piled up to terrorise the population in general. Presently the Kishans are undergoing metamorphosis under the influence of Rajmohim Devi of *Bapu Dharam Adi Sabha* or of the Christian missionaries who give them work and grain under Food For Work Programme and, thereby, convert them into their fold.

NOTES

1. Letter No. 4T dated 14th January, 1894 from H. G. Cooke, Officiating Superintendent, Tributary Mahal, Orissa to the Secretary, Government of Bengal. (Available with National Archives of India).
2. *Report of the Feudatory Chief on the Kishan-Oraon Rebellion in Sirguja State 1918* — (Political Police File No. P-5, R-3 of 1919) p. 13. (Available with Bihar State Central Record office, Patna).
3. *Ibid.*
4. Letter dated 25th April, 1919 from Sir Benjamin Robertson, Chief Commissioner Central Provinces, to Sir Edward A Gait, Lieutenant Governor of Bihar and Orissa. (Political Police File No P-5, R-3 of 1919). (Available with Bihar State Central Record Office, Patna)
5. *Ibid.* para 4.
6. Letter dated 2nd June, 1919 from Sir Edward A Gait, Lieutenant Governor, Bihar and Orissa to Sir Benjamin Robertson, Chief Commissioner, Central Provinces. (Political Police File No P-5, R-3 of 1919). (Available with Bihar State Central Record Office, Patna)
7. Report dated 20th June, 1918 from F. L. Crawford, Political Agent, Chattisgarh Feudatory States. para 6.
8. Letter dated 7th March, 1919 from Sir Edward A. Gait, Lieutenant Governor, Bihar and Orissa to Sir Benjamin Robertson, Chief Commissioner, Central Provinces.
9. W. B. Brett's Personal Assistant to Inspector General of Police, Bihar and Orissa,

noting on page 29 of The Police File No. P-5, R-3 of 1919.
(Available with Bihar State Central Record Office, Patna)

10. Letter dated 8th May 1918 from B. Folley, Commissioner, Chota Nagpur Division, to H. Macpherson, Chief Secretary, Government of Bihar and Orissa. (Political Police File No. P-5, R-3 of 1919).
(Available with Bihar State Central Record Office, Patna)
11. Letter No 352 TC dated 14th May, 1918 from B. Folley, Commissioner, Chota Nagpur Division to H. Macpherson, Chief Secretary to the Government of Bihar and Orissa. (Political Police File No. P-5, R-3 of 1919).
(available with Bihar State Central Record Office, Patna).
12. Same as 2 above.
13. Personal diary of Father Dehon, a contemporary Roman Catholic Missionary. The dairy is preserved in Roman Catholic Mission Archive, at Mahudanr. It was made available to the author by Father Crottis and the author has got a photocopy of the diary.
14. Same as 11 above.
15. *Ibid.*
16. *Ibid.*

PART V

Revolution of Conflict, Analysis and Conclusions

16

ANALYSIS AND CONCLUSION

HISTORIOGRAPHY OF a community has to contribute a lot in understanding the community of living people as a whole. It is in serious form not only the recollection of old inhabitants but also such documentary records of the community as exist in libraries and archives so that the researcher is able to make a considered and fruitful comparison of the same community at two different times in its history. Evans-Proitchard's explanation of this phenomenon makes the understanding of the concept clearer:

> "Beyond the annual cycle, time reckoning (history) is a conceptualisation of the social structure, and the points of reference are a projection into the past of actual relations between groups of persons. It is less a means of coordinating events than of coordinating relationship, and is, therefore, mainly a looking backwards, since relationship must be explained in terms of the past."[1]

Redfield too used History in his understanding of the little community and he called his historiography as 'little history', 'a history of accomplishment'.[2] His is the story of how these villagers, leaders, and followers made up their minds to do something and then did it. The unity of the history lies in the central fact of the conspicuous collective effort of these people to make their community the progressive chief community of their region and, therefore, his history is the 'history of development'.[3]

In this very light, the little history of some of the communities, living in Bihar and its adjoining border States, have been attempted in foregoing chapters which is certainly not the history of a nation or an empire, but it is the study of the sequence of events by which they tried to attain their end. These sequences of events become beads on the historical thread. The settling of the community, the establishment of some sort of authority; the schools and the church; the struggle to restore their authority in the communal lands which was usurped by the outsiders, coming of the fresh outsiders, petty traders, service class people; the European administrators, tax collectors and missionaries; the opening of roads; the recognition of some sort of their autonomous political institutions; passing of certain welfare acts and taking of several regulatory executive actions to safeguard the interests of indigenuous communities etc. are some of the signal events among which a student of social history such as this author would like to find out 'aesthetic unity of the tale', the suspense and resolution of the problem set themselves and the human interest of the little story. The author like Postan using the historical method in social sciences would like to make microcosmic (capable of reflecting world larger than themselves) of the 'microscopic problems' of historical research.[4]

It is in this reflected flicker of truth, the revelations of the general in the particular, that the contribution of the historical method to social sciences will be found. The struggle of the tribal communities such as Santals, Korwas, Gond, Khond, Mundas, Hos, etc. with the problems of injustices heaped on them by the neo-*zamindars, Katkindars, Sezawals* and distant 'European' officials through their new technology, trade, education, fresh ideas and thereby the break down of the old traditional way of life is a microsopic account of what may be seen as microcosm, a great world represented in a small one. As a matter of fact this way of looking at these little histories would call for a look at history as a whole. It is the entire tale of these communities that stands for the much larger tale of modern man that pulls the big problems down to village size. However, the nature of these events of social unrest are discussed typology-wise which will bring forth our conclusion of the study of these tribal unrest.

Nature-Man-Spirit Symbosis

A student of human ecology might find relevant to his general understanding of ecological processes through which various communities in the hilly terrain of Chota Nagpur and Santal Parganas and in their near abouts passed through. Evens-Pritchard's 'Nuer' and Redfield's "The Little Community" followed by his student Vidyarthi who tested Nature-Man-Spirit concept in his 'Maler' and others have discussed ecological control on the eco-system and subsistence system of people. The concept of ecological system takes into account much of the whole community when that community is one, that is, closely dependent upon the land resources and the seasons. Primitive communities exist in such dependence; and in primitive communities we find it possible to describe concurrent regularities of man and nature in such a way as to include much of the life of the people and to describe the unique character of that people.[5]

To a naturalist, the ecological system is a system of organism in a natural environment, not a mental environment, but if this system is stretched to men as done by Evans-Pritchard, Redfield and Vidyarthi and others then mental environment attains prominence. The environment of men is not only artificial but also mental too. Redfield has, very rightly, pointed out:

> "In towns and cities, men build their environments into their very houses and streets so that the land and the weather are pushed outside of system. And in every community, primitive or civilised, what most importantly surrounds and influences the people are the traditions, sentiments, norms and aspirations that make up the common mental life. The world in which plants and rabbits live is made up of more or less adaptive responses to the natural features immediately around the rabbits and the plants. The world of men is made up in first place of ideas and ideals. If one studies the rise of urban communities out of more primitive communities it is the change in the mental life, in norms and in aspirations, in personal character too, that becomes the most significant aspect of the transformation."[6]

The ecology affects the social groupings and there is intimate connection between the ecological system and the value and character of the people. Take for example the situation of Bihar and adjoining States, we find the Wild Korwas, Kodkus, Kisans, etc. heavily relying upon their rocky hilly fastednesses as their impregnable fortress against the British forces and the Surguja Raj retainers. The difficult rocks and dense forests were their havens which emboldened them and other Tribal groups to carry on their depredation even in the presence of the police force on the *Pat* area. Turbulence of the Wild Korwas as seen during 1878-81, very rightly gives them the epithet of '*Bouldermen*' whose apprehension by British forces was simply wild goose chase because the Korwas living in such ecology could climb these high boulders like monkey and the Government had to accept defeat temporarily.[7]

Similarly, when the Kishans (Nagesia) rebelled in 1918 in the same *Pat* area, they gave a difficult time to the British and the Raj forces sheerly on the strength of the geographical situation and the local eco-systems. The same could be true with the Gonds of Bonai State (now in Orissa) when they rebelled against their Raja and the unjust enhancement of their fixed rent by the Commissioner Hewitt in 1888. The same ecology and difficult terrain helped the Gonds and made them turbulent enough to have it sorted out with the authorities. The Khonds also rose in revolt against their Rajas in Nayagadh and their turbulence was attributed to their natural surroundings which afforded great protection to them. The Bhuiyans of Keonjhar remained in a state of insurgency from 1867 to 1893 in the hills and forest of Keonjhar (now in Orissa) against their Raja much due to their natural strongholds in hills and forest and such factors which their ecology afforded. Coming to the present time, the Sibo Soren Sarkar movement, known also as Shivaji Samaj Movement and Jharkhand Mukti Morcha during 1970-73 in the hills and forest of Giridih, Hazaribagh and Dhanbad could show its militancy only because the eco-system worked well, the area was inaccessible and because of these the fury of revolt raged for years together. Similarly, Tana Bhagats in the interior inaccessible area remained recalcitrant so far as the payment of state revenue was concerned. Also in the interior areas of outlying districts in the Ruam Jungle of Singhbhum, the tribal groups such as the Lodhas, Santals etc. had the confidence enough to wage war against establishment shoulder to shoulder with the Naxalites of Bengal. Thus, these comparatively less advanced tribes reacted to outside intrusion or local injustice because they had the tradition of leading an isolated antonomous life in commune system duly buttressed by natural fortifications. It would, therefore, be deducted that these rebellions of minor tribals were apt to be local affairs, an isolated event in a particular area marked by the geographical feature of inaccessibility away from the seat of administration.

The resilience of these minor tribes was due to their being a people who had to live under conditions of continual and imminent wants with precarious food supply so much so that they had to depend on their hunting and food gathering activities and abilities for their subsistence which some of them are pursuing even today. A harmony between their natural environment and the traits of character could very well be found. Evans-Pritchard has rightly said that the occasional scarcity of food and the narrow margin of sufficiency at all times are the causes of much of interdependence among the members of the smaller local groups and that in turn these factors result in an ideal practice of sharing food with one another. This is very evident with wild Korwas, Bhuiyan, Khonds etc. who showed wonderful unity at the time of their rebellion. Thus we have the study of the insurgency of these minor tribes in the context of nature-man-spirit and it is for the ethnologists of future to search detail of these elements in these primitive tribal groups who rose in rebellion against the authorities. We have also found that the rebellions of wild Korwas, Gonds, Bhuiyas, Khond etc. are apt to be local affairs. They are apt to be an isolated event in a particular area marked by geographical feature of inaccessibility away from the seat of administration. We have found that to quell these risings in outlying border areas in the Gujarat Mahals of Orissa and Central Provinces (now Madhya Pradesh) the Chota Nagpur authorities had to rush with armed forces, men and materials. Apart from this generalisation, it can also be added that the risings of these wild Korwas, Kisans, Gonds, Bhuinyas etc. may be due to their ecological settings and the upheavals were more turbulent and marked by excesses on the both sides than what we found in the rebellions of other tribal communities living in comparative accessible areas.

It could also be said that the aftermath of these turbulent risings of these minor tribal groups was marked by setting up of police thanas, quartering of armed police pickets, but very few administrative ameliorative actions whose whole evidence in other open area were found in abundance to meet the situation. Perhaps the British thought to find out military answer to quell the militancy of these people which is evidenced in their killing, pillaging and burning of their hideout villages etc. It is not the armed rebellion or resistance which is important. Rather nature, man and spirit is noteworthy which together make up the resistance of these turbulent little groups in inaccessible areas.

Acceptance and Avoidance

The rebellions during the time that British Crown assumed the responsibility of governing the area directly were certainly typologically different from those which took place during the rule of East India Company in this part of the country. While the early British penetration in the area met with violent retaliation and fighting e.g. the

Paharia Resistance, 1772-80, the Tamar Insurrection, 1795-1800, the Chero Rising, 1802, the Great Kol Rising, 1832, the Bhumij Revolt, 1833, and the Santal Hul, 1855. The rebellions during the period of British Crowns early administration was that of a movement of "prayer, protest and petition" e.g. the Santal Discontent of 1860 and 1871, the Kherwar Movements of Bhagirath 1871 and Dubia Gossain 1880, the Sardar Movement of Mundas and Oraons 1858-1895 and the Birsa Movement 1895-1900. If there were some violence in Birsa Rebellion, it was negligible in comparison to the rebellions of earlier regime of the East India Company. Of course, the minor tribes living in hilly fastnesses reacted more violently than the settled tribes. Therefore, taking up the responsibility of running the administration of these areas by the British Crown directly involved challenge and response which could be evident from the study made in the Chapters 6 and 7 on discontent in Santal Parganas and in Chapters 8-10 in Chota Nagpur.

Early encounter of the British with the tribals was met with stiff resistance, a phenomenon not unique for Bihar only as it has been the same in other parts of India also. Confrontation and hostility marked the relations of the British with the tribals in most parts of the country during the early stage of extension of the colonial rule. After the fateful year of 1857, there was a general anxiety shown by the British Government in and outside British Parliament to give a responsible Government to the people and mitigate their sufferings by a thorough system of paternal non-regulation system of administration.

Nonetheless, every tribal group resented loss of liberty in their own way as a reflex action. Even if they were suppressed and brought under the arms of administration they would have intermittently resented the slightest fault in the working of that machinery which sought to provide protection to them. Therefore, the whole nineteenth century in tribal Bihar is a saga of furtherance of British administration as well as wresting of various concessions and safeguards that go to make up the personality of the present day tribals here, alienated, withdrawn, somewhat hostile against the people with whom they had the tradition of living more or less peacefully for centuries. Government administrative machinery, land laws, western education and western Christian missionaries and such other factors acted as catalytic agents, as made out in Chapters 1-5.

It is possible that during the course of the tribal struggle a qualitative transformation had taken place or was taking place in many cases. A distinct change could be noticeable in the behaviour pattern of rebellions of major tribal groups. This change could be studied at two levels. First, one can perceive in the ferment caused by the Santals, the Oraons, and the Mundas the centering around their rights in land and forest in more organised manner, sometimes giving vent to their ideas, ideals and goals through the preaching of revivalistic creeds like Kherwarism of Bhagirath, Tribhuvan, Dubia and Bhagatism of Birsa and Jatra Tana Bhagat. The Kherwarist Sapha Hors among the Santals, Bhagats among the Oraons, Mundas and Hos were the people who rose in sporadic isolated revolts inspired by the primieval dream of freedom, Abua Raj and Suraj (Swaraj) sought to attain by restructuring totally their primitive system which was crumbling under the heavy weight of colonial system. These groups underwent self-discipline of high order and sustained their movement through well-knit organisation, may be the stimuli imbibed from outside.

It is these group of people who very enthusiastically responded to the call of Mahatma Gandhi on his tour of this part of the country with his aides after 1920. Their leaders called Bhagats steeped deep in *Bhakti* tradition, instinctively, understood and responded to the Gandhian message and programmes and threw themselves heart and soul, as shown in chapters 8-10 for the attainment of higher goal, i.e. emancipation of the whole motherland from British foreign domination. These Bhagats and Sapha Hors became the standard bearers of national struggle and they fully integrated themselves in national milieu. Of course, to them freedom from British Raj always meant freedom from oppression of bureaucracy aided by the landlords, money-lenders etc. and Ram Raj as restoration of tribal world of primitive freedom of the golden age of the race, of their ownership of land and forest, of their freedom to move without paying any tax, fare etc. To the traditional Bhagat, the idioms of purity, temperance and teetotalism were added *Swaraj*, *Gandhi Raj*, non-payment of Taxes, *ahimsa*, *Charkha* etc. Naturally the tribals seized upon these idioms to express their agrarian hunger. They stood as a solid phalanx of the followers of Congress and Gandhi in most unfavourable circumstance, pitted against the missionaries, the establishment and the distillers. Large number of them courted imprisonment, trekked distances mostly on foot to attend the sessions of the Congress held in different parts of the country, propagated the message of the spinning wheel and the national flag, all the while hoping that when *Swaraj* would come, they would get back all the land they had lost to the aliens, they would not pay rent and they would get legitimate place in the body politic of the country.

Sapha Hors under Santal leaders of Santal Parganas and Bangam Manjhi of Gumia (Hazaribagh) also were attracted towards Congress movement for national emancipation. Hos under Duka Ho also called Hori Baba also led a movement in 1930 against village spirits and witchcrafts and styled themselves as the disciples of Gandhi and used to recite *Angrez Bahadur Noy* (No More British) *Gandhi Mahto Ki Jai* (Victory to Gandhi Mahto) and thus promoted Gandhi as tribal functionary. Similarly, the Bhumij also underwent self-purification, teetotalism and declared Mahatma Gandhi as the new Raja of Bhumij and sought to raise themselves to the high status of Rajput. Thus these tribal movements of Bihar emerged as precursor of the champion of tribal rights not at variance with the nationalist interests and acted as a great integrative force. It is understood that given time and opportunity and orientation these tribal groups can still play an important role in integrating the tribals in the mainstream of the national life, a goal set by the Constitution of India. Those who want to find nationalism and tribalism incompatible with social ideals, are proved as false prophets in the situation as stated above. The tribals can be hostile and they can also be integrative. It is only the situation and approach that counts and matters. Some people who dreamt for autonomous *diku* free State and craved for non-diku social ideals can also fight for integrative national ideals in a particular situation. Thus we can find that honest leadership of Mahatma Gandhi, Thakkar Bapa and other Gandhites in freedom struggle drew the tribal groups such as Tana Bhagats, Sapha Hors, Hori Baba's followers and so called Kshatriya Bhumij etc.

Besides this integrative aspect of behaviour pattern of tribal movements in tribal Bihar, we find at the second level of abstraction the rise of a separatist movement in terms of ethnicity transforming into a regional movement. In his study K. S. Singh has enumerated many causes which were responsible for Chota Nagpur being the ideal centre of the separatist movement, but it is also the fact that these reasons of Chota Nagpur being most advanced of tribal regions in points of literacy, political consciousness and industrial progress having the tribal concentration into a geographically distinct regions and coming of the Christianity in Chota Nagpur in a big way etc. were also the antithesis of the assertion of its being the craddle of separatism. It has been seen in chapters on Evangelical activities as factor of conflict and tension and on Jharkhand Movement that as the

Christianity spread, "it performed many roles. It gave them a history and a myth, it accentuated the notion of private rights in land and forest, it promoted educational and medical care, but the Church, it also, emphasised a sense of separateness from the rest".[8]

The chapter on Jharkhand movement gives a description of how the Christian missionaries engaged themselves in shaping the demand for political emancipation which not necessarily meant political independence from the British control but it always meant freedom from Diku control to be achieved in an ethnic state. Right from the Dacca Student's Union movement days to the blossoming forth of the political consciousness of the neo-literate tribal (mostly Christian) into a mighty Adivasi Mahasabha and later on into Jharkhand Party under Jaipal Singh, the *Marang Gomke*, the inspiring hands of the Christian missionaries could be seen so much so that to a patient students the inter-denominational conflict to control one faction of political party of the tribals and other could well be perceived. No doubt the slogans for separatism were catchy and were popular in some urban centres like Ranchi, Jamshedpur, Chaibasa, Hazaribagh and Dumka but forgoing of a pan-tribal sentiment remained always weak. Though Christians dominated the party and provided basic leadership, general masses of tribals, by and large, provided unmistakable tribal core to the separatist movement because in 1952 and 1957 general election 7,50,000 votes were bagged by the Jharkhand party whose leaders remained Opposition leader in the Bihar Legislature for years. The Jharkhand party has emerged as the major party in Chota Nagpur Santal Parganas region, but this hegemony of Jharkhand had contradictions inherent in it because soon non-Christian tribals rallied round Kartik Oraon, a British trained Railway Engineer who represented their urge of self-determination (but mostly in non-Christian Oraon area). Again the Jharkhand party merger with Congress in 1963 further accentuated the chance of a national party like the Indian National Congress to engulf the wavering separatist Jharkhandis of yesterday and thereby paved the way for other national political parties to spread their ideas in the bastion of Jharkhand, a feat which was practically impossible without the slaughtering of the election symbol Cock. Therefore, the electoral politics eroded the last vestiges of ethnicity. The demand of separate state in terms of an Eldrado, free from exploitation in tribal area remained a catching slogan for all the parties whether Congress, Janta, Swatantra S. S. P., Jan Sangh and C. P. I. Marxist. The more these different parties talked about separation the greater was the chance of their showing the mockery of these feigned slogans.

Nonetheless, the mockery of working of Constitutional safeguards, blatant exploitation by powerful sections of community, both tribal and non-tribals, ineptness of the administration, slothful leadership, communication lag etc. are some of the factors operating in the tribal areas of Bihar which still keep the embers of separatism alive and make the political leaders wooing the electorate on a separatist manifesto. Every political party got chance to be represented in the Bihar Cabinet but they remained ineffective either in stamping out the exploitation or removing the poverty, illiteracy and diseases. Once out of the cabinet they go in political wilderness and once again start talking in terms of separatism because they always felt that tribal electorate can understand this shiboleth better. But elections in 1977 for the Parliament as well as the State Legislature have repeatedly shown the ineffectiveness of the shiboleth of separate Jharkhand throwing confirmed separatist like Laloo Oraon (ex-Chairman of Birsa Seva Dal) as champion of non-separatist stand and Kartik Oraon former Member of Parliament and anti-separatist leader now as the top leader of separatist movement. Bharatiya Jan Sangh constituents of Janata Party joined by Congress legislators boycotted meeting when Karpoori Thakur, the Chief Minister refused to listen to them on separate Jharkhand issue or give any assurance on that point on 16th January, 1978. Therefore, except their being headline news in some newspapers people by and large understood their gimmicks well. A summary of our observations in this area is as follows:

1. How the integrative leadership composed of national leaders such as Gandhiji, Thakkar Bapa, Rajendra Prasad and other Gandhians could win the hearts of very virulent groups of people such as Tana (Oraons), Birsa Bhagats (Munda), Sapha Hos (Santal), Hari Baba (Hos), Kshatriya Samaj (Bhumij) and welded them into the integrative national movement of liberation of the mother country for which they took part actively with a lurking hope that after the struggle is over they would get back *Abua Raj* (their Kingdom) and *Disum* (their country) back to their pristine glory.
2. We have found that some groups of tribals responded heartily to the call of the leaders of Adivasi Unnati Samaj, Adivasi Mahasabha and Jharkhand party such as Ignes Beck, Bandi Ram Oraon and Jaipal Singh to coalesce together an ethnic front to wrest the political powers for creation of Diku free separate state

of Jharkhand where there would be hegemony of the tribals of different ethnic origins. May be these leaders found the parochial leaderships from among the Christian, business magnates and Muslim League as their allies to put pressure on the them provincial government run by the Congress Party for wresting a separate state, but once the Congress Ministry resigned in 1939, the leaders of this separatist movement turned into leaders of National War Front as if resignation of the Congress Ministry was the only sought goal of these separatists.

3. When the country got freedom the separatists raised their heads once again and curiously enough the Jharkhand Party under the dynamic role of Jaipal Singh remained the regional party of great importance till he got his separatist Jharkhand party merged in the Indian National Congress in 1963 and thereby separatism (Jharkhand) merged in integration (Congress).
4. The separatist movement anyhow was kept alive to suit the ends of the interested groups so much as that the separatist stance has caught hold of many of the national parties like Bhartiya Jansangh, C.P.I. (Marxist) and Congress (Indira Gandhi) who want to focus their own party's image in the mirror of separatism because they seldom feel that integrative role can presently pay any dividend.
5. Apathy by the *Dikus*, neglect by the distant administration, breach of faith by the provincial leaders, incapacity of the indigenous leadership all force the pace of separatism as the main plank of the political movement which accidently is more understood by the corps of social scientists, newsmen, and others than tribal communities today with their integrative aspiration and movement. Language of bows and arrows, parading on the main streets of the urban centres with clenched fists, displaying placards with a parochial slogans are taken note more than the millions of tribals taking part in national festivals and occasions, taking part in the fair and processions of greater community etc. in an integrative manner.
6. It is for the intelligent section of the community to mould the tribals either in integrative mould or allow the tribals to have a personality alienated, dissatisfied, grumbling, emitting venom of separatism duly tutored by such sections of the population which are ever busy fomenting dissatisfaction.

Categorisation by Type

The different rebellions and movements as depicted in the foregoing chapters can be categorised in terms of Roy Burman; suggested sevenfold typology:

1. Revolt against territorial encroachment.
2. Revolt against economic exploitation
3. Revolt against cultural imposition and social domination.
4. Revolt against loss of resources.
5. Movement for entry into existing structure of power.
6. Movement for generation of alternative structure of power.
7. Movement for entry into existing structure of prestige without visualising any alternative structure of power.

This categorisation may not be final because unrest surfaces in problem manifestation but it has been used only to have some convenience in understanding the typology of some of these movements. While serial nos. two and four are practically the same and serial nos. six and seven are also more or less identical, but we have not omitted any of these traits in comprehension of the overall phenomenon of unrest.

Thus from the above we can clearly find that there was no revolt against territorial encroachment during the year (1858-1990) under review. Far-fetchedly, we can place Birsa *Ulgulan* in this category also because one of the orders of Birsa was to drive away the British and their accomplices like Christian missionaries and Zamindars and in this Birsa preceeded Mahatma Gandhi by 43 years in asking the British to '*Quit Abua Disum*'. The main reason of no rebellion against territorial encroachment may be that on assumption of administration by the British Crown in 1858 and extension of all areas of Government, missionaries, schools, market economy, bureaucracy, courts, health dispensaries, roads, railways etc. the British rule got entrenched in this country and it was very difficult for people to think of dispensing with the British rule rather "prayer, protest and petition" remained the main method of protest or unrest. Birsa Bhagats and Tana Bhagats were the people who could ask the British to go away from the country.

Most of the unrest centred around the system of economic exploitation which became unbearable to the tribal people. In this category we find Rai Movement, Sardari Larai, Birsa Ulgulan, Tana

Bhagat, Wild Korwa Rebellion, Khond Rebellion, Gond Rebellion, Bamanghatti Upsurge, Santal unrest of 1861 and 1871 etc. This is evident that enquitious tenancy system, tyrannical landlords coupled with equally tyrannical lower bureaucracy always goaded the tribals to seek redress through protest either by show of battle-axe or bows and arrows or by representing to the *Bara* or *chota Lat Sahab* at Howra (Calcutta) or Queen Victoria for "decree" or by resorting to revivalistic *creed* under a *Babaji* or *Gossain.*

No Movement under the study was found against cultural imposition and social domination of the Greater community like the Hindus but some of them such as Birsa Ulgulan, Kherwar Movement of Bhagirath, Dubia Goassain Movement, Sapha Hor Movement, Sardari Larai had something to do with their avowed opposition to the Christian missionaries who wanted to convert them. However, Christian-based leadership of Jharkhand movement showed some stance against the Hindu dominance, but Theble Oraon and in recent time Kartik Oraon and other Jansanghi Tribal leaders Kalyan Ashram, Vanvasi Kendra people were against the Christian dominance in their body politic of Chota Nagpur and they succeeded in wresting most of the reserved constituency representation from the Christian leaders who were the habitual representatives. However, Kartik Oraon also demanded that dancing in Murma Mela should be stopped as that was a system of past when Hindus dominated Oraon scene. Shibu Saren also forbade such dancing by tribal maidens in fairs.

There was no revolt against loss of resources in literal sense of the term. However, passionate appeal to past where there was no want, poverty and there was plenty of every thing and when the tribal groups passed their lives in pristine glory has always been the motive force behind some of the movements like Santal's Sapha Hor yearing for *Chai Champa days*, Tana Oraons of their old *Kurukh Raj* and Birsa Munda's *Abua Disum* and far fetchedly Jharkhandis is clamour for *Jajkhand Raj.*

Most of the movements wanted to generate alternative structure of political power, establishment of Diku free Raj in which they would perpetuate their hegemoney on ethnic lines, Kisan Tana Rising stood for the Raj of Bigu, Birsa's Abua Disum was to be free of mission, Zamindars and British, Jharkhand Mukti Morcha etc. for expulsion of outsiders are some of such instance.

There are some movement for entry into the existing power structure. In this category we find Tana Bhagats trying successfully to integrate themselves with nationalists. The tribals professing loyalty to nationalist cause and party like Kartik Oraon and others were there. So was the Bhumij Kshatriya Movement. Even Jharkhand's merger was brought about to share power with the Congress.

Tana Bhagat's Oraon, Hori Baba Hos, Bhumiji Kshatriya movement, Sapha Hor's Bangam Manghi etc. are the movements for entry into existing structure (mostly Congress) of prestige without visualising any alternative structure of power because by and large their association with Gandhi and the Congress programme was without any reservation. The leaders of the Sardars movement also wanted to be peasant proprietors paying rent to the Government directly and not through Zamindars.

Besides these above seven categories pointed out by Roy Burman another category could be added, that is, revolt against political encroachment or imposition. In this category comes the rebellion of Bamanghatti under Bhagwan Das who had lost his patrimony which was given to Raja of Mayurbhanj.

By using Roy Burman Typological classification, the various rebellions and conflicts get classified as follows:

1. **Revolt Against Territorial Encroachment**

(i) Birsa Rebellion (1895-1900)
(ii) Tana Bhagat (1914-1990)

2. **Revolt Against Economic Exploitation of Unbearable Tyranny**

1. Tana Bhagat (1914)
2. Kisan Tana Rising(1918)
3. Wild Korba Rebellion
4. Birsa Ulgulan (1895-1900)
5. Khond Rèbellion of 1893 in Nayagarh
6. Gond Rebellion of 1888
7. Bamanghatti Upsurge
8. Santal discontent (1860-61)
9. Santal Unrest (1871)

3. **Revolt Against Cultural Imposition and Social Domination**

1. Tana Bhagat

2. Jharkhand Movement
3. Sapha Hor Movement
4. Kherwar Movement
5. Birsa Movement
6. Rae Movement
7. Kisan Sabha of Theble Oraon
8. Karticism
9. Sardari Larai

4. Revolt Against Loss of Resources

Nil

5. Movement for Generation of Alternative Structure of Political Power

1. Kisan Tana Movement
2. Jharkhand Movement for Separate State
3. Birsa Sewa Dal Movement
4. Shivaji Samaj Movement or The Movement of Jharkhand Mukti Morcha
5. Kherwar Movement
6. Rae Movement

6. Movement for Entry into Existing Structure of Power

1. Tana Bhagatism
2. Independence Movement among Tribes
3. Karticism
4. Bhumij Movement
5. Khewar Movement

7. Movement for Entry into Existing Structure of Prestige without Visualising any Alternative Structure of Power

1. Tana Bhagat
2. Hori Baba
3. Kshatriya Bhumij Sudhar
4. Sapha Hor Movement
5. Bangaon Manjhi Movement

6. Sardar Movement

8. **Revolt Against Political Encroachment or Imposition**

1. Bamanghatti Movement of Bhagwan Das
2. Bhuiyan Rebellion of Keonjhar (1867-1893).

Typology of Leadership

Without going into the different criteria of classification[9] of leadership we can attempt here the typological difference in the leadership of the various movements and unrest detailed above. It is noticeable:

1. that on the level of initial leadership traditional leaders such as Manki-Munda-Parganait-Suba etc. supplied the initial leadership to any movement;
2. that such leadership and movement remained confined to their own realms and made it a localised affair;
3. that if region of influence is sought to be extended it required the help of other vehicles of communication which may not be invariably based on indigenous model and traditional leadership;
4. that in event of getting the traditional leadership diffused there are cases in which individual self-aggrandisement becomes evident; and
5. that in event of atmosphere surcharged with emotion warranting bigger action, the people threw up leaders who may not belong to the traditional office-bearer class of the community, who may not even be a tribal leader at all and still could start a revivalistic and revitalisation movement among the community.
6. that at the level of the decision-making at the highest level concerning the fate of the statehood for the tribal areas in nineties, it is neither the traditional tribal leaders nor their known ally; but some of the bureaucrats, social scientists and resourceful influential *Dikus* of yesterday became the potential leader of today.

While the earlier rebellions during the John Company's days were led by the traditional leaders it was not true in the early days of the British Crown's administration e.g. Chuari Larai of 1795-1800; the leaders were Manki and Mundas led by their Thakur (Raja) Bhola Nath

Sahi. They rose against the introduction of a new system of revenue collection under *Sezawal* and other tyrannies of the money-lenders and others. The area of revolt remained confined to *Chuar desh* (Tamar, Pachet, Silli, Jhalda and Reghunathpur etc.). The leaders of the Kol Rising of 1831-32 were Singhrai and Brinda Manki, Sooie Munda etc. when they sought to spread the rebellion to other territory, they got instant support from Rautias, Larka Kols and Oraon's Sardars. Naturally, the area of rebellion grew from Sonepur Pargana to Seraikella, Tamar, country of Larka Kols and Oraons. The same is evident from the Mutiny in Chota Nagpur. The Mutiny was led by Thakur Biswanath Sahi of Barkagadh Estate supported by his able Diwan Ganpat Rai. Of course, local traditional leadership remained at the back of it so much so that it retained its popular character. But when the leadership failed to get the active support of leadership of different ethnic groups, the movement flopped and further it was crushed. Similarly in the Bhogta rebellion 1858 also Lilamber Sahi and Pitambar Sahi could not carry on for long for want of support of other areas. Santal Hul only succeeded with fierceness because the initial leadership was supplied by four brothers Sidhu, Kanhu, Chand and Bhairab dully supported by Santals, Manjhis, Parganaits, Subas etc.

Coming to the time of the British Crown administration, character and the complexion of the leadership changed altogether. The leaders of this period were not that impulsive. Rather, they were emulative, reformative, nativistic, charismatic and revivalistic. This change in the character of leadership of the movement might have something to do with the change of the character of the rebellion and unrest. From militaristic to persuasive, from direct action of pillaging, killing, looting etc. to the deliberative stance of 'prayer, protest and petition', was the change. After, successive military actions, wisdom dawned upon the people that adventurous and violent action provided no solution to their problems.

In 1861, the Sathals under their *Parganaits* rose against the European landlord Barnes and the administration of Naya Dumka under Soonder Manjhi. The *Parganaits*, the traditional leaders of Santals, convinced the high administration through persuasion and there was no killing. This type of leadership was repeated against another European Zamindar Graham in 1871 who sought to introduce indigo cultivation with attended tyranny. But these traditional leaders localised their interest to wrest a few concessions from the Government and never succeeded in getting bigger things done, but the latent discontent found vent in the Kherwari movement led by Bhagirath in 1871-75 who was not a traditional leader but was anointed as king to lead them in a revivalistic creed which forced the government to take ameliorative action on some bigger scale. Again Sapha Hor Movement in 1880-81 resisted under Dubia Gossain the first census operation a Saintly person from Lucknow who gave the Santals a creed and welded the Santal and Kurumbis as one people known as *Sapha Hors*.

The great agrarian struggle of the Chota Nagpur Oraons and Mundas known as Sardari Larai was waged not by the traditional leader but John Munda, Daud and others who were the earliest of the converts. So is the case with Birsa Ulgulan of 1895-1900 which was led by Birsa Munda, Gaya Munda, Donka etc. for the safeguard of Khuntkatti rights and it would not be an exaggeration to say that the C. N. T. Act, the *magnacarta* of the tribals of Chota Nagpur, was passed in 1908 and Survey and Settlement Operation in 1902-1910 was instituted much due to the type of leadership given by those martyrs. When that too failed to satisfy the Oraons of South Ranchi there was Jatru Oraon of Chingri propagating a new Kurukh Dharam, Tanaism, a millenarian movement, bordering on Cargo cult as Tana's leader declared that German Emperor Wilhem Kaiser was coming to them with a cart load of gold through which they would end their misery. Thus these reformative and emulative non-traditional leaders made deliberate, organised and conscious effort to construct a more satisfying culture. This leadership contained both emulative and resistant traits and were charismatic and nativistic.

The aftermath of World War I saw a different type of leadership all together. If Tanas choice was to fully integrate themselves in the national struggle launched by Mahatma Gandhi and his followers, there were other leaders like Ignes Beck, Bandi Ram Oraon and later on Jaipal Singh to carry on resistance movement as well as demanded a Diku free separate state of Jharkhand. The leadership at both levels, integrative as well as separatist, were deliberative, brooding and manouvering type whose main aim was to woo the electorate as well as supporters for better political strength. It is quite a different thing that Tanas, Hori Baba, Sapha Hors and reformed Bhumji remained confined to Congressmen, but the bulk of the people voted in first three general elections for Jharkhand Party and were under the spell of *Morang gomke* Jaipal Singh till Jharkhand party was merged in Congress in 1963. This merger left the electorate high and dry not understanding the shifting stand of different political parties and their local supporters so much so that in 1977 general election, the traditional aspiration of getting a separate state under the banner of Jharkhand got the final blow. But the ghost of Jharkhand remained dogging Janta, Congress legislators who boycotted Audrey House (Raj Bhawan) meeting on 16th January 1978 when Karpoori Thakur, Chief Minister and the Chairman of the Meeting, refused to discuss the demand for separate state. Thus, this traditional leadership failed the tribal masses while their misery multiplied day by day.

Model of Tribal Movements

Two hundred years of history and increasing social tension have been depicted in this study, but this is suffice to highlight the essential points, the entry of cash in farter economy, the loss of lands on which integrity was built, recourse of missionaries and the Christian influence, the attempt to gain redress by legal procedure etc. Only after all these had failed, did the Oraons, Mundas, Santals and Hos etc. attempt to transcend their difficulties by recourse to militant activities. The integrity of these tribal groups had been slowly eroded over several generations. But eventually when the time seemed ripe, they asserted themselves. And they are still doing so. Social scientists have worked on different models of tribal movements in Chota Nagpur, but it is very difficult to accept any of the models discussed below. One can only arrive at some conclusions about the typology of these movement.

Edward Jay[10] discussed the movement among the Mundas, the Santals, the Oraons, and the Bhumij and attempted to structure the various movements outlined above in terms of the current anthropological perspective provided by Coser, Linton, Redfield, Govet, Wallace and others and interpreted them in terms of their roles as mediators between the Great and Little Traditions of India. His model could be used well for one or two movements, but it cannot universally be utilised.

Surjit Singh[11] in his review of *Tribal Solidarity Movements in India* criticised N. K. Bose's Sub-nationalism model (which is generally generated in economically backward communities of an emerging nation) for having over-emphasised the role of the elite self-interest in the recent tribal movement. In contrast to this, Roy Burman's model of differentiation of Infra-nationalism and sub-nationalism has appealed to him. In infra-nationalism tribes are envolved in a progressive movement in a phase of expansion from a primitive stage of tribalism towards nationalism. But sub-nationalism is essentially a product of social disorganisation where already acculturated elites of a tribe get involved in contra-acculterative contraction of relationship. Sinha[12] criticised Martin Oraon's enunciation of Rank Concession Syndrome to the dominant Hindus, but resent their low position and desire to attain high position for under-estimating the communication gap between the elite and the masses. He also criticised Wallace's frame of "revitalisation movement otressed too far on the rise of charismatic messianic leaders and on the reorganisation of the total cultural system". He rather suggested to find out to what extent the solidarity movement is 'genuine' or 'spurious' to use Edward Sapir's terminology.

Nature and degree of involvement of tribal groups in solidarity movement depend on number of factors rightly suggested by Surjit Sinha[13]:

1. Location of tribal group *vis-a-vis* the core peasant martix;
2. Number of tribals *vis-a-vis* non-tribals in a region;
3. Degree of exposure to and socio-economic and cultural inter-relationship with the Hindu peasantry;
4. Level of economy of the tribe;
5. Level of education of the elite and of the tribal masses;
6. Historical experience in the encounter with the advanced peasantry and urban population;
7. Cultural orientation of the elite Hindu, Moslem and European Christian;
8. Pattern of articulation with non-tribal political associations.

These factors, of course, are responsible for co-relating the intensity of tribal movement but we have seen how among movement or unrest of the minor tribes such as Wild Korwas, Gond, Bhuiya, Khond, Kisans the factors of ecological isolation, nature-man-spirit, go to make up the severity of revolt, but at the same time leaving these unrest as local affair, an isolated event in a particular area marked by the geographical feature of inaccessibility away from the seat of administration. Historically speaking, the locational and ecological isolation shaped the personality of these people and has left them still on the rung of primitivism, bereft of new elite, literacy, prosperous economy etc. Thus the major root of the tribal solidarity movements may be traced to their socio-cultural isolation, economic backwardness and feeling of frustration about a lowly status *vis-a-vis* the advanced sections.

Apart from this Stephen Fuch[14] tried to prove every movement among the tribe as messianic and more charismatic leaders as *messiah*. Mahapatra[15] also surveyed social movements among tribes of India and categorised them as (i) reactionary, (ii) conservative, (iii) revisionary, (iv) revolutionary, (v) revivalistic etc. Besides these typologies, he also mentioned about religious or secular, political and non-political, emulation reinforcing or solidarity reinforcing movements. He mentioned the important criterion of leadership as a basis of typology.

These traits discussed above may fit in some of the tribal movements of recent past and current ones; but they can hardly be model for our historical experience, for the movement held before the First World War. Revolts and rebellions are not an isolated episode but accumulation of certain historical processes confined for certain period of time. These rebellions were not against the violent intrusion of different people, but they were clash of culture in peaceful meeting of two different societies. Such clashes could be found in traders peddling the petty trades, business men settling in the interiors with their wares, introduction of landlordism in the wake of Permanent Settlement of land and revenue, missionary activities, *beth begari*, enhancement of rent, ejectment, under-weighing, over-weighing etc. were some of the passive elements to which tribals sometimes reacted violently because they had the tradition of leading a peaceful isolated life in commune system. Therefore, in all these eventful main clashes like Paharia Rebellion, Chuari Larai, Kol Rising, Santal Hul, Birsa Ulgulan one finds that the economic and social degradation mostly was resented by the tribals and their leaders who retaliated to see that encroachment is put to an end, forced *begari* is not given, *rakumat* is not paid and injustices to them are resented. Land to the settled tribals like Oraon, Munda, Santal, Ho, Kharia etc. was inalienable, held in lineages, a sacred trust from the first-comers and founders who had handed it on to their descendents. They found their integrity in being land-owners. They found relative prestige among themselves by comparing the skill and industry with which households and lineages exploited the resources of land. Money entered their economy and money-lenders were perhaps the only means of supplying the cash to the villagers to whom the villagers mortgaged their land to find cash. When the first

European administrators and missionaries arrived in Chota Nagpur, the situation had already reached a breaking point. Though the administrators seem to have appreciated the situation quite accurately, they had only their own legal conventions to work with which forced them to confirm the intruders in possession of tribal land. The tribals were helpless. Without deed, a (Munda said *Sasandiri Ko Horo Hon Ko'a patta* — Burial stones are the title deeds of the Mundas), without papers, not knowing how to write the tribals were helpless. They looked up to the missionaries, but all in vain. Thus with passionate desire to reassert ones' integrity they started millinary movement and they asserted themselves. That much is their ideology, that much is their philosophy of rebellion. It is fruitless to search ideological questions in these tribal movements and unrest. Ideology presupposes an advanced situation which could not be expected in the preliterate tribal groups of Chota Nagpur and Santal Parganas. The whole argument can be summed up as follows:

1. Ecological and sub cultural-isolationism shaped the little histories of the minor tribes such as the wild Korwas, Kisans, Khonds, Gonds, Bhuiyas so much so that their rebellions, though remained largely localised affairs, were marked by excesses from both sides, tribal as well as the British forces and were fiercer than the rebellion or unrest of the major tribal groups.
2. Rebellions of the tribes after assumption of administration by British Crown were typologically different from the rebellions of the tribes during the day of East India company so much so that the rebellions during the Crown administration days took the shape of unrest, discontent and conflict in which not usually the battle-axe or bows and arrows; but prayer, protest and petition remained largely the manifestation. Lanternari proposed similar classification in Prophtic movement.
3. The protesting tribals ultimately not only lent the main vigour for attainment of their tenurial rights, but also provided the atmosphere for the struggle for political emancipation in which the Christian missionaries and tribal new literate elite joined to find their own identity.
4. On the level of leadership it has been found that tribal traditional leadership such as *Munda, Manki, Paraganait, Suba, Manjhie* etc. supplied the initial leadership in any discontentment, but if they choose to extend their discontentment to wider area they had to

give way to non-traditional official functionaries, so much so that a few non-tribal leaders came to the tribals for their socio-political amelioration.

5. In twentieth century, the tribals aligned themselves with the national struggle for freedom launched by Mahatma Gandhi and others. The other groups of neo-literate in the influence of western Christian missionaries, Muslim League and other outside elements remained separatist to the hard core and carried on resistance and movement for a separate state.
6. The tribal ethnic and solidarity movements are class by themselves and are the by - product of historical experiences that the group had and they can hardly be categorised in any general frame.

Resolving The Conflict

It is not the intention to prescribe a panacea for all the ills of Chota Nagpur and Santal Parganas here, but some observation in this regard has been made.

The locational and ecological isolation has created two distinct types of tribal patterns. In one, isolation had led to poor economy, illiteracy and lack of new elite while in the other a section of the tribe received education, embraced Christianity and operated as the new elite. The present day discontentment among the section of people on the ground of not getting a separate state has become all pervasive when the constituents of Janata Party as well as separatist Jharkhandis and defeated Congress leadership have joined hands together and has rendered the prospect of an ethnic Diku free state for tribes dimmer and dimmer. We can discover in this discontentment both a process of progressive enlargement of socio-political and cultural experience beyond the primitive tribal units and also a process of drawing solidarity boundaries around the expanded horizon *vis-a-vis* the Indian core.

Integration of the tribes in the mainstream of the national life is the goal of Indian Constitution by extinguishing all forms of exploitation, the pace of integration among the tribes, shall have to be accelerated without encroaching upon "the cultural autonomy" of the Tribals. There should be wide awareness of the integrative tendencies of the tribes than what we have presently observed. There should be arrangement for greater acquaintance with the emerging core of Indian national culture so that the elite as well as the masses are oriented towards the core pattern rather than seek an escape model in their search for new identity. It is also suggested that proto-nationalist aspiration of the people of this area is understood. It should also be our endeavour to welcome the genuine solidarity movement. The extent to which we are able to properly identify the "genuine" tribal aspiration from spurious and meet them with 'genuine' nationalist, our task of building a new nation by integrating the relatively isolated tribes will be successful.

Although the region of Chota Nagpur-Santal Parganas is a thoroughly unconnected area and is predominantly the home land of the tribals, the over enthusiasm to integrate them in the main stream of national life has made the political aspirations take precedence over economic consideration. The reservation and safeguards are being implemented in some form or the other, but no plans are there for economic betterment. The strategy of planning has been changing and changing the economic opportunities instead of permeating a broad base of the population. Regional approach has been made instead of community approach. Wood has been taken for tree.

Chota Nagpur-Santal Parganas plateau accounts for 46. 3 per cent of the total area of Bihar. This is nearly about the double the size of the state of Kerala and nearly equal to that of the state of West Bengal. Out of the total area 45 per cent is not available for cultivation, about 30 per cent is covered by forests, 7 per cent is barren and uncultivable, 6 per cent is put to non-culturable use and 1.6 per cent is permanent pasture. Out of 55 per cent of land available for cultivation, net sown area is only 32 per cent and balance 23 per cent is classified as culturable waste, current fallows and other fallows which are generally *tanr* (upland) land. Thus there is limited agricultural possibility due to undulating terrain, deficient soil and paucity of irrigational facilities (only about 7.8 per cent of the cultivable area get assured irrigation presently). Half of the working population of the area is cultivator peasant-proprietor and one quarter is agricultural labourer. In one decade the percentage of agricultural workers has risen from 9 per cent in 1961 to 28 per cent in 1971. This shows landlessness is increasing — 5.5 per cent are engaged in mining, 4.7 per cent in manufacturing processes other than household industries. The result is that the sons of soil feel great deprivation and find their way to distant tea gardens in Assam, road building projects in Bhutan, brick kilns in Uttar Pradesh and farm labour in Punjab and Haryana where the worst type of trafficking in human labour exists. At home due to landlessness they have to mortgage their own labour and remain bonded to well off agriculturists for generation.

Even in present time due to industrialisation and urbanisation neo-colonisers have alienated tribal land by hook and crook in spite of protective legislation under the very nose of the administration. Agriculture sector failed to expand production on account of the weak infrastructure and shortage of inputs. Thus, super imposition of new industrial growth (large number of heavy and medium industries were opened in this area) upon a predominantly agricultural economy without effective steps for integrating the agricultural and industrial sectors has not produced beneficial results all around for the present. Rather it has created ferment every where. The oasis of little prosperity here and there cannot possibly exist peacefully in the vast desert of poverty, want, squalor for long. Hence in every land acquisition proceeding, we find regular agitation of one type or other going on through out the area. Installation of big projects are initially resisted, even survey and settlement operations are opposed.

Excessive drinking opportunities have been provided to the tribes so much so that till a few months back large revenue were collected from liquor shops in the area. This worsened their condition and the new government has started phase prohibition, but illicit distillation has continued unabated. Rural indebtedness per capita of rural population is Rs. 296 and infrastructure of institutional finance is very weak. Therefore, village Shylocks had an upper hand in all matters inspite of so many legislations to control their activities.

There is systematic operation of exploitation machinery in the rural area and the common mode is under pricing of agriculture produce of the tribals and over-pricing of articles of daily needs, medicines and other stores to be purchased by the tribals. The exploitation of tribals by petty officials, survey staff, police etc. has reached its nadir. There are practically no medical and health facilities worth the name. Schools are run on paper. Meso projects (I.T.D.P.) are being run just in perfunctory manner and practically are in suspended animation. Abject alround neglect is the rule.

Thus Christian missionaries step up in the shoes of the absent and distant governmental machinery. Of course, conversion is main aim of the missionaries but that too creates ferment. The people complain that their misery is being exploited by the Christian missionaries and agencies of *Sudhikaran* run by Hindu mendicants, Birla Charitable

Trust, Arya Samaj etc. They also say that *Madhya Pradesh Dharam Swantantrya Adhiniyan*, 1968 (Act 27 of 1968), and Orissa Freedom of Religion Act, 1967 (Orissa Act 2 of 1968) protect the people in two bordering adjoining states. But the same kind of legislation is not forth coming to them in Bihar. Therefore reprisal in the aftermath of Father Kerkol expulsion and *Niskalanka* propaganda and lynching of a few Hindu in village *hats* in Sundega occur and they are retaliated by Arya Samaj, Vaovasi Kalyan Kendra, Viswa Hindu Parishad.

The solution to these problems has been attempted by the Ministry of Home Affairs, Planning Commission and others. It is very difficult to prescribe, but it could be suggested that there should be equitable income generation and gainful employment opportunities so that tribal migrant labour do not face cultural and economic hardship. There should be integrated approach in a package deal to solve the problems in the rural area by inducting a separate sympathetic administrative and implementing machinery. In place of usual unit schools, Ashram school in some complex be opened for children. Rural industries should be opened in growth centres and there should be full utilisation of rural electrification programme, dry land farming opportunities, services of several voluntary agencies. There is the need of State Government decentralising its power as the administration of these areas shall have to be run on separate lines as recommended by the Haldipur Study Team of the Planning Commission. To meet the situation, the states should introduce the concept of District Autonomous Council with sufficient powers of making local plans and execution on the lines of Sixth Schedule so that the misapprehension regarding separate state is removed. The opportunities of education both modern as well as traditional be available in appropriate manner to the tribal areas.

There is need of transfer of technology in agriculture as well as other crafts. We have seen that agricultural possibility of the area is practically bleak and it is very difficult to effect transfer of technology among the root and fruit gatherers and shifting cultivators of yesterday. There is therefore, the need of rationalisation of minor forest produce for which a M. F. P. Corporation is the need of hour. Government and Institutional credit facility be so arranged that village Shylocks are ejected from their lucrative trade. There should be campaigns against drinking habits and Tana Bhagat volunteers could be employed for picketing liquor distillation hideouts.

In short everything has to be done to make the area and its people enjoy the blessings of planning and development and then only the situation of conflict of the area can be resolved. For example presently there is a great ferment on account of the Survey and Settlement Operation[16] because Mundari Khuntkattidars of Khunti and Tamar area feel that their rights are too disturbed by the clever Survey officials and they have at place forced them to close the survey camps. Therefore things should be so managed that apart from survey operation and other administrative action confidence of the people is won because inspite of hundreds of years of administrative procedure the area still respond in primitive way, sometimes against their own interest may be because of the colonial approach of the administration.

NOTES

1. E. E. Evans-Pritchard, *The Nuer*. OUP, 1940, p. 108.
2. Robert Redfield, *The Little Community*. Stockholm. 1955, pp. 96-112.
3. *Ibid.*, p. 100.
4. M. M. Postan, *The Historical Method in Social Science*. Cambridge University Press, 1939 p. 36.
5. J. H. Steward, *Basin Plateau Aboriginal Socio-political Groups.* Washington, Smithsonian Institution, 1938.
6. Redfield, pp. 30-31.
7. 1884, Foreign Department, Internal A. Proceedings. para 69. (available with National Archives of India)
8. K. S. Singh, *Tribal Movement in Chota Nagpur in Dissent, Protest and Reform in Indian Civilisation.* Simla, IIAS, 1977 pp. 318-19.
9. L. P. Vidyarthi, ed. *Leadership in India*, Bombay 1967.
10. Edward Jay, Revitalization movement in Tribal India *in Aspects of Religion of India Society*. Meerut, 1961.
11. Surajit Sinha, Tribal Solidarity Movement in India: A Review *in Tribal Situation in India.* Simla, IIAS, 1972, p. 415.
12. *Ibid.*, p. 418.
13. *Ibid.* p. 419.
14. Stephen Fuch, *Rebellious Prophets: A study of Messienic Movements in India* . Calcutta, 1965.
15. L. K. Mahapatra, Social Movement among Tribes of India *in Tribal Situation in India. Simla,* IIAS, 1972.
16. Proceedings of Seminar on Efficiency of Survey and Settlement Operations in Tribal Areas held at Bihar Tribal Welfare Research Institute, Ranchi, 27-29th January 1978.

17

EPILOGUE

ONE CANNOT ignore the operation of different phenomenon which very much warrant a new look at the tensional situation in Chota Nagpur and Santal Parganas or for the matter of fact for the demand for a separate state of Jharkhand. Incorporating important changes which changed the socio-political complexion of the following decades (1971-1990) has become an imperative.

I

Administrative Reorganisation : Breaking the Tribal Territorial Solidarity

We have already seen earlier that administration has been a great source of conflict. Some of the frequent and fleeting changes introduced in the last two decades by the State Government to meet the exigency of time though on *ad hoc* basis, have definitely created great confusion at the level of administration in Tribal Bihar. In the year 1976 Chota Nagpur Division was bifurcated into North and South division. North Chota Nagpur division with Headquarter at Hazaribagh comprised the districts of Dhanbad, Hazaribagh and Giridih. South Chota Nagpur division comprised of the Districts of Singhbhum, Ranchi and Palamau. The old Ranchi district was again trifurcated into Ranchi, Lohardaga and Gumla districts, leading to a great agitation against this reorganisation. The old Ranchi district was occupying the first position in the country to have more than 15 lakhs tribal population as such a centre of a great importance, but now it was brought down from such high pedestal. Again in January 1990, Singhbhum district was also bifurcated in two districts, Singhbhum East with Headquarter at Jamshedpur comprising predominantly industrial and Santal area and Singhbhum West with headquarter at Chaibasa which had to remain contented with Kolhan and dominant Munda and Ho area of Chakardharpur. The eighties also witnessed the creation of Santal Parganas division out of Bhagalpur division and the old Santal Parganas district was sub-divided into the Districts of Godda, Dumka, Sahebganj and Deoghar.

Thus administrative reorganisation was done hastily without referring it to the Bihar State Tribes Advisory Council which should have been done in Part V Schedule State like Bihar. Great many doubts have been raised in the minds of the people that in the garb of administrative reorganisation interested section wanted to break up the solidarity of tribal dominated area by bifurcating and trifurcating the tribal dominant districts.

The demographic pattern of the different zones of Tribal Bihar is well revealed by the table and map overleaf. With a tribal population of 5810867, Bihar has third largest concentration of Tribal population in India as per 1981 census. 91.71 per cent of Bihar Tribals inhabit the districts of Chota Nagpur and Santal Parganas divisions which together practically constitute Tribal Bihar. Both territorially and spatially, the tribals have been vital constituent of Chota Nagpur and Santal Parganas population and as such their rights and privileges in land and forest and tenurial protection are enshrined in the local tenancy acts such as Santal Parganas Tenancy (Supplementary Provisions) Act (1949) and Chota Nagpur Tenancy Act (1908); but in course of time in later seventies and early eighties these tenurial protection lay torn asunder practically without making commensurate amendments in these tenancy acts locally in operation. This actually led to great tensional situation.

Decline in Tribal Population

If we compute the population figures from 1931 to 1981 we can find that it declined during the past fifty years. In the Table 17.1 it will be clear that the Tribal population declined from 54.08 to 44.08 per cent in old Singhbhum from 62.72 to 54.61 per cent in old Ranchi, from 42.90 to 36.80 per cent in Santal Parganas and from 11.45 to 9.04 per cent in old Hazaribagh and from 20.94 to 18.33 per cent in old Palamau.

One of the reasons for this decline is attributed to the large scale immigration of non-tribals from other parts of the country to some growth centres, mining areas, heavy industries etc. which were opened in the wake of implementation of Five-Year Plans. The causes of immigration are historical socio-cultural and developmental. 'Pull' and

'Push' factors attracted the people from outside to migrate into the region, particularly when the migration barriers, such as inaccessibility, danger of various diseases and wild animals, etc. have been removed with the improvements in road system, and medical and other social facilities. New opportunities were available with the opening of new mines, heavy industries, Universities, Colleges, Institutes, apex training organisations, market and transport, and so on. Operation of all these forces turned the once tribal dominated area into non-Tribal dominated area and the Tribals became overall minority so much so that in Chota Nagpur Santal Parganas only 30.26 per cent of population are tribals as against 69.74 per cent of population who are not scheduled tribe, and hence non-tribals. While the different local tenancy laws regulating the tenancy situation between the raiyats and the State, heavily overweighed in favour of scheduled tribes or "aboriginals", and imparted a special complexion to the area though now redundant; but continued blessedfully.

TABLE 17.1: Proportion of Scheduled Tribes to Total Population at different censuses (1931 to 1981)

Districts	1981	1971	1961	1951	1941	1931
Santal Parganas	36.80	36.22	38.24	44.67	41.50	42.90
Palamau	18.33	19.09	19.24	17.45	20.06	20.96
Hazaribagh	9.04	10.99	11.30	13.81	12.53	11.05
Ranchi	56.41	58.08	61.61	60.47	69.73	62.72
Dhanbad	9.11	10.61	11.08	15.10	14.43	16.37
Singhbhum	44.08	46.12	47.31	44.94	59.94	54.08

The Table 17.2 shows that in the 12 Tribal Sub-Plan Districts only in Lohardaga and Gumla Scheduled Tribes are in majority otherwise it is said that in all the districts the purpose of covering by separate Tenancy Acts has practically no meaning. (See Fig. 17.1)

This has definitely created irksome situation such as the non-functioning of the Rules and Regulations, Tenancy Acts etc. of the area and if they are forced to be observed they are observed more in their breach. Bihar State Tribal Advisory Council, a constitutional body remained non-functioning for years together and if at all it was convened in 1989 it made a mockery of its functioning which will be evident from its proceedings. The Governor who has the constitutional responsibility to report annually on state of affairs of Tribal areas to the

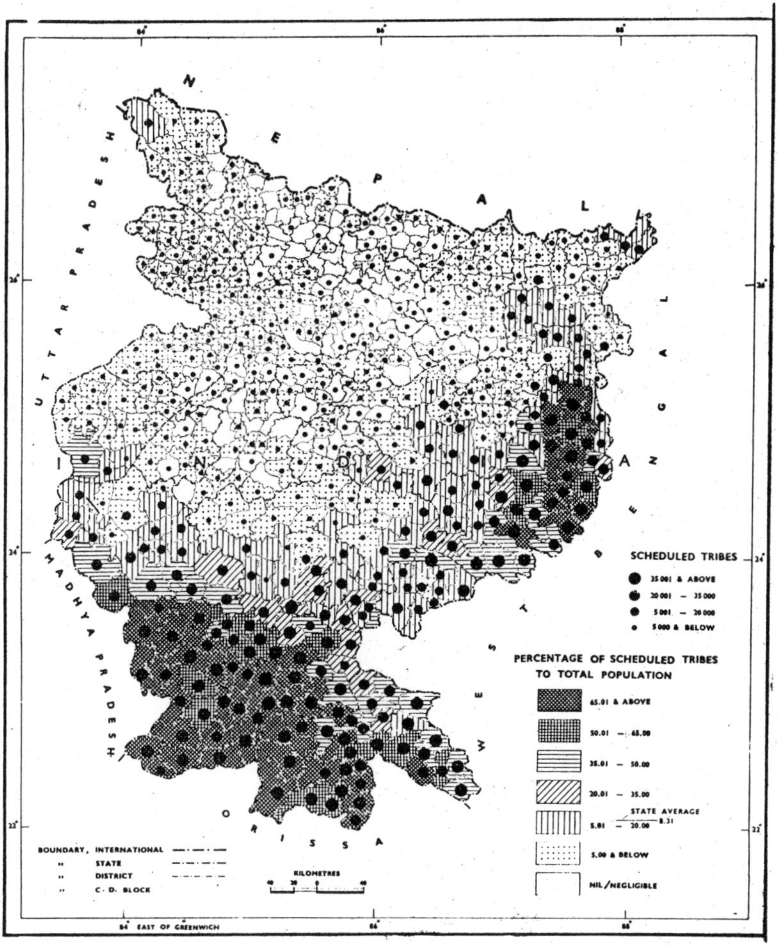

FIG. 17.1: Bihar Scheduled Tribes 1981

President of India remained a defaulter for years together. This is reflected in the Annual Reports of Commissioner for Scheduled Castes and Scheduled Tribes placed on the table and discussed in Lok Sabha. The whole administrative edifice of Chota Nagpur Santal Parganas looks like square peg in a round hole only because the tribals have turned into minority so far as the demographic pattern of this region is concerned. The general rule is that more the tribal population the greater is the thrust of Tribal predominance, the lesser the tribal population minimal is their importance. This is amply not reflected in implementation of rules, regulation and acts in the state of Bihar meant to protect the tribal interest. This is stoutly resented by the tribals who feel alienated and suffer from deprivation syndrome.

TABLE 17.2: Districtswise Comparative Figures of Scheduled Castes/Scheduled Tribes Population According to Census of India (1981)

Sl. No.	Name of Districts	Total Population	Scheduled Castes Population	Scheduled Tribes Population	Percentage of Population	
					SC	ST
1.	Dumka	1,215,542	100,255	574,347	8.25	47.25
2.	Godda	1,177,559	77,907	462,777	6.26	39.30
3.	Deoghar	708,828	93,210	108,434	13.15	15.30
4.	Sahebganj	615,599	40,429	222,310	6.57	36.11
5.	Dhanbad	2,115,010	330,767	192,777	15.64	9.11
6.	Giridih	1,731,462	225,993	224,878	13.05	12.99
7.	Hazaribagh	2,198,310	414,971	198,792	18.88	9.04
8.	Palamau	1,971,528	478,225	351,432	24.94	18.33
9.	Ranchi	1,824,322	98,094	865,594	5.38	47.45
10.	Lohardaga	229,786	8,280	134,854	3.60	58.69
11.	Gumla	1,016,324	51,725	731,584	5.09	71.98
12.	Singhbhum	2,861,799	137,005	1,261,504	4.79	44.08

The other reasons contributing to the proportionate decline of the tribal population is low rate of population growth of tribals as compared to the general population. The increase in Tribal population was much below the average with only 16.6 per cent during 1961-71 decade compared to the average increase of 27.19 per cent in the case of non-tribal population. In Bihar under Scheduling of communities as tribes is also a cause of lower population figures of tribes. Even now in 1981 as many as 74 blocks out of total 193 blocks of the region have majority of tribal population. 112 blocks of the Tribal Sub-Plan area are covered by 14 Meso Project Areas. They contain about 50 per cent of the total population.

Change in Character of Tribal Population

In the State of Bihar, in all 30 categories of tribal communities (including unspecified groups) have been scheduled in the Presidential Order of 1952 and are characterised by their cultural peculiarities and are living on different rungs of cultural development lending to a non-Plan Tribal situation because all the ethnic groups live with separate identity. The most numerous among the tribal communities are the Santals (20.61 lakh). Next to them are the Oraons (10.54 lakh) the Mundas (8.46 lakh) and the Hos (5.36 lakhs) as per 1981 census. They are mostly settled agriculturists and somewhat developed. The less numerous are the Banjara (411), the Khonds (1264), Bathudi (1575), the Baiga (3551), the Gorait (5206), the Birhor (4377), the Savars (3014), the Birjia (4057) etc. who are at a lower stage of development and are scattered over interior hilly parts of the tribal districts. Thus we can very well understand that out of 30 categories of communities scheduled as scheduled tribes in 1952 still denominated as Tribals although hardly ten communities are significant while the rest are insignificant and the mistake committed in 1952 is being perpetuated by stubborn delay in drastic revision of state list which other neighbouring States such as Orissa and M.P. have already done many a time registering high tribal population figure. Similarly problem of surnames and synonyms and usurpation of the status of tribals by the offsprings of mixed marriage or others, creation of new killi names etc. also plague the situation of existence of tribals in Bihar. Many deserving remained gaping while their advantages are usurped by clever.

The Tribals range from settled agriculturists such as Santals, Oraons, Mundas, Hos to the root and fruit gatherers such as Birhor, Birjia and Hill Kharia, Iron Smelters such as Asur, Shifting cultivators such as Sauria Paharia etc. In terms of rank of caste hierarchy and social stratification Cheros, Kherwars, Bhumij and some of the Mundas consider themselves as superior and sometimes call themselves as Rajputs, while Mahali, Lohras, Chick Baraiks, basically artisan communities consider themselves occupying lowly position in tribal society.

While many among the settled agriculturist have adopted advanced technology and have taken up white collared jobs and are leading a sedentary life of a town dweller and cannot possibly be taken as "backward, poor, rustics, illiterate tribals". Their literacy has increased;

but the Ministry of Home Affairs have officially recognised some minor communities as Primitive tribes for their backwardness, illiteracy, living in precarious abode in interior hilly surroundings and following the practices of hunting, roots and fruits gathering and slash and burn primitive cultivation. They show backward trend in their literacy decrease.

The occupational distribution of the scheduled tribes in Bihar, according to 1981 Census is in Table 17.3. This shows that majority of them are non-workers. While the primary sector might have registered some marginal increase in the last two decade in secondary and tertiary sector it has shown a decline. This is a unhealthy trend in as much as the already overburdened primary sector has to take more land of economy whereas relatively less untapped secondary and tertiary sector leave much more to be done. There lies the reason of practically over all alienation of the sons of the soil with the 'new temples of development', high dams, mining complexes and industries etc. whose opening are invariably and unknowingly opposed tooth and nail by the locals because some of those Projects have the capacity to wipe out the misery of monocropping.

Again even if those who have some work to do in agriculture sector they have to content with subsistence cultivation leading to bondage and impoverishment of various kind. As a matter of fact landuse pattern of Chota Nagpur-Santal Parganas has been such that one cannot expect much and therefore large scale migration to the farms of Punjab and Haryana, brick klins of U.P. and Bihar, road construction in Rajasthan, Tripura, tea gardens of Assam and Bengal, etc.

Chota Nagpur-Santal Parganas districts have an average 27.87 per cent of its area as Forest, 7.34 per cent as barren land, 6.46 per cent as land put to non-agricultural uses, 1.46 per cent as pasture and grazing land, 0.84 per cent as miscellaneous crops and grove, 4.52 per cent as culturable waste, 8.61 per cent as other fallow land, 10 per cent as current fallow land and only 32.90 per cent as net sown area. We can very well understand the inevitability of poverty and subsistence agriculture in a region where 44 per cent almost half of the land is not available for any cultivation, only about 33 per cent of cultivated with old and archaic technology. Only about 11 per cent of the net sown area is irrigated. We can understand the underlying significance of the tribals anguish and their propensity to commit crimes as we find more often in the paddy growing area or in Naxalite infested Palamau-Chatra etc. where the Naxalite and Sunlight Army have been waging a war against each other, the local landed gentry and establishment.

As about 75 per cent of the scheduled tribe live in the Sub-Plan area, the occupational distribution in respect of the scheduled tribes population of Bihar speaks truely about the cause of misery of the scheduled tribes in Sub-Plan area.

TABLE 17.3: Showing Occupational Distribution of Scheduled Tribes in Bihar

	Year 1981 (in lakhs)	Percentage	Remarks
1. Total population	58,10,867	100	
2. Total main workers	21,57,664	37.13	
(i) Cultivators	13,60,636	63.06	Against the Percentage of total main-workers
(ii) Agricultural labourers	5,00,606	23.20	
(iii) Manufacturing processing, servicing and household Industry	38,718	1.79	
(iv) Other workers	2,57,704	11.94	
3. Marginal workers	5,10,803	8.79	
4. Non-workers	31,42,400	54.07	

Thus we see that more than 50 per cent of the tribal population have no work and they are idle non-workers and are a people easy to be exploited by the vile politicians. These are mostly the people who are readily available to swell the number of one procession or another, in forcible land grabbing, harvesting of paddy and carrying on depredations if "Direct Action" call is given and thereby contribute to tensional situation.

Instead of doing more and more to improve the lots of people economically and that too in effective manner. The state government preferred to try with one idea or another to create this edifice or that to stem the tide of disaffection in the Tribes of Chota Nagpur and Santal Parganas. One such phenomenon following the field of administrative change is the attempt to grant autonomy to the people of this area.

II

Quest for Home Rule

The story of Autonomy to the people of Chota Nagpur Santal Parganas can be dated from the days of Kolhan and Damin-i-Koh system in

Singhbhum and Santal Parganas respectively as a part of British dispensation of Autonomy given to the people of this area in the last century when they were subdued by the British forces. In course of time the Autonomy was diluted and after the independence of India it started eroding due to number of causes such as administrative reforms made on *ad hoc* basis, opening of many Police Thanas, Community Development Blocks ignoring Tribal Traditional leadership such as Manki, Munda Parganaits and Manjhi as well as the rules and regulations and their untidy implementation of local Tenancy and Protective Act etc. These forced the situation in which more and more restlessness started to be perceived by tribes who accused the administration for their persecution and depriving them of them of their traditional rights. This feeling was accentuated all the more when Jharkhand under Jaipal Singh merged in Congress in 1963 and Binodanand Jha was Kamrazed.

Regional Planning and Development Board

By a resolution of the State Government in 1964 the Regional Planning and Development Board was opened in the main hall of the then Secretariat of Summer headquarter of Bihar Government at Doranda which new houses the Ranchi Bench of Patna High Court. Thus the Board was inaugurated with great funfair and merry making. The jurisdiction of the Board extended not merely over the districts of Chota Nagpur division and the districts of Santal Parganas, but also over certain individual Blocks in other districts where tribals were found in sizeable numbers, namely, Chanun and Katoria of Bhagalpur, Chakai of Monghyr and Adhaura and Nauhatta of Sahabad district. The Chief Minister, Bihar was the Chairman of the Board, while Shri S.K. Bage, the then Minister for Community Development and Gram Panchayat was made its Vice-Chairman. The Board had seven Ministers, including the Chief Minister as Members apart from eleven non-officials. A number of officers of the State Government were designated as Associate Members. The term of office of the Board was fixed ordinarily to be concurrent with the period of the Five Year Plan. In its meetings the Board appeared to have confined itself to a review of schemes being executed by various Departments and the various suggestions made by the members were passed on to the Departments. Annual report was prepared and published by its Member. Secretary who was ex-officio secretary of Tribal Welfare, Patna.

The political instability in the State eversince 1967 gave these group leaders an excellent opportunity to pressurise ruling camp in this respect of wresting political powers. Successive Chief Ministers during 1967 to 1971 tried to wean the Adivasi leaders.

Consequently the so-called "full autonomy" was granted to Chota Nagpur and Santal Parganas in 1971 the *Chota Nagpur and Santal Parganas Autonomous Development Authority (CASDA)* . Act envisaged for its "all round development", according to an observer the Chota Nagpur and Santal Pargana Development Authority was the "Child of political give and take".

Though the 'Authority', was constituted, but it did not satisfy all the Adivasi leaders fully, but apparently it generated great hopes amongst them that ultimately the region would get adequate share of prosperity and that they would have their say in the formulation and implementation or the development plans for the area.

In his inaugural address on 13th November, 1971 the then Chief Minister Bhola Paswan Shastri and the then Planning Minister, Mr. Chandra Shekhar Singh promised great future for this "Authority". Far from it, the actual working since its inauguration has belied all such hopes. In fact, the 'Authority' started working only when Mr. Shastri nominated Sri Kartik Oraon, M.P. as its Deputy Chairman and 11 other members.

Chota Nagpur and Santal Parganas Development Authority created by an Act of the legislature (Act 8 of 1971) marked the culmination of political and regional pulls and pressures exercised by many Adivasi as well as non-Adivasi leaders.

The Autonomous Authority was located in the building of the Audrey House and was planned to have various wings of Development Department if it was allowed to function fully. It can hardly be denied that the Development Authority has tremendous potentialities and prospects. The laudable five points objective enunciated in the Act appear self-explanatory – (i) to prepare short- and long-term plan for all round development of the area; (ii) to advise the State Government in evolving developmental schemes and assist effectively in their execution; (iii) to assist in accelerating the pace of development of the tribal belt and recommend to the State Government about steps to be taken for the same including disciplinary action against erring personnel; (iv) to review and evaluate the progress of various development programmes; and (v) to call for reports and returns from developmental departments and issue directions to them.

It is needless to add that this 'Autonomous Authority' if clicked for the purpose it has been incorporated may rise to the stature and strength it deserved for the fulfilment of the objectives. But history is witnessed that its Dy. Chairman Sri Kartik Oraon made herculian attempt to enliven it, but it is said that Patna always functioned like a doubting aunt resulting in its practically non-functioning.

Observers have assigned three main reasons for the sluggish crawling of the 'Authority'. Firstly, it was apprehended that the then ruling group was presumably not genuine in its *bona fide* when it acceded to form the so-called Autonomous Authority. Otherwise the provisions of the Act would not have been framed with an amount of so many reservations. What cannot be overlooked was that admittedly the Government did not vest 'autonomous authority' with any autonomy as such.

The size of the 'Authority' (80 members) swelled as its executive committee precluded any serious discussion for the purpose of giving any definite directions to the policy. 'Actual decision-making was not possible by such a large body', remarked an experienced officer.

Secondly, the Autonomous Authority appeared to be a mere recommendatory body and its decision, according to the provisions of the Act, may not be acceptable to the Government. In fact many Sub-committees formed by the 'Autonomous Authority' on 13 and 14th November, 1971 held several dialogues and made some impressive recommendations, but all in vain, lack of political will stood in the way.

Thirdly, as laid down in the Act all the personnel of the Autonomous Authority was to be deputed by the State Government. In other words, the Autonomous Authority has no authority over its functionaries and manpower.

Fourthly, the State Government reserved the right to dissolve or supercede the Autonomous Authority whenever it may so please. Even a casual observer could hardly escape noticing the unbusiness like manner in which its meeting was conducted on the inauguration day. Members were allowed to make speeches off the agenda, and the sub-committees were formed without any procedure of guideline etc. It seemed that it was merely a completion of some formality and that was all. Nor has this Autonomous Authority a building of its own or sanctioned quota of officers, and other staff as suggested by Governor Dev Kant Barua or a fund.

Another factor for the sluggish functioning of the Autonomous

Authority appeared to be bureaucracy's indifference towards it. The various departments of the Government particularly the Planning Department which happened to be its parent department, appears to have cold shouldered the Autonomous Authority, in as much as, it reflected some erosion of their power.

In fact, the Autonomous Authority had no framework of rules and byelaws to conduct business. The powers and functions of the various functionaries viz. Chairman, Dy. Chairman, Member-Secretary etc. were not spelt out by the Government fully simply posting an officer of the Senior Commissioner's rank was not expected to serve any purpose. Similar was the case of the Deputy Chairman who remained starved of power and fund. Nor the fund of the Autonomous Authority was reported to have been created. The worst part was the non-posting of the staff. State Welfare Department doled its role of saviour of the region to the Planning Department which to some was one of cause of its debacle.

Dr. Ram Dayal Munda talked about Mr. Kartik Oraon's participation in the Authority 'CASDA' as the spirit of fighting from inside the system and characterised Mr. Oraon as a great cooperator perhaps because he was throughout a Congressman and was near to the then Prime Minister Late Smt. Indira Gandhi. Some say that Mr. Kartik Oraon was able to wrest from the Government the organ of planning and development of this region so that the development process of this area is reinforced. Unfortunately it is said that the so-called CASDA and all hopes to development of this area foundered the rock of intrasigence and unwilling political will at Patna.

This kept Kartik Oraon fighting for the developmental autonomy of his area. While the then Prime Minister Mrs. Indira Gandhi lent lip sympathy to Kartik's overtures and she addressed the Authority many a time at Ranchi and this way developmental questions of Chota Nagpur and Santal Pargana could not be taken to further extent except it somehow got reflected in Annual Plan prepared by the Authority; but it is said that Planning Department at Patna and the then Planning Commissioner had minimal involvement with this. The Member-Secretary of the Authority prepared plan annually and the Plan, it is said, remained a document in the archive of the State Government. The Central Government, Ministry of Home Affairs first insisted on perspective planning by preparing fourteen Meso area ITDP reports, and then backed out and clung to a tiny Annual Plan containing 'only small schemes of greater importance' and in this way

Patna and Delhi in their own way stood in the way of the functioning of the Authority, ITDP remained in 'suspended animation'.

Sri Devkant Barua, the then Governor of Bihar while inaugurating the Authority on 12th November, 1971 had very emphatically laid down seven conditions for the success of the Authority, the first and foremost being a responsible sympathetic pro-poor, pro-tribal and pro-down trodden bureaucracy specially created for developmental job for this region. But Patna never agreed to this and the bureaucracy of Bihar remained a square peg in round hole. And it is still a big question mark that can a highly objective, unresponsive, autocratic, colonial tools of regulatory function of the state coming from the British time without much change in its character could deliver the good in Chota Nagpur and Santal Pargana? Kartik Oraon was always irked on this and specially the imperial attitude of the Heads of Department of different development departments who followed the concept of ruling over the departmental Empire was agonising. The Member-Secretary of the Authority K. Ramanujam came into lime light for ventilating the grievances of the sons of the soil through the Authority documents. The Jharkhand Party under N.E. Horo, Theodore Bodra and Bagun Sumbrai was also intensifying the struggle for Jharkhand State. Kartik Oraon was under great pressure. In meanwhile a fact finding team under Mr. Hamid, Additional Secretary, Minister of Home, New Delhi visited this area and submitted a detailed report justifying immediate revamping of the administrative machinery and setting up a clear goal for the emancipation of this area.

During the rule of Janata Party after Emergency under Karpuri Thakur's Chief Ministership another death blow to the Authority was made by trifurcating it into three basing one each at Ranchi, Hazaribagh and Dumka and creating a Branch Secretariat under Regional Development Commissioner who was also made the Ex-officio Member-Secretary of these three Authorities. Later on the officer of the Tribal Welfare Commissioner, a functionary of Welfare Department was also created under the Regional Development Commissioner the Branch Secretariat miscalled Mini-Secretariat remained functioning and with 29 transferred sectors though on mini scale. It remained preparing its annual plan and got funds from tribal sub-plan budget and Central Special Assistance and also allocations under Article 275 of the Constitution except this there was no iota of autonomy. Thus reliance was put on unbriddled bureaucracy and the organs of self-governing authority could not be managed well and they were allowed to languish.

This chance of responsive self-rule was lost which had wide repercussion. Kartik Oraon in disparate mood once shared the same platform with N.E. Horo. Theodore Bodra and Bagun Sumbrai. But nothing was to be achieved.

Thus case for Home rule and Autonomy was lost for the time being State Government substituted the autonomy with "controlled dosage of administrative arrangement" under Tribal Sub-Plan system as a part of national exercise to eradicate the tribals backwardness and misery.

Tribal Sub-Plan Area

Thus as a Tribal Sub-Plan strategy the Tribal Sub-Plan area constituting the above schedule area in Bihar was formed during the Fifth Five-Year Plan. Scheduled Tribe population in the State numbered 58.11 lakh against the total population of the state at 699 lakhs in 1981 Census. The tribal population constituted 8.3 per cent of the states population. The Schedule Tribe population in Tribal Sub-Plan area is 43.29 lakhs. Out of its total population of 87.56 lakhs which constituted 12.5 per cent of state total population. 43.29 lakh Schedule Tribe population in Tribal Sub-Plan area comes to 49.44 per of the total population of the area. The Tribal Sub-Plan area, therefore, was created as Sub-Plan strategy with main purpose to narrow the gap between the development in tribal area and other area while improving the quality of life of the tribal community. As a part of the above strategy the Tribal Sub-Plan area has been territorially divided into 14 ITDPs popularly known as Meso areas, one Meso area constitutes mostly a sub-division and placed under an official of Addl. Collector rank while the sub-divisional Magistrate of that sub-division is declared as the Ex-officio Addl. Meso Area Officer.

The object of the Integrated Tribal Development Projects are as follows:

(i) to bring the tribals socially and economically at par with others so that they may mingle in the mainstream of life;
(ii) to remove bottlenecks in the development of the area so that smooth functioning of programmes could be realised;
(iii) to prepare resource inventory suiting of the felt need of the area;
(iv) to administer the area on right lines.

Perspective Plans for each of the 14 ITDPs were prepared focusing on the felt needs of the people; but they remained unimplemented and instead tiny annual plans were preferred under which small schemes of larger significance were taken up. May be the state failed to procure large funds for perspective plans. The Meso area officers were given the responsibility restoring the alienated lands of the tribals in 1988; but he was not taken seriously and he remained in the area as an officer out of contest "devoid of significance regulatory administrative duties". This ineffectiveness of this machinery has forced the ITDP to be in "suspended animation".

Main reasons of .failure of this administrative and development manoeuvring might have been its non-starting character, non-working bureaucracy, departmental empire system and overemphasis on IRDP and other general programmes etc. ITDP remained languishing and presently the whole sub-plan area divided into 14 Meso Projects looks a great fraud on the working of Developmental Plan in the area.

About 75 per cent of Scheduled Tribal population in Bihar live in Tribal Sub-Plan area spread in eight districts. Areawise Tribal sub-plan area constitute 25 per cent of the geographical area of the State of Bihar. With a Branch Secretariat under Regional Development Commissioner (successer of Member-Secretary and Area Development Commissioner (CASDA) as Principal Secretary of all the transferred developmental Departments). Tribal Sub-Plan is prepared in Branch secretariat keeping in view to allocate 25 per cent of the state outlay. In the biginning only creation of infrastructural facilities promised benefit and raised the level of the life of the people. Instead they invariably preferred to use all gimicks to wrest a separate Jharkhand or Vananchal state as if creation of separate state is the panaces of all their ills. Little do they understand that if they get the so-called Jharkhand whatever available reservations, safeguards, protective discrimination and advantages actually implemented the Eldrado could be reached. They hardly remember the martyrdom of Sidhu-Kanhu and their which had secured a *Megnacharte* for them in peasing of Santal Pargana Tenancy Regulation 1872. They forget *Birsa Bhagwan's* great heoric fight and supreme sacrifice due to which Chota Nagpur Tenancy Act (1908) secured practically a Jharkhand for them.

Instead the leaders preferred to flitter away their energy in organising this movement or that, this *bandh* or that, parading on the streets, holding endless meeting, etc. Issuing statement, holding parleys and sometimes indulging in violence. Polarisation of interest led to the formation of pressure groups such as· Sivaji Samaj Movement,

Jharkhand Mukti Morcha, Jharkhand Coordination Committee, Kolhanistan Movement, etc. regarding whose debut in early seventies one can recount with great profit. Therefore, a small study of these new trends have been made in the following paragraphs.

Shivaji Samaj Movement

In this State of confusion in 1969 Sibu Soren, 'an insignificant worker of Birsa Seva Dal based at Paterwar came into prominence. He started an agitation in collusion with Vinod Bihari Mahto of Baliapur (died on 20 December, 1991) and A.K. Roy a Trade Union Leader of Dhanbad. They started a drive against *Diku*, the outsiders. They have slogans like *A.B.C.D. Bhag Jao, Hamari Jamin Bapas Karo*, and other such much known Jharkhandi slogans which were raised under the banner of Shivaji Samaj Movement. There were firings by the police on irate mob and parallel government under Shibu Soren worked in hilly fastnesses of Giridih forest areas for many months.

On 4th February, 1973 (Dr. S.P. Sinha: Peasant Organisation in Chota Nagpur, Ranchi, 1988) Jharkhand Mukti Morcha evolved out of Shivaji Samaj Movement with much support of Kurmis, Marxists and it is said also with the blessings of the Christian Missionaries. In 1972 elections Congress secured clear majority. Kedar Pandey became new Chief Minister of Bihar. The regional party once more faced eclipse. The All India Jharkhand Party was divided into Bagum and Horo factions and could get one seat each while Hool Jharkhand Party divided into two factions and got one seat each.

In these frustrating days N.E. Horo took upon himself the responsibility to revive his party as a Jharkhand Party on 12th March, 1973 and demanded an area of 187646 sq. km. with population of 3050899 which was to be carved out of 6 districts of Bihar, 4 districts of Orissa, 3 districts of Bengal, and, 2 districts of Madhya Pradesh. Jaipal had asked for a bigger Jharkhand in 1954-55 which was practically commensurate with the South West Frontier Agency created by the British Government in 1832.

But the demand of separate State of Jharkhand by any Jharkhand Party now remained an academic question because 1971 census brought home to the people the truth that tribals in so-called Jharkhand State of their demand were in State of overall minority and separate State for Tribal home land as an ethnic State became once for all a far cry.

Emergency was clamped in June 1975 and this ended only in March 1977, ushering Janata Rule in Centre and Bihar. Mr. Jaipal Singh was already dead in 1972 and Jharkhandis kept themselves away from J.P. agitation although this author is witness to a nocturnal meetings of number of Jharkhandi youth with J.P. at Tiril Ashram, Ranchi, when J.P. actually pronounced his opinion in favour of a smaller State, but dissuaded the tribal youth then from demanding a separate big State like Jharkhand which was not to be feasible as a separate State. The emergency was followed by Janata Rule in State when Shibu Soren became a mass leader, Mrs. Indira Gandhi is said to have come to terms with Jharkhand Mukti Morcha leaders and did not allow her candidates to contest against Jharkhand Mukti Morcha candidates in Santal Pargana and in this way Shibu Soren and his men practically "got walk over" and "entered in the legislature practically with Mrs. Gandhi's help".

Once more in 1980 Shibu Soren aroused a dream for a Jharkhand State; but the Congress did not allow the dream come true by patronising Shibu Soren. Events following it brought about the disruption in the Morcha when it is said that Shibu parted company with A.K. Roy and Vinod Bihari Mahto. Bagun Sombrai had again changed his party and joined Congress. Kartik Oraon was dead on 8th December, 1981. A.P. Sharma (Social Change, New Delhi, 1988) rightly wrote "that grandiose project of a tribal State mooted by Jaipal Singh and sustained by leaders like N.E. Horo and Shibu Soren was left with only academic value. The industrialisation and urbanisation in Chota Nagpur had provided employment to many while reservation in services had created a tribal elite that was not disgruntled; but satiated and it was this elite that used the separatists demand as a leverage for further gains".

Role of Regional Tribal Language Department of Ranchi University.

In May, 1980 one important phenomenon appeared on the scene of Chota Nagpur, that was the opening of the Tribal and Regional language Department with Dr. Ramdayal Munda as the Head. Dr. Munda had returned from America after pretty long stay with Dr. Norman Zide, an Internationally known Linguist. Dr. Munda basically is an Anthropologist, Poet, Social Reformer, Musician, cultural hero all rolled into one. He came to become the centre of the local aspiration.

Picked boys and girls were admitted to study regional language which became the symbol of localism. He was joined by different faculty members like Dr. B.P. Keshri, Mrs. Rose Kerketta and others. Accidentally they became the potential leaders of movement for a separate Jharkhand State, they supplied the much publicised talents to Intellectual Forum spearheaded by Dr. Nirmal Minz. The pressure on administration to appoint tribals on important posts in University and elsewhere. Along with others Dr. Ramdayal Munda was made the Acting Vice-Chancellor in June, 1986 and subsequently Vice-Chancellor Ranchi University and it is alleged that University Campus was the happy recruitment ground for Chota Nagpur Santal Pargana Sangharsh Vahini, Intellectual Forum. It will not be travesty of truth that when Jharkhand Coordination Committee was formed in 1987 at Ramgarh the Department of Tribal Regional language supplied it with a Convenor and several active members who ultimately sat with the Jharkhand Affair's Committee's Parleys in New Delhi in 1989-90. In December 1987 Jharkhand Coordination Committee also memoralised to the President of India on issue of separate State. Thus may be due to the personality of cultural hero like Dr. Ramdayal Munda, an University Department rose to supply the deliberative leadership to the call of Jharkhand, the Home land.

Jharkhand Coordinations Committee

Concomitant to this was the formation of All Jharkhand Students Union (AJSU) in June, 1986 when stormy petrel like Suraj Singh Besra, became its Secretary and Prabhakar Tirkey became its President. Number of rallies, conferences and *bunds* were organised by AJSU. Sometimes they talked of violence and they were reported to be in contact with outside movements in North Eastern States and wanted to organise Assam type movement such as *Rail Roko Andolan, Jharkhand March*, organising provincial government etc. On August 8, 1987, Nirmal Mahto, the President of Jharkhand Mukti Morcha was killed at Jamshedpur, Dr. B.P. Keshri took upon himself the mentle of Convenor of Jharkhand Coordination Committee in a Conference at Ramgarh held on 11th to 13th September, 1987. This Conference was attended by 438 delegates representing 48 organisations and groups including the factions of JMM, JKD, AJSU, Jharkhand Party, IPF, MKSS and others. 23-point demands were made out including the demand of Jharkhand State consisting of 21 districts of four States carved out from such as Bihar, Orissa, M.P., and West Bengal.

Kolhanisation Movement

In the meantime Kolhanisation movement under Narayan Zonko as President and Krishna Chandra Hembrom as Secretary raised their heads for autonomy of Kolhan and Manki-Munda system in Singhbhum district. In September 1981 the two above named Ho leaders along with Christ Anank Topno, Ranchi based lawyer visited London and Geneva and presented memorandum before the Commonwealth Conference. The Kolhan Raksha Samiti reportedly let loose terror in the area by killing those who did not obey them. This resulted into their arrest under National Security Act. *Times of India* smelt foul in this movement and castigated the role of foreign missionaries and C.I.A. in this movement". World Council of Churches founded a branch at Ranchi in June 1987 naming Indian Council of Indigenous Tribal People (ICITP) which it is said provided another forum to the separatists. Between 3 to 7 August, 1987 ICITP sent some of its member to Geneva who participated in meetings of the Working Group organised by the UNO and there they raised the issue of Jharkhand very seriously. Xavier Institute of Social Sciences, Ranchi has been blamed in some quarter to have provide a ready platform for "separatists" and "dissenters" "where ICITP and other such organisations held their conferences. Xavier Institute of Social Sciences became a forum for a big seminar on High Dams and questioned the developmental strategis of the State Government in 1988. It is said to have encouraged the Jansangathana in Torpa and Basia against Koel Karo Hydel Thermal Power Project and it tenanciously secured from Supreme Court some of the best advantages for the would be displaced persons due to the Koel Karo Project.

Operation Brahmputra

Some columnists in National daily talked of "Operation Brahmputra", a CIA Plot, masterminded to de-estabilise tribal areas of north-east and middle India. Unfortunately all the movements run in Santal Pargana and Chota Nagpur areas are very loosely attributed to CIA connections. It is very difficult to investigate and see in the agitation of Jharkhand a patronage of CIA and the Christian Missionaries. But West Bengal Government branded number of Christian Organisations getting CIA help and thus banned their operation in its area. These organisations had tentacles in this area also. This might create some doubt in some quarter. Unfortunately, the functional role of these proto-nationalistic movements are not realised and recognised.

It is said that the distant administration, irresponsible bureaucracy, poor accountability, seething discontent and growing unemployment, poverty, ill health, wants, high prices crowned with unsympathetic little bureaucracy and non-functioning tendency legislations and reservation clauses etc. created such a situation that it is very difficult to stem the tide of separatism. It is difficult to separate wheat from the chaff. In post Father Korkove expulsion era some of the Missionaries organs might have gone furious, the pages of *Niskalanka* excited legal action. But branding all the movements as whole as a CIA and Christian Missionary oriented would be definitely far from truth. At best this movement of separatism can be one form of protonationalistic movement in which the motor force into rally round a leader with the desire to have a separate State ruled for better developmental prospect and amelioration of weaker sections of the society. If it cannot be a search for Home Land, it can easily be the quest for Home Rule.

Committee on Jharkhandi Affairs

The Jharkhand Coordination Committee got its respectability when through perhaps the active support of Mrs. Sumati Oraon the then Minister, Welfare Government of India and the then Home Minister Buta Singh varied assortments of separatists and locals tribals and Sadans were brought to a common table for several rounds of talks with the Central Government Committee on Jharkhand Affairs known as Lali Committee at New Delhi. Several memorandum were placed before the Central Government. With the fall of Rajiv Gandhi government a sense of frustration was created in their hearts although Jharkhand Mukti Morcha had won 19 seats and Jharkhand Party won one seat of the Bihar Legislature and four seats in Loksabha in 1989-90 General Election. Fortunately National Front Government picked up the thread of talk on Jharkhand Question and it looked that on 14th and 15th May, 1990 the protagonists of Jharkhand were about to get something when Lali Committee Report was submitted and discussed thread bare. Matter is still tossing between Patna and Delhi and date lines are fast changing. In October 1990 another set of Jharkhandis, mostly the members of Jharkhand Mukti Morcha and AJSU were taken to New Delhi for talk and that has led to heart burning among others because earlier negotiators were totally ignored.

Akhra Mahasabha

AJSU has recently started a movement afresh and resolved on its foundation day i.e. 22nd June, 1990 to carry movement to its Akhra (dancing grounds) by forming Akhra Mahasabha which will be the substitute for the Legislative body for the Jharkhand. It proposed to show black flag on 15th August and start connecting the terrorist organisations already agitating in North-Eastern state. This has once again created a deep suspicion as to whether the Jharkhand state would be state for the tribal or for others also because other than the tribals may not be the part of so-called Akhra legislature. It was regarded that Shri Shibu Soren also declared at Ranchi meeting in September 1990 that Brahmin, Rajputs etc. were to be thrown out from Chota Nagpur.

Thus the Jharkhand movement starting from a Chotanagpur Unnati Samaj days of 1913 to the present has travelled long way and has undergone many changes. Emanating from the urge to get a separate State for the Adivasis, that is, ethnic state it turned into a demand a regional State. But there remained always a confusion that the proposed State would house only the locals or the tribals because sometimes from the platform of AJSU and others the years 1971 is declared as cut year on the line of Assam agitation for expulsion of outsiders. This created a suspicion in the minis of people who had the tradition of living in this part of the country for the hundreds and thousand of years perhaps even before coming of the several types of Tribes in Chota Nagpur. Chota Nagpur and Santal Pargana is a region of mixed population out of which only thirty categories of ethnic communities has been scheduled as yet as Scheduled Tribes under Presidential Orders while others are still clamouring for that status on the basis of their backwardness, illiteracy, living in hills and forest, sharing deprivation which the tribals who are scheduled are facing.

Therefore, when Coordination Committee for Jharkhand was formed it was virtual take over of Jharkhand movement by Kurmis, Telis, Suris, Nagvanshis, Ansaris, over and above the Tribals who have had the common bond of speaking Nagpuria or low Bengali dialect, the Panchpargania. Regional Language Department of Ranchi University again became a catalytic agent for bolstering up the image of "Jharkhand for the locals". This linguistic Chauvinism still has its negative role to play which bifurcated this plateau population into two; one who speak local dialect and the other who do not. The tradition of *Zamindari Zulum* perpetrated by *Zamindars* and their men in the State and by Hindu and Muslim traders in *hats* and *Bazar* were perhaps being forgotten. Curiously enough the potential exploiters of Tribals and poor local for generation became the mouthpiece of Jharkhand demand it is they who sat in the parleys at New Delhi and Patna, 1981 population figures made it all the more clear that the tribals are in hopeless minority except in districts such as Ranchi, Lohardaga and Gumla, Sahebganj, Dumka. Therefore, outside these districts the tribal are now living in some pockets only although once they were humming with their considerable population. So this reality dawned upon Jharkhand Tribal leaders to allow their so-called Diku's as their Co-sharer of the Platform for Jharkhand agitation.

According to Dr. Dilwar Hans, the word *Diku* taken from Hindi word *Dik* is now loosely understood as one who troubles and disturbs; but it is definitely the perverse form of Mundari's *Inku* (they) contradistinguised from *Aingku* (We). It is a question of "insider" and "outsider", joining together against new settlers of Chota Nagpur and Santal Pargana who came in the wake of urbanisation and nationalisation of mines, industrialisation, opening of trade and commerce, establishment of heavy industry and universities starting of new avocatious and in a way they are also claiming a place in the sun becausing they have also contributed in augmenting the wealth of Chota Nagpur and Santal Pargana by their sweat of their brows.

Vananchal

The strain of new settlers mixed with other, demanded *Vananchal* by holding rallies, meetings, blockade and recently publishing a book which was released by Sri Tarakant Jha, the Chairman of Bhartiya Janata Party, Bihar on 16th June, 1990 at Ranchi. The protoganists of Vananchal do not look serious about the name of proposed Jharkhand state. They feel that "after all what is there in name". In the crucial meeting of 15 and 16th May, 1990 all the legislators and M.P.'s belonging to different political parties irrespective of their political affiliation endoresed the demand for a separate State, the lone dessentor being Sri Karamachand Bhagat, Tribal Welfare Minister in Bihar who wanted a very broad based body to look into the demand of Jharkhand state very consistently and sincerely. Sri Ram Bilas Paswan, formerly, Welfare Minister, New Delhi is clear in his mind that Jharkhand cannot be decided in an isolated way different from the demand of Bodoland and Uttarakhand.

Thus we have seen that what could not be achieved by agitation, bunds, ballot box, and other deliberative democratic process could now about to be achieved by the willing New Delhi to carve out a separate state out of the allegedly "unprepared and complacent Bihar". This has been creating a murky situation and perhaps *Balkanisation of Bihar* is on the agenda of Lali Committee Report which has been sent to Bihar Government as well as the Ministry of Home Affairs when recently in December 1991 Shri S.V. Chavan, Home Minister declared that centre can think of creation of separate state for Jharkhand provided the adjoining States of West Bengal, Orissa and M.P. also agree. It is said that there is practically no ripple on Patna's political quarter, no anxiety to save Bihar from biffurcation. Some Congressman of course tried to put Vishal Bihar movement on the rail but all in vain.

During S.R.C. days (1955) the Government of Bihar fought a battle royal to stop its territories being doled to other States by encouraging number of voluntary agencies like Bihari Association and others who filed their own memorandum against such division. But the present government prepared to befriend to JMM leaders and promulgated creation of Jharkhand Development Council in July 1991.

Thus demand of separate State for Jharkhand was justified on the ground that the tribal and downtrodden have been exploited long and they must be given back their due. For many a decades the Jharkhandis fought and many of them perished in the struggle; but will they get Jharkhand of their demand, territorywise and political advantagewise? The territories outside the State of Bihar having dominant tribal population were now out of the question because Coordination Committee for Jharkhand could not attract a single representative from Madhya Pradesh, Orissa and West Bengal on the parleys table. Moreover, three adjoining states practically prevented the Committee for Jharkhand Affairs from visiting their area to solicit the people's wishes regarding their joining the Jharkhand State. Therefore, it is clear that now if the Jharkhand State is created by the Central Government it will not be Jharkhand State of Jaipal Singh, N.E. Horo, Bagun Sumbrai, but it will be a New Jharkhand State dominated by so-called Dikus and non-tribals because of their numerical strength. Not it will no more be called anti-national supported by C.I.A. and Foreign Missionaries; but will be a Nation State supported by all the Political Parties of different hues.

Jharkhand is far away, *Delhi door ast* (Delhi is far away) Dr. Ramdayal Munda's document of demand placed before the Central

Government gives the impression that he wanted a substitution of Bihar Tribe Advisory Council and some sorts of Autonomous Union Territory. AJSU want a separate State. Vananchal wants a regional State of Chota Nagpur and Santal Pargana. So-called Diku leaders and their supporters in bureaucracy are more adamant in demand of separate State of Jharkhand than the tribal leaders themselves. That is the impression of Delhi based National Fellow. The ball is in the courts of Government of India. Modality has to be settled. Legislation shall have to be passed. It looks legislation for Chota Nagpur State would sub-plant the earlier Act on Chota Nagpur and Santal Pargana Autonomous Development Authority (1971). Only the horse is going to be changed not the rider. The poverty, ill health, wants and squalor will perhaps remain hurting the people of Chota Nagpur. While the working of Jharkhand State will not make any real difference from the level of administration in other backward areas of these States, the future activists, would have very difficult time to convince people that them meant this and they got what. Neither the Jharkhandi would get their homeland nor their home rule; but some thing might be better than none.

APPENDIX I

MUNDA THEORY OF RENT

IN ORDER to appreciate the tribal attitude to the enhancement of rent, it would not be out of place here to discuss the Munda theory of rent. The history of rent in every village is a history of struggle between landlord and *raiyots*. Neither the traditional theory of rent in England as *redditus* or "compensation for land demised" nor the proportion theory of the Permanent Settlement Regulation of Bengal (1793) have any application to the concept of rent in Chota Nagpur.

Bengal theory of 'rent' as a *certain customary* proportion of the rent produce of a holding cannot be applied to the case of aboriginal *raiyots* in Chota Nagpur, what is called 'rent' in Ranchi district originated in voluntary nominal contributions in the nature of 'tribute' or 'aid' which the Munda peasant proprietors paid to the Maharaja of Chota Nagpur. These rents were originally fixed without any reference to the yield of the holding and *at no period of their history represented a certain proportion of the produce, or its money value*, and that consequently neither any permanent rise in the prices of staple food crops nor any other ground will be available to the 'landlord' to enhance the rate of 'rent'. 'Rent' payable by aboriginal tenants was neither "competition rent" as in Bengal and Bihar, but stands as a class apart which may be termed "tribute rent". To understand this phenomenon, a look at the antecedents of Munda Tenancies is imperative.

Earliest of the Mundas founded a village by clearing the primeval jungles and reclaimed the lands which now comprised their tenancies. They continued to hold the village as Mundari Khuntkattidar (peasant proprietor) and in time came to pay through their headmen, a nominal tribute for the whole village to the ancestors of the present Maharaja of Chota Nagpur, initially in the shape of presents of jungle produce like *hanrua, barni, sabai, Kampi* etc., and assistance in war, and later, in the shape of annual contribution of a few rupees for the whole village.[1] Much later in the twenties of the last century, the Maharaja of Chota Nagpur granted in Jagir the Pargana to his relations as maintenance grant. These relations latter began ruthless campaign of expropriation of the Khuntkattidar Mundas of the village. Not content with the small annual contributions then payable by each village in lump, he began by forcibly expanding the amount of annual contributions from the village. Not satisfied with this, too, he cast about for means to breakdown the communal ownership of the village by the Munda.[2] He found willing instruments to effect his designs in adventurers who had come in the train of the extension of British administration to this part of the country as small traders, money-lenders, *Daroga, Mukhtearys amlas* etc. To them he gave leases or *Thikas* of the villages. These overtures though strenously resisted in the beginning, at length succeeded in reducing the Mundas from *Khuntkattidars* owners of villages to the position of Bhuinhars in respect of the lands which they respectively cultivated. This was effected, first by realising small payment from each *Khunt* separately as its share of the tribute, miscalled 'rent' of the village, and then by managing to realise by way of rent at fixed rates from the *Parjas* or Jeth Raiyots (all aboriginals) who came after the Khuntkattidars or Bhuinhars and cleared jungles and reclaimed lands and whom the original Khuntkattidars had established on some of their own lands. The *Khorposdar* or Thakur and his *Thikadars* began to call such holdings by the name of *rajhus* (or lands from which the Raja's or superior landlords demand was to be met). The tenancies of the descendants of the Munda founders of the village they named *Bhuinhari*.

The *Thikadars* did not stop there. They vigorously prosecuted the ruthless policy of reducing the status of the Munda descendants of the original founders of the village by still further reducing the area of *Bhuinhari* lands (which one comprised all the cultivated lands of the descendents of the aboriginal founders of the village). The *Thikadars* forcibly seized and appropriated some of the best of these lands for their own cultivation and called them *manjhihas* (the *manjhi's* or *Thikadar's* share) and *Zerait* or *Saika* and settled some of them with other new-comers whom the Zamindars and Thikadars brought into the village as their adherants to serve as a counterpoise against the aboriginal tenants and to further the landlords' schemes of aggrandisement.

Even this did not satisfy these Zamindars and their Thikadars, they went on further reducing the area of *Bhuinhari* lands. After having arbitrarily separated most of the tenant's lands from the *Khuntkattidars* or *Bhuinhari* stock to which they had all originally belonged, the

Thikadars called them *Korkar* land and began to assess them to a small fixed rent of two annas or four annas per *Kat*. These *Korkar* lands or rather the bulk of them were in their turn wrongfully reduced further to the status of *Rajhas*, lands to be burdened with *rajhas rents*. It may be noted that this insidious method of conversion of *'Korkar'* into *Rajhus* continued till the other day with the help of settlement *amlas*, for some of the lands which were recorded as *Korkar* at the last settlement in (1902-10) have been mysteriously recorded as *rajhus* at the Revisional Settlement in 1937.

On the basis of both oral and documentory evidence, S. C. Roy found that the landlords and their *thikadars* made repeated attempts to enhance the rent by force and trickery and lost no opportunity of seeking on some pretext or the other to screw more out of the tenants than was their due. These *Thikadars* began to sell the trees of jungles which the tenants had saved from the axe and preserved and treated as their own. Even the sacred *Sarnas* did not escape their unholy aggressions. The ancestors of these Mundas resisted, as best as they could, these and other attempts of the landlords and *thikadars* to bring them down to the level of ordinary raiyats such as were the *sadan* cultivators.

During the regime of Lt. Col. Evans Gordon under the management of the Court of Wards Tehsildar Bikramajit was deputed to prepare a *jamabandi* of the village. He demanded bribes for making correct entries, and on Mundas tenant failing to satisfy his illegal demands, some of the *Korkar* land were entered by him as *rajhas* and in some cases the areas of their holdings were exaggerated. The Court of Wards authorities thus misled by Tehsildar Bikramajit and also through their zeal in the interests of their Ward, arbitrarily, wrongfully and illegally assessed most of the lands of their holdings with *rajhas* rents. The *Hukum* of *hakim* prevailed. Tehsildars was regarded as '*Sorkari Hores*' (men of administration), object of fear and awe. The aboriginal tenants were further led to believe by the *Tehsildars* and other creatures of the landlords that the rent they assessed would never be enhanced any further. But they found that it was a mendacious hoax and false assurance.

The successive stages of disintegrations of Mundari-Khuntkatti villages could be found in the systematic history supplied by J. Reid[3] in the Settlement Report of Ranchi District:

"All that is certain is that the aboriginal tribes the Mundas, the

Uraons and the Kharias penetrated the country and reclaimed it from the virgin forest. There is no doubt that Mundas were the first comers. . . . In very early period, possibly in the tenth century of the Christian era, the ancestors of the present Maharaja of Chota Nagpur appear to have established themselves as Chief of the primitive Munda tribes who then inhabited the country. The Uraon who arrived in the country considerably later than the Mundas, appear to have acquiesced in the rule of these chiefs.

On the organisation of the primitive Munda Community, the whole country was divided into *Parhas* consisting of from 15 to 20 villages each over which a chief presided. It is probable that these chiefs elected of their own free will the Khukra chief (a Munda) as their feudal superior. As the family prospered, they intermixed with the Rajput families of Pachete and Singhbhum and eventually with others. When the familly joined the Hindu community, it became a great object of the chief to induce other Hindus to come and settle in the country, and they succeeded in inducing numbers of Rajputs, Brahmins, Baraiks and others to settle, by making grants of villages on lineral conditions. The Hindu population and contact were there prior to this.

With their help, the Chota Nagpur chief succeeded in maintaining his position against neighbouring Rajas, and in managing and controlling the aborigines so effectively, that the latter have in course of time been generally reduced to the status of cultivators pure and simple. So much is this case, that there is no part of the Ranchi District in which the aborigines have succeded in retaining any considerable share of their proprietory rights in the soil, save a small area in the present Khunti sub-division, where the Mundari Khuntkattidars have succeded in retaining their ancient rights unimpaired to this day. The Muhammadan Government was always content to leave the administration of the country of the Raja, provided he remitted a small annual tribute. He was thus free to deal with his subjects as he liked."

The next step was to impose rent on the villagers who were the clearers of the soil and were recognised as the owners. They rendered light services or paid a small tribute to their local chief and he in turn rendered service and tribute to Raja. Rent in the common sense was none rather it was a small subscription or *Chanda* to the immediate landlord for the whole village.

But the adventurers and the hordes of middle-men rendered themselves obnoxious not only to the Manki but to cultivators when they used all means to dispossess them with the help of their patron the *jagirdars* and *khorposdars*. The result was the Kol Rebellion of 1831-32 which cleared the country of aliens for a time, but the insurrection was put down with a strong hand, and, though several remedial measures were passed, the havoc and destruction brought by the aborigines during the brief period of their ascendancy had naturally exasperated the landlords. They retaliated severely, and a considerable disturbance of peasant proprietary tenure undoubtedly occurred. The suppression of the revolution was followed immediately by a number of administrative reforms, but the question of rents payable by the great mass of the agricultural Kol population was, however, left untouched so that the so called reforms merely affected the fringe of the trouble. After the Kol Insurrection was put down, the tide of official favour turned against the Zamindar. The establishment of courts and the officers ignorant of local customs played havoc with the aboriginals right. The consequence was that in the main the disputes about rent charges were not settled through their agency, but in the village themselves, and the criterion was the relative strength of the parties of their ability to enforce or resist demands. This state of affairs existed down to quite recent times:

> "Closely connected with the disputes about rent charges and paraedieal conditions is the question of possession of fields. The refusal of the aborigines in parts of the country to comply with the exorbitant demands of the Zamindars from the beginning of the second quarter of the nineteenth century led to the reprisals and counter-reprisals. When the raiyats refused to pay increased demands, the Zamindars began to dispossess them by force and take their lands into their *khas* cultivation, or to sublet them to Hindus at enhanced rates. The aborigines being on 'a much lower plane of civilization' and lacking the power to combine, lost heavily at first. The balance was to some extent redressed by the advent of the European Missionaries, who took the side of the *raiyot* (converted) and the agrarian struggle for the past 30 years have been a tug of war with the landlords and Hindu raiyats, who are locally known as *Sadans* on one side, and the aborigines supported by the missionaries on the other."[4]

Before the Sonepur Pargana was granted by the then Maharaja of Chota Nagpur as *Khorposh* to his younger brother, Kuar Harnath Sahi, all the villages of the Parganas maintained their *Khuntkatti* status intact. The whole pargana was divided into a number of circles, each consisting of a number of villages over which there was a *Manki* who collected a tribute of Rs. 5 to Rs. 10 or Rs. 12 from each village and remitted it to the Maharaja, his own remuneration being the *chandas* collected from his *chaputa* village. Kuar Harnath Sahi through the agency of his *thekadars* succeeded in breaking down this system in the great majority of villages in the Sonepur Pargana. The *Khuntkatti* breaking, Bhuinhari reducing and *Rajhas* making period of Kuar Harnath's regime was followed by then Bhuinhari breaking and Rajhas-swelling and Manjhias grabbing period of his successor Thakur Indranath. But ever since Kuar Harnath Sahi took over the jagir his *thekadars* and *Katkindars* remained busy in expropriation of the Bhuinhars of the Oraon country and reducing most of them to the status of ordinary *raiyats* by transferring most of their Bhuinhari lands into Rajhas, by forcibly enhancing their rents beyond the customary rate of Rs. 3 per *poa*, and by levying all sorts of illegal imposts whose number in time swelled to thirty six, so that the great bulk of their Rajhas lands were finally converted into *Chatisa* and with the few exception of few *Kats* of *tanr* land allowed as *lagan tanr*, the remaining tanr lands of a raiyats holding were converted into *damgat* or rent-paying. It was then that the *Rakumat* were first ushered into being and came to be levied only for *lagan tanr* lands attached to *Chhatisa* holdings. These were prevalent in Oraon country in the central, north eastern portion of Ranchi, besides the Panchparganas of Ranchi district and Tori and Opa Parganas of Palamau and they were reported by Mr. Webster and Mr. Slack. In the villages of the Khunti and Torpa, thanas in Sonepur Parganas as the village notes show, there was no *Chatisa* land with a fixed proportion of lagan *tanr* could be introduced and no *rakumats* could be levied. It was Thakur Indranath who lived during the *Bhuinhari* Survey of 1869-1880 and caused the greatest havoc among the *Khuntkatti* and *Bhuinhari* rights of the Mundas by breaking down the *Khuntkatti* and *Bhuinhari* villages, converting some *Bhuinhari* lands into *Majhias*, and by converting most *Bhuinhari* or *Korkar* lands into *Rajhas* but he never thought of or succeeded in assessing rent on *tanr* lands or imposing *rakumats*.

Messrs Slack and Lister in their joint note have described the origin of the rent in the Mundari area as follows:

"There is little documentary evidence regarding the early history of the Munda but it appears to be a common feature in all their traditional stories that the relation of the primacy of the Maharaja of Chota Nagpur was a voluntary act on the part of the majority of the village communities, and this recognition was the first denotation from the rights of full properietorship of the village community agrees with *a priori* inferences in ascribing a very small value to the dues renderable to the Maharaja. For it is quite certain that the money dues must have been light up to the period of the British occupation, and even now Rs. 5 is the normal annual rent payable by an intact *Khunkatti* village. *Begari* even if ever rendered at all, must have been an insignificant and rarely recurring service in the case of villages at all, remote from the Maharaja's residence, and, if "aid" were rendered, they must, being perishable goods, have been limited in amount to the capacity of consumption in the Maharajas establishment. The story of Mundaris is shortly: "The Maharaja delegated his rights to Khorposdars or to his Hindu proteges, and contributions of *begari* and *aids*, which had been unfelt when distributed amongst a thousand villages, became onerous when borne by a few only. Moreover, these petty tenure-holders were not content with receiving the small sum which constituted the village quit rent payable to the Maharaja. They began by demanding a portion of the cultivated land for their maintenance, the cultivators of which were to pay rents direct to the tenure-holder. This *Rajhas* as it is called, in Thane Tamar (where its origin is so recent as to be unambigous) was extended by the inclusion of all lands subsequently added to the cultivated stock and the area of *Khuntkatti* land was thus intended to become fixed."

Thus the theory arose that in a typical Ranchi village, there are three classes of land viz., (1) Bhuinhari or the original clearings of the village clan, (2) *Rajhas* or the rest of the cultivated villages lands, (3) those portions of cultivated land which has come into the personal cultivation of the tenure holder. This theory fits in with the appearance of existing facts, and supports the claims of the tenure-holders to be considered landlords, in the Bengal sense, of the whole of the village, but historically, it is demonstratively false. The true facts are not only indicated by the Mundari tradition, but on proved by the evidence of the villages exhibiting at the present day each successive stage of decay from the intact Mundari Khuntkatti type; whilst the impossiblity of applying the ordinary theory is conclusive proof of its historical falsity.

Now the grievances of these Mundaris are peculiarly emanate from the fact that the successive loss of all the rights of ownership until their present status has become practically that of ordinary *raiyats* has been brought about, not by the deliberate decision of Government based on a full review of the facts, but by the imperceptible operation of impersonal legal principle, the suitablity of which to the local environment was never adequately considered. Lord Macaulay in his speech on the need of codification emphasised value of uniformity where informity is possible. Had the attendant working regarding diversity being headed, the Mundaris of Chota Nagpur, a race whose languages proves them to belong to their early stage of human development, would not have been given an agrarian law and elegal principles derived from the peculiarities of historically unconnected races. The Evidence Act and the Civil Procedure Code may not be suited to the needs of advanced commercial communities, for jungle tribe they are grotesque instruments of oppression.

NOTES

1. S. C. Roy, "Munda Theory of Rent", *Man in India*, XXVI, Ranchi, (1946), p. 156.
2. *Ibid.*, p. 157.
3. J. Reid, *Survey Settlement Operations in Ranchi District* (1902-10) Patna, 1910 p. 83.
4. *Ibid.*, p. 34.

SELECTED BIBLIOGRAPHY

ARCHIVAL SOURCES

National Archives of India, New Delhi

Foreign Department, Internal : A Proceeding, November 1884, pp.264-266.

Home (Public) Proceeding, December 1888-89, Nos. 1-3, pp. 42-43.

Home (Public) Proceeding, August 1892, Nos. 273-52, pp. 24-33.

Home (Public) Proceeding, June 1861, No. 26-28, pp. 329-331.

Home (Public) Proceeding, May 1861, No. 8 and 12.

Home (Public) Proceeding, 1862, No. 38.

Home (Public) Proceeding, January 1868.

Home (Judicial) Proceeding, February 1879, No. 136.

Revenue Department Proceeding dated 27th May 1860, No. 4.

Revenue Department Proceeding, December 1903, No. 5.

India Office Collection Revenue Despatch dated 9th July, 1862, No. 14.

Foreign Department Internal A Proceeding, September 1889, pp.137-139.

Foreign Department Internal A Proceeding 1888 No. 84-85.

Foreign Department Internal A Proceeding May, 1891 No. 105-110.

Foreign Department Internal A Proceeding September 1868 No. 1083.

Foreign Department Internal A Proceeding September 1893 No. 121-124.

Foreign Department Internal A Proceeding June 1892 No. 227-234.

Forign Department Internal A Proceeding September 1893 No. 121-124.

Paper concerning the Birsa Risings were collected by the author in the years 1953-55 and they have been preserved now in the National Archives, New Delhi. They consist of:

- Judgment in Birsait cases, Lower Court, Ranchi.

- Deposition in the Lower Court of some of the important Birsaits.
- Confidential reports from the Deputy Commission, Ranchi and Singhbhum.
- Secret files of Mr. Forbes, Commissioner, Chota Nagpur, containing day-to-day information with notes and comments by the Commissioner.
- Correspondence between Commissioner, Chota Nagpur and Legal Remembrancer and the Secretary to the Political Department, Government of Bengal.
- All these papers belong to 1899-1900.

Imperial Gazeetters of India, Bengal, Vol II 1909.

West Bengal Secret Record office, Calcutta

Foreign Select Committee Proceedings, No. 734, Fort William, 14 August, 1768.
Revenue Department Proceedings, No. 529 dated 30th August, 1875.
Revenue Department Proceedings, No. 4 dated 27th May, 1860.
Revenue Department Proceedings, No. 23 dated 28th September, 1860.
Revenue Department Proceedings, No. 24 dated 12th September, 1860.
Revenue Department Proceedings, No. 2975 dated May 1872.
Revenue Department Proceedings, No. 3 dated August, 1870.
Revenue Department Proceedings (Board of Revenue), No. 3 dated 30th June, 1850.
Revenue Department Proceedings, No 5294 dated 30th August 1875.
Revenue Department Proceedings, (L. R.) No. 2955 dated May, 1872.
Revenue Department Proceedings, (L. R.) No. 3 dated August, 1870.
Revenue Department Proceedings, No. 24 dated October, 1891.
Revenue Department Proceedings, No. 5 dated February, 1904.

Famine in Bengal, last V 1874, Calcutta.

Bihar State Central Record Room, Patna

Revenue Department L. R. Branch May 1892 No 20/22 File No 11/7.
No. 812 dated 13th November, 1901
No. 88-89 dated 11th June, 1902
No. 3400 dated 24th Novemver 1903 Part I
No. 12 dated 13th November, 1901.

Police file no. Pol. 5R-3 of 1919.
Series of letters from Lal Mritunjay Nath Sahideo, Sub-Inspector of Police, Khunti to the Deputy Commissioner of Lohardaga, Ranchi.
Series of letter from Commissioner of Chota Nagpur Division to the Chief Secretary to the Government of Bengal No. 33, August-November, 1895.
Series of Demi-Official letters from Father G. H. Lusty of Murhu to Mr. Meares, District Superintendent of Police, Ranchi, 1895 (Secret file).
Notes by Mr. Bompass, Deputy Commissioner, Singhbhum (Secret file).
File No. 38-46 of Police (1895).
Series of letters from Deputy Commissioner, Ranchi, to the Commissioner of Chota Nagpur (from 1895-1901).
Bengal Police Abstract of Intelligence, Calcutta, from 1895 to 1900.
Series of letters from Deputy Commissioner, Ranchi to District Superintendent of Police, Lohardaga (from 1895-1901).
(As these papers have not yet been catalogued and arranged in the State Archive, the writer is unable to quote Accession or Rack Nos.).

G. E. L. Mission Archives, Ranchi

Sri N. E. Horo supplied me the manuscripts of Abhiram Pracharak, Nistar Heranj, Kalyan Krist Sorin, etc.
Burju Parish-Old Registers of Baptism.
G. E. L. Mission, Chaibasa-Register Conformendum G. E. L. M. E. School old records, Inspection reports, etc.

Patna High Court Archives, Patna

Judgment of F. B. Taylor, Judicial Commissioner, Chota Nagpur, in *Empress* Vrs. *Chamon and 86 others*, Trial No. 1 of Ranchi Sessions, 1900.
W. S. Coutts, Joint Magistrate, Judgment in Appeal No. 184 of 1901, Paper Book, Part II.
Criminal Appeal No. 462 of 1901 in the Court of Hon'ble Justice Ghosh and Hon'ble Justice Brett, Calcutta High Court.
Criminal Appeal No. 184 of 1901 in the Court of Hon'ble Justice Ghosh and Hon'ble Justice Brett, Calcutta High Court.

Manuscripts

MSS of Abhiram Pracharak, a contemporary of Birsa Munda, Memoir of Birsa Bhagwan, translated by Master Topno, Pathal Kudwa, Ranchi (with the author).

MSS of Gangu Pahan, a contemporary of Birsa Munda, Maranghata, aged 95 years (with the author).

MSS of Heranj Nistar of Malgo-Birsaiti Hallagalla (Mundari) (with the author and Sri N. E. Horo, Ranchi).

MSS of Sagu Munda of Chandor, Khunti (with the author).

MSS of Sukh Singh Munda, a contemporary of Birsa Munda, Bangaon, aged 90 years (with the author).

MSS of Surin Khrist Kalyan–*Birsa-Bhagwan Bornika* (Mundari), Jaldega, P. S. Raeboga, Raj Gangpore, dated 23rd February, 1939.

MSS of Tigga Julius of Ranchi–*Mahatma Birsa* (Hindi) with Mr. Tigga.

MSS of Father Lievens and others at Bishop's Archives, Ranchi.

MSS of Father Dehon and others at Mahmadanr Minior.

SECONDARY SOURCES

Books

Ahluwalia, M. M., *Freedom Struggle in India* (1858-1900), Delhi, 1965

Allen, B. C., *Census of India*, 1901, Vol. IV, Assam, Shillong, 1902

Altekar, A. S., *The Vakataka Gupta Age*, Lahore, 1946, (reprinted later)

Atchinson, C. V., *A Collection or Treaties, Engagements and Sunnud Relating to India and Neighbouring Countries*, 14 Vols. Calcutta, 1862.

Baden-Powell, B. H., *The Land System of British India*, 2 Vols. Oxford, 1892.

Basu, B. D. Rise of Christian Power in India, Calcutta.

Bave-Brown, J., *The Chota Nagpur Mission.* London, 1870

Biswas, P. C., *The Santals*, New Delhi, 1950.

Bodding, P. O., *Tradition and Institutions of the Santal*, Oslo, 1942.

Boddi, P. O., *His Diary* (MS) Mahadanr Mission.

Bowen, F. J., *Father Constance, Levens : Apposite of Chota Nagpur.* St. Louis 1936.

Bradley-Birt. F. B., *Chota Nagpur : A Little Known province of the Empire,* London, 1903.

Bradley-Birt, F. B., *The Story of the Indian Upland.* London, 1905.

Buchanan, F. H., *Account of Bhagalpore District in 1810-11*, edited by R. N. Martin, London, 1838.

Buckland, C. E., *Bengal under the Lieutenant Governor*, Calcutta, 1901.

Cohen, Bernard S., Structural Change in India in Rural Society 1549-1885 in *Hand Control and Social Structure*, London, 1969.

Coser, L. A., *Towards Sociology of Social Conflict*, Columbia University, 1954.

Coser, L. A., *Functions of Social Conflict*, Glencoe, 1954.

Crook, W., *Tribes and Castes of North Western Province of Oudh*, 3 Vols., Calcutta, 1890.

Dalton, E. T., *Descriptive Ethnology of Bengal*, Calcutta, 1872.

Datta, S.N., *The Chota Nagpur Tevavly Act, 1928.*

Desai, Mahadeo, *Gandhiji in Indian Villages.*

Dhan, R. O., "The Problem of Tana Bhagats of Ranchi District" *Bulletin Bihar Tribal Welfare Research Institute, Ranchi*, Vol. 2, No.1, 1960.

Dhan, R. O., *These are my Tribes, Oraon*, Ranchi, 1968.

Diwakar, R. R., *Bihar Through the Ages*, New Delhi, Orient Longmans, 1958.

Dube, S. C. (ed), *Tribal Heritage of India*, New Delhi, Vikas, 1977.

Duff, Alexander, *The Indian Rebellion: Its Causes and Results*, London, 1858.

Duff Alexander, *India and Indian Missions*, Ed 2, London, 1840.

Dutta, K. K., *The Santal Insurrection,* Calcutta, 1940.

Dutta K. K., *History of Freedom Movement in Bihar*, 3 Vols. Patna, 1957.

Dutta, R. C., *The Economic History of India under Early British Rule.* London, 1901.

Ekka, Phillip, Revivalist Movement Among the Tribal of Chota Nagpur *in Tribal Situation in India*, Simla, 1972.

Evans Pritchard, E. E., *The Nuer*, Oxford, 1940.

Fidelis, De Sa, "The Crisis in the Mission of Chota Nagpur & Reaction of the Landlord Public", *Indian Ecclesiastical Studies* (Bangalore), Vol. 8, 1969.

Fuchs, Stephen, *Rebellous Prophets: A Study of Messianic Movement in Indian Religion*, Bombay 1965.

Firminger, W. R., *Fifth Report* Vol. II, Calcutta, 1917.

Frykenberg, Robert Eric (ed), *Land Control and Social Structure in Indian History*, London, 1969.

Ganguly, P. G., *Separatism in the Indian Polity in Anthropology and Archaeology*, Oxford, 1969.

Ghury, G. S., *Social Tension in India*, Bombay, 1968.

Grey, Alexander, *Indian Mutiny: Causes and Effect*, Gudon, 1859.

Hamilton, Walter, *Geographical, Statistical and Historical Description of Hindostan*, London, 1820.

Hand, J. R., *Early British Administration of Bihar*, Calcutta, 1894.

Hobsbausm, E. J., *Primitive Rebels*, London, 1971.

Hoffmann, John *Encyclopaedia Mundarica*, 13 Vols., Patna, 1930-1950.

Hunter, W. W., *Annals of Rural Bengal*, London, 1868.

Hunter, W. W., *Old Missionary*, Oxford, 1896.

Hunter W. W., *Statistical Account of Bengal*, 20 Vols, London, 1877, Vol. XIV Bhagalpur and Santal Parganas, Vol. XVI, Lohardaga.

Jay, Edward, Revitilisation Movement in Tribal India *in Aspects of Religion of Indian Society*, Meerut, 1961.

Jay, Edward, Tribal community of Middle India in *Leadership in India.* Bombay, 1967.

Jha, J. C., *The Bhumij Revolt*, Delhi 1967.

Jha, J. C., *The Kole Insurrection in Chota Nagpore*, Calcutta, 1964.

Jha, J. S., Missionary Education in Chota Nagpur Division in Bihar *Journal of Historical Research, Ranchi* (1961).

Joshi, P. C., *A Survey of Research on Land Reforms in India*, New Delhi, ICSSR, 1972.

Keith, A. B. *Speeches and Documents in Indian Policy*, Vol. I, 1922.

Kerketta, Kushal, *Biography of Rev. Joel Lakra*, Ranchi, 1974.

Koichi Sugiyama : *A story of the Mundas Village Life in India: Hill Peoples surrounding in Ganges Plain*, Tokyo, 1969.

Lanternari V, "*Incivilments dei barbari*" (Bari, Dedals Libre, 1983).

MacDougall John, *Agrarian Reforms, its Religions Revitilization: The conditions of Two Social Movements Among the Tribals of Bihar, India, in the late Nineteenth Century*, Connticut, 1974 (MSS).

MacDougall John, *Land and Religion*, Manohar, New Delhi 1984.

Macphail, R. M., *The Story of Santal*, Calcutta, 1922.

Mahato, S., *Hundred Years of Christian Mission,* Ranchi, Gosner Press, 1968.

Mahapatra, L. K., Social Movement among Tribes in India *in Tribal Situation in India*, Simla, 1972.

Mazumdar, D. N., The Korwas of United Provinces in *Man in India.* IX (1922).

Mind, W., Report on Native Schools in the Few Districts in H. S. Reid, *Report on Indigenous Education of Vernacular Schools NWP*, Agra, 1852.

Mishra, B. B., *The Central Administration of the East India Company*, Manchester, 1959.

Mishra, B. B., *The Indian Middle Class,* Oxford, 1961.

Mishra, B. B., *Administrative History of India 1934-1947*, Oxford, 1957

Muller, S., *A Brief Review of Ten years of Missionary Labour* (1852-61), 1863.

Mukherjee, R. K., *The Dynamic of Rural Society*, Berlin, 1957.

Mukherjee, R. K., *Rise and Fall of the East India Company*, Berlin.

Nottrott, Alfred, *Gosner Mission unter dir Arbeit 1974-87, Pictures from the life of a Missionary*, specially translated for the Author by J. Macdoughall, Bilderans dem, Missuousleben. Halle Richard Muhlmann, 1874.

Oldham, W. M., *Introduction in Reprint of the Laws of the Santal Parganas*, 1889.

O'Malley, L. S. S., *Modern India and West*, Oxford, 1968.

O'Malley, L. S. S., *Santal Parganas District Gazetteer*, Calcutta, 1910.

O'Malley L. S. S., *Santal Parganas District Gazetteer*, Patna, 1938.

O'Malley, L. S. S., *The Indian Civil Service,* London, 1955.

O'Malley L. S. S., *The Census of India 1911*, Vol. I, Part I.

Posten, M. M., *The Historical Method in Social Science*, Cambridge, 1939.

Prasad, Nerbadeshwar, *Land and People of Tribal Bihar*, Ranchi, 1961.

Prasad, Satyanarian, Tribal Education in Bihar, in *Man in India*, Vol. 51, Part 4, December 1971.

Rai, Hardwar, Political Administrative Bases of Indian field-Administration : The Pattern of the District Officer System under the British in *Journal of Indian Institute of Public Administration*, Vol. 16.

Reid, Henry Stuart, *Report on Indigeneous Education of Vernacular Schools, NWP*. Agra, 1852.

Reid, J., *Survey and Settlement of Ranchi District* (1902-1910), Patna, 1910.

Reid, J., *The Chota Nagpur Tenancy Act*, Calcutta, 1908.

Redfield, Robert, *The Little Community,* Stockhohm, 1955.

Rickets, *Reports of Chota Nagpur*, 1854.

Risley, H. H., *Tribes and Castes of Bengal*, Calcutta, 1891.

Rosner, Victor, Leadership among the Korwas of Jaspur *in Leadership in India*, Bombay, 1967.

Roy, Ramsharay, *The Congress Party in Bihar*, New Delhi.

Roy S. C., "A Religious Movement Among the Oraon in *Man in India*, Vol, I, No 4 (1921).

Roy S.C : *Munda and their Country*, Calcutta, 1912.

Roy S.C : "The Effect of the Aborigines of Chota Nagpur on Their Contact with Western Civilization", in *Journal of Bihar and Orissa Research Society*, Patna, Vol. XVII, part IV.

Roy S.C : "Ethnographical Investigation in Official Records" In *Journal of Bihar and Orisa Research Society*, Patna, Vol VII part IV

Roy S.C., *The Oraons of Chota Nagpur*, 1915.

Roy S.C., *The Oraons Religion and Customs*, 1928.

Roy S.C., *The Kbarias*, 1937.

Roy S.C., *The Hill Bhuiyas of Orissa*, 1935.

Roy S.C., *The Bishors, 1925.*

Russell, R. V. *The Tribes and Castes of Central Provinces of India.* Vol VIII(1916).

Sahay K. N., *Under the Shadow of Cross,* Calcutta, 1977.

Sachchidanand, *Profile of Tribal Culture in Bihar*, Calcutta, 1965.

Sandwar, A. N., *The Korwa of Palamau: A study of their Society and Economy*, Ranchi (University) 1972.

Shifton, James, *Revisional Survey and Settlement Report, Supplement.*

Singh, Jaipal, Adivasi and Nation Security, *The Organiser*, Depawali Issue, 1963.

Singh. K. S.(ed), *Tribal Situation in India*, Simla, 1972

Singh K. S., *Duststorm and Hanging Mist.* Calcutta, 1966 (Reprinted by Oxford in 1983).

Singh K. S., Tribal Movement in Chota Nagpur *in Dissent, Protest and Reform in Indian, Civilisation,* Simla, 1977.

Sinha, A. N., *Mere Sansmaran*, Patna, (in Hindi).

Sinha, R. N., *Bihar Tenantry* (1783-1833) Bombay, 1968.

Sinha, S. P., *Problem of Land Alienation in and around Ranchi District* (1955-1965), Patna, 1968. Restudied in 1989-90.

Sinha S. P., *Life & Time of Birsa Bhagawan*, Patna, 1963. Hindi Translation published by Rajbhasa, Patna, 1988.

Sinha S. P., Calcutta Press Reaction on Birsa Rising *Calcutta Review* (1959).

Sinha S. P., Election Studies in Tribal Constituencies of Bihar, *Bulletin of Institute of Public Administration*, Patna University, (1972).

Sinha S. P., Gandhi's Impact on the tribals of Chota Ngpur (1920-1930) in *Gandhi and Social Sciences*, New Delhi 1970.

Sinha, Surajit, Presidential Address of Forty Ninth, Indian Science, Congress Session, Anthropology Section.

Sinha, Surajit, Tribal Solidarity Movement in India: A Review 1959 *in Tribal Situation in India*, Simla, 1977.

Sinha, Surjit et. al "The Concept of Diku among the Tribes of Chota Nagpur" *in Man in India*, Vol. 49, No. 2(1969).

Sorokin, P., *Social and Cultural Dynamics*, London, 1957.

Spradley James, P. *et al.* (ed.), *Conformity and Conflict: Readings in Cultural Anthropology*, Boston, 1971.

Steward, J. H. Basin, Plateau Aboriginal Social-Political Groups Washington, Smithsonian, Institution, 1938.

Stokes, Eric, *The English utilitarian and India*, Oxford, 1959.

Sunnder D. H. E., *Survey and Settlement Report of the District of Palamau*, Calcutta, 1896.

Thakkar A. V., *Tribes of India*, Delhi, 1950.

Trevelyan, C. E., *The Education of the People of India*, 1938.

Tribal Solidarity Movement in India: A Review 1959 in *Tribal Situation in India*, Simla, 1977.

Tucker H. W., *Digest of S. P. G. Records* (1891-1892), London, 1894

Vidyarthi, L. P. (ed), *Leadership in India*, Bombay, 1967.

Vidyarthi, L. P., *The Maler: A Study in Nature-Man-spirit Complex*, Calcutta, 1963.

Vidyarthi, L. P., *Dynamics of Tribal Leadership in Bihar*, New Delhi 1963.

Vidyarthi, L. P. (ed), *Aspects of Religion in Indian Society*, Meerut, 1961.

Vidyarthi, L. P. and Benay Kumar Rai, *The Tribal Culture of India*, New York, 1970.

Reports

Hansard of different years during 1856-1859/Reports on Famine Comission 1880.

Report of Excluded and Partially Excluded Areas (other than Assam) 1950.

Report of West Bengal Police (Secret Section).

Selections from Educational Records, Bureau of Education, India 1920, Part I.

Report on Indigeneous Education of Vernacular Schools, NWP, Agra, 1852.

Selections from Education Department (S. D. E.) Calcutta, 1868.

Report on Public Instruction, Calcutta for the year 1876-77, 1870-71, 1878-80, 1885-86, 1886-87.

Report of Progress of Instruction, Yearly Report, 1888.

Report of Education in Bengal, 3rd Quenquiennial Review (1902-3 to 1906-7).

Paper Relating to Agrarian Disputes, Vol. I & II, Calcutta 1890.

Report on Chota Nagpur by Ricketts, 1854.

Slack's Report 1888 Section VIII. Calcutta, 1890.

Progress of Education in Bengal, 4th Quenquiennial Review 1907-8 to 1910-12.

Census of India, Bengal Vol. VIII, 1911.

Santal Parganas Enquiry Committee Report, 1938.

Bengal Harkaru, Calcutta, 1832.

Proceedings of Bihar and Orissa Legislative Council, Vol. I.

Administrative Report of Bengal for 1865-66.

Administrative Report of Bengal for 1867-68.

Administrative Report of Bengal for 1869-70.

Administrative Report of Bengal for 1871-72.

Administrative Report of Bengal for 1892-93.

T.W. Bridge, Survey and Settlement Operation in Palamau District.

J.D. Shifton, Survey Settlement Operation in Hazaribagh

D.H.E. Sunder, Survey and Settlement Operation in Palamau District.

L.R. Forber, Ryotwaree Settlement in Palamau.

John Reid, Survey and Settlement Operation in Ranchi District.

W.G. Lacey, Dhalbhum Survey Report.

B.K. Gokhale, Manbhum Survey Report.

A.D. Tuckey, Kolhau Resettlement.
A.D. Tuckey, Settlement Operation in Porahat.
A.D. Tuckey, Settlement Operation in Seraikella and Khorawan.

Journals

Journal and Proceedings of Asiatic Society of Bengal, Calcutta
Journal of Bihar and Orissa Research Society, Patna.
Journal of Indian History.
Journal of Historical Research, Ranchi.
Bengal Past and Present, Calcutta.
Man in India, Ranchi.
Bulletin of Bihar Tribal Welfare Research Institute, Ranchi.
Proceedings of Historical Records Commission, The Calçutta Review, Calcutta.

Gazetteers

Gazetteers Bihar & Orissa District Gazetteers: Ranchi by M. G. Mallet, Patna, 1917.
Gazetteers Bihar & Orissa District Gazetteers, Palamau by L. S. S. O'Malley, Calcutta, 1907.
Gazetteers Bihar & Orissa District Santal Parganas by L. S. S. O'Malley, Calcutta, 1910.
Bihar & Orissa District Gazetteer, Patna, 1938.
Recent Gazetteer of Districts of Chota Nagpur and Santal Parganas by P. C. Roy Chaudhury.
Imperial Gazetteer of India by W. W. Hunter, Oxford, 1909, Vol. VII, XV, XIX, XXI, XIII.

Newspapers

The Gharbandhu, Ranchi, 1890-1900.
The Christian Intelligencer, June 1860.
The Indian Ecclesiastial Studies, Bangalore, 1969.
The Pioneer, Calcutta, 1890-1900.
The Indian Daily News, Calcutta, 1890-1900.
The Statesmen, Calcutta, 1890-1990.

The Friends of India, Calcutta, 1880.
The Hindoo Patriot, 1878.
The Englishmen, Calcutta, 1880-1885.
The Searchlight, Patna, 1930-1945.

INDEX